THE REMINISCENCES OF
Vice Admiral Eugene P. Wilkinson
U.S. Navy (Retired)

INTERVIEWED BY
Paul Stillwell

U.S. Naval Institute • Annapolis, Maryland

Copyright © 2006

Preface

One of the many benefits of oral history is that it not only records for posterity the accounts of events, but it also reveals the personality of the individual who is interviewed. That is especially true in the case of Admiral Wilkinson. By telling of his entire life and career in the interviews that follow, he provided one example after another of the factors that made him successful in his professional endeavors. He also demonstrated a sense of humor that was at times devilish and thus entertaining to read about. He enjoyed playing tricks on people.

From the time of his boyhood, Wilkinson was an extremely competitive person, as illustrated, for instance, by his success at marbles. He practiced hour after hour, and, as he said in remembering the experience, "I always beat all comers, and I always played for keeps." That was true as well in his prowess as a poker player, in which his skill is widely recognized. In the oral history he says, with false modesty, that he was quite lucky. There was obviously much more to it than that. He talks at times of putting on his "poker face" in naval situations, as if he just happened to come out on top through some odd circumstance. The real explanation was that he was shrewd to begin with, then worked harder than others to make sure he did as well in war games and other endeavors as he had in marbles.

Success in poker calls for much more than having the right cards; it requires the ability to read people. Wilkinson used that ability time and again; he is a master psychologist. One amusing example occurred during his time as a student in Submarine School in 1942. Though he was outworking many of his classmates and doing better on tests, his class standing didn't reflect that, because he was still a reserve officer rather than a regular. So he approached the head of the Submarine School and said he wanted to drop out, because he apparently wasn't suited to be a submariner. With his poker face expression, he implied his class standing was the result of his own shortcomings rather than a biased system. The skipper saw through the charade and fixed the system.

Another facet of the Wilkinson personality is loyalty. One example after another in the following narrative tells of his sticking up for his men, so that they knew he was looking out for their interests and making sure they gave their best for the Navy. The old saying has it that loyalty downward produces loyalty upward, and his crewmen repaid him by performing superbly under his command. Some of the examples he cites in this memoir are case studies in effective leadership.

Still other aspects of his success were stamina and a can-do attitude. He knew whether or not the construction of the world's first nuclear submarine, the *Nautilus*, was going well, because he was at the shipyard at 2:00 in the morning. He also conned the crew of another submarine, the *Seawolf*, into believing he had simulating sinking her because he was awake in the wee, small hours of the morning on that occasion as well. When the defective diesel engines in his submarine *Wahoo* were making operations difficult, he didn't complain to higher authority. He expressed confidence that his men could solve the problem, and they did. In these interviews he expresses the idea that subordinates will outdo themselves to live up to expectations, and many times his men did just that. He gave them a sense of swagger. Because he told them repeatedly that they were the best, they sought to be just that. His charisma drew them into his circle.

On top of the personality traits, especially the desire to succeed, there was a great deal of native intelligence—especially a gift for dealing with numbers. An individual who recognized and capitalized on this package of attributes was Admiral Hyman G. Rickover, the father of the Navy's nuclear power program. Even though Wilkinson was not a Naval Academy graduate, he received the plum assignments to be the first commanding officer of the *Nautilus* and later the nuclear-powered cruiser *Long Beach*. This oral history contains a great deal on Admiral Rickover, as revealed through the eyes of someone who was with him from the beginning of the nuclear-propulsion program. Admiral Rickover eventually established himself as the powerful czar of the program, but in the beginning he needed Wilkinson more than Wilkinson needed him. That's why Wilkinson didn't heed Rickover's recommendation that he specialize in engineering. He preferred to remain an operational naval officer, and he had the self-confidence to know that he could succeed in an arena of his choosing.

Interviewing Admiral Wilkinson was an interesting experience, because he did it his own way. We had five long, long sessions, parts of which were on tape and parts were not. Often he would bring up topics when we were just chatting in his den or having a meal. Sometimes he said he was telling the stories "just for fun" rather than for the record. When I'd subsequently raise the topics while the tape recorder was running, he was a good sport about it and repeated the tales for the record. At other times he just talked about whatever topic happened to be thinking about, a stream-of-consciousness format that demonstrated how his mind worked but wasn't necessarily conducive to a linear, chronological telling of the story. Thus the stories were at times repetitious and often out of sequence.

George Van, himself a former naval officer, did a marvelous job in producing the initial raw transcript. My challenge then was to do a considerable amount of rearranging of the many bits and pieces so that the narrative is now essentially chronological and thus easier for a reader to follow. I also added a number of footnotes and checked statements against existing documents, such as wartime submarine patrol reports and ships' histories. Admiral Wilkinson has reviewed the rearranged sequence, added a number of corrections of his own, and given his blessing to the result.

I am grateful to Captain Jim Hay of the Naval Submarine League for supplying some questions that led Admiral Wilkinson to discuss the submarine force as a whole; to Wilkinson's daughter Marian Casazza, for helping track down details for the biographical summary; to Ann Winters, Wilkinson's biographer, for her help in facilitating completion of the transcript; and to Ann Hassinger, my long-time assistant, for her unfailing support on this project and many others.

Finally, the Naval Institute expresses its gratitude to the donors listed prior to the text and to the Tawani Foundation and the Pritzker Military Library of Chicago for their generous financial support of the oral history program that produced this memoir.

Paul Stillwell
U.S. Naval Institute
July 2006

VICE ADMIRAL EUGENE PARKS WILKINSON
UNITED STATES NAVY (RETIRED)

Eugene Parks Wilkinson was born in Long Beach, California, on 10 August 1918, the son of Dennis William and Daisy Parks Wilkinson. He attended Holtville, California, High School and San Diego State College. He graduated from the latter in 1938 with a Bachelor of Arts degree with a major in chemistry. He taught chemistry there for a year. He also filled in and taught a course in mathematics. During this year he attended the University of Southern California. The next year he had a teaching fellowship in chemistry at USC. During those two years he completed all of the course work for a doctor's degree but never did a thesis or received any graduate degree. Commissioned ensign in the U.S. Naval Reserve on 12 December 1940, he was transferred to the regular U.S. Navy on 28 August 1946.

Wilkinson's commissioned service began in the heavy cruiser *Louisville* (CA-28), in which he had duty in the engineering department until December 1941. He was detached in San Francisco, with orders to the Submarine School, New London, Connecticut, for instruction in submarines. After completing the course in March 1942, he served in the engineering department of the submarine *R-10* in April and May, after which he was ordered to the submarine *Blackfish* (SS-221). After the commissioning of that boat in July, he served on board for one year, making four war patrols. He had commissary, engineering, and electrical duties. During his time in the crew the submarine participated in the North African operation (Algeria-Morocco landings).

From June 1943 to October 1944 Wilkinson was in the crew of the submarine *Darter* (SS-227), which participated in four war patrols, including the Truk attack and the Battle of Leyte Gulf. Officially detached from the *Darter* in November 1944, following her loss the previous month, he returned to the United States. From January to March 1945 he was an instructor at the Submarine School, New London, Connecticut. He next served as executive officer and navigator of the submarine *Menhaden* (SS-377) from March to October 1945 and had similar duty on board the submarine *Raton* (SS-270). Upon his transfer from the Naval Reserve to the U.S. Navy, he was ordered to the General Line School, Newport, Rhode Island, where he completed the assigned course in May 1947.

From June 1947 until April 1948, Wilkinson was executive officer and navigator of the USS *Cusk* (SSG-348). From April 1948 to April 1950, he completed assignments at the Oak Ridge National Laboratory in Oak Ridge, Tennessee; the Argonne National Laboratory in Chicago as an associate engineer, and at the U.S. Atomic Energy Commission in the Pittsburgh, Pennsylvania, area, as chief of the operations branch and Bureau of Ships representative. In May 1950 he assumed command of the submarine *Volador* (SS-490), in which he participated in action in the Korean area from 12 August to 2 November 1951. From January to May 1952 he fitted out the submarine *Wahoo* (SS-565) and on her commissioning on 10 May of that year became her first commanding officer.

In February 1952 Wilkinson had temporary duty for one month as commanding officer of the submarine *Sea Robin* (SS-407). He was detached from the *Wahoo* in June 1953. He then carried out a series of temporary assignments by way of preparation for becoming prospective commanding officer of the USS *Nautilus* (SSN-571), the world's first nuclear-powered submarine. He took command of the ship upon her commissioning on 30 September 1954 and held that billet until relieved in June 1957.

After spending the following academic year as a student at the Naval War College, Newport, Rhode Island, Wilkinson served as Commander Submarine Division 102 for a year and had brief temporary duty as commanding officer of the *Nautilus*. In September 1961 he became the initial commanding officer of the guided missile cruiser *Long Beach* (CGN-9), the U.S. Navy's first nuclear-powered surface ship. After completion of that command, he reported on 1 November 1963 as Director of the Submarine Warfare Division (OP-31), in the Office of the Chief of Naval Operations, Navy Department, Washington, D.C. While in that billet he was promoted to the rank of rear admiral.

On 23 November 1966, he assumed duties as Chief of Staff for the U.S. Forces in Japan. After earning the Distinguished Service Medal for his service in Japan, Admiral Wilkinson assumed command of Submarine Flotilla Two on 6 June 1969. He was promoted to vice admiral upon becoming Commander of the Atlantic Fleet Submarine Force on 12 February 1970. He had additional duty as Submarine Operations Advisor for Polaris Operations, Atlantic Command and Supreme Allied Command Atlantic, Commander Submarines Allied Command, and Commander Submarine Force Western Atlantic. His final billet on active duty, from 1972 to 1974, was as Deputy Chief of Naval Operations (Submarine Warfare), OP-02, on the staff of the Chief of Naval Operations.

Following his retirement from active duty in 1974, Admiral Wilkinson had a number of jobs in civilian life, including service for Data Design Laboratories and as the first head of the Institute of Nuclear Power Operations (INPO). He has served on several corporate boards.

Family Personal Data:

Wife:	Janice Edith Thuli, married 28 March 1942
Children:	Dennis Eugene Wilkinson, born 11 April 1944
	Stephen James Wilkinson, born 22 August 1945
	Marion Lynn Wilkinson, born 12 August 1948
	Rodney David Wilkinson, born 15 July 1949

Dates of Rank:

16 September 1940	Midshipman
12 December 1940	Ensign
16 June 1942	Lieutenant (Junior Grade)
1 December 1942	Lieutenant
27 July 1945	Lieutenant Commander
1 January 1951	Commander
1 November 1956	Captain
1 July 1964	Rear Admiral
12 February 1970	Vice Admiral

Chronological Record of Service:

Jan 1941-Dec 1941	USS *Louisville* (CA-28)
Jan 1942-Mar 1942	Submarine Base, New London, Connecticut (Instruction)
Mar 1942-May 1942	USS *R-10*
May 1942-Jul 1942	Electric Boat Company, Groton, Connecticut, commissioning and fitting out of *Blackfish* (SS-221)
Jul 1942-May 1943	USS *Blackfish* (SS-221)
May 1943-Sep 1943	Electric Boat Company, Groton, Connecticut, commissioning and fitting out of *Darter* (SS-227)
Sep 1943-Nov 1944	USS *Darter* (SS-227)
Jan 1945-Mar 1945	Instructor, prospective commanding officers' course, Submarine School, New London, Connecticut
Mar 1945-Jun 1945	Manitowoc Shipbuilding Company, Manitowoc, Wisconsin, commissioning and fitting out of *Menhaden* (SS-377)
Jun 1945-Feb 1946	Executive officer, USS *Menhaden* (SS-377)
Feb 1946-Jun 1946	Executive officer, USS *Raton* (SS-270)
Jun 1946-May 1947	Student, General Line School, Newport, Rhode Island
Jun 1947-Apr 1948	Executive officer, USS *Cusk* (SSG-348)

Apr 1948-May 1949	Argonne National Laboratory, Chicago, Illinois
May 1949-Apr 1950	U.S. Atomic Energy Commission, Pittsburgh, Pennsylvania
Apr 1950-Dec 1951	Commanding officer, USS *Volador* (SS-490)
Dec 1951-May 1952	Portsmouth Naval Shipyard, Kittery, Maine, commissioning and fitting out of *Wahoo* (SS-565); temporary additional duty as commanding officer, USS *Sea Robin* (SS-407) in February 1952
May 1952-Jun 1953	Commanding officer, USS *Wahoo* (SS-565)
Jun 1953-Aug 1953	Student, Armed Forces Staff College, Norfolk, Virginia
Aug 1953-Nov 1953	Atomic Energy Commission, Division of Reactor Development
Nov 1953-Sep 1954	Electric Boat Company, Groton, Connecticut, commissioning and fitting out of *Nautilus* (SSN-571)
Sep 1954-Jun 1957	Commanding officer, USS *Nautilus* (SSN-571)
Jun 1957-Jun 1958	Student, Naval War College, Newport, Rhode Island
Jun 1958-Sep 1959	Commander Submarine Division 102
Sep 1959-Sep 1961	Bethlehem Steel Company, Quincy, Massachusetts, commissioning and fitting out of *Long Beach* (CGN-9)
Sep 1961-Sep 1963	Commanding officer, USS *Long Beach* (CGN-9)
Oct 1963-Nov 1966	Director, Submarine Warfare Division, OP-31, Office of the Chief of Naval Operations, Washington, D.C.
Nov 1966-May 1969	Chief of staff, Commander U.S. Forces Japan
Jun 1969-Feb 1970	Commander Submarine Flotilla Two, New London, Connecticut
Feb 1970-Jun 1972	Commander Submarine Force Atlantic Fleet, Norfolk, Virginia
Aug 1972-Aug 1974	Deputy Chief of Naval Operations (Submarine Warfare), OP-02, Office of the Chief of Naval Operations, Washington, D.C.
1 September 1974	Retired from active duty.

Medals and Awards:

Distinguished Service Medal (three awards)
Silver Star Medal
Joint Service Commendation Medal
Legion of Merit
Navy Commendation Medal
Navy Unit Commendation Awarded the USS *Darter*
American Defense Service Medal with Fleet Clasp
American Campaign Medal
European-African-Middle Eastern Campaign Medal
Asiatic-Pacific Campaign Medal
World War II Victory Medal
National Defense Service Medal with one bronze star in lieu of second award
Korean Service Medal
Philippine Liberation Ribbon
Second Order of the Sacred Treasure (Japan)

Navy Meritorious Public Service Citation (civilian award)
George Westinghouse Medal (American Society of Mechanical Engineers)
Oliver Townsend Medal (Atomic Industrial Forum)
Gold Medal (Uranium Institute)
Henry DeWolf Smyth Nuclear Statesman Award (American Nuclear Society)

Deed of Gift

The U.S. Naval Institute is hereby authorized to make available to individuals, libraries, and other repositories of its choosing the tapes and/or transcripts of five oral history interviews concerning the life and naval career of the undersigned. The Naval Institute may also, at its discretion, use the material in electronic/digital format, including posting on the Internet. The interviews were recorded on 17 January 1998, 18 January 1998, 19 January 1998, 20 January 1998, and 21 January 1998, in collaboration with Paul Stillwell for the U.S. Naval Institute.

The undersigned does hereby release and assign to the U.S. Naval Institute the rights and title to these interviews, with the exception that the undersigned retains the right to use the material for his own purposes, as he sees fit. The copyright in both the oral and transcribed versions shall be the sole property of the U.S. Naval Institute. The tape recordings of the interviews are and will remain the property of the U.S. Naval Institute.

Signed and sealed this 14th day of May 2004.

Eugene P. Wilkinson
Vice Admiral, U.S. Navy (Retired)

The United States Naval Institute

gratefully acknowledges

Alyce Boyd and Captain David S. Boyd

LCDR Robert L. Cox, USN (Ret.)

Ann Robinson Joyce and Captain Jack B. Joyce in honor of O. P. Robinson, Jr.

Vice Admiral Joe Williams, Jr., USN (Ret.)

Exelon Corporation

1 Anonymous Donor

for their generous support in

underwriting the oral history of

Vice Admiral Eugene P. "Dennis" Wilkinson, U.S. Navy (Retired)

Interview Number 1 with Vice Admiral Eugene P. Wilkinson, U.S. Navy (Retired)
Date: Saturday, 17 January 1998
Place: Admiral Wilkinson's home in Del Mar, California
Interviewer: Paul Stillwell

Paul Stillwell: Admiral, I'm delighted to be here and to meet you for the first time. I've heard so many things about you and am eager to get your history on the record. Could you please talk initially about your boyhood and your parents?

Admiral Wilkinson: My dad was killed in an automobile accident at an early age, and my mother also died at an early age.[*] I grew up with my grandparents in a place in Imperial Valley: Holtville, California. It was a small town, then about 1,000, and I was there from grammar school through high school. Then I left home and worked my way through San Diego State College, from which I graduated in 1938 with a degree in chemistry, minors in math and physics. I was 19 when I graduated from college, and I had a good reputation at the college. I got a job the next year teaching chemistry at San Diego State, which in those days had 1,800 students. After World War II the bulldozers never stopped, and there must be 30,000-40,000 out there now. There were only three teachers in the chemistry department, and they were shorthanded in math, so I taught a mathematics course also.

At the same time that I was teaching there, I was doing graduate work at the University of Southern California in Los Angeles. I would drive up there two nights a week and take courses. I took mostly lab courses, where I could do the work away from the college while I was teaching out here at State. The next year I took a teaching fellowship in math at the University of Southern California, although I was also offered one in physics. While I was at USC in the teaching fellowship I finished my course work for an advanced degree but never got it because I never did a thesis. My work at USC was in chemical engineering.

---

[*] His parents were Dennis William Wilkinson and Daisy Parks Wilkinson.

Paul Stillwell: Please tell me what you remember about your father.

Admiral Wilkinson: I don't remember too much except a great sadness when he was killed. I was quite young. But he was a fabulous person. He was very popular. He was quite an athlete. He was captain of the baseball team in high school, and baseball was the sport in those days, not football. He was the valedictorian, and my mother was the salutatorian. After he went to work he managed a creamery and was doing quite well financially when he was killed in an automobile accident. He was a good horseshoe pitcher and in fact was the horseshoe champion as an amateur for the state of California. He was greatly missed by my sister, who's four years older, by me, and especially by my grandparents.

Paul Stillwell: Please tell me about that national competition in horseshoes.

Admiral Wilkinson: In those days that was the big thing, and it was in Akron, Ohio. I think it was under Goodyear, and my dad went back as the champion from California. My grandfather went with him. Back there he placed third. He averaged 42 ringers out of every 50 throws, which if you've ever pitched horseshoes is phenomenal. But that and baseball were the sports in those days.

Paul Stillwell: What did somebody have to do to win if 42 was only third?

Admiral Wilkinson: I don't know except the guy that was the winner was also a trick artist. As I understood, he could stick matches in wood and strike them with the horseshoe. [Laughter] So he must have been a lot better. [Laughter] But my dad was good.

Paul Stillwell: I wonder if you inherited a competitive instinct from your father.

Admiral Wilkinson: I don't know about inherited, but I do have a competitive instinct. I work harder when the competition's tougher.

Paul Stillwell: How long did your mother live after your birth?

Admiral Wilkinson: Not very many years. I don't know exactly.

Paul Stillwell: What do you remember of her and things that you learned from her?

Admiral Wilkinson: I don't remember my parents that well. It's my grandparents that I really remember. My grandfather died when I was 15, and I had a different feeling in those days. I had good grades in high school, and I was offered a scholarship to a private college up here. But in my mind in those days that would have been being beholden. Years later I was happy to get scholarships for my kids to go to college, but back then I didn't want to be obligated, so instead of taking a scholarship in a college I came to San Diego State and worked my way through school.

You've got to think back to the time of the Depression.* I graduated from high school in 1934. Things were really bad, and I had a job that summer irrigating corn. I worked seven nights a week, 12 hours a night, from 6:00 P.M. to 6:00 A.M., for 15 cents an hour. By the time the summer was over I had saved $42.00, and that's what I started college with. Four of us joined together and rented a house over here in San Diego that's sort of on the minority borderline. We paid $16.00 a month for a two-bedroom, one-bath apartment and our utilities. Split four ways, that's $4.00, and our utilities averaged about $2.00 apiece, and we chipped in.

One of the young men ran the vegetable counter at the Piggly Wiggly store. They'd have a big sale every Saturday night, and we'd buy lots of vegetables for a penny for so many pounds of it. So we chipped in $5.00 a month apiece for food. And our bus pass was three dollars a month, which got me to school and back. So four and two are six and five are 11 and three are 14. You're not talking a lot of money. And in those days the registration for a two-semester year was $18.00 a semester. So I worked my way through college at a time when it didn't take much money to go. I made and saved more money, relatively, during my four years working my way through college than I ever

---

* Following the crash of the New York Stock Exchange in late October 1929, the United States plunged into the Great Depression, from which it did not recover until the nation geared up for World War II at the beginning of the 1940s. The Depression was marked by high unemployment and many business failures.

have since. [Laughter] I started college with $42.00, and four years later I owned a house and lot and 100 shares of B&O Railroad stock, which was at four and an eighth, and had a year-old car.* [Laughter]

Paul Stillwell: How close a relationship did you have with your sister?

Admiral Wilkinson: My sister and I are very close, although she's four years older than I. She was valedictorian and won the sports award, which had always gone to a boy before. Her husband was the salutatorian. She became a very devout Christian, and she and her husband were going to go to China in '39 as missionaries. Just four or five days before the sailing he fell down a cliff and fractured his elbow, and so they never went. About ten years ago I was able to take my sister and my wife and my wife's sister to China, and it was a tremendous thing to her because she never got to go as a missionary.

What was also sort of interesting was that we were in Tiananmen Square the afternoon before the attack.† That day we were off seeing the Great Wall, and as we came back we saw the army trucks rolling in. The day before, my sister and my wife and my wife's sister, all of whom are pretty women-libber, independent-type women, were around giving thumbs-up signals to these kids pitched in their tents with the red flags there. I said, "Hey, cool it, will you? There are people taking pictures of you." [Laughter] But they never bothered us.

I'd been planning to come down the Yangtze with my three women, and we'd popped for a very expensive cruise ship, luxury, out on deck, gourmet food, coming down the Yangtze, see the three gorges and all that. Well, all the tour groups were hustled out of China after Tiananmen Square, and all that stuff was cancelled except us. We weren't in a tour group. The four of us were going independently, and we were going to rendezvous with a ship up there that day. When we got there, all that was cancelled. We went down the Yangtze in what they called a common carrier, you know,

---

* B&O – Baltimore and Ohio Railroad.
† In May 1989 100,000 students and workers staged a march in Beijing, China, to demand political reforms. After the unrest spread, on 3-4 June Chinese tanks and armored personnel carriers rolled into Beijing's Tiananmen Square to crush the pro-democracy demonstrations. All told, some 5,000 people were killed, 10,000 injured, and hundreds of demonstrators arrested.

with a benjo and whatnot, and we didn't have all the luxury accommodations.* The scenery was just as good.

Paul Stillwell: Right.

Admiral Wilkinson: So those are great memories for my sister and my wife and her sister. I digress. Sorry I took so long to answer your question. My relationship with my sister is very close. We talk all the time. I talked to her this morning. You heard me wishing her number-two boy a happy birthday. Her husband has passed away, and she lives in Seattle.

Paul Stillwell: What's her name?

Admiral Wilkinson: Her name is Lillian Hancock, and her number-one son is quite a famous eye surgeon. Of her other three boys, two of them live right there in Seattle with her. She taught school in the Seattle area and worked up to where she was the person in charge of the teacher training for the university. When their kids go out and take teacher training, she'd set that up, so she's pretty well known in the educational system in Seattle.

Paul Stillwell: Did your grandparents provide some of the values and discipline that parents normally would?

Admiral Wilkinson: We never had to worry about discipline. We never considered doing anything wrong. That was never a problem. As for standards, our grandparents just expected us to excel, and both my sister and I did do that. I have a feeling that people have a tendency to live up to what is expected of them. In ship after ship, in job after job, I found that to be true of my people. There isn't any doubt that our grandparents really thought in their hearts we were going to be the best, and we seemed to work toward living up to that.

---

* Benjo is a name in the Orient for a crude sort of toilet.

Paul Stillwell: Were these your mother's parents or your father's parents?

Admiral Wilkinson: My father's parents. We lived with them after our parents passed away.

Paul Stillwell: Please tell me about your marble-shooting prowess.

Admiral Wilkinson: Well, we were talking earlier, before we got this tape recorder started. I've had ups and downs in my life, some good things and sometimes not so good. But I guess the high point in my life compared to my contemporaries was in the little town of Holtville between about the fourth grade and the first year in high school when I retired myself from active combat. For all those years I was the marbles champion; I never lost. For five years I was *the* best marble player, and that was my world. There's a much bigger world, but I wasn't aware of that bigger world. As far as I was concerned, I was the best marble player there was, and I might have been too. I won thousands of marbles back when marbles weren't mass-produced. They were three for a nickel, and in the Depression time that was a lot of money. Agates were more, and I had sacks and sacks and sacks of them, because I always beat all comers, and I always played for keeps.

Paul Stillwell: What skills were required to be so good at that?

Admiral Wilkinson: I practiced probably five or six hours a day. My hands were chapped. The knees of my trousers were worn off. My shoes were scuffed, which was a distress to my grandparents. There are lots of different marble games. There's fish ring, and there's bullring, and there's where you run along like croquet shooting into holes, etc. Sometimes a marble will run erratically along the ground, but I could put one hand up on the other and shoot through the air and hit marbles farther than you can believe. Across the room you could put a marble on the ground, and in free flight I could hit it every other time at least.

Paul Stillwell: It sounds as if you also had some innate hand-eye coordination that was very useful.

Admiral Wilkinson: I was a good marble shooter, but I probably spent thousands of hours of practice.

Paul Stillwell: So a combination of native skill and hard work?

Admiral Wilkinson: Yes. Compared to my contemporaries that was the highest point of my life. I tell that story, and my wife just thinks it's ridiculous, but it wasn't at the time. You've got to put yourself in the mind of a fourth grade boy.

Paul Stillwell: Please tell the outcome of what you did with the marbles and how you later rediscovered them.

Admiral Wilkinson: Well, I buried them under the house, sack after sack of them. Years later, when I was almost through college, I bought that house that my grandparents rented and my grandmother lived in. You've got to think back in the Depression context. I bought that house and lot for $400.00, and after my grandmother passed away I sold it for $3,000. I went back to visit my grandmother frequently. One time when I went there, I crawled under the house, and I dug up those sacks and sacks and sacks of marbles. There were literally thousands of them. She had a birdbath like that, and I'm measuring here two or three feet, and I filled it with marbles. I planted tulip bulbs in it and put it out in my grandmother's yard, and she liked those flowers in among those shiny pretty marbles. Then for a couple of years kids would run in there and steal a handful, and eventually they were gone. But that's what happened. I lost my marbles—but to a good cause.

Paul Stillwell: How diligently did you apply yourself to your schoolwork as you were coming along?

Admiral Wilkinson: I guess I never did apply myself real diligently, because I was book smart enough that it came easy for me, and so I'd get all ones or all A's. I didn't work as hard at it as I should, and so when I went to college and I was working nights and whatnot, it was a little more of a strain to do it. In grammar school and high school I didn't have any trouble at all. As a matter of fact, I skipped a grade in grammar school, and I skipped a grade in high school. I skipped the grade in grammar school because my teacher was mad at me. I guess it was the third grade I skipped, and by that time I could do arithmetic up to fractions and division before I ever went to school. I guess that was because my folks had worked with me. And I could read because I learned to read from the comics before I could go to school. So when we got to third grade the math teacher said arithmetic was getting harder. It would be two columns or whatnot; the teacher would put the problems up, and I'd just write the answer down. She said, "You have to show your work."

I said, "That's all the work there is." [Laughter] So she marked me with a zero. So the next time they had the thing I just wrote down the answers. For about, oh, six weeks or something I got all zeros. I said, "I don't have any work. I'm sorry." So finally they got mad at me and skipped me to the next grade.

Paul Stillwell: So you were working these in your head, I take it.

Admiral Wilkinson: Yes, I could, but I wasn't as smart at that as my grandfather and my father. They were really good with their numbers. My grandfather would have a column of numbers and I'm talking like $152.62 and so on, a page full of numbers. He just added it up all up and wrote it all down at once. He didn't do it column by column. Well, I can do that, too, for a couple of columns [laughter], but my grandfather could do that for five whole columns of figures. Numbers come easy for me. I don't remember things. I'm very bad with names and things like that, but I can remember numbers to this day. I remember the phone number when I was dating my wife in college.

In high school one summer I worked for Seaside Service Station in Holtville. I used to hate it. I used to pick up that phone and say, "Seaside, smiling service," and that didn't appeal to me at 14. One day a Model A Ford came in, and I had checked its oil and whatnot. There was a can tied under the distributor, which was leaking gas. The guy would catch it. As he pulled out of the station after I'd serviced him, the car caught on fire, and so I ran in and got the fire extinguisher and put it out. Eventually the boss came back and said, "What happened?" I told him proudly, and he said, "That guy wasn't even in our station." This was the Depression, you remember. "His wheels were out on the pavement. That costs 90 cents to refill that fire extinguisher." So I told him what he could do with his service station. [Laughter] And he said that if I wanted to get paid I could stay the rest of the day. So the rest of the day, I can remember, instead of saying, "Seaside, smiling service," I said, "Seaside, what the hell do you want?" [Laughter] I was so pleased with that. I'd hated saying, "Seaside, smiling service." [Laughter]

Paul Stillwell: You told me before we started that you graduated high school at 15.

Admiral Wilkinson: At 15.

Paul Stillwell: How was the interaction with your classmates when you were chronologically younger and probably didn't have as many social skills as they did?

Admiral Wilkinson: Well, there were things to be desired there. Remember my sister, I told you, had been valedictorian and her husband salutatorian in high school. Well, I didn't get to be valedictorian because I graduated in three years, so they didn't count that. So I missed that, although our little high school was funny. If anybody got an A in a subject every marking period, every six weeks, out on the bulletin board they listed all the people that got A's and how many. I mean like Eugene Wilkinson, so many A's. Well, I'd have all A's.

One of my classmates and competitors was a bright young fellow named George Brown, who later was elected to Congress and is now the senior member of the Committee of Science in the Congress.* And George liked to do well. In high school

---

* George Edward Brown, Jr., born 6 March 1920, graduated from Holtville Union High School in 1935. As a Democrat, he served in the U.S. House of Representatives from 3 January 1963 to 3 January 1971 and from 3 January 1973 until his death on 15 July 1999. He was chairman of the House Committee on Science, Space and Technology.

you had to have 17 credits to graduate. You got four credits a year, four fours are 16, and then you had one quarter of a credit for athletics. So I would have enough credits to graduate at the end of three years except you had to have four years of athletics. Isn't that stupid? So I said, "Well, okay, I'll take athletics twice." And so my senior year I did two years of athletics. I signed up for six classes instead of four, no study hall, so I had to come in an hour early every day and take an extra hour of athletics. Well, that was all right, because I'd come in and play tennis for an hour early in the morning.

Our tennis coach, who also taught Latin and Spanish, had a simple grading system. If you made the team you got an A. Well, I was on the tennis team, and I took two athletics, so I got two A's plus A's in my six subjects. So every time the marking period came out I always led off with "Wilkinson, eight A's, which really frustrated George Brown. Although he got all A's, that gave him only six. He could not ever get at the top of the list, and he was quite a competitive person and a crackerjack. So that last year in high school I got two A's for athletics, but I was immature physically.

You asked me how I was with my classmates. I hadn't got up to girls yet. I was only 5-foot-5 at 15 when I graduated from high school. I was six feet when I graduated from college, so a lot of my growth came late, and I was not social. I was on a team, and I'd won the county championship in tennis, but I didn't date or those things.

Paul Stillwell: You mentioned before we started that you're universally known as Dennis. Your initials are E. P. How did the "Dennis" name get hung on you?

Admiral Wilkinson: My name is Eugene P. Wilkinson, and the P. stands for Parks, which is the family name of my mother's side of the family. But I was so high on my father, and my father's name was Dennis, my grandfather's name was Dennis, and I thought highly of them both. They were both smart and quick with numbers, which I admired. So when I signed up in college, I signed myself as Eugene D. instead of P. Wilkinson. The D. was for Dennis, and it wasn't really my name. But my wife started calling me Dennis, and pretty soon everybody refers to me as Dennis, and now it's a problem, because my name legally is Eugene P. Wilkinson. I'll get correspondence; I get checks made out to Dennis Wilkinson, and I have to endorse them "Eugene P. 'Dennis'

Wilkinson" to make things come out right. But everyone refers to me as Dennis and sometimes as Dennis the Menace. You could look at this pile of correspondence. It's all addressed "Dennis." That's not really my legal name, but it is my operating name.

Paul Stillwell: How much of an effect did the Depression have on your family?

Admiral Wilkinson: Very much. The Depression was really tough, and my dad would have been well off, because he was making good money and owned his own creamery. But when he was killed, my grandparents didn't have a lot of money. My grandfather first and then my grandmother worked, and they didn't get paid too much. My grandfather owned a service station and owned a restaurant, and in the Depression neither one of those was very successful. So there wasn't a lot of money to spare.

Paul Stillwell: So you had to pick up the odd jobs where you could.

Admiral Wilkinson: I worked a little bit in high school, earlier actually, and I had saved some money. When the Depression came and the banks went broke, I lost my money that was in the savings account, except just before the banks went broke I had drawn $5.00 out to buy a used bicycle. I was so happy with that. So really all I started college with was the money I had earned that last summer that I mentioned—15 cents an hour. That seems incredible, doesn't it?

Paul Stillwell: It does, especially with today's prices.

Admiral Wilkinson: Yes, but people would work for a dollar a day and board and room in those days.

Paul Stillwell: Did you have life goals at that point when you had graduated from high school and you were moving on towards college?

Admiral Wilkinson: Not really. I had confidence. I had no doubt that I could do okay. As a matter of fact, never did I do quite as well relatively as the four years I was in college. I would work every summer and save money for winter. Between the junior and senior years I had enough money so I didn't have to worry about the senior year in college. So that summer I took off for six weeks or so. You're not old enough to remember, but things were really tough in '37. I went to Northern California, and I would go from town to town and get jobs washing dishes, picking hops, picking prunes, whatever. After six weeks of that that summer, I had no doubt ever about being able to get a job.

As a matter of fact, I never have had any trouble. I always worked, and so it's always easier to get work and make money than you think. It's never been a worry to me. I should have planned a career, but I was taking a major, and I thought I'd be able to do something in that career. I made a mistake being a chemist. I should have specialized in business or something, because that's what I've enjoyed more since, the numbers. I've been on the boards of directors of quite a few companies. As a matter of fact, I'm chairman of the board of a little company up here in Laguna Niguel right now. And I'm on the board of directors of a company back in Maryland. The company I'm the chairman of the board of was quite successful. We make money.

Paul Stillwell: What other jobs had you had in the previous summers during college?

Admiral Wilkinson: I worked more than just the summers. I worked at night one year. I've worked for oil companies. The most interesting job I had was one year I did the coroner's work for San Diego. If a person died under suspicious circumstances or where they couldn't attest the cause, then they had to do an autopsy. As a guy with a chemical background, I had a job doing the city coroner's work for San Diego. I'd get $20.00 a head. They would give me the liver, spleen, lung, heart, kidney, stomach and contents, sample of blood and urine. If there was no poison or anything in there, I'd go through everything, and it would take me about 18 hours. If you were lucky enough to get somebody that was poisoned [laughter], you could do it faster. Once I had two people from cyanide, and I finished it all off in about three hours. Forty dollars—gee, that was half a month's pay.

One summer I worked in a creamery over in Yuma, and that was a bad thing. They asked me when I went there not only to work but also to see if I could find out where the dishonesty was. It turned out to be the manager who was selling part of the product and pocketing the money.

I was living in a boarding house in Yuma, and that must have been '36. I played a lot of poker, and I've played poker all my life. I was fortunate enough in poker that in a game of stud I had aces back to back, and I got a third ace. I had not bet the aces back to back, and somebody had three 7's, and he pushed it all the way. I called, and finally I had a cinch winner. Anyway, I won that pot, and it had over $80.00 in it, which was more than I made in a month. So the summer working in the creamery in Yuma was an interesting one. Also, I did water samples for the city of Coronado. I made money lots of different ways. I worked for the NYA, National Youth Administration, for 40 cents an hour. But I did lots of different jobs, and I didn't spend a lot. Finally in '38 I bought myself a 1937 Chevy, which was, I think, $400.00.

Paul Stillwell: Your skill at poker is legendary. I have heard about this from anybody who knows you.* What was the secret of your success?

Admiral Wilkinson: I'm a highly overrated poker player.

Paul Stillwell: I doubt that.

Admiral Wilkinson: I have not won a fortune at poker, but I won consistently. When I went to college, we played poker once a week in the honorary fraternity I belonged to. It was a five-chip limit, and chips were worth a half a cent, so the maximum bet was two and a half cents. Sometimes I'd have a successful night and maybe win 95 cents or something. Well, that might not sound like much, but you've got to put yourself back in

---

* See, for example, the Naval Institute oral history of Vice Admiral Joe Williams, Jr., USN (Ret.), who discussed Admiral Wilkinson's poker prowess.

1935. That was a lot of money. So I played a lot of poker at low stakes, and I was a very cautious player. And I'm good with numbers. I remember all the cards.

Now, if we were playing stud and I threw my hand away, I always remembered what my hand was. Now, if you were to manipulate it so that hand would come up, for example, in everybody's hole card on the next deal, that would be dishonest and cheap. I'm not. I have never lied or cheated or been dishonest in my life, but I do remember. If by chance that happens, that's a big advantage to know. Strangely enough, although you shuffle, it doesn't always change all those things, so once in a great while you may know what your next card's going to be. That is an enormous advantage, and so I do remember.

But, forgetting all that, I'm a careful player. I don't draw to shorts, and I'm quite lucky. I used to think that I was a much better poker player than I am. Actually, all during World War II, both at sea and at playing poker, I was enormously lucky. The submarine I was on, the Japanese were being pushed back, and they were still in New Guinea.* We went into Biak Harbor in Northern New Guinea, and we sank a cruiser-minelayer, and it took us hours. See, we were depth charged for about four hours getting out of there, but that's another story. But six or eight months later we were going into Biak to fuel. One afternoon and evening playing poker in Biak Harbor I made 13 consecutive one-card draws. I don't mean in consecutive hands. Are you a poker player?

Paul Stillwell: No.

Admiral Wilkinson: Well, you draw one card if you've got four to a straight, and I'm not talking an inside straight but where you could hit either end or four to a flush or two pair. One card. Well, the odds are at least five to one against making that. If you take five to one and raise it to the 13th power that is an astronomical number. I can work it out for you if you want.

Paul Stillwell: I'm sure you can.

---

* The submarine was the USS *Darter* (SS-227).

Admiral Wilkinson: But one afternoon and evening, not in consecutive hands because you don't get consecutive opportunities, I made 13 consecutive one-card draws, and the 13th was the most interesting one of all, because it was a five-card draw poker game. Guts. I didn't have to have anything to open, and I was right under the gun. I looked at my cards, and I got three aces. I passed. The most fortunate thing that could happen did happen. The second player opened. It went around to the fourth player over there, who had more money than anybody else in the game except me. He had $300.00 or $400.00 and I wanted it, and he raised. So when it got back to me I said, "You know, I've been very lucky this evening. I've made 12 consecutive one-card draws, and I'm not superstitious. I've got another one here, and I can do it again, and so I'm going to raise you." Actually I had three aces. Remember I told you.

Paul Stillwell: Right.

Admiral Wilkinson: "So I'm going to raise you." So the opener dropped, and the guy that raised over there didn't much like that, but finally he put his money in. I kept a five with my three aces and said, "Deal it right there." I got one card, and everybody could see that I didn't look at it. He drew two cards, and I knew I had him. Actually he had three nines. The opener dropped, so it was his bet, and he checked. I didn't look at my cards, and I said, "Well, like I told you, I'm not superstitious about 13. I can do it again, so I'm going to bet you all the money you've got." So I did, and I hadn't even looked at my card. Well, the odds are five to one against a one-card draw, and he agonized and he agonized. He finally called, and I shuffled my cards up and remember I told you 13. I had paired the five. I had aces full. I didn't need them. Three aces would have been enough. He wanted to know if I drew the ace or the five. [Laughter] But that was pretty damn lucky.

Paul Stillwell: Yes.

Admiral Wilkinson: Jumping ahead in years, our country gave the Brits nuclear submarines, and the young officers who were going to man their first one came over to our country for training. Since I was commander of the only nuclear submarine division, Submarine Division 102, they were put under my tutelage.* I discovered to my shock that those people in their intelligence briefing before they came over had been advised not to play poker with me. [Laughter] Can you imagine that? That's an international reputation. They couldn't wait.

Paul Stillwell: And how did they do?

Admiral Wilkinson: I will say that we used to play poker for very limited stakes on the *Nautilus*. I jump back now. I was on the *Nautilus* for four years.† We never had a visitor come and go away a winner. Once Ralph Kissinger almost did.‡ The last round I wiped him out. I was a very lucky poker player.

Paul Stillwell: But there must have been more than just luck. I think in addition to knowing the cards there are some psychological games that are involved as well.

Admiral Wilkinson: There are. Years later I was assigned as Chief of Staff, U.S. Forces Japan, and that was with the Air Force, the jet pilots.§ They were hot pilots, and they flew back to the States and stopped by Las Vegas and played poker with the big boys and won. They were good. We used to play poker every week with them, and I could tell you the stories, but I had a lucky streak. Two and a half years, and I never lost one time, and that really used to frustrate them.

Paul Stillwell: What are the little psychological gimmicks you used? Two and a half years cannot be just luck.

Admiral Wilkinson: I was a rear admiral. The head of the Fifth Air Force was a three-star Air Force general, and he had a deputy in the Air Force that was a two-star guy,

---

* Wilkinson commanded Submarine Division 102 in 1958-59.
† As a commander, Wilkinson was prospective commanding officer, then CO, from 1953 to 1957.
‡ Captain Ralph J. Kissinger, USN.
§ Wilkinson had this duty from 1966 to 1969.

same as I was a two-star guy. They were both jet pilots, and there was a certain amount of competition between them as such. Tim, the deputy, used to say in our little game that the first time he played he won. He said to my wife, "It's not fair. We're anteing 50 cents. I bet $30.00, and everybody drops out and I win. It's not fair for me to play with those."

My wife, who has a certain amount of confidence in me as a poker player, said, "Tim, only time will tell." Well, the second night we were playing, I don't even remember my hand now, but I remember how the betting went. There were seven of us, and we'd anted 50 cents, so there was $3.50 in there. I opened for $3.50, size of the pot. Another guy called, which made $10.50 in there. It came to Tim, and he said, "I'll see your $3.50, and I'll raise you $30.00"

It came back to me, and I said, "Tim, that's a terrible way to play. We're playing guts." That's open on anything. "You bet $30.00. Everybody drops. You take the pot. Nobody knows who had the best hand. I said, "I'll tell you what I'll do. I'll see your $30.00, and I'll raise you to $75.00." So I did. We didn't have a damn thing. So he looked down for a while. Now it was another $75.00 to him. So he threw his hand in, and I took the pot. And I said, "See, Tim, nobody knows who had the best hand."

Well, his boss jumped up and ran all around the table. He said, "Goddamn, Tim, are you gutless to let a guy in the Navy do something like that?" [Laughter] I remember that hand well.

Paul Stillwell: Did you have a better hand than he?

Admiral Wilkinson: I don't know. [Laughter] Probably, probably. I don't remember the hand, but I had opened, and I didn't open on nothing, and so I probably had a fair hand. He picked the wrong time. But with six weeks to go out there I gave a little speech to them. I said, "Gentlemen, I've got my orders now back to the States, and I want to tell you guys in this group who socially are together a lot here how much I've enjoyed my tour out here, how much I've enjoyed working with the Air Force. Of all the things, how much especially I've enjoyed this poker game." I had never lost. [Laughter] I said, "You know, there's one thing that has really worried me about it. I've been afraid it wouldn't last, that you'd quit playing, but now there's only six weeks more to go, so I don't have to worry about that, and you guys are all friends of mine, so I want to tell you. All this time I've been holding back for fear the game would stop, and now I'm not going to do that anymore. You guys are friends of mine, so I'm warning you now it's no holds. Watch out. Yap, yap, yap, yap, yap." I made that speech just for fun.

Paul Stillwell: You're a master psychologist.

Admiral Wilkinson: Never in my life have I had such a lucky streak. So I won a ton of money the last six weeks, and my wife would go out to the dirty dish shops and buy this or that, and I'd tell her, "Honey, you're just not spending the money fast enough." So we really acquired a lot during our last six weeks in Japan. We're here in the den, and there's some *Nautilus* stuff and Navy pictures in here, but if you went in the rest of the house you'd think we'd never been anywhere but Japan.

Paul Stillwell: I have seen those things, yes.

Admiral Wilkinson: I was in the Navy mostly in submarines, and that meant San Diego and New London and Norfolk, and my wife would say to me, "If we're in the Navy, why don't we go somewhere?" and she didn't mean New London and Norfolk. She meant somewhere overseas. Finally I got banished to Japan, and that was our overseas tour, but to my wife that's the best thing that ever happened to us. She loved her tour in Japan. The Commander Fifth Air Force in Japan had had a special poker table made, and after I got back to the States and was here a while they sent it to me. [Laughter] It's out in the garage there now. I've made it sound like I'm a great poker player, and I'm really not. I'm a careful, cautious player, and there were periods in my life when I was enormously lucky. I still do play poker every two weeks with a really good group here who are mostly scientists or teachers over at the college, and I manage to make a little profit.

Paul Stillwell: Still be lucky.

Admiral Wilkinson: Yes.

Paul Stillwell: Did you play baseball or other team sports like your dad?

Admiral Wilkinson: No, I tried to run track, but I was too small and too slow. The only thing I did as a sport to any success was play tennis. I played hours a day, and I practiced at it. Although I was small, I kept hitting the ball back, and I did win the county championship. When I came home and told my grandmother that, which I was quite pleased with, she said, "Oh, isn't that great?" Then finally she slipped and said, "Your dad won all four years." [Laughter] He was a tennis player.

Paul Stillwell: How much religious exposure did you have growing up?

Admiral Wilkinson: I belonged to the Christian Church in Holtville, and I went every Sunday to Sunday school class and to Christian Endeavor, but it never really took with me very much. Now, my sister and her husband at the time in high school got into it, and they became very devout. My sister's husband became a Presbyterian minister, and my sister worries about me and prays for me all the time. Her whole congregation is praying to get this knee well, but personally I haven't been very religious.[*]

Paul Stillwell: What led you to major in chemistry when you went to college?

Admiral Wilkinson: That was a mistake. When I first started college I was going to be premed. I was very unlucky in that it just happened that the premed group at that time were very cooperative with one another and would exchange papers. In their fraternity or whatever they had files of papers and files of past exams, and they all in my opinion cheated. I don't lie and I don't cheat, and I don't approve of it. I thought maybe all doctors were like that. They're not. It was just a sad little situation, and I was not going to associate with that group, so I quit being a premed. I'd already taken chemistry, so I

---

[*] At the time of the interview Admiral Wilkinson was having problems with a knee that had become infected after a joint-replacement operation.

just shifted into a chemistry major. That worked out, because by the last year in college I was the senior lab assistant, and the next year I was teaching at the college. Chemistry's changed an awful lot since then. It's amazing how little you know. It used to be technique. Now it's all with the special equipment, cryotography and whatnot.

Paul Stillwell: Were you getting more involved socially in those college years?

Admiral Wilkinson: No. As I said, in high school I was physically immature, and I played tennis there a lot of hours. I wasn't attracted to girls, I guess, or wasn't attractive to girls [laughter], and I didn't do that. Then in college I was working all the time. One year in college I worked nights. I was hard pressed for sleep at school. I'd come out and sleep an hour between classes or something. So it wasn't till about my senior year I met my wife, Janice, at San Diego State.* She came over to get some nitric acid to take a wart off, and I told her, "No, you don't want nitric acid." We got acquainted. But I didn't have much of a social life at State. It wasn't then that I wasn't old enough and wasn't attracted to the girls. It was that I was working.

Paul Stillwell: Well, you said that high school was not that much of a challenge. Did you have to work harder in college?

Admiral Wilkinson: Had to work harder in college with the time I had to put on it. See, I was working at jobs that took hours and hours, and that didn't leave a lot of time for sleep. So I guess I didn't have trouble with the amount of time I put in. But college was harder than high school.

Paul Stillwell: So you had to have good study habits to fit the study into the time available.

Admiral Wilkinson: Yes. Yes.

---

* Her name at the time was Janice Edith Thuli.

Paul Stillwell: How did you land the teaching position after you graduated?

Admiral Wilkinson: I'd been the senior lab assistant in the chemistry department my senior year, and the next year they were going to add an instructor, and, oh, they had an awful lot of applications. The head of the department thought well of me, so he hired me instead of all the applicants they had.

Paul Stillwell: You told me before you started that some of your students were older than you were.

Admiral Wilkinson: Especially in that math class. Well, 19 is not real old. A lot of kids don't start college till they're 18 or more. I was quite successful with my math class. I filled in teaching a course in college algebra. There were two sections, and the head of the math department ran the other section. He taught his section, and I taught mine, and I worked hard with mine. I taught them to help each other. It was hard to get them all to do all their homework, so every day I would end up giving them a little quiz. Frequently I'd leave the room while they were doing it. That put pressure on them, and they would cheat and help one another, and afterwards I'd throw those papers away.

When it was time to take the final, which was most of the grade for the class, the head of the department made the exam out. I said, "Sir, would you like me to give you some problems for the exam?"

"No, no," he said. "I'll make it."

I said, "I don't think that's right. You've got a section, and I've got a section. We've each been teaching our people, and I think I should be able to contribute half the exam so only to be fair to my group."

He said, "Get lost," or words to that effect. "I'll take care of it. I'll make the exam out," which he did. Then he brought them all in, and now this was the real thing. There was no cheating. My class, on a basis of 100, averaged 21% higher than his did, which was a real shock to him. And that was my success as a math teacher. But I finally got them so they would do the work. They worked helping each other and learned how to do it.

Paul Stillwell: So this was a deliberate device on your part when you left the room.

Admiral Wilkinson: Oh, yes. Sure.

Paul Stillwell: Was it more than just them cooperating with each other that got them to learn more?

Admiral Wilkinson: It was cooperating with each other. It was doing sequentially everything that we did in the class and actually doing it under pressure and getting it done. See, the hard part was getting everybody to do the homework, but I got them so that by the time that year was up they had done everything in the book and done it themselves. If you've done something, you're more apt to do it on an exam, especially in college algebra.

Paul Stillwell: Did you enjoy teaching college?

Admiral Wilkinson: I really did. I had every intention of coming back after the war and teaching and finishing off my doctor's degree, for which I did the course work but never did the thesis and got the degree. But rum and gin and destiny play funny tricks, and some way or other I never went back. I always regretted not finishing off and accomplishing something and getting my doctor's degree, but years later I had dozens of Ph.D.s work for me, so I guess it didn't make any difference.

Incidentally, later on in life I had the pleasure of being on a very highly capable, technically capable, advisory group to the CIA.* The membership was classified secret. [Laughter] We would advise them on some of the information they had collected, what it really meant. If they got some information, for example, from Russia we'd say, "Well now, this is what that shows, and this is what you ought to look for." We had quite a capable group. There were ten of them, and two of them were Nobel Prize winners, which means something.

---

* CIA – Central Intelligence Agency.

Paul Stillwell: Yes, it does.

Admiral Wilkinson: I've had the good fortune later on in my life to be associated with some pretty famous people: Nobel Prize winners, scientific advisor to the President, heads of this and heads of that. You know, I've heard all my life about these guys that could memorize a page at a glance and all that stuff. Paul, I've never met one of those people. I've met some of the best and the brightest, and the ones that do the very best work real hard at it. Those guys really did their homework and put it in, and I think that's the way it really is.

Paul Stillwell: What were the satisfactions you derived from teaching?

Admiral Wilkinson: I really enjoyed teaching, and I enjoyed the association with the students. There was an awful lot of it that was on a one-on-one basis. Not giving a lecture to 100 people, although I've done that a lot, too, but I was helping them learn how to do their experiments, learning how to work out the problems and whatnot, and there's a lot of satisfaction when a person makes improvement. I guess more than anything else, it's when you get the good rapport, and the guy appreciates it. I lived on that appreciation; I enjoyed it.

Paul Stillwell: And you could see visible evidence of progress.

Admiral Wilkinson: Yes, and I guess I hadn't thought of it that way until you asked me, but I guess what meant the most was when the people really appreciated your association and what you'd done for them.

Paul Stillwell: So you got a lot of feedback in that way.

Admiral Wilkinson: Yes, yes.

Paul Stillwell: What was the focus of your doctoral studies?

Admiral Wilkinson: I was taking chemical engineering, but actually it was in organic chemistry related to oil. I had finished some here from San Diego, some in summer session, some when I had the teaching fellowship. I had finished all the coursework, which was only 48 units. It may be more now, but I had finished all the coursework. I had 46 units of A and two units of B. I had passed my scientific German and was about to pass my scientific French without ever having taken French. I can't pronounce scientific French, but I could read it. I had studied that, and I was about to pass that. The thesis and the French were all I had left to do.

Paul Stillwell: What intervened to prevent you from finishing the thesis?

Admiral Wilkinson: The military service.

Paul Stillwell: Okay. Well, could you get into that, please, and how you wound up getting involved with the Navy?

Admiral Wilkinson: Well, the time came when there was going to be a draft. There was an opportunity to get a commission in the Navy and do a year's active duty. You signed up, and you did a month's training as a midshipman at sea. Then you went to V-7 Officer Candidate School, and they had them all over the country.[*] The first one was on *Prairie State*, and I went to the second OCS class, the first one at Northwestern.[†] There were 400 of us went there, and they were, I believe, all college graduates. You took your three months of academics plus a little of marching around, which I didn't do very well, and then you got a commission in the reserve as a (D), deck volunteer general, USNR. You did one year's active service, and then that completed your military obligation, and you didn't have to be drafted.

---

[*] V-7 was a Naval Reserve officer-training program in which individuals with enough college education (normally a bachelor's degree) were trained as deck officers for surface ships.
[†] The pre-dreadnought battleship *Illinois* (BB-7) was commissioned in 1901. After her active service she was loaned to the New York Naval Militia in 1921 to serve as a training ship, stationed in the Hudson River west of New York City. In January 1941 she was renamed the *Prairie State* so the name "Illinois" could be used for a projected new battleship. Construction of the new ship started in January 1945 but was canceled in August of that year because World War II was about to end. Northwestern University in Evanston, Illinois, was the site of one of the midshipman training schools.

My year would have been up December 12, 1941, which was just a little too late. So I was in for the war, and by the time the war was over I never got around to getting out. I did pretty well in OCS class except my aptitude was poor, so I stood only second in the class. I was first academically, but the guy that was first had a 3.9 in aptitude and that counted a quarter of your standing, and so I stood second. They had three courses: navigation, ordnance, and seamanship.

I had two roommates, and they put us under a very rigid military thing of marching right and cornering and all this. You had compulsory study hours, and one night the duty officer came in, and everybody was at rigid attention. My roommates were studying, and I was writing a letter to Janice. The guy said to me, "What are you doing?"

I said, "I'm writing a letter to my girlfriend, sir."

He said, "This is compulsory study hour."

I said, "Well, sir, there's so many compulsory study hours. There's just not that much material."

He said, "Oh, yeah?" The quarterly standings had come out. He said, "Where did you stand in navigation?"

I said, "Number one, sir."

He said, "Where did you stand in seamanship?"

"Number one, sir."

"Where did you stand in ordnance?"

I said, "Well, number two, sir."

He said, "Well, work on your ordnance." [Laughter] But his heart wasn't in it. [Laughter] I still hear from those two roommates of mine, because they say I helped them get through. The bookwork came easy for me.

Paul Stillwell: Was the opportunity to get a commission the thing that steered you to the Navy instead of one of the other services?

Admiral Wilkinson: Earlier, in '39, an Army guy came in my lab and offered to get me a reserve commission in the Army, and I thought he was out of his mind. But a year later the draft was coming, and I preferred the Navy to the Army anyway.

Paul Stillwell: Why?

Admiral Wilkinson: I don't know. Just, I guess, growing up and living in San Diego. But when I went in the Navy I had no intention of staying in and making a career out of it. I didn't even consider that. But by the time the war ended, I was the exec of a submarine and had lots of responsibilities, taking care of people and doing everything to get everybody out, and we had a very good submarine. Later I got my orders to new construction and never got around to getting out. Then I got into the nuclear business, and that was exciting. And then if you're skipper of the *Nautilus* you don't get out, and if you're skipper of the *Long Beach* you don't get out. I was going to get out on 20 years as I was leaving the *Long Beach*, but then I got selected admiral early, and that didn't seem right. So the first thing I knew, I was in for 34 years.

Paul Stillwell: The Navy had you hooked.

What are your recollections of being around Chicago and Evanston, Illinois? This was a long way from your background in California.

Admiral Wilkinson: Well, as I said, I went to the first Officer Candidate School at Northwestern in the V-7 program. That was during the last three months of 1940, and I didn't get around very much, so I don't remember too much of that at the time. When the people would have liberty, they would wander off as far as they could go, but I didn't do that much.

There were some very talented people that came into the service in World War II. And some of the different officer candidate schools around the country became the dominant forces in football and other sports. Iowa Preflight or some preflight had the guys that were equivalent to the Heisman Trophy winner.* I mean, they had the All Americans. They could beat any college in the country.

For example, in our little group of 400 at OCS I think we had Hank Luisetti, who was a great basketball player.† The University of Northwestern challenged our group to a basketball game. Well, we ought to be able to get a basketball team up, so they got one up, and we went over and watched. I remember they just ran over us and picked up a big lead for the first few minutes. But then suddenly talent will tell. They were almost caught up, and the second half was a slaughter. Our people just wiped them out going away, because although they hadn't practiced as a team, individually each one of them was better than his opponent. So we had some crackerjack people.

Paul Stillwell: How much had you traveled in your growing-up years? Had you mostly just stuck around Southern California?

Admiral Wilkinson: I guess I had never been anywhere except Southern California and over to Yuma, Arizona. I'd worked in Yuma one summer, and maybe across the border to Mexico. But I had not traveled at all until I went off and rode the *Wyoming* as a midshipman for a month and then off to OCS school at Northwestern.‡ I've sure traveled since, and I've been to all the states and an awful lot worldwide. But at the time that I was going to OCS, there wasn't much time off. When there was liberty you were in

---

* Nile C. Kinnick of the University of Iowa earned the Heisman Trophy as the best college football player during the 1939 season. After graduation he entered the university's law school but dropped out to serve in the Navy during World War II. He became a naval aviator and on 2 June 1943 was killed during a training flight from the aircraft carrier *Lexington* (CV-16).
† Angelo "Hank" Luisetti was a two-time All-America at Stanford University (1937, 1938) and is in the Basketball Hall of Fame. He is credited with devising the running one-handed shot at a time when two-handed shots were the norm in basketball.
‡ USS *Wyoming* (BB-32) was commissioned as a battleship in 1912 and served in that role until being demilitarized as a result of the 1930 London Treaty on the limitation of naval armaments. She was redesignated a miscellaneous auxiliary, AG-17, on 1 July 1931 and thereafter served into the mid-1940s as a training ship for gunnery and for midshipman cruises.

midshipman uniform, and you wandered off as far as you could. I guess I did that along with others but not too much.

Paul Stillwell: How much was there of a disciplinary organization teaching you the military-type things like customs and traditions and saluting and so forth?

Admiral Wilkinson: Well, they tried to put pressure on for three months in marching and being military, but it was a tough group for them to work with, because most everyone there was a college graduate, and they didn't adapt to that real quick.

Paul Stillwell: It sounds like you weren't all that adaptable either.

Admiral Wilkinson: No, although I think the young man that got such a high aptitude mark at 3.9 was the son of a senior military guy. He probably had great aptitude. My aptitude wasn't really that poor. It's just that they had to average marks out.

Paul Stillwell: Well, it's interesting you mentioned you were in the *Wyoming* for your midshipman training. I've just been interviewing Admiral King, and he was in that same ship at about the same time.*

Admiral Wilkinson: Is that a fact?

Paul Stillwell: Yes. What do you remember about your first shipboard experience?

Admiral Wilkinson: I took the midshipman training tongue in cheek and with a little grain of salt. Thought it was sort of humorous in a way, because again they were putting great pressure on putting four years of military indoctrination on a group that were pretty mature. I think all of us were college graduates, and so it was a little harder on people who have never had that background to impose it on them instantly. So we pulled a few jokes on people.

---

* See the Naval Institute oral history of Vice Admiral Jerome H. King, Jr., USN (Ret.).

Paul Stillwell: What were some of the jokes?

Admiral Wilkinson: Oh, you wander into a room with 20 or 30 guys. You would know a guy's name and say, "Paul Stillwell, Paul Stillwell, they want you down at the exec's office." Then you'd wander off and wonder what happened when Paul got down to the exec's office. [Laughter] Well, that's a terrible thing to say, but we'd pull those kinds of jokes and forget it.

Paul Stillwell: What was the relationship like with the enlisted crew members of the *Wyoming*?

Admiral Wilkinson: Not much because there were so many of us. They had the place overloaded with midshipmen and marched us around. The three months at OCS are a little hazy, because it was just going through some intense academic stuff. Then when I went to active duty in the fleet, things were really different, because suddenly I had a function, a responsibility, authority. I was an officer. I was on a cruiser—this was the year before the war—and promotion was slow in the Navy. The Navy didn't expand as fast as the Army and the air people did. A couple of years later I was back, and I think I was a lieutenant by then. Kids that I'd taught in college were majors, and I thought "Wow."

Paul Stillwell: Well, back to the *Wyoming*. What sort of operations did she do while you were on board?

Admiral Wilkinson: She steamed around to train these midshipmen in the Atlantic, and I don't remember much except we went aboard. We did the evolutions. We put our hammocks up and took our hammocks down.

Paul Stillwell: Holystoning and swabbing the deck?[*]

---

[*] Holystoning refers to the practice of cleaning a ship's wooden decks by scraping them with bricks pushed back and forth across the planks by means of wooden handles. It is a laborious operation.

Admiral Wilkinson: Yes, yes. It's all hazy in my mind. I don't remember much about it except having a little fun running people around.

Paul Stillwell: Was the commissioning done out there at Northwestern?

Admiral Wilkinson: Yes, December 12, 1940.

Paul Stillwell: Was there some sort of ceremony?

Admiral Wilkinson: I had stood high. I stood second in the class and the guy was shaking hands. They got him mixed up, and he complimented the guy behind me, but that was okay. I didn't really care. From there I was ordered to the cruiser *Louisville*.[*]

Paul Stillwell: Was that your choice?

Admiral Wilkinson: No, I don't think we had a choice. I don't remember ever being asked for a choice. They sent us off for our reserve training and not all from Northwestern, but I remember it took us some time to catch up with the *Louisville*. She had been down in South Africa and made a run back. And then out to Pearl, so we had to travel out to Pearl to get to the *Louisville*.[†] As a matter of fact, they sent us on another cruiser for transport, the *Vincennes* I believe, so I didn't get to the *Louisville* for six weeks or so after I was commissioned.

Some other reserve officers were coming, and there were ten of us that reported aboard all at once. They had us down on the well deck on reporting aboard, and now they had to assign us to different divisions for training, and none of them really had vacancies. None of them really wanted us. These were just extra officers out for

---

[*] USS *Louisville* (CA-28), a *Northampton*-class heavy cruiser, was commissioned 15 January 1931. She had a standard displacement of 9,050 tons, was 600 feet long, 66 feet in the beam, and had a maximum draft of 16 feet. Her top speed was 32 knots. She was armed with nine 8-inch guns and four 5-inch guns. The *Louisville* served throughout World War II and was eventually decommissioned 17 June 1946.

[†] In October 1939 the Navy Department directed the establishment of a Hawaiian Detachment of the U.S. Fleet, which was then based in California. In the spring of 1940 the bulk of the fleet remained in Hawaii after going there for Fleet Problem XXI. Thus the major ships of the U.S. Pacific Fleet were operating out of Pearl Harbor at the time the Japanese struck in December 1941.

training, and all the other hundreds of OCS graduates were off to other ships in the same way. They weren't fulfilling a function yet. They were on some ship for augmentation to get indoctrinated and trained. They were trying to decide which divisions to assign the ten of us to. They said, "Well, we have one vacancy in engineering. Who knows anything about engineering?"

I thought to myself, "Gee, it must be better to be one of one than one of ten," so I said, "I do." Actually I did have a considerable technical background, having taken technical courses and physics courses and worked in a service station and whatnot. So they sent me down to engineering, which turned out to be very good because there were mostly warrant officers there. One of the line officers got lost, and then another one got transferred, so there was a lot of pressure from the warrant officers on me to get qualified to stand watches. So I qualified as an engineering watch stander on a heavy cruiser in six weeks. I worked hard at it.

Then in three months something happened to the assistant engineer, who was out of the class of '31; I ranked with the class of '41.[*] The chief engineer didn't like any of the line officers that he had had for a few months and transferred them on up to the deck divisions. He told me I could be the acting assistant engineer, and eventually I became the assistant engineer. So I was the assistant engineer, which may not sound very much, but in 1941 on a heavy cruiser assistant engineer was a guy with at least ten years' service in the Navy, and I had three months. So suddenly, instead of just a fill-in for training, I was a person with responsibility, authority, accountability, a working job. So my last seven months on the cruiser I was the assistant engineer.

The ship's damage control was out of date and not filled up. I was a bachelor and took most of my warrant officers' duties at night because they had families ashore. I stayed aboard, and I rewrote the ship's damage control books, so I thought that was of value to the ship after I was gone. So I had a good tour on there. The chief engineer, who was a fellow named George O'Keefe out of the Naval Academy class of 1925,

---

[*] These refer to members of Naval Academy classes.

thought highly of me.* As I just showed you a minute ago, I just got a letter from him here a couple of weeks ago. Gosh, he's got to be over 90.†

Paul Stillwell: Yes.

Admiral Wilkinson: I've got to answer that before he dies.

Paul Stillwell: How sophisticated was shipboard damage control in that era?

Admiral Wilkinson: Not very sophisticated, but the lineups and the marking of the valves and the designation of what was closed and what was opened under what conditions should have been up to date and right. There were a lot of errors in it, and that's all I was doing. I wasn't changing philosophy or anything. I was just bringing records up to date. I've overemphasized what I was doing, but I worked hard at it.

Paul Stillwell: Well, I think the damage control got better. As the war went on, the Navy incorporated lessons from combat experience.

Admiral Wilkinson: Part of damage control had to come from lineups. Part of it needed to come also from design and integrity of systems. Nowadays a ship should be checked every 18 months to make sure that there aren't any leaks when it's lined up. I suspect that that wasn't true. I suspect it isn't true in a lot of ships today either. I suspect that you could be all lined up and there still would be leaks. Unless you check on something with a test and plug leaks, there's going to be some. It's not like a submarine that's really watertight. Surface ships, you need to work at that. There are a lot of bulkhead penetrations. I sounded grander than I was when I said I reorganized the damage control. I didn't really change it. I just went around and checked and brought it up to date.

---

* Lieutenant Commander George F. O'Keefe, USN.
† O'Keefe was born 6 December 1903.

Paul Stillwell: What was involved in the propulsion side of your job as assistant engineer?

Admiral Wilkinson: We had a very old-fashioned 300-pound steam system with eight boilers, two screws.* We had 225 engineers in our different engineer divisions and warrant officers for each one of them plus me.

Paul Stillwell: And you could make pretty good speed with that 300-pound plant.

Admiral Wilkinson: Oh, yes. We could make 30 knots, maybe 31.

Paul Stillwell: You told the story before the tape started about the competitiveness in fuel economy during those years. If you could repeat that please.

Admiral Wilkinson: The cruiser *Louisville* was stationed in Pearl Harbor, but before that she'd been in the Atlantic and she'd been sent on special missions to South Africa.† That was independent duty, so she had been absent from being an integrated unit of the fleet for a long time. So she had fallen behind in doing competitive training years and whatnot. So *Louisville*, after it got to Honolulu and joined up there, was in an intensive period to try to schedule all the different kinds of exercise and training functions that they had not done when they were off operating independently.

There were different competitions. There was seamanship and there was gunnery. She had 8-inch guns. And she would do competitive training things. As a matter of fact, I had a battle station as Spot 2, spotting some of turrets at one time. But my interest was in engineering. They had an intensive engineering competition with many exercises to do. You competed with eight cruisers in different competitions, and one of them was on fuel economy. That was probably the most important one, and our cruiser did win that.

---

* The standard steam pressure for U.S. warships built later, during the World War II era, was 600 pounds per square inch.
† In 1940, as a neutral ship at a time when World War II was under way in the Atlantic, the *Louisville* had transferred $148 million in British gold from Simonstown, South Africa, for deposit in the United States.

Paul Stillwell: Please tell the tape how your cruiser won that one.

Admiral Wilkinson: I'm embarrassed to tell you that story.

Paul Stillwell: No, no. That's a good one.

Admiral Wilkinson: Well, when I was going to graduate school and living up in Los Angeles, I worked nights for Union Oil Company. Because I was a chemist, I did their chemistry work at night. I had a gentleman there that worked with me who had just retired from the Navy as a chief petty officer with 20 years' service. Then I went on my way to *Wyoming* and Northwestern and transported on the *Vincennes* to the *Louisville*. I was in engineering, and the *Louisville* needed to fuel. The first day we had 825,000 gallons of fuel to get, and at that time in this engineering competition of eight cruisers in our group we were standing fifth. This was fuel economy, and they would shut off the showers to not spend as much fuel evaporating water, and they would turn the lights down low and many other economies.

You got your fuel allowance depending on the speed you were supposed to make. You had a different allowance for every RPM. And so at the end of the hour our people would very carefully control the revolutions so that we would average just at a half so you'd get the fuel allowance for the next half RPM, because the fuel allowance was for every integral RPM. And if you had a casualty, that counted against you. The competition really was made up of casualties and meeting commitments and fuel economy.

As the line officer, not a warrant, they gave me the job the first day of being in charge of fueling. When I went down to the fuel barge that was tied alongside, lo and behold, the skipper of the fuel barge was this Navy chief I'd worked with at nights for a year. He had now been called back to active duty. I'd bring him some coffee maybe and some stuff for his barge, and although we never said a word about it, some way or other every time we fueled I'd get extra fuel. I'm quite quick with numbers, and I had to keep records. I can remember to this day, and that's a long time ago, 1941, that I had a 4 1/8% percent meter error, so really I was getting 4% more fuel than the record showed.

Paul Stillwell: You claimed it was in error.

Admiral Wilkinson: That was enough for us to win the engineering competition going away. I got a commendation for that, which I always thought was a little unfair, because it was just because I knew that chief.

Paul Stillwell: So essentially you would get more fuel on board than the books would show you got?

Admiral Wilkinson: Right, some way. I don't know how it happened.

Paul Stillwell: You can guess.

Admiral Wilkinson: All I know was I'd sign up for so much fuel, and I'd have an extra tank full.

Paul Stillwell: Very helpful.

Admiral Wilkinson: Well, there's always some meter error.

Paul Stillwell: Did you do any speculation on how you would have done vis-à-vis the other ships if you got exactly what you were accounted for?

Admiral Wilkinson: No, but I'm sure 4% was significant. We didn't win by that much. That's a big amount of fuel. I mean, the first time it was 30,000 gallons extra. That runs you quite a ways. That guy and I had worked closely together. I thought highly of him.

Paul Stillwell: Of course you would.

How did the regular officers in the *Louisville*'s wardroom react toward the new reservists?

Admiral Wilkinson: There was a certain amount of hazing. The most hazing, strangely enough, came from the other ensigns. In those days you were an ensign for three years before you could get promoted to jaygee.* We had what they called the bull ensign, the senior ensign, who was out of the class of '38, and we were here ranked with the class of '41. So, strangely enough, the hazing and the pushing the weight around weren't from senior management. It was from rather senior ensigns. They happened to be Naval Academy, not that that means anything. They were just in a senior position, and so there was a certain amount of taking advantage of that.

We had one young officer in our group that the bull ensign put a lot of pressure on him because he put his revolver on. You cannot wear a revolver until you've passed the qualification. You've just jogged my memory. I'd forgotten that for years. The young reserve ensign he was picking on just happened to have been the pistol champion for the state of Arkansas, and so they took him out to the firing range. Whtt. Whtt. They were all bull's-eyes. So, to the reserve officers in our group, that hazing was a big joke. I took that all with a grain of salt.

Paul Stillwell: What other forms did the hazing take?

Admiral Wilkinson: Just only if you would accede to it. I didn't because I was an engineer, and I had nothing to do with those deck people. They didn't order me around.

Paul Stillwell: But I suspect that you won their respect by the way you did your jobs.

Admiral Wilkinson: With your bosses. Maybe not among the other group of ensigns. The bull ensign, whose name was Walsh, picked on me once.† I said, "Listen, when you see me coming I just want you to do one thing. Get to the other side of the ship and get out of my way. Don't you give me any more crap." And what could he say? I mean, he

---

* Jaygee – lieutenant (junior grade).
† Ensign John J. Walsh, USN, Naval Academy class of 1938.

didn't have any authority over me. Later on, as a matter of fact, he had a nervous breakdown. Not from that. He was mentally disturbed, but that made it tough on some of the others. I think he was emotionally disturbed.*

Paul Stillwell: How much contact did you have with the senior officers in the ship?

Admiral Wilkinson: Very little other than my own boss, Commander O'Keefe, who was head of the engineering. I was head down, tail up, working in the engineering outfit, and I didn't do much else.

Paul Stillwell: Did you have to make the traditional calls on senior officers?†

Admiral Wilkinson: By the time we got to submarines we did. Out there, no. One, we didn't have a lot of families there in Hawaii. The ship was operating on a very intensive schedule trying to catch up on its training years and whatnot, and there was little of that. Later on, even during the war, there was calling, but there wasn't much of that with the *Louisville*. If we called on our boss, a bunch of us got together and called on him as a group and got it over with.

Paul Stillwell: Please tell me about the sailing competition.

Admiral Wilkinson: Now you're going to embarrass me again.

Paul Stillwell: Well, I'm sorry for that, but it's a story worthy of the record.

Admiral Wilkinson: Well, all the cruisers and all the battleships, and it's hazy in my mind whether the carriers were involved, but the capital ships every Saturday had a sailing whaleboat competition. They took a regular whaleboat and put a mast in it and a sail and got one of their young officers who had had sailing and some of the seamen from

---

* Walsh died 21 September 1941 at Pearl Harbor.
† It was expected that officers newly reporting for duty would make brief calls at the homes of senior officers to become better acquainted.

his deck division, and they'd take out their boat, and they'd compete with all the other major ships.

I remember the scoring system. If your sailboat won the race, and there may be 30-odd sailing whaleboats there in that race, you got ten points. If you were second you got five points. If you were third you got three points, and if you were fourth you got one point. And so on the *Louisville* with our deck divisions, some young ensign that had had sailing at the trade school, at the Naval Academy, would go out and sail with some of his seamen. In all the time they'd done it, they had never placed in the first four, so *Louisville* had zero points.

At the officers' landing over there by the club there was a posting of the standing for this championship for the year. And, of course, we were down in the group at the bottom with zero points. So each time the chief engineer would go over and come back to the wardroom he'd say how embarrassed he was to go over there and see the standing of the *Louisville*, and he was ashamed to face his classmates. He was ashamed to admit that he was on a ship with such poor seamanship talent that they couldn't ever make any points in sailing and seamanship. He said that if the deck-apes up there, the deck divisions, couldn't do it, perhaps they'd like to have the engineers do the sailing. He wasn't serious. He was just rubbing salt in the wounds of his contemporaries in weapons and seamanship.

One Saturday it was worse, because not only did they not get any points, but they also ran aground. They ran aground at high tide, and they had a hard time getting off. That time the chief engineer really got into it. And this had come up to the attention of the captain—that the boat was aground and special provisions had been taken to get it off at high water.

Paul Stillwell: Where were the races held?

Admiral Wilkinson: In Pearl Harbor. There was a course around in there. It was quite a long race. It would take two or three hours.

Paul Stillwell: Around Ford Island?

Admiral Wilkinson: I've forgotten, but it was a considerable distance, and there were considerable legs. Finally there were words from the captain to the exec and the gun boss and Towner, the navigator, who was the third senior officer on the ship.[*] They were afraid, and they were commanders. So when Lieutenant Commander O'Keefe got into his diatribe, they said, "All right. The engineers can sail it next time," which was a shock to him.

This was Sunday. He called me up to his room and asked me what I knew about sailing, and I said, "Nothing, sir."

He said, "That's too bad, because you have to sail the sailing whaleboat next Saturday."

I said, "Commander, I grew up in the Imperial Valley. I learned to swim in an irrigation ditch. I've never seen a sailboat. I don't know anything about it. You got the wrong man."

He said, "That's too bad, because you are going to do it next Saturday."

I said, "Commander, who do you think is winning you this engineering "E"? I'm busy. I'm correcting the damage control bill."[†]

He said, "Listen. You're going to run that."

So the next the morning, as assistant engineer of this cruiser, I got all my engineers out on deck, and I told them we were going to sail the whaleboat race with the engineering force next Saturday and asked who knew anything about sailing. I had 225 guys, and they all sat on their hands. There wasn't anybody that knew anything about sailing. So I said, "Let me start over. Let me tell you what's been going on up in the wardroom." So I waxed eloquent and told them about the chief engineer and what he said about the deck apes, and if they weren't capable enough or didn't know any more seamanship than that, perhaps we should get the engineers who were good at everything to come up and sail for them.

So then I talked quite a while along that vein, which appealed to my guys' sense of humor, and then I told them, "Now, I don't know anything about sailing or what you

---
[*] Lieutenant Commander George C. Towner, USN.
[†] An "E," for excellence, is generally awarded to a ship or component of a ship as a result of top performance in competition with other ships during a given time period.

do to a sailboat. Whether you wax its bottom or wash its sails or what you do, but whatever you do, we're going to do it, and we're going to take off every afternoon this week instead of working. I'm going to get the beer and the steak sandwiches, and we're going to go out there and practice, and next Saturday we've got to sail this damn whaleboat. Now, who knows anything about sailing?"

Suddenly some guys knew about sailing. We had a little second class metalsmith. God, I wish I could remember his name. In his youth he'd won countless championships in the Chesapeake Bay in sailing competitions. It was a different Navy in those days. We had quite a few people in that engineering gang that had had experience with sailing—more than eight. We had a lot of talent, and we did what I said. We got the boat out of the water, and we cleaned it up and spiffed up the sails and the tackle and the lining, and I got the steak sandwiches and the beer, and we took off every afternoon that week and practiced.

There were ten more weeks of this competition year, and I'm telling you there'd be 30-odd boats out there. One week we were in just perfect position and crossed the starting line just after the gun burst. About 20 minutes later there was a total wind shift, and suddenly we were in last position. We never could beat our way all the way back up, and that day we ended up second. But the other nine weeks we won, and 95 points was enough to beat all the other ships and win going away. My boss, the chief engineer, was happy with that, and I still didn't know a damn thing about sailing. But one day, when we were well ahead of everybody else and going straight downwind, I even held the tiller once. But mostly my second class metalsmith did that.

Paul Stillwell: You may not have known how to sail, but you knew how to motivate people.

Admiral Wilkinson: I was lucky enough to find some guys in that engineering gang that were really good at it. A young officer going to the Naval Academy takes some sailing, but he doesn't get to do it as much as my little second class metalsmith had done.

Paul Stillwell: Well, the way the Navy system works you got credit for that.

Admiral Wilkinson: Yes, I got all the credit, and I didn't know a damn thing about it. [Laughter] That's the system, isn't it?

Paul Stillwell: That's right. And it works just the opposite, too, if something bad happens.

You mentioned you were in Spot 2 during some of the gunnery exercises. What did that involve?

Admiral Wilkinson: Before I became assistant engineer I needed a battle station when I first went to that cruiser. They gave me the battle station of Spot 2, which for the after turret sat up there above. After the 8-inch shells were shot and hit, you made a report that they were 200 yards over or 200 feet over or whatever it was. And you could actually see those 8-inch shells in the air from that position.

Paul Stillwell: Were you in the main top, all the way up?

Admiral Wilkinson: Yes.

Paul Stillwell: How good was the *Louisville*'s gunnery?

Admiral Wilkinson: I don't really know. I didn't get into that much. Seems like to me it was pretty good.

Paul Stillwell: Did she do a lot of shooting?

Admiral Wilkinson: A lot of practice. They had missed a year's training, so they were doing a lot. This was before the war, but it was all training. We operated a lot, and we did an awful lot of evolutions, but my main interest was toward engineering. As soon as I got out of that battle station and down to an engineering battle station I never thought much of it anymore.

Paul Stillwell: You probably stood your regular underway watches in engineering, didn't you?

Admiral Wilkinson: Yes. I had that battle station till I became assistant engineer, but then I had a battle station in engineering, and I never stood any watches except engineering. After I qualified as an engineering officer watch in six weeks, then I stood watches as the person in charge. I was a DV(G), and so eventually I wrote a letter in to BuNav asking them to reclassify me as a deck-engineer, volunteer, general, which they did.* I became a DEV(G), USNR.

Paul Stillwell: Did you stand these in main control?

Admiral Wilkinson: Yes.

Paul Stillwell: And you mentioned that the warrants were eager to get you qualified, because presumably they wouldn't have to stand watches as often then.

Admiral Wilkinson: Yes, yes.

Paul Stillwell: What did you do ashore in Hawaii when you went once a week?

Admiral Wilkinson: Not much. I was a bachelor, and I didn't go ashore much. Went to the beach. It's all a little hazy in my mind. But I remember one story. I had two roommates who were also reserves like I was. They had reported aboard the same time. One of them later became the mayor of one of the boroughs in New York City, and the other one was George Peabody Gardner, Jr.† George Peabody Gardner's a good name in Boston, and he became chairman of the board of United Fruit. I got a letter from him right over there this Christmas.

---

* BuNav – The Bureau of Navigation made officer assignments to various duties in the years prior to World War II. In 1942 it was renamed the Bureau of Naval Personnel, a more fitting description.
† Gardner was an ensign.

Paul Stillwell: Who was the one who became a mayor of a borough in New York.

Admiral Wilkinson: McDowell.* We had some crackerjack people in the reserves that came in early during the war or probably all during the war. There were no flies on either one of those guys. They were good people. But George Peabody Gardner didn't need money. George never drew his pay, so it just collected on the books. Finally, after six or seven months, just before the war came, he had $1,200 or something on the books, so he figured he'd better do something with it. So he went and drew it out, and he went over and he bought a half interest in a bowling alley. [Laughter] Bang. The war came. There was a sudden influx of people in Hawaii—people standing in line to do anything. Standing in line at the bowling alley. Made a mint of money. [Laughter] The rich get richer.

Paul Stillwell: That's right.

Admiral Wilkinson: So when we'd go over we might do something like that, go bowling or go to the beach. Having no family and no people with domiciles to visit, you didn't do much.

Paul Stillwell: Did you get to the Royal Hawaiian at all?†

Admiral Wilkinson: Not then, but when the war started the Royal Hawaiian was taken over. It was given to the submarine force as a rest camp, and so I've been to the Royal Hawaiian since but not before the war.

Paul Stillwell: When Admiral Kimmel became the fleet commander in chief he was very active in trying to get the fleet prepared.‡ How much operating did the ship do in addition to the training you mentioned?

---

* Ensign Lester L. McDowell, USNR.
† The Royal Hawaiian is a luxury hotel on Waikiki Beach in Honolulu.
‡ Admiral Husband E. Kimmel, USN, served as Commander in Chief Pacific Fleet from 1 February 1941 to 17 December 1941.

Admiral Wilkinson: Well, all the operation was training, and it did a lot. That's all it did was go out and train, train, train.

Paul Stillwell: How hectic a pace of operations was it?

Admiral Wilkinson: I don't remember, but it was a lot. We were under way a lot, but we were in every weekend.

Paul Stillwell: Oh, I see.

Admiral Wilkinson: We'd just operate during the week.

Paul Stillwell: Did you have a feeling at that time that war was imminent for the United States?

Admiral Wilkinson: No, no, no. Maybe I should have in retrospect, but I was young and totally immersed in what I was doing and probably didn't read the paper every day. I had no inkling that something was going to happen. Later on, by the time we got out to the Philippines, where I was just before Pearl Harbor, then we knew there was something going on. My cruiser passed a Japanese fleet three or four days before the seventh.*

Paul Stillwell: Well, please tell me about that trip.

Admiral Wilkinson: They decided they needed to send supplies out to the Philippines, and so there were two big ships loaded with supplies for the forces in the Philippines. They decided they needed an escort and they sent us, a cruiser, to escort those two ships to Manila or Cavite or wherever they went.

---

* In late November 1941, the Imperial Japanese Navy dispatched from the Kurile Islands in the North Pacific a task force built around six aircraft carriers. A force of some 350 fighters, dive-bombers, and torpedo planes attacked U.S. military installations on the island of Oahu, Hawaii, on Sunday, 7 December 1941. The principal focus of attack was the collection of American warships at the naval base at Pearl Harbor. The U.S. Congress declared war on Japan the following day.

Paul Stillwell: Were they merchant ships?

Admiral Wilkinson: Yes, but they were big special cargo ships loaded with supplies for out there and weapons and armament and tanks maybe. I don't know what all.

Paul Stillwell: Any destroyers with you?

Admiral Wilkinson: No. Just us to escort them out. We left Manila on the first of December, having unloaded, and we were given the mission of escorting these ships back. They sent them back, so somebody must have known something was going on. On the seventh we were down between New Guinea and Australia, escorting these ships back, and we got into Honolulu I think on the 19th.

Paul Stillwell: What do you remember about getting the news from Pearl Harbor of the attack?

Admiral Wilkinson: We were on a ship under way at the time, and so we didn't get papers or anything like that. Just the word to the ship, and it was a large amount of unbelief. As I said, undoubtedly senior people somewhere knew the problem was happening, but we on our ship didn't.

Paul Stillwell: Did it make a difference in the ship's operations once you got the news? Was there increased readiness?

Admiral Wilkinson: No, we were escorting these two ships back to Honolulu, and we did that. Then the *Louisville* was scheduled to go to the West Coast, and once we got to Honolulu they had cut people out of the bottom of a battleship there.* I got some of those

---

* On 8 December 1941, 32 crew members of the battleship *Oklahoma* (BB-37) were rescued through holes in the ship's bottom a day after she had capsized during the Japanese attack. For a firsthand account by one of the 32, see Stephen Bower Young, *Trapped at Pearl Harbor: Escape from the Battleship Oklahoma* (Annapolis: Naval Institute Press, 1991).

people on board, and one of them wouldn't sleep below decks. We got as far as San Francisco, and I had my orders, and I was transferred.

Paul Stillwell: What do you remember of steaming into Pearl Harbor on the 19th? What was the sight that greeted you?

Admiral Wilkinson: It was a shock to us. We had thought this was the invulnerable bastion of the United States. It was appalling.

Paul Stillwell: The feeling was that the Japanese could not be capable of such a thing.

Admiral Wilkinson: Right.

Paul Stillwell: How had you gotten orders to submarines? Did you volunteer for that?

Admiral Wilkinson: I volunteered for that when it was obvious that we weren't going to get out of the military service when our year was up. So there was a recognition of the fact that something was going on. I mean, there had been action in the Atlantic, and the word was out, but that didn't involve the Japanese. The action that was imminent related to Germany. There wasn't the same awareness on our part that something was happening related to Japan.

Paul Stillwell: Why did you choose submarines instead of something else?

Admiral Wilkinson: Small ship, responsibility quicker. Chance to get three months back in the States and see my girl and some time at home. It got me back home. That was part of the reason, probably a big part.

Paul Stillwell: Was there anything other than early responsibility that appealed about submarines specifically?

Admiral Wilkinson: No, it was getting home and seeing my girl, to be honest. [Laughter]

Paul Stillwell: And so history was changed.

Admiral Wilkinson: Yes.

Paul Stillwell: And I presume you'd been in touch with her all this time while you were in the cruiser.

Admiral Wilkinson: Somewhat, of course, letters, yes.

Paul Stillwell: But you knew that you wanted to be back with her.

Admiral Wilkinson: Yes, yes. When I came home, we got engaged. Then I went back to Submarine School. I knew I wouldn't be able to get any time off to come to San Diego to get married after the school ended. Her mother had a broken leg, so Janice came by herself to New London, and we got married the day Sub School was out, March 28, 1942.

Paul Stillwell: Well, please tell me about the experiences in New London. What did the training involve?

Admiral Wilkinson: I went to Sub School from January to March 1942. We did a lot of operation on O-boats, the old submarines, and training in the various trainers, including the attack teacher, which is a mathematical thing.* I was pretty good at that. And we had courses in electricity and engineering and whatnot. Your class standing in submarines was based on the marks you got on exams plus your aptitude mark, which all the officers were given.

---

* The early U.S. submarines were designated by letter-number combinations rather than names. *O-1* through *O-16* were commissioned in 1918.

Paul Stillwell: Who determined the scores on that?

Admiral Wilkinson: The senior officers in the Sub School.

Paul Stillwell: The instructors?

Admiral Wilkinson: The instructors, yes. Our Sub School class had 60 people, and we had 30 reserves and 30 regular Navy. Some different problems then than there were later on. The 30 regulars had the 30 best aptitude marks, and the 30 reserves had the next 30. There wasn't one overlap, which was a little odd.

Paul Stillwell: Yes, it was.

Admiral Wilkinson: Yes, a little odd. So every Saturday morning we'd have a special exam, and that exam was supposed to count one quarter of your aptitude mark plus the evaluations of the teachers. The aptitude mark was important, because it counted one quarter of your class standing. And you got your duty assignments according to your class standing. Well, as it happened, they gave this exam every week for several weeks in a row, and by some good fortune I had cracked it. Just by chance one week they threw in a surprise exam on buoyage. I had got interested in that, and the week before I happened to have read that and studied it thoroughly. There wasn't anybody knew all these things about buoyage except me, and so I had a 4.0, and everybody else was down there further and further and further.

Then they had one on Rules of the Road, and the same thing happened to me. It happened that several weeks in a row I had had a 4.0 on that surprise any-subject quiz. And I'm telling you, the average of those quizzes was probably 2.5 or something. So, as it happened, if I took my marks and counted them a quarter and measured them with my aptitude and mathematically, I had more aptitude than they'd given me down here, which was pretty good among the reserves. It was top third, but it was probably about 40th in the school. So my aptitude from all my senior instructors had to have been under 2.5. In other words, they had never done what they said, got aptitude marks and averaged them.

So nobody was less than 2.5 in aptitude except I had to have been on account of these quizzes I had cracked. So, tongue in cheek because I'm a humorist, I went around and asked for an appointment with the CO of the school, who was a crackerjack guy.

Paul Stillwell: Was that Karl Hensel?

Admiral Wilkinson: Hensel, yes.* Good man, smart. Really good at fire control and approaches, and he ran the teachers' training thing for that. And I was good at that. So I went in and told him how much I liked submarines and how bad I felt that I didn't measure up. "What are you talking about?" he said, because I was doing pretty well scholastically in that school.

I said, "Well, here's what I had on the quizzes. Here was my aptitude. And all the senior people. It's obvious mathematically that I'm rated as unsatisfactory in aptitude by these people that I admire as leaders," and whatnot and etc. Butter wouldn't melt in my mouth. Absolute poker face. [Laughter] I was really putting it to him, you know, and asked when I could expect other duty. If I didn't have the aptitude for submarines, I felt really bad. He looked at me for a long time. He told me, "I'll square it away. Get the hell out of here."

I said, "Aye, aye, sir." And the next month all the aptitude marks were read.

Paul Stillwell: Were they fair?

Admiral Wilkinson: I don't know whether they were fair, but they certainly weren't like they had been, and I was marked number one in tactics. [Laughter] Hensel was attack teacher in submarine approaches and all.

Paul Stillwell: Well, I again say you're a good psychologist, because that was a masterful job on Commander Hensel.

---

* Commander Karl G. Hensel, USN, served as officer in charge of the Navy's Submarine School from August 1941 to December 1942.

Admiral Wilkinson: Yes, I did that nicely. I did it tongue in cheek. Remember, I had no intention of making a Navy career at that time. I was in to do my service. The war would be over. I'd be out. So I wasn't intimidated by any seniority or hierarchy from doing what I thought was right. So to me that was fun like, "Hey, Paul Stillwell, they want you down at the office." I mean, that was just humor.

Paul Stillwell: No, but you did it in such a way that you made it appear that you were at fault rather than his people.

Admiral Wilkinson: Oh, yes. Oh, yes.

Paul Stillwell: That was clever.

Admiral Wilkinson: Poker faced too. That was funny. I've forgotten the exact figure now, but I think when I finally retired I had probably sat on nine selection boards. Finally I sat on a selection board that determined which admirals after five years we could keep.

Paul Stillwell: The plucking board.

Admiral Wilkinson: In the beginning it really made a difference whether you were a reserve or from the trade school. Hey, now it doesn't make a damn bit of difference at all. All they care about now is the quality and performance of the guy. I saw that change during my time in the Navy. And I was on the inside where I really knew. I don't know now, but I saw that totally change, and it was good that it did.

Paul Stillwell: Well, for example, now there are four-star admirals who are not Naval Academy graduates, and even 10 or 20 years ago that was not the case.

Admiral Wilkinson: Yes. And I saw that change, but in the beginning our treatment as reserves when we reported to the *Louisville*, those aptitude marks at Sub School, almost unbelievable. But it all changed. The war partly changed it, but then we were at tension for years after the war. It was more than the war that changed it. It was the years to follow.

Paul Stillwell: But the war was important because people would move up on merit. Talent was recognized.

Admiral Wilkinson: And we got some awful good people in the service during the war.

Paul Stillwell: Who are some of the classmates you remember from Submarine School who were going through with you?

Admiral Wilkinson: Some of them have been killed. I don't remember.

Paul Stillwell: What do you remember of the instructors?

Admiral Wilkinson: They were good people. There was Tommy Dykers.[*] There was Hensel. They were sincere. I don't know who did what I said or how, but they really believed those guys had more aptitude. [Laughter] It was an honest mark on their part. And maybe they did, because an awful lot of reserves did have tongue in cheek. The war changed them too.

Paul Stillwell: Were the staff members and instructors role models for those of you who were aspiring to go into submarines?

Admiral Wilkinson: No, I don't believe so. Not at all. They were just running courses and running us through. We did two things. We rode submarines at sea, O-boats, and got some familiarity, and we did an awful lot of training on the training devices, attack teacher and the diving trainer, and we covered a lot of technical material in coursework. I wouldn't say that we considered the instructors or the department heads as role models.

---

[*] Lieutenant Commander Thomas M. Dykers, USN.

Paul Stillwell: One disadvantage you had was it was still so early in the war that you didn't have the benefit of any lessons learned from the combat experiences.

Admiral Wilkinson: No, we didn't. No one that was there as an instructor had been in combat. Later on they brought some people back from combat and put them in the Sub School as instructors. In '44, for example, I became for a short time the TDC instructor, but I got out of that quickly and back to a submarine.* We did have some experienced people later on, but in the beginning, of course, you couldn't have.

Paul Stillwell: Well, one name I've heard is Roy Benson.† A number of people have mentioned how useful he was telling them what it had been like in combat.

Admiral Wilkinson: Oh, but that's years later.

Paul Stillwell: Oh, absolutely.

Admiral Wilkinson: He was terrific, and he really could keep track of what was going on in his head, the whole approach. Afterwards he could tell you just what happened at such and such a time, such and such a thing. He knew what he was doing. He was a crackerjack guy.

Paul Stillwell: Did you use the *Marlin* or *Mackerel* at all in your training?‡

Admiral Wilkinson: Johnny Davidson had been the early skipper of one of those boats, the *Mackerel*.§ No, we did not. We used the O-boats.

---

* TDC – The torpedo data computer was a piece of equipment that figured approach courses for torpedoes to take on their way to a target and set the torpedo gyros prior to firing.
† In 1943-44 Commander Roy S. Benson, USN, ran the prospective commanding officers' course at the Submarine School. The oral history of Benson, who retired as a rear admiral, is in the Naval Institute collection.
‡ USS *Marlin* (SS-205) was commissioned 1 August 1941 and the *Mackerel* (SS-204) on 31 March 1941. Their range was too short to serve the role that the fleet boats did in World War II, so these two were used primarily as training submarines.
§ Lieutenant Commander John F. Davidson, USN. The oral history of Davidson, who retired as a rear admiral, is in the Naval Institute collection.

Paul Stillwell: What do you remember about making approaches in those? How much useful experience was that?

Admiral Wilkinson: Approaches. Oh, yes. We did do that. We would group up and be a whole fire control party, or we would observe that. But we didn't do much of that. Mostly that was for people in PCO school, prospective commanding officers' school. As the Sub School student you more observed fire control parties than you did the actual approaches yourself. Now, we made the actual approaches on the attack trainers.

Paul Stillwell: Did the O-boats have a TDC in them?

Admiral Wilkinson: No.

Paul Stillwell: So did they still use the is-was?*

Admiral Wilkinson: Yes.

Paul Stillwell: What about practicing diving a boat, keeping it in trim, and so forth? Where did you get that knowledge?

Admiral Wilkinson: Again in the diving trainers. They wouldn't have trusted us to do that in the shallow water of Long Island Sound. Oh, no. We probably didn't really learn that till we got out to the fleet.

Paul Stillwell: What do you remember about the escape trunk, ascending in that?

Admiral Wilkinson: We made an escape from 100 feet.

Paul Stillwell: And did you get out into the community of New London at all on liberty?

---

* "Is-was" was the nickname for a circular slide rule that calculated a target ship's future track on the basis of where it had been.

Admiral Wilkinson: Not a great deal. I didn't have a car, and I was going to get married at the end of Sub School. I was saving my money and writing home, and I really didn't do much of that. Probably didn't do any.

Paul Stillwell: So no sightseeing?

Admiral Wilkinson: I had a good friend named Jimmy Antrim on one of the boats.[*] See, I lived in the BOQ and he lived in the BOQ, and we'd go up to the club and have a beer together, and later on he married my wife's sister.[†] So I socialized with him quite a bit, but I didn't go out into the surrounding countryside. Looking back, not really at all, and didn't even miss it.

Paul Stillwell: Was there any clue at all yet about the torpedo problems?[‡]

Admiral Wilkinson: No. No.

Paul Stillwell: What do you recall about finishing up in New London?

Admiral Wilkinson: The day Sub School was over, my girl Janice came out from California, and we were married. Because it was wartime, we didn't have any leave, just orders to proceed and report. That gave us four days plus travel time of two days, so we had six days to get to our next duty station, which was our honeymoon.

At Sub School they had an interesting system: depending on how you did in class, you could get your choice of duty assignment. I was in the enviable position of getting most any duty assignment I wanted. So at the end of Sub School, gung ho, the war was on, and all the people were putting in for an operating boat in the Pacific. I put in for duty on a training submarine in Key West, Florida, and everybody said, "Hey, what

---

[*] Ensign James E. Antrim, USNR, was serving in the crew of the USS *O-7* (SS-68).
[†] BOQ – bachelor officers' quarters.
[‡] During the early part of World War II, U.S. torpedoes were notorious for running deeper than the designed settings and for malfunctioning or poorly functioning exploders in cases in which the torpedoes did hit their targets. For details see David E. Cohen, "The Mk-XIV Torpedo: Lessons for Today," *Naval History*, Winter 1992, pages 34-36.

are you doing? You avoid the war and the war will be over. The Japanese won't last very long." Distances are vast out there, and they didn't understand that, and besides I was just getting married. But the Navy kept faith and gave me orders to the *R-10*, down in Key West, and they left me there for six weeks before they transferred me too.* [Laughter] So I had a few weeks with my bride in Key West, and then I got orders to a fleet boat.

Paul Stillwell: It turned out the war lasted long enough.

Admiral Wilkinson: The war lasted long enough. It lasted plenty long.

Paul Stillwell: Was the *R-10* time useful at all just for on-the-job training and to build on what you had learned at New London?

Admiral Wilkinson: No, I didn't qualify in submarines on the *R-10*. I qualified as a duty officer and watch stander, but I didn't qualify in submarines, which took longer until I was on the *Blackfish*. I qualified in submarines on *Blackfish*, and I qualified for command on the *Darter*.

Before the war a guy was an ensign for three years, which seemed like a long time then. By this time they were bringing people into the service right and left. When I was an ensign on this submarine in Key West, a young guy came in, and he accosted me. I've forgotten what his name was. He was reporting for duty, and it turned out his dad owned a cruiser down there, and so he had been commissioned in the service without going to OCS. Through some kind of connection he got his commission as a lieutenant (junior grade), and so he was just now reporting for duty. He wanted to report in there. So he asked me where the paymaster was, and I told him, "Well, it's over there."

He said, "Let me show you. I've got these orders." And they said lieutenant jaygee. He said, "What does that mean?"

---

* USS *R-10* (SS-87) was commissioned on 20 August 1919. She was 186 feet long, 18 feet in the beam. She displaced 569 tons surfaced and 680 tons submerged. She was armed with one 3-inch gun and four 21-inch torpedo tubes. She had a top speed of 13.5 knots surfaced and 10.5 knots submerged. She served until eventually decommissioned 18 June 1945.

I said, "Mister, it doesn't mean a goddamn thing." I'll never forget that. I was ensign for 19 months, and then I made lieutenant jaygee. In two years I made lieutenant. Suddenly things accelerated.

Paul Stillwell: Right.

Admiral Wilkinson: Took you a lot longer.

Paul Stillwell: Well, no, I made jaygee in 18 months. That was the norm in the '60s.

Admiral Wilkinson: Then it took the rest of the war to get promoted again. I didn't make lieutenant commander until the war was over.

After six weeks on the R-boat, I was very fortunate. I got orders to new construction, the *Blackfish*, and I had a superb skipper, Johnny Davidson, who was a terrific person and smart.[*] He later became the submarine detailer, which helped me because he had to do with my duty assignments. Then he became Superintendent of the Naval Academy. Johnny Davidson, a crackerjack guy.

I might have been the junior officer. I was the communicator, and they put me in charge also of this new device they had called the radar because it was electronic, and I had the radiomen in communications. And because I was quick with numbers, I was the torpedo data computer operator at battle stations. During my time on the *Blackfish* we fired some torpedoes, and it turned out one of them didn't run right. Maybe more than one.

After the *Blackfish* had finished her construction and training, which didn't take long—we're talking a couple months—instead of sending us to the Pacific they sent us to participate in the landings in North Africa.[†] We went, and we were stationed off of

---

[*] USS *Blackfish* (SS-221) was a *Gato*-class submarine commissioned 22 July 1942. She had a displacement of 1,525 tons on the surface and 2,410 tons submerged. She was 312 feet long, 27 feet in the beam, and had a draft of 17 feet. Her top speed was 20 knots surfaced and 9 knots submerged. She was armed with ten 21-inch torpedo tubes and a 3-inch deck gun. See Davidson's Naval Institute oral history for his recollections of the submarine and of Wilkinson.

[†] Allied forces invaded Casablanca in French Morocco on 8 November 1942. The French forces in the port resisted, so American ships bombarded the port.

Dakar to make sure the French battleship *Richelieu* didn't come to sea.* It didn't come to sea, so our mission was successful. [Laughter] But we sat out there.† That's 100%.

Paul Stillwell: That's the essence of deterrence.

Admiral Wilkinson: But for nearly 24 hours we were at war with France until the French forces in Africa came over to our side. So it's a good thing we didn't plug the *Richelieu*, because now she was on our side. But during the 24 hours that we were off there waiting for her, a French ship did come along, and we plugged it and we sank it. So we're one of the few ships that sank a French ship. So that gave us a successful patrol. Then another patrol we were patrolling down off Spain.

Paul Stillwell: Bay of Biscay.

Admiral Wilkinson: Bay of Biscay off Spain to make sure to try to intercept any blockade runners that the Germans might be bringing around from the Far East to bring some precious supplies in. We never saw any blockade runners, but one day two German destroyers were out, 10 knots, in column.‡ We eased up for a perfect shot, 700 or 800 yards, dead on, couldn't miss. We punched out two torpedoes at that one. Punched out two torpedoes at the next guy, all of which should have hit. Now, only one of those torpedoes went off. The others obviously ran too deep and ran under them. The one that went off on the second one sank him.§ But the first guy turned right down the tracks and unloaded on us. We were only at 170 feet deep, and that really shook us up.

---

* The 35,000-ton French battleship *Richelieu* was completed at Brest in early 1940. When France collapsed in the spring of 1940, the ship was ordered to Dakar, French West Africa, where she was subjected to British attacks. In 1943, following Allied landings in Northwest Africa, the ship was sent to the New York Navy Yard for repairs and rearming. After that was completed, she operated as part of the Royal Navy.
† The *Blackfish* arrived off Dakar and sighted the *Richelieu* on 7 November, the day before the Allied invasion in North Africa.
‡ The *Blackfish* patrol report described them as ASW trawlers.
§ This action occurred off Bilbao, Spain, on 19 February 1943. The *Blackfish* spotted German colors on two antisubmarine trawlers it was tracking. The submarine reported scoring a hit on one trawler and then undergoing a heavy depth-charge attack that cracked the conning tower doorframe. As Wilkinson recalled, the *Blackfish* also damaged a sound head when she hit bottom. Postwar analysis attributed no sinkings during the period to any boats of Submarine Division 50, of which the *Blackfish* was a part.

Paul Stillwell: What do you recall about that shaking?

Admiral Wilkinson: Well, insulation and piping, which was tight to the bulkhead, so there was nothing in between. It was an inch away from the bulkhead. The light bulbs broke. Glass was flying. Cork was flying from the insulation. I was in the conning tower, and just to my left was the conning tower door, and that split. A stream of water came across right in front of my face, and we're talking only a foot and a half or two feet from me.

I was right there with my hands on the torpedo data computer, and in between me and it was the little stream of water, and the water was cold. Ocean water is cold. The ship was shaking from the depth charging, and then this stream of water hit the helmsman. He went, "Hah," and fainted dead away. [Laughter] We had to abandon the conning tower and go down. We lost depth control, and we hit bottom. Actually we were closer to Spain than we should have been, navigation error. [Laughter]

We hit bottom maybe 100 feet over our test depth, and that knocked off one of the sonar domes. It ruptured some air bottles, and we also had some fuel leaking out. So up to the surface were going air bubbles and fuel, but there was a strong current there, and that guy for the rest of the day would wheel around and come back and drop one depth charge. He must not have had too many. He kept dropping one at a time. That would shake us up, but we were not where the stuff was coming up. He never got that quite calibrated because they never hit us again. The one at 170 feet was what did the damage. That night we got up on the surface, drained out the conning tower, got on the bridge, and ran for England.

Paul Stillwell: Was there any concern about electrical shorts or other problems?

Admiral Wilkinson: No, no. We ran for England, and we went into Land's End. It was really bad visibility. I won't say there was fog, but there were clouds down to the surface. Suddenly one of these Spitfires came out of the fog on one side and saw us.[*] A submarine to everybody was just a medal down there. I had the deck. The pilot cut loose

---

[*] The Spitfire was a British fighter plane.

with everything. Here was a stream of tracers. He hit 300-400 feet over our head. We didn't have any damage. I didn't dive or anything. I just kept on. He never came back.

We did end up in Plymouth to get worked on and get repaired.* Also, this was liberty for our crew, but we didn't have any money, so we made arrangements for the British to pay us. And they didn't pay their people as much. It was about $10,000 we wanted, and they brought it down. They must have had $500 worth of silver in pence and shillings and whatnot. Wish I'd have kept it. And because I'm quick with numbers and all, the captain had me be the paymaster and pay people. When they got all through, when I'd paid everybody, including some of my own money, all the silver left was mine.

So I had these pounds of silver, and it was really quite interesting because I went over to a bank. You can't imagine. There was a rug on the floor and three guys behind counters. There were no customers in the bank. The three cashiers were wearing striped trousers and morning coats, and I went up there and said, "I've got this silver. I'd like to turn it in for some paper money."

"How much is it?" I've forgotten what it was, but it was more than 500 pounds. The guy reached in the drawer and pulled out two of the kind of tins that you buy candy in. There was so much money. He scraped it in there, put it on a scale, looked at it, gave me the money I'd asked for, and put the coins in the drawer. Here's the thing. With their striped trousers and morning coats, they didn't count it or anything. It really was an amazing thing.

Every day they had different air raid alerts. If a plane took off over France, that was close enough for some kind of an alarm. If he got closer, there was another kind of alarm. Something else was that trucks were running around with balloons on cables.† The first time there was an air raid alert, we were up in dry dock. Bang. Well, we'd just been damaged, it was a war and we were in England, and now there was an air raid alarm, and so we went to battle stations. All we had were some .50-caliber machine guns. [Laughter] Well, we had the 5-inch guns, but we were not going to shoot them at planes.

---

* The *Blackfish* underwent repairs at the Royal Naval Dockyard, Devonport, England, from 22 February to 5 March 1943.
† Helium-filled barrage balloons were tethered to cables as a means of protection against enemy aircraft. The idea was the low-flying aircraft might snag on the vertical cables.

Zoom, Brits came running down and said, "If a guy's diving right at you, shoot at him, but otherwise don't shoot. The shells will fall back on the city." And so, God, were we embarrassed. We secured battle stations and said, "Hey, let's go up to the club and get a drink." [Laughter] The whole rest of the time in England I don't care what kind of air raid alarm it was—and we had some right up the street—we ignored them, just the same as the Brit Navy did. We paid no attention to that at all. Air raid alarm, planes coming over, we walked right up the street just like it belonged to us. [Laughter] But I remember how embarrassed we were when we went to battle stations at the first alarm. Probably some plane that was taking off over France.

Paul Stillwell: What do you remember about Davidson's qualities as a skipper?

Admiral Wilkinson: Davidson was a very smart guy, and he was very personnel oriented. He was good on the periscope, but we unfortunately didn't have many opportunities to shoot. We shot only twice. We sank a ship both times, so you can't do better than that, but in four patrols those were the only opportunities we got. Another time we were sent up off Norway to see that the *Tirpitz* didn't come to sea, and it didn't.[*] But we didn't have much opportunity to see him in combat action, because in the Atlantic we didn't have many opportunities. As far as being a remarkably personable human being, interested in people, a crackerjack guy, he was all those things. Charming. Smart. But I never got to see him in action that many times.

Paul Stillwell: Was he a cool customer during the depth charging?

Admiral Wilkinson: None of us were. [Laughter] I was terrified. We had a guy on there named Butch Elliott. He was ex-merchant marine, and he was a man full of baloney. He said, "I wasn't a bit afraid." He'd been keeping the log. I went and got the book and said, "Then tell me what you wrote in here." You couldn't read it. [Laughter] So everybody was scared. It's how you perform when you're scared that makes the

---

[*] The German battleship *Tirpitz* was a sister ship of the *Bismarck*, which was sunk by the British in May 1941. To avoid a similar fate, the *Tirpitz* holed up in Norway for protection. After being damaged by a midget submarine attack in September 1943, she was sunk by aerial bombing on 12 November 1944.

difference. Or whether you let the scaredness inhibit you from doing what you should have. When Johnny Davidson was in action, a vein would throb in his throat, but it didn't keep him from doing what he ought to be doing.

Paul Stillwell: That was your first experience with depth charging, wasn't it?

Admiral Wilkinson: That was it when they really hit us. I was depth charged many times later but never like that again. Did you see the movie *Das Boot*?[*]

Paul Stillwell: Yes.

Admiral Wilkinson: Do you remember those guys panicked? Let me tell you, that was for the movies. I don't believe those German guys panicked. They were competent submariners. We had almost an identical depth charging. Knocked to the bottom, upset all this stuff. But there wasn't any panic. Everybody still went about doing their job like they should.

So here I was at war, and I really wanted to go home and see my wife. The only way you could get home was new construction. And to get new construction you had to have four patrols. So eventually we got four patrols in. They had one vacancy for new construction, and they settled it in an absolutely reasonable manner. We were over there in England. They called all eight of us to the office and said, "There are eight of you eligible for new construction, and we've got one vacancy." And, "Roll the dice. High man goes." So old Butch Elliott rolled just in front of me, and he rolled 65. I picked up those dice and bounced them off the wall, 66. And that's the way I got to the *Darter*, and that's when our first son was conceived.[†] And I could have done it again. [Laughter]

Paul Stillwell: Well, just to show you how memories differ, I talked to Admiral Davidson about this point.

---

[*] *Das Boot* was a 1981 German film that depicted in fairly realistic fashion the claustrophobic lives of a U-boat crew in World War II. A dubbed English-language version, titled *The Boat*, appeared in 1982.
[†] Dennis Eugene Wilkinson was born 11 April 1944.

Admiral Wilkinson: Yes?

Paul Stillwell: He said he promised that the junior officer who did the best job in his boat would get the new construction slot, and you did the best.

Admiral Wilkinson: They rolled dice, and I rolled a 66.

Paul Stillwell: He also remembered—

Admiral Wilkinson: Yes, he might have. Maybe that cut it down to the eight. It was more than our ship. What did he say he promised?

Paul Stillwell: That the junior officer who did the best job would get the chance to go to new construction.

Admiral Wilkinson: Well—

Paul Stillwell: Were you the only one from *Blackfish*?

Admiral Wilkinson: No, there were two of us on the *Blackfish* that went up, and Butch Elliott was a good man, too, so maybe he sent two. The other eight weren't off *Blackfish*. There were other submarines, too, that he didn't control, like the *Herring* and whatnot, so he may have done that on the *Blackfish*.

Paul Stillwell: Another thing Admiral Davidson remembered was a possible encounter with a U-boat. He said there was something out there; it may have been a German U-boat, and it may not have been.*

---

* On 14 April 1943, as recounted in the submarine's patrol report, the captain of the *Blackfish* spotted what might have been a periscope.

Admiral Wilkinson: That's true. We sighted a periscope, and the periscope was really up. We didn't do a thing. When the guy pulled the periscope down, we turned toward them, angle on the bow zero, and went right toward them, and we never got shot at or never saw them again. But we did see a periscope, and that's what we did. That was in the Atlantic, on the way over to Africa. That's the way it was, because I had the deck. [Laughter]

Paul Stillwell: Do you remember any special ceremony associated with getting your dolphins?*

Admiral Wilkinson: No. I think Johnny Davidson pinned them on me.

Paul Stillwell: Was it a fairly rigorous training program you had to go through to get those in addition to fighting the war?

Admiral Wilkinson: It was an extensive qualification, so you became very familiar with your ship, plus the other requirements. Had to be qualified diving officer and qualified OOD.† Of course, I was both those things long before that, but then you're qualified in the submarines and went through the boat with people. I didn't have any trouble qualifying because I was on a ship at sea days on end. Later on I helped qualify literally hundreds of troops; I was quite meticulous about it and believed in doing it thoroughly and extensively. So when I think of qualification, I think more of what I did with my people than doing it myself, because we were on an operating submarine at sea, and I was there all the time. I very quickly knew the boat—probably long before I'd met the time requirements and was qualified.

Paul Stillwell: Well, you couldn't help but learn in that atmosphere.

---

* The insignia for a qualified submariner is a metal pin worn above the left shirt pocket. The pin is gold for officers, silver for enlisted men. The design features a pair of dolphins and a portion of a submarine. An individual earns his dolphins by a rigorous qualification process.
† OOD – officer of the deck.

Admiral Wilkinson: That's right.

Paul Stillwell: Admiral Davidson remembered that the engineer did not want to go on the patrol up north to the Arctic Circle with the *Tirpitz* and all, and so he was left behind, and you fleeted up to be engineer. Is that your recollection?

Admiral Wilkinson: The engineer was a pretty good man, but he was emotionally very intense, and I don't know why. I might have contributed to it. He was very tied up in his wife, and he was very organized. I'm going to tell you a sea story now. He was Clay Tucker.* Every evening after dinner, since he didn't have that watch, he would open up his safe and get out his wife's and children's pictures and lay them out like a little shrine and write a letter to his wife. I'm telling you a story now. It's true, but I'm not fully proud of this. He put the letter to his wife up in a slot on his desk, and the next night he'd do the same thing. In the meantime I hadn't written my wife a letter, and then another day would go by, and there were three letters and then four and then five. And then finally we'd get in port, and his wife would call my wife up and say, "I just got 56 letters. How many letters did you get?"

And, you know, I'd written my wife a letter the day we got in port and said, "Hey, we're back in, Honey, and I love you and I miss you and all that." But 56 letters is a lot, and I guess that used to bother me a little bit. Each officer had a safe at his desk, and when the ship went in commission he set the combination on his safe and wrote it in an envelope and gave it to me, and I locked it in a big safe. I was the communicator, and I had the big safe in the radio room. The combinations to all the safes were there in double sealed envelopes. But when it was set I saw it, and I'm quick with numbers, so I really remembered everybody's safe number. And even though it had been six months by now and they were all sealed, I really knew his safe combination. So one day when he was up on the 12:00-to-4:00 watch, I was thinking about this. I went in, opened his safe, changed the combination, and closed it again.

---

* Lieutenant (junior grade) Houston Clay Tucker, Jr., USN.

That evening, when he went to go through his ritual of erecting the shrine, the safe wouldn't open. So he told me, since it was all sort of under me, "Dennis, my safe is broken."

I said, "Hey, Clay, I've got to go do this now, but, you know, we've written all those combinations, and they're sealed in there in the big safe. When we get a chance we'll go and open it up. You've forgotten your combination."

After all, he did open it every evening, and he said, "I haven't forgotten my combination. It's broken."

"Now, come on, Clay," I said. "You know those things. They don't break." So this went on a couple of nights. No letter. No letter written. Twist, twist, twist. Twist, twist, twist. So he said, "I've got to get in my safe and get my wife's picture out."

I said, "Clay, when you come down from watch tomorrow, we'll go in, and we'll get the combination and open that damn safe."

"It's broken," he said.

So the next day, when he was up on watch, I opened the safe and set back the original combination. And now the scene was set. When he came down from watch, I said, "Clay, did you ever get that safe open."

"No, it's broken," he said.

I said, "Why don't we go in and get the combination and open that damned safe?"

"It's broken," he said. So I went in and made a big thing of opening the big safe, taking out the thing, ripping open his envelope. I said, "Here," and I slashed it open. He knew that wouldn't work, but I knew it would. So I twisted the dial, opened it up, and I said, "Clay, you ought to write that down somewhere." [Laughter] Well, the letters started up again, so his wife didn't get that many letters. In retrospect I feel bad about that, but it seemed humorous at the time. [Laughter]

Paul Stillwell: You certainly were playing with his mind.

Admiral Wilkinson: He was a very bright, very capable guy, but he worried a lot, and I guess time away from home and family and the time at sea preyed on his mind. It's all a long time ago. He was a good man. I liked him. Liked his wife. Sorry I changed his safe combination.

Paul Stillwell: That was a feather in your cap, though, to make chief engineer as a jaygee.

Admiral Wilkinson: Oh, I wasn't chief engineer. I probably was acting.

Paul Stillwell: I see, but even so that says something.

Admiral Wilkinson: I came back from that ship to the *Darter*, and I became the gunnery officer.* Then I finally became the engineering officer on the *Darter*, the third officer, senior watch officer, in charge of qualification and compensation, diving, except if we were going to shoot torpedoes. Then I manned the TDC until we fired, and then I went down and took the dive.

Paul Stillwell: Please talk about the *Darter*'s commissioning and the workup for battle.

Admiral Wilkinson: You had at least 25% experienced people on each crew, and the other people that came were new people into submarines. So as construction was being finished, you were checking on the ship, you were writing ship's orders and organization, you were training people. For the two or three months it was a very intensive period. We went through that, working hard at it, and trained new people.

By that time the submarine force recognized it had trouble with torpedoes. We had the interesting assignment, among others during our shakedown, of going up and firing 19 torpedoes against the cliff up in Maine to check them out.† So we had the fun of firing a full load of torpedoes from the *Darter* when torpedoes were precious.

---

* USS *Darter* (SS-227) was a *Gato*-class submarine commissioned 7 September 1943. She had a displacement of 1,525 tons on the surface and 2,410 tons submerged. She was 312 feet long, 27 feet in the beam, and had a draft of 15 feet. Her top speed was 20 knots surfaced and 9 knots submerged. She was armed with ten 21-inch torpedo tubes and a 3-inch deck gun.

† From 3 to 5 October 1943, according to the *Darter*'s patrol report, she fired 19 war shots at Bald Porcupine Island, just east of Bar Harbor, Maine, to test exploder mechanisms for the Bureau of Ordnance.

Then we were assigned to the Pacific and sailed away. Left my wife. Eight months later my first youngster was born. When I got home 16 months later, he was eight months old, so I was gone a long time for my four patrols out in the Pacific.

I was still the gunnery officer when the *Darter* went through Pearl Harbor on the way out, and they gave us an inspection there.[*] One of the things was to battle surface and shoot at a big weather balloon that was floating out there on the water about 2,000 yards away. So from SubPac we got various inspections because we hadn't made a first patrol yet.[†] We battle surfaced, and we zipped up and manned that 5-inch gun, and there was a big red balloon skipping across the water over there with the wind behind it. We wheeled around, and as luck would have it we hit it direct the first shot. Bang. The balloon. And thinking about that quickly I said, "Train in and secure. Clear the deck. Bridge, target destroyed. Gun secured. Going below." The inspector didn't know what to do. We'd fired only one shot. Target destroyed.

Paul Stillwell: What more do you need?

Admiral Wilkinson: So I have nothing to answer your question with from that. If you hit the first time, what can you do? If you miss, you spot up or spot down or something. They're more accurate than you think, though.

Paul Stillwell: Well, it was strictly direct fire, it sounds like.

Admiral Wilkinson: Yes, yes. And, of course, we had a 20-millimeter and the 40-millimeter and eight .50 calibers and a couple of .30 calibers and then a bunch of BARs.[‡] We could throw a lot of small arms in the air if it came to that.

Paul Stillwell: Who was the commanding officer?

---

[*] The *Darter* arrived at Pearl Harbor on 26 November, en route to her first war patrol.
[†] SubPac – Submarine Force Pacific Fleet.
[‡] BAR – Browning automatic rifle.

Admiral Wilkinson: Our skipper's name was Stovall, and he was an experienced guy, but he wasn't as fully aggressive as Dave McClintock, who came later.* I have great respect and admiration for Dave's performance as a wartime skipper. He wasn't ever going to not get it in there.

Paul Stillwell: How soon did he take over after the ship went in commission?

Admiral Wilkinson: I'm not sure. I guess Dave had two patrols with me on there.

In the *Darter* we went into Perth and went into Brisbane, and the Japanese were in New Guinea. The Japanese were coming down with the Tokyo Express to attack our forces that had landed in Guadalcanal, and so we were supposed to load and get up and head up there as fast as we could. So we sailed a day earlier than we would have otherwise, loading as fast as we could.† I remember well we were supposed to pick up 1,600 pounds of beef among our supplies. They brought us down all the supplies, and we loaded them on board. We were on our way. They gave us a case of rabbit. We said, "Rabbit?" You've got to remember the eating habits of young Americans have changed. Two-thirds of your people wouldn't eat shrimp. Shrimp? What's that? I mean, now there are not enough shrimp to go around in the world. But we said, "Rabbit? Where's our beef?"

"Oh, it's over there," they said. So we got to sea and started opening the boxes on our way out, 1,600 pounds of beef, and every bit of it was filet. We got up to Guadalcanal, and the Army and Marines were over there eating K-rations. We invited a few of them aboard, and we were serving them filet and feeling a little guilty.

Paul Stillwell: If memory serves, when Stovall died his widow then married John Davidson.

---

* The *Darter*'s first commanding officer was Commander William Shirley Stovall, Jr., USN. He was relieved by Lieutenant Commander David H. McClintock, USN.
† The *Darter*'s first war patrol ended in late February 1944, and then she refueled and refitted at Brisbane, Australia, from 29 February to 17 March. Commander Stovall was the skipper during the second war patrol, which began after the boat topped off with fuel at Milne Bay, New Guinea, on 21-22 March 1944. On 30 March the *Darter* sank the 2,829-ton cargo ship *Fujikawa Maru*.

Admiral Wilkinson: I didn't know that. Yes. I liked her. And Johnny Davidson's wife had passed away, huh?

Paul Stillwell: I think they were divorced.

Admiral Wilkinson: Oh, divorced, right.

Paul Stillwell: Do you have any memories of dealing with Australian civilians? I've heard they're very hospitable, friendly people.

Admiral Wilkinson: Remember that when we first went in there, the Japanese were still in New Guinea, and the Aussies had trenches dug north of Brisbane, so they were pleased to see us. Their men were all absent over in North Africa. They considered the submarine people fighting men. They talked about some of the liaison people they had down there, and they called them lounge lizards. [Laughter] When we were out on the economy, the Australian people were very friendly and really nice to us and pleased to see us, and there was no friction or bad feeling with us at all. If you talked to them, they really differentiated between the guys that were fighters and the guys that weren't, or at least that was my impression.

Paul Stillwell: Well, there was a lot of gratitude to the United States for protecting them from invasion.

Admiral Wilkinson: In that bigger sense I don't know. In the little sense that I was at, I was a young fellow then, and we were into Brisbane a couple of times and we were in Perth the one time.* When we came back in the second time, my captain, Dave McClintock, wanted to get a 40-millimeter gun so we'd have something to fight surface ships, to fight spit kits with. He went through official channels, and he couldn't get one. We also had some 20 millimeters and eight .50 caliber and whatnot. He said, "I really want to get a 40-millimeter mounted up here, but I can't get one."

---

* During the second visit, the *Darter* was at Brisbane from 8 to 31 August 1944.

I said, "Captain, what's hard to get around here in transportation. If you'll get me a truck, I'll get you a 40-millimeter gun." So he had enough authority as the captain of a ship to get a truck, so he got a truck and I went out to the Army and talked to a guy. I said, "I'm on this submarine here, and we're going out on a war patrol. We'd like to get a 40-millimeter gun, and you've got all these 40-millimeters. You haven't got anybody to fight with. Why don't you give me one of those 40-millimeter guns?"

The guy said, "I'm signed for those."

I said, "Jeez, I'll sign for it." I was a lieutenant, and I signed to the Army for a 40-millimeter gun and spare barrel. Put them on the truck, and I had them back to the base in less than two hours. We mounted that 40-millimeter gun on the *Darter* and serviced it all the time and never fired it in combat.

Paul Stillwell: How would a gun like that be protected when you submerged?

Admiral Wilkinson: It was greased, and then we'd get up every night, and we'd clean it and grease it. And we had a spare barrel. In case the barrel corroded, you could just change barrels. The spare barrel was in a watertight container.

Paul Stillwell: Well, and you'd have to get some ammunition too.

Admiral Wilkinson: Oh, we had plenty of ammunition. That was below decks. Many of the submarines out there armed themselves to the teeth to shoot up spit kits if they got into that situation.

Paul Stillwell: I guess you wouldn't have any fire control. You'd just point it at the other ship.

Admiral Wilkinson: Yes. Then McClintock took over from Stovall.* When we lost our exec, Ernie Schwab was promoted up to exec, and I became the chief engineer as third

---

* Lieutenant Commander McClintock relieved Commander Stovall on 15 June 1944.

officer.* I did the compensation for the ship as diving officer when we went to battle stations unless we were going to shoot torpedoes. If we were going to shoot torpedoes, I was on the torpedo data computer. If it was just a normal battle station other people had those things, but if we were going to shoot then I went up and did it until we had shot, and then I went down and became diving officer for the depth charges.

Paul Stillwell: You were a busy man.

Admiral Wilkinson: No. No. It's just that I was good at that. And I had done it a lot and practiced. I could do it blindfolded. One crank was four degrees.

We went on patrol. Dave McClintock was a crackerjack skipper and good. One day we sighted a convoy, and there was heavy air cover so that we couldn't get close on the surface. It was daylight, and these people were steaming by out of our range. But we figured if we ran as fast as we could, a little over two-thirds speed, and ran for an hour and a half, that we maybe could get within range of the last ship in the column. We couldn't get up to the surface because there were Japanese airplanes up there.

It's sure bad to shoot at somebody when you don't have any battery left, but we used almost all our battery to get to position. I'm going to bring this back to the TDC in a minute, because that's what got me off on this memory. We were not going to get in a good enough position to fire. When the guy went by, we were going to be at 6,000 yards.

We had some Mark XXIII torpedoes that would only go high speed, but a Mark XIV would shift into two speeds. You could make 4,500 yards at 45 knots, or you could make 9,000 yards at 30 knots with the torpedo that we had during the war. And because two-speed torpedoes were a little more complex and cost more along toward the end of the war, they gave us mostly XXIIIs that would only go high speed, 4,500 yards. As an aside, there were some electric torpedoes. That's another subject.

But we could see that in an hour or so we were going to get to 6,000 yards from the closest ship. So we shuttled around, and we changed torpedoes, and we got four XIVs up in the tubes forward that we could shoot in low speed at 30 knots if we had to. And, sure enough, what we'd figured out came true, and we got to the point where it was

---

* Lieutenant Commander Ernest L. Schwab, Jr., USN, was executive officer and navigator of the *Darter*.

a 6,000-yard run. By now our battery was down pretty damn low. And the torpedo data computer would only track and compute at high speed. It would only do the 45 knots. So mathematically I figured out what we ought to do with a 30-knot torpedo.

Paul Stillwell: You were the human TDC.

Admiral Wilkinson: Well, less complicated than that. This was the lead angle that you want to use for 30 knots at 6,000 yards. And now we could shoot a spread, more chance of hitting. But we said, "No, there's no sense in shooting a spread. At 6,000 yards the natural dispersion of those torpedoes will spread them out a little." So as they came by we had our four Mark XIVs up. We had them set at 30 knots and put 6,000 yards as the range, and we punched out four torpedoes in a natural dispersion. At 30 knots, 6,000 yards, it takes a torpedo six and a half minutes to run that far. That's a long time after you've shot to wonder what's going to happen.

So after we shot Captain McClintock sat there and berated himself and me. He said, "I'm really stupid to let you talk me into that. The sea is absolutely calm up there. There's all this air cover. We've thrown four XIV torpedoes away. They're making a wake up there. The airplanes are going to come down and bomb us. I'm foolish to have wasted those four torpedoes."

I said, "Captain, it's only been three minutes. They're just not there yet." So six and a half minutes—bang, bang, bang. One of those torpedoes didn't hit, but three of them did and sank the ship, and we didn't even get depth charged. They were so far away. We'd been worried about getting away with no battery left.*

But it's an interesting thing because that's the second longest successful shot of the war. And the longest shot was 9,000 yards. Can't remember the name of the submarine. It was a good submarine. But they shot a guy that was anchored [laughter], and they missed him the first time. It exploded against the beach, and they put a spot on the next one for that distance to the side that they'd missed with the first one that the current had carried it. Then they shot the second one, and they plugged him at 9,000

---

* The *Darter*'s patrol report says this was a day periscope attack on 12 October 1944. She fired at two overlapping tankers at a range of 6,000 yards. The report said the *Darter*'s crew heard two hits on one tanker and one hit on the other. The ships were damaged but escaped through through Balabac Strait.

yards. But for a shot at a running ship at sea the old *Darter* had the second longest shot of the war, and we made three hits out of four fish. But I had to compute it not with the torpedo data computer. It would just set to track a target and give you the lead angle with a 45-knot torpedo.

Paul Stillwell: Well, you sort of eliminated the lead angle, didn't you, by coming up directly astern?

Admiral Wilkinson: No, no. We fired broadside, see, so you had to make a lead angle for six and a half minutes of run.

Paul Stillwell: I see.

Admiral Wilkinson: How far is he going to travel in six and a half minutes? And what angle, how many degrees is that at 6,000 yards? That's a simple calculation.

Paul Stillwell: Trigonometry.

Admiral Wilkinson: Yes. What angle, and again if your ship wasn't pointed exactly that way, you'd have to add some more degrees of gyro to the torpedo if it had to turn. If I was firing directly ahead, I'd only have the lead angle of the distance that he was going to run in six and a half minutes and how many degrees that is at 6,500 yards. But if my ship was not pointed exactly at him, which it was probably not, if it was two or three degrees off, I had to add that many degrees of gyro to the torpedo, so all I had to figure was the lead angle. The machine would add the degrees depending on the target not being directly on the bow. It's a simple calculation.

But the point I was trying to make, it had to be done by other than the TDC. The old TDC was a very antiquated piece of equipment. Now they have very sophisticated things that compute it with computers instantly. No human being could match that. But in those days you only corrected on a TDC by a trial and error system of if it didn't track making a difference to speed or range or something.

Paul Stillwell: Did the TDC set that gyro angle into the torpedo?

Admiral Wilkinson: Yes.

Paul Stillwell: How did you set the gyro angle in this case when you weren't using the TDC?

Admiral Wilkinson: I knew what I wanted to set, and I just cranked it in.

Paul Stillwell: How was that physically achieved?

Admiral Wilkinson: There's a signal goes from TDC up to the torpedo and you can match.

Paul Stillwell: So you manually put it into the TDC?

Admiral Wilkinson: Yes, yes.

Paul Stillwell: Well, the skipper had acquired quite some confidence in you by that point then.

Admiral Wilkinson: Yes. We went into Biak Harbor and shot a cruiser-minelayer too.* McClintock was a crackerjack skipper, and he knew what he was there for.

Paul Stillwell: That takes some guts to do it in a harbor. There aren't that many ways to escape.

Admiral Wilkinson: No.

Paul Stillwell: And relatively shallow water probably.

---

* The *Darter* was credited with sinking the 4,400-ton minelayer *Tsugaru* on 29 June 1944.

Admiral Wilkinson: That was really a disappointing day, because there were a couple of destroyers. They picked us up, and they were depth charging us, and we broke contact. When you were being depth charged, you were at silent running, there was no ventilation, the water out there was hot, and everybody was sweating. You were very silent, silent running, nobody making tapping, nothing for the other person's sonar to hear or anything. We had broken contact for, I've forgotten now for sure, but three or four hours, and then they picked us up again. Never have I seen such a letdown in emotion and morale as when we had thought we were home free and away when we were picked up again. But then we broke contact again and got away.

Then the next patrol we were up in the straits off Borneo. We moved around quite a bit during that patrol, but finally we were around the Philippines and were fortunate enough to pick up the Japanese fleet, which had been in radio silence when they came down to oppose the landing.* I was up manning the TDC, and we picked these guys up at midnight. And, oh, boy, were we lucky to pick them up, because the angle on the bow was about 80 degrees and they were 34,000 yards. We just barely picked them up on our radar.†

Then we started running with them. We closed in a little, and we could see there were more and more and more and more Japanese contacts. These people had been in radio silence, and they were coming up, 15 heavies and 16 destroyers—31 ships to oppose that landing—and nobody on our side knew where they were. So our getting a radio message off and saying "Here they are" was the most important thing. We kept calling our base in Australia, and they wouldn't answer. Finally who came up and took our message but Radio Washington, D.C.? That message had to be decoded, sent across the States, re-encoded and sent to Pearl, decoded, re-encoded onto the submarine fox, and sent out.‡ It all was out there in our submarine fox in two hours. So we knew that our message had been received and understood. And so during the course of the night, as we

---

* On 22 October 1944 the U.S. Sixth Army under Lieutenant General Walter Krueger made an amphibious invasion of the island of Leyte in the Philippines.
† Samuel Eliot Morison, *Leyte: June 1944-January 1945* (Boston: Little, Brown, 1958) is Volume XII of *History of United States Naval Operations in World War II*. On page 170 it reports that the *Darter*'s radar detected the Japanese at 1:16 on the morning of 23 October. The Japanese were then 30,000 yards away, at the southern entrance of Palawan Passage, approaching the Philippines from the southwest.
‡ "Fox" was the word for the letter F in the phonetic alphabet of the day. The fox schedule referred to the messages sent on the fleet broadcast.

got closer to them and saw more and more ships, we sent more messages. Finally we said, "We're out in front of them now, and we're going in to attack."

Just before dawn we dived out in front of the 31 ships. We'd been getting information by radar, and they were making 15 knots. I was solving that on my TDC machine, we had two plots that were solving it, and we were all getting 15 knots. Then we dived down to test depth to check all our deep submergence and everything. When we came back up, we weren't tracking the same ship anymore and we weren't with radar. The captain was taking a stadimeter range, and it was a different ship.[*] But the Japanese had speeded up. At dawn they speeded up to 18 knots. It was around dawn, so it was dim light still. It was a questionable angle on the bow, because they'd speeded up. So I said, "Captain, they've speeded up to 18 knots."

He said, "What have you got, plot?"

Plot One said, "Fifteen." Plot two said, "Fifteen." So we took another observation. And the captain was looking maybe at the same ship as before, maybe a different ship. But, anyway, there was a certain uncertainty in this, but we zeroed in, and we happened to shoot the flagship, which was a heavy cruiser called the *Atago*. Big cruiser, 16,000 tons. The second ship in that line was a cruiser called the *Takao*. As we were coming down, it was time to shoot, and both those plots were still reporting 15 knots. But I was saying, "Captain, they're 18 knots."

He said, "Dennis, do you want to split it with them?"

"No, sir," said I.

"Fine," said he. So I put in 18 knots, which was what they were making. And Captain Dave McClintock said, "Cover 125% spread." So we punched the first torpedo, and I muttered, "There's one ahead." And I guess that annoyed David, so he turned to me, and he said, "Dennis, put the rest of them in the ship length."

"Aye, aye." So we punched off five more fish at that one and then we spun and shot the four stern tubes at the next one, all within the ship length.[†] I don't know which fish missed, but we made four hits in the *Atago* and two hits in the *Takao*. I'm sure that

---

[*] The stadimeter is a mechanical device for measuring the range to another ship when the height of her mast is known or estimated.
[†] At 6:32 in the morning the *Darter* fired a spread of torpedoes at the *Atago*, flagship of Vice Admiral Takeo Kurita. Shortly after that she fired four torpedoes at the *Takao* from her stern tubes.

they were making 18 knots. But that's a lot. I really respected Dave McClintock because he backed me up on using the 18-knot solution.

Paul Stillwell: How could you be so sure they were making 18 knots?

Admiral Wilkinson: Well, because I was computing it from the information I was getting and also from where they were before and where they are now. They speeded up at dawn while we were down there. They weren't where they should have been at 15 knots. And then every observation I was getting confirmed that. Dave McClintock was a fantastic, really super guy on the periscope. I did many an approach when he was running on the scope, and if he told you the angle on the bow was seven degrees it was seven degrees. He was perfect from zero to 30, and then you absolutely couldn't place any reliance on what he said from 30 to 60, and from 60 on he was perfect again.

Paul Stillwell: That's amusing.

Admiral Wilkinson: Dave had all the guts in the world.

Paul Stillwell: What else did you admire about him?

Admiral Wilkinson: He was a good poker player. [Laughter] Well, Dave never panicked. He was good with people. He was a quiet guy, but he had total guts. He wasn't ever going to back down from the enemy. He was going to go in there. As a matter of fact, he terrified us. We almost went in a couple of places that were mined. We didn't know it until afterwards, but Dave was one to get right in there. He was an ideal skipper and warrior. I'm sure Slade Cutter was like that too.[*] Dave wasn't afraid of anything. Some people were, you know. Everybody's afraid. I'm afraid, and I'm sure Dave McClintock down deep had some fear somewhere, but he never showed it, and it never affected what he did.

---

[*] Commander Slade D. Cutter, USN, earned four Navy Crosses while commanding the submarine *Seahorse* (SS-304) from September 1943 to August 1944. He and McClintock were 1935 classmates at the Naval Academy. The oral history of Cutter, who retired as a captain, is in the Naval Institute collection.

Paul Stillwell: Well, they shared that trait, but McClintock certainly has a more low key personality than Slade Cutter.

Admiral Wilkinson: Oh, yes. Yes.

Paul Stillwell: You sank the *Atago* and damaged the *Takao*. Captain McClintock tried to finish off the *Takao*.

Admiral Wilkinson: The *Darter* ran aground on Bombay Shoal after our attack on that Japanese fleet. I don't remember what time it was.* Must have been about midnight.

Paul Stillwell: I talked to Captain Schwab, who was the navigator at the time, and he said that the reason he never got prosecuted for running aground was that there's something in Navy Regs that says if you do this when you're in hot pursuit of the enemy, there's not a problem.† What's your reaction to that?

Admiral Wilkinson: We had been in active contact with the enemy for at least 48 hours, and there hadn't been an opportunity to take star sights. As the fire control guy, the guy that ran the thing, I also really controlled the courses that we took. We were in and around trying to catch this *Takao* that was being towed away. We wanted to plug it one more time and sink it, and so I was running the courses. I went over, and Ernie was dozing with his head on a chart. I banged him up and down and said, "Ernie, show me where we are on this damn chart. I'm running an attack here." I was really recommending courses to the captain on the bridge. I said, "I'm running at attack. I want to see where we are."

He said, "Goddamn it, you take care of the attack. I'll take care of the navigating." So I went back to my thing of running the attack, and 20 minutes later we

---

* During the Battle of Leyte Gulf, the submarine *Darter* (SS-227) torpedoed and damaged the Japanese cruiser *Takao*. The *Darter* and her sister ship *Dace* (SS-247) pursued the crippled cruiser through the channels of Palawan Passage in the Philippines. Just after midnight on 24 October 1944 the *Darter* grounded on Bombay Shoal. Efforts to free her were unsuccessful, so the crew evacuated to the *Dace* and rode safely to Australia.
† Captain Ernest L. Schwab, Jr., USN (Ret.), has been interviewed as part of the Naval Institute's oral history program.

ran aground. That never came out. But that doesn't have anything to do with it. What Ernie says is exactly true. We were in contact with the enemy. We hadn't had a chance to take a star sight for at least two or three days.*

Paul Stillwell: So it was understandable but unfortunate.

Admiral Wilkinson: Yes. We probably could have taken some sights with a bubble octant, because you can take those in the middle of the night if you know what you're doing. But even in the middle of the night we had limited access to the bridge. We were in active contact with the enemy. So Ernie's right. I was skipper a long, long time. I've been skipper of five different ships for 11½ years, and navigation is one thing you really worry about. And navigation isn't something that requires great brilliance. It just requires doing it all the time. And I guess maybe it's because of the *Darter* and that background, but as a skipper I always knew right where I was—exactly.

Paul Stillwell: What happened next?

Admiral Wilkinson: When we ran aground a Japanese destroyer out there closed in to— I've forgotten for sure now, but I think it was about 14,000 yards. We had contact on this guy, and, God, we were immobile, couldn't dive. We manned our guns and everything, but then he went away. We would have been helpless, except we would have shot. We ran aground at midnight. This probably was 1:00 o'clock or something like that.

Paul Stillwell: I see.

Admiral Wilkinson: The *Dace* was operating in our vicinity, in company with us. She found what course we'd come in on, and she got us on that bearing and came in up our stern and stopped just before she reached us, so she wasn't aground. We went aground with four engines running at 75-90 RPMs. We really ran up on that thing, so that we lost suction in the engine rooms all the way back to maneuvering. I went over the side and

---

* The *Darter*'s patrol report said no star sights for 30 hours.

swam around the ship and dived down under it. I came back and told the captain, "We'll never get off." We probably had only seven or eight feet of water instead of our usual 17. We were up high and dry.

So we sallied the ship and did all those things, but at the same time we were destroying the communications and setting the explosive devices. When we finally left the ship, we had these 50-pound charges to destroy the ship, and they'd been planted and the timers started at 20 minutes. And then we'd started a fire. In my opinion the fire burned through the leads to the destruction devices in the 20 minutes, and they never went off. We'd set three explosive devices, one forward and one aft and one amidships. We had lots of men who volunteered to go back and try again. But by that time we were all over on the *Dace*.

I had been the first person to leave. The captain said, "Who will take a line to the *Dace*?"

I was younger and could swim better then, and I thought, "My god, we might all not get off, so I better go first." So I said, "Captain, I will." I had a chance to be a hero. I could have put a knife in my belt and swum over, taking that line, but instead I popped the rubber boat and paddled over. [Laughter] What a clown! Then we used all the rubber boats and back and forth, back and forth, down that line. We got everybody off and everybody on the *Dace*. The *Dace* got there at 4:00, so we got off just before light. We were all over in less than an hour.

After we all got on the *Dace*, they backed off, and it was decided that they would torpedo us and destroy our ship, although we had destroyed all the cryptographic stuff and had planted the destruction charges. So they backed off and fired their torpedoes at it, but they all hit the reef and exploded and none of them hit the ship. After all, we had really run aground. Probably only had seven or eight feet of water left. I guess a shot right at the stern might have hit the ship, but from any other way it was protected by the reef. So they expended their torpedoes; I think they had four left and never made a hit. Around 7:00 A.M. a Japanese destroyer came and stopped and put a boat over to go over to the *Darter*, but by then the *Dace* didn't have any torpedoes left.

Later on, the submarine force had one of the big ships with the 6-inch gun, *Narwhal* maybe, stop by and fire 55 rounds into it. But the *Darter* stayed up on Bombay Shoals for years and years and years.

Paul Stillwell: I have heard that.

Admiral Wilkinson: Finally I guess in some storm it was gone. But it was there for years and years and years.

Paul Stillwell: It must have been a terrible feeling to be in the *Dace* shooting torpedoes at your own ship.

Admiral Wilkinson: Well, it was just like we had destroyed all the cryptographic aids and set off the explosive devices which never worked, and destroyed a lot of equipment, the special gyro and whatnot. We destroyed a lot of equipment before we left—once we knew we were going to leave.

The *Dace* had been extended on patrol, which had run them low on fuel. The *Dace* was free to go back to Perth in Australia, but they didn't have enough fuel to run down on two engines. We had to go at a more economical, one-engine speed to Australia. So with two crews on board we were making seven or eight knots down to Australia. And they ran very low on food. We were down to mushroom soup and peanut butter sandwiches. [Laughter] And with two crews on board there was no place to sleep. We flaked out on deck, and one thing we did do. We spent a lot of time in the wardroom, and we played poker. I'm ashamed to say on the way down to Australia we won all the *Dace*'s money playing poker.

Paul Stillwell: Well, one other story I heard is that before abandoning the *Darter* you made sure that the log of the poker winnings was transferred.

Admiral Wilkinson: Let me show you something here. The picture I just showed you of my wife was mounted in my stateroom on the *Darter*. As we were about to leave the ship, I ran back down, and I didn't get my wife's picture. I got the poker book, in which I was ahead and the one most ahead in the book. My wife to this day has never forgiven me, even though I got the picture duplicated. I've got it in there now. She's never forgiven me for taking the poker book instead of her picture. As we got on the *Dace*, the captain said, "Well, at least one thing. We start a fresh book."

"Oh, no," I said. "Here's the poker book right here." [Laughter]

Paul Stillwell: Well, the marriage has survived anyway.

Admiral Wilkinson: Yes. There's another thing. We really knew the war was almost over, and I had every intention of getting out of the Navy as soon as the war was over. So on that last patrol there were times when you were in action, but there were other times when it was dullsville. You were just sitting on the surface or cruising on the surface waiting for something to happen or looking for something to happen. And every once in a while we'd see one of these Japanese fishing balls. You know, beautiful balls.

Paul Stillwell: Glass balls.

Admiral Wilkinson: Yes. I'd say, "Captain, I've got to have that for my patio when the war's over and I go home. Let me get that."

So the captain would say, "Dennis, if a plane comes along, I'm going to leave you."

"That's okay. I'll be here. Come back and pick me up later," I said. So I'd dive over and get a fishing ball, and finally I had six or seven beautiful fishing balls. I didn't like to do laundry at sea, so I had 60 pair of socks and skivvies, and I'd come in with a lot of dirty laundry. It annoyed me that the Navy wouldn't pay me for those either when the *Darter* was lost. But, anyway, the patrol was almost over, so I had 60 dirty pair of skivvies and socks. I had these fishing balls wrapped in them and in my clothes closet. I couldn't take those either. I had to leave those there, and I've always wondered what the Japanese thought when they boarded and searched that ship and found all those glass fishing balls in there with my dirty laundry.

Afterwards I put in a claim for what I'd lost, and I didn't put anything in that I hadn't lost. I didn't put a watch. I don't wear a wristwatch. I didn't put any of that stuff. I put exactly item for item what I lost, which was 60 pair of skivvies. And they disapproved it. Said the full bag is eight pair. And so they only paid me for eight pair of skivvies. That didn't seem right to me, so I took the difference and put it in as a loss claim on my next income tax return. And they gave me the same jazz. They said, "Hey, you had a loss, and the Navy paid you for it."

I said, "Friend, my job is to fill out this form. Your job here is to take it and process it. I've done my part. Here. Don't give me any of that crap." You know, as they processed it they never complained, because they accepted that on the income tax return. But the Navy never paid me for those other 52 pair of skivvies. [Laughter] Silly story.

Paul Stillwell: We now have that on record.

Admiral Wilkinson: Yes. They owe me. [Laughter]

Paul Stillwell: Well, was it a case that you could take only the poker book or your wife's picture? You couldn't take them both?

Admiral Wilkinson: I probably should have taken them both, but the time was short, and the picture was screwed to the bulkhead in a metal frame. And it wouldn't have been as easy to carry.

Paul Stillwell: Right.

Admiral Wilkinson: And, after all, it was dark at night, and I was taking a line over to the *Dace*. In retrospect I could have done it. It would have been harder.

Paul Stillwell: Right. We've got that on tape.

Admiral Wilkinson: I've never told her that.

Paul Stillwell: What do you remember about your time in Australia after that ride where you were running out of food and no place to sleep?

Admiral Wilkinson: We came into Perth, Australia, which is a climate much like San Diego here. I had my orders waiting for me to go back to Submarine School in New London and be the torpedo data computer instructor. So as soon as they could get me transportation I left Perth and went back to the United States.

In the time that I was waiting we had some trouble with the behavior of some of our people. Our chief of the boat named Turner, who was a crackerjack guy, was over in Perth, which is some 28 miles or so from where we were in Fremantle, and he couldn't get transportation back.* He couldn't get a taxi, so he went down to the rail yard cars. There was a switch engine there, so he drove it back. [Laughter] They arrested him, and we had to go over and rescue him from the judge the next day. We explained to her he was a good man, and we'd take care of him. She said, "Well, that's fine, but I'm going to fine him 100 pounds," which was $322.80. He just reached in his pocket and paid it. [Laughter] He was a good man. But other than a few little incidents like that, Australia was a great place to be.

Paul Stillwell: Well, please tell me about it.

Admiral Wilkinson: Rest camp was great, like a club. You had tax-free liquor, so a drink, as I remember, was ten cents, and they made so much profit from that so that the beer on tap was free. [Laughter] We had a rest period, and you could catch these fabulous blue point crabs. Throw a net over and pull it up, there'd be 20 crabs on it. You'd get enough in one throw to eat all the crab you could for the rest of your picnic day. But I wasn't there very long, because I had my orders and came right back to the States and reported in to New London.

---

* Fremantle is the port for the city of Perth.

Paul Stillwell: How did you get from Australia back to the States?

Admiral Wilkinson: I waited till there was a flight, and they flew me back. I sat with a seatmate, Commander Bakutis, who had been the head of the fighter squadron on the *Enterprise* and had been shot down there in the Philippines and was waiting for transportation back.[*] I got to fly back with him and talk to him, and I really admired that guy. He'd been in the water there for seven days floating around in his raft, every night taking his parachute and changing it into a sail and trying to sail somewhere and in the daytime pulling it down so no airplane would spot him. As he told the story to me, he had a Very pistol with some rounds in it that he could have fired up there to attract attention. He said, "I saw planes every day, U.S. planes, but none of them came close enough. I was waiting for one to fly overhead before I fired my Very pistol." Finally one night as he sailed along, a submarine pulled up alongside and asked him if he'd like a ride.[†] [Laughter] So that's how he got to Perth, you see. The submarine took him back down to Perth, and he was waiting at Perth for transportation. I got to fly back to the States with him and hear that story, which I thought was tremendous.

Paul Stillwell: Sure. Please tell the story about McClintock getting another command.

Admiral Wilkinson: The head of the Navy was Admiral King, and his aide was Dusty Dornin, who was out of the class of '35, a classmate of my skipper, Dave McClintock.[‡] And that was a pretty great patrol we had. After all, we did sink the flagship of the Japanese fleet and gave warning to our Navy, which was making the landings in the Philippines, where the Japanese fleet was and where they were coming.

Paul Stillwell: And wounded the *Takao*.

---

[*] Lieutenant Commander Fred E. Bakutis, USN, commanding officer of Fighter Squadron 20 from the *Enterprise* (CV-6), was shot down in the Sulu Sea on the morning of 24 October 1944.
[†] Bakutis was rescued by the submarine *Hardhead* (SS-365), which then transferred the aviator to another submarine for transportation to Australia. The *Hardhead* then resumed her patrol. Bakutis later became a rear admiral and eventually retired in 1969.
[‡] Admiral Ernest J. King, USN, was Chief of Naval Operations and Commander in Chief U.S. Fleet. His aide was Commander Robert E. Dornin, USN, who had been skipper of the submarine *Trigger*. The Naval Institute oral history of Dornin, who retired as a captain, tells of his service with Admiral King.

Admiral Wilkinson: And then we damaged the *Takao* with torpedo hits. So McClintock as a skipper had done real well, even if we did run aground. So he was in calling on his classmate, Dusty Dornin. Dusty Dornin said, "Let me take you in to see the boss," and the boss was pleased to see him, because this guy had done quite a successful or famous operation out there. He was asking Dave if he was going to get his crew back to put a new submarine in commission. And Captain McClintock said, "Admiral, I understand that's not the policy anymore."

"I don't know anything about that. Dusty, fix it up." So, although we'd all been ordered elsewhere, they arranged then for the *Darter* officers and crew to go back to put the *Menhaden* in commission. That was the next-to-the-last submarine being built at Manitowoc, Wisconsin, which was a tremendous place to go and put a ship in commission. Ernie Schwab had been the exec and navigator on the *Darter*, but Dave and Ernie weren't 100% compatible. So, after I'd been on shore up in New London for a couple of months, Dave called me up and said, "Dennis, Admiral King said we can put a new submarine in commission. Would you like to come and be my exec?"

I said, "Dave, as long as you don't tell my wife you asked me." [Laughter] So I got out of shore duty at Sub School. I was there only three months as instructor on the torpedo data computer, and I went up and got to put the *Menhaden* in commission as the exec. In the meantime, our people had dispersed a little. Two of the officers had fleeted up to being execs, but they'd lost those jobs. They came and were the third and fourth officers on the *Menhaden*, and I hadn't been exec yet. So when we got there, I said, "I don't want a damn bit of advice. Don't tell me a thing."

Paul Stillwell: I take it you were senior to them.

Admiral Wilkinson: Yes.

Paul Stillwell: Well, please tell me then about reporting in at New London to teach the torpedo data computer.

Admiral Wilkinson: I was flown back to the States and then traveled to New London and reported in to the Submarine School. That was in late '44, and I worked in the gunnery department as the TDC operator.

My boss, the head of the gunnery department, was Chester Nimitz, Jr., the son of the famous Admiral Nimitz.[*] Chester Nimitz, Jr., was probably as capable a person as I've ever known, and he was a pistol. He was my boss and an interesting guy to work for. Because he was my boss, my wife and I became quite well acquainted with him. Janice and I are the godparents of their third youngster. He got out of the Navy because his wife really didn't want him to be in the shadow of his father and also wanted him to make more money. So at 20 years he got out and went through two or three jobs and finally became the head of Perkin-Elmer, a big company.[†]

Paul Stillwell: Did very well.

Admiral Wilkinson: He did very well. He's a very capable guy.

Paul Stillwell: Well, I hope you'll repeat the story you told me before about your discussions on who was the better TDC operator.

Admiral Wilkinson: Well, I hate to do that. That sounds a little funny. Understand that Chester Nimitz was very capable. He had set up a TDC course for the people at Sub School that was very good and trained them to do everything in a mathematical way, which is the right way to approach the problem. And they practiced and trained that way. Then when I reported aboard, he told me the first day that really we people from the fleet were not up to speed on how to properly run a TDC. He said that these kids approaching the problem mathematically there were all more capable and more competent running it than we people were that were out in the fleet doing it.

---

[*] Commander Chester W. Nimitz, Jr., USN, was the son of the five-star admiral who was then Commander in Chief Pacific Fleet and Pacific Ocean Areas. His oral history interview about his dad is in the Naval Institute collection.
[†] Nimitz, who was in the Naval Academy class of 1936, retired on 1 August 1957 and received a one-grade "tombstone promotion" to rear admiral upon retirement.

And he told me that for two or three days. He was my boss, so I swallowed my spit and didn't say anything. [Laughter] Finally, on about the third day, at the end of the course, he said, "Now, we're going to have a graduation exercise for these 20-odd guys. Any one of those, having been through this, can run that TDC better than you can. Go ahead. You take one of the machines there and try to run the problems at the same time they're doing it, and you'll see what I'm talking about."

I said, "Commander, I don't want to take issue with the method of doing it, but regardless of how it's done, let me tell you there isn't anybody can run that TDC better than I can. And mathematically is the way to approach it. That's the way to do it right. That's the way I've always done it." And I pulled out my wallet, which had some 400 and some odd dollars, and I said, "Commander, all or any part of that. Pick any three of them you want. Pick any three people you want and let's run the exam. Pick any three you want, including you if you want, Commander." He wouldn't take me up on that. It sounds silly in retrospect, but I think that that helped me make my reputation with my boss, Chester Nimitz, because I really could run it better than anybody else.

Paul Stillwell: Well, did you in fact match off against these three students?

Admiral Wilkinson: No. He backed away. He wouldn't bet. Smart man.

Paul Stillwell: Well, please tell me about your subsequent runoff with Nimitz himself.

Admiral Wilkinson: Well, one of the training devices there was a theater in which there were a lot of different films. They showed airplanes zooming out of the sky from dead ahead or one side or the other at different distances, at different speeds. You would lead them with a simulated gun and push down the button, and how much time you would have been hitting you'd get a score. I was quite dexterous with movements in three dimensions, and that just came naturally to me. So two or three times a week Chester would say, "Let's go up and shoot a training film to see who pays for lunch."

I'd say, "Yes, sir." And we'd go up and do that, and he'd buy my lunch. This went on for three months, and he always bought my lunch. After a couple of months I discovered that as the head of the gunnery department he would go up in the morning, pick out the film, and practice it three or four times before he'd sandbag me into betting for lunch. Then he still had to buy my lunch, and it really frustrated the hell out of him. [Laughter] But I was quite dexterous at being able to wheel the thing one way with one hand and the other way with the other and keep on tracking something.

Paul Stillwell: I'll bet this was related to your marble skill also.

Admiral Wilkinson: No, the marble skill went back to hundreds and hundreds and hundreds and hundreds of hours of practice, and the manual dexterity I think was just a God-given trait.

Paul Stillwell: But I suspect that the dexterity helped out in the marbles too.

Admiral Wilkinson: Oh, probably did. Yes, I see what you mean.

Paul Stillwell: What do you remember about teaching the course and the content?

Admiral Wilkinson: Actually, Chester was right. The way they had set up to do it was the proper way to do it, so that when you first get an observation you should note all the mathematical information and the time and mathematically compute and make your spots and changes from that, not by trial and error. He was absolutely right in the method of doing it, and they had set up good methodology, and that's the way we trained. But that wasn't the way I'd always done it for years and years.

Paul Stillwell: How was yours different? Was it sort of a seat-of-the-pants instinct thing?

Admiral Wilkinson: No. I did all that in my head, and I could do it faster. It just came almost instantaneously, like a computer.

Paul Stillwell: Were you working the solution in your head faster than the TDC could do it mechanically?

Admiral Wilkinson: The TDC was an old and antiquated thing. It wasn't a computer. It just tracked and you took a new reading, and depending on the difference you tried a new solution in the TDC. If you had a target going at a certain speed and a certain bearing and you got new information on the target a certain length of time later, you made an adjustment in the course and speed you'd assigned the target to try to make it be closer on the next observation. You could be more accurate if you made a very accurate calculation of exactly how much range difference there had been for such and such an angle difference for a certain length of time. If you did that, if you made the calculation easy in your mind by taking the next observation, for example, exactly a minute later, it was an easier mental calculation than a minute and 22 seconds.

If the target had been coming exactly towards you, and it was only a range difference, it's a much easier mental calculation than if the thing's at 15 degrees and you have to apply a sine or cosine factor. I don't want this to sound wrong. It doesn't matter to me if it's 22 degrees off and so many yards and a minute and 32 seconds. I can do that calculation in my head just as easily. It's the easy one, see. So if you dummied up a problem for the students that was set for observation, a minute or something, they went through a trial and correction methodology.

Now, if you want to make that harder and make the problem a minute and 22 seconds, to me I'll get the answer faster because it's a computer-type computation made with your mind. I couldn't compete with a computer now, but with the old TDC, which was just a mechanical device that was tracking something, it was easy to do it in my head. The machine didn't figure out the error. If the range was wrong, you made your target go faster or slower a certain amount. If you made that amount exactly accurate the first time, the next time it would track right on, so if you took ten observations you'd slowly get to the right solution. But I had a tendency to get pretty close to the right solution after one observation. Does that make sense to you?

Paul Stillwell: Yes.

Admiral Wilkinson: The TDC was a very antiquated piece of equipment.

Paul Stillwell: You didn't have all that much respect for the machine, but still you were required to teach it.

Admiral Wilkinson: Well, I had a lot of respect for the machine at that time. It did its job. I didn't know anything about computers that were to come someday. You've got to look at the situation through your eyes at the time. It's just like our submarine through today's eyes didn't amount to much, but it was the right ship for the job at the time. Our submarine carried a lot of fuel and had a long cruising range. Carried a lot of torpedoes, and the Japanese didn't have any effective radar yet, and we raised hell with them because we really had the right weapon for the time.

That old antiquated submarine wouldn't be worth a damn today, but it did a good job then. Same with the TDC. I didn't know any better. I used to spend hours practicing on that machine. I could close my eyes and run it in the dark. I remember one crank, four degrees. And every day I'd get the people up on the regulators in the torpedo room that matched to make sure that we were getting the right gyro there, and we would practice together for 15 or 20 minutes every day. I spent an awful lot of time on that machine. I was good in the use of the equipment we had at the time, because I spent hours and hours and hours and hours fiddling with it and practicing with it.

Paul Stillwell: How capable were the students at picking it up?

Admiral Wilkinson: Chester Nimitz was right. That was the right way to do it, and that was the right way to teach them. You could make it easier to start with by, as I say, giving easy time units between observation, something that was easier to compute. Depending on how you set your problems up, it would be easier to get a solution than if you set a more difficult problem. For example, a 37-degree angle on the bow with a high-speed target it would be harder to make a computed correction. Now, if I wanted to have the guy zigging or changing speed, I could make the problem very complicated, or I could make it very simple. But doing the mental calculation, no matter what, is better than doing trial and error. So he was right, and that was the right way to do it. But then that was the way I'd always done it.

Paul Stillwell: It was probably a time of mixed feelings for you. On the one hand you got to spend time with your wife. On the other hand, you weren't out in action.

Admiral Wilkinson: I'd much rather spend time with my wife.

Paul Stillwell: Okay, good. [Laughter]

Admiral Wilkinson: But it was the war, and things were different in World War II. It wasn't like Vietnam or Korea. Everybody went in the service. That was the thing you did. Millions of people were in, and we were going to be in until the war was over.

Paul Stillwell: Well, we've talked about your being recruited for the *Menhaden*.

Admiral Wilkinson: *Menhaden* was built in Manitowoc, Wisconsin, from Electric Boat Company plans.* When the ship was finished, we took the ship from Manitowoc to Chicago. We went through the Chicago drainage canal and down to the upper reaches of the Mississippi, where we got in a floating dry dock. The guaranteed depth in the upper reaches of the Mississippi in those days was nine feet, and in the floating dry dock we drew only about seven. At New Orleans we got out of the floating dry dock and finished the outfitting of the ship, some things that needed to be put on it, and sailed away.

Paul Stillwell: Do you remember any incidents from the trip down the river?

Admiral Wilkinson: Yes. First of all, all the people in Manitowoc, the shipbuilding people and the local citizens, were there when we left. As we sailed away, we had to go

---
* USS *Menhaden* (SS-377) was a *Balao*-class submarine commissioned 22 June 1945. She had a displacement of 1,525 tons on the surface and 2,424 tons submerged. She was 312 feet long, 27 feet in the beam, and had a draft of 15 feet. Her top speed was 20 knots surfaced and 9 knots submerged. She was armed with ten 21-inch torpedo tubes, a 5-inch gun, and a 40-millimeter gun.

through a couple of bridges, and they were all there to wave good-bye. As we got ready to set sail to be under way that night and get to Chicago the next morning, we took in a stern line and twisted out. With the bow line still over, the loudspeaker blared, "Bridge, this is maneuvering. We've lost lube oil suction." We had already waved good-bye to everybody. I was the exec and navigator. So we waited 15-20 minutes till they got squared away in maneuvering.

During those 15 or 20 minutes my good quartermaster, Bob Gallic, came up to me and pointed out this beautiful blonde over on the dock. Let me digress a minute. The crew had their option there of riding the ship down the Mississippi River or taking leave and meeting us in New Orleans. Out of a crew of 64 we had maybe 50 that wanted to ride down the Mississippi.

In those days I think there were only nine bridges over the Mississippi. You didn't see a damn thing except cane breaks on both sides, but we didn't know that. Since we didn't really need everybody, it was all right for a guy to get off. But in these 15 or 20 minutes that we were waiting, my quartermaster came up to me, and he said, "Commander, my girl and I want to get married. I'd like to take leave and meet the ship in New Orleans."

His eyes looked like two red holes in a blanket. He had obviously been up partying all night the night before. I said, "Gallic, we're just about to get under way. There is no way I'm going to let a guy off to get married at this time in your condition. If you still feel that same way tomorrow morning when we pass through the Chicago drainage canal, I'll pull over to the side and let you off."

So he went and talked to his girl, and they made that arrangement. I guess they were serious. The next morning we got there, and she was waiting in a convertible with the top down. We pulled over to the side, and he clambered up and went off. Then they got married and sat in New Orleans. I just got a Christmas card from them over there. He got out after the war and became vice president of his company.

Paul Stillwell: That's a neat story.

Admiral Wilkinson: Yes. But going down the Mississippi was quite an experience in those days. We finished whatever we had to do with the ship. It just took a day or two, and then we sailed across the Gulf of Mexico and through the Panama Canal, and then we stopped and did training there. They had a training element. We fired 77 torpedoes in ten days, which our guys made ready for training against multiple ships.

We had a super fire control team. Remember this is the outfit that had sunk the *Atago*. We fired 77 practice torpedoes in the ten days, and we had three erratic runs and 74 hits, and I mean real torpedoes, under the target. But we were good. Then the war ended, and we never got the *Menhaden* into combat.[*] It was a slick-looking ship. They sent us to Honolulu.

Then, when they wanted to relieve Admiral Nimitz they decided to do it on a submarine.[†] They came down and looked at all the submarines to see which one looked best, and obviously ours looked best, so that's where the change of command for Admiral Nimitz was. We had a good crew and good spirit; and we were not like regular new construction that's 25% experienced guys and some other people. We had a fully qualified crew. We probably had almost everybody from the *Darter* who was on the *Menhaden*. The war was over, thank goodness.

Paul Stillwell: Where were you when you got the news that the war was over?

Admiral Wilkinson: There in the Perlas Islands.[‡]

Paul Stillwell: What was the reaction on board?

Admiral Wilkinson: Oh, everybody was happy probably.

---

[*] V-J Day – Victory over Japan Day, marked the end of the war in the Pacific on 15 August 1945. Because of the time difference it was 14 August in the United States when combat ended.
[†] On 24 November 1945, on board the *Menhaden* at Pearl Harbor, Admiral Raymond A. Spruance, USN, relieved Fleet Admiral Chester W. Nimitz, USN, as Commander in Chief Pacific and Pacific Ocean Areas.
[‡] The Perlas (Pearl) Islands are in the Caribbean Sea, near the coast of Nicaragua.

Paul Stillwell: Slade Cutter was in the *Requin*, which was out in Hawaii at the time.[*] He said there were a couple of the junior men who were disappointed because they hadn't qualified for the submarine combat pin, and he told them to swallow their disappointment because they were still alive.

Admiral Wilkinson: Everybody on *Menhaden* had been out there on *Darter*. We weren't disappointed. We all had combat pins.

Paul Stillwell: That's true. [Laughter]

Admiral Wilkinson: We were happy, except we would have rather not been in Panama. We would have rather have been up in the States. And because we were a new boat they sent us out to Honolulu, when everybody else would have rather gone home. Nobody there had family in Honolulu. That was the only bit of dissatisfaction.

Paul Stillwell: Well, here was a crew that was all trained up, a ship in great condition.

Admiral Wilkinson: And ready to go.

Paul Stillwell: And ready to go.

Admiral Wilkinson: And the war was over, thank goodness.

Paul Stillwell: And no mission, so what did you do then?

Admiral Wilkinson: Oh, she just became one of the submarines that were left. A lot of ships and submarines were put out of commission at the end of the war, and obviously the *Menhaden* wasn't because she was one of the newest.

---

[*] Commander Slade D. Cutter, USN, was the first commanding officer of the submarine *Requin* (SS-481), which was headed toward combat when hostilities ceased. See his Naval Institute oral history.

Paul Stillwell: Did you stay around Hawaii for a while?

Admiral Wilkinson: Not I. When I decided to stay in the Navy at the end of World War II, a crackerjack officer that had been my boss was the submarine detail officer, Johnny Davidson.[*] He gave me orders to go put the submarine *Dogfish* in commission, SS-350.[†] I proceeded to New London and reported to the supervisor of shipbuilding for duty in the pre-commissioning detail of the *Dogfish*. It was a sort of a bad situation. I guess Johnny Davidson had been in a hurry to get me some orders now that I had decided to stay in the Navy.

Also, I put my request in for a permanent commission, because I was still a reserve. There were some unusual provisions in the law concerning the way seniority worked at that time. All regular Navy personnel were senior to all reserves with the same date of rank. As a part of the pre-commissioning detail there was an officer for *Dogfish* that was out of the Naval Academy class of '41, which was commissioned in February 1941. In the reserve I had been commissioned December 12, 1940. We happened to have both made lieutenant commander on 7/27/45. So since we had the same date of rank in our present rank of lieutenant commander, the regular Navy officer out of the class of '41 was senior to me. But if my request for regular Navy were approved, which eventually it would be, I would become senior to this officer from the class of '41.

This would be a really bad situation on a ship where one guy would be exec for seven, eight, nine months, and then the third officer would become senior and become exec. So I went around and talked to the prospective commanding officer and said, "Hey, this is a bad situation on this ship. You should make a decision and have only one of the two of us stay and be exec, and the other one should go and get some other duty elsewhere."[‡]

---

[*] Davidson, who had been Wilkinson's skipper in the *Blackfish* during the war, was now a commander.
[†] USS *Dogfish* (SS-350) was a *Gato*-class submarine commissioned 29 April 1946. She had a displacement of 1,525 tons on the surface and 2,410 tons submerged. She was 312 feet long, 27 feet in the beam, and had a draft of 15 feet. Her top speed was 20 knots surfaced and 9 knots submerged. She was initially armed with ten 21-inch torpedo tubes and a 5-inch deck gun.
[‡] The first commanding officer of the *Dogfish* was Commander Thomas S. Baskett, USN.

He said, "Gee, I hadn't realized that, and you're absolutely right. I agree with you and I choose—" He chose the other guy [laughter], which was a shock to me, because I was pretty proud of myself.

So I said, "Well, sir, I think you just made a mistake, but I thank you for doing it." So I left the pre-commissioning detail of *Dogfish* and went hunting myself for another job. Fortunately, Fred Janney, who was a crackerjack guy, was the CO of the *Raton*.[*] He wanted to get a new exec, and quickly I got orders and became the exec on the *Raton*.[†] But it was a blow to my pride when the PCO of *Dogfish* chose my contemporary instead of me to be the exec. He just made a mistake, that's all. [Laughter]

The military was cutting down in size as fast as they could. People were being shipped out right and left that were in for the war. Ships were being put out of commission, and the submarines started to become shorter and shorter on personnel. All the boats in New London had less than full complements. There was a provision that if your enlistment was up and you got out, you could reenlist within a certain period, I think it was 30 days, and lose no seniority. A lot of people wanted to shift locales. For example, a person in submarines on the West Coast, and whose family was in New London, would finish his enlistment, travel at his own expense across country, and ship over aboard a ship in New London. Then he'd be on duty in New London instead of Honolulu. It was a strange provision at the time, but there was a real shortage of people due to everybody getting out faster than they could put the ships out of commission.

We were quite shorthanded on the *Raton*, but pretty soon the *Raton* attracted some of these men. The *Raton* had a good reputation, and we had a lot of people who came from the West Coast, got out, came over, and shipped aboard on the *Raton*. Eventually we were way over complement. Everybody else was down in the 45 and 50 range instead of 64, and we had 75 or 80.

Paul Stillwell: Where did you put them all?

---

[*] Lieutenant Commander Frederick E. Janney, USN.
[†] USS *Raton* (SS-270) was a *Gato*-class submarine commissioned 13 July 1943. She had a displacement of 1,525 tons on the surface and 2,424 tons submerged. She was 312 feet long, 27 feet in the beam, and had a draft of 19 feet. Her top speed was 20 knots surfaced and 9 knots submerged. She was armed with ten 21-inch torpedo tubes and a 3-inch deck gun.

Admiral Wilkinson: Well, we weren't operating very much, only out in the morning and back in the evening. The boats then weren't going out for the week like they do now. We became the training boat for prospective commanding officers. We would carry the PCOs out where they'd do their fire control training and approach training and whatnot. The *Raton* was a very high-morale, high-reputation boat, and Fred Janney was really a good ship handler. He ran a nice approach. Ran his ship safely. He let me run it like the exec should as far as all the rest of the details went. But he was very capable. I'm very high on Fred Janney.

Paul Stillwell: What do you remember about the administrative part of the job?

Admiral Wilkinson: The exec does that on a ship. When I reported aboard, Fred Janney had not been there very long as a skipper. They had a rather sorry bunch as officers, and a lot of the troops were being paid off and getting out. So they weren't paying much attention to taking care of the mail and doing those things. When I reported aboard and Fred Janney offered me the job as exec, I sort of walked through with the acting exec. In the yeoman's office there were just drawers full of mail, maybe been there a month, never been opened. I remember well I went in the wardroom and opened the thing, and the chronometers were all stopped in their boxes. They hadn't been wound for 23 days. And after about two hours of walking around I went back to see Captain Janney, whom I didn't know from Adam at that time. I said, "Captain, a—"

He said, "Never mind. Just relieve as exec."

So I went back and said to the guy, "Well, thanks. That's all the dope I need. I'm ready to relieve you." I did, we transferred him, and I became exec.

The ship hadn't operated since Janney had been aboard, I don't think. All the boats had come back there at the end of the war, and as people walked away it took a while to get things straightened out. I hate to tell these stories, but one of the things I did after I became exec I inspected the ship, and I went through the wardroom area very thoroughly. There was a built-in bureau in the submarine and there were drawers. If you were to pull them all out, there was some space down under the lowest drawer, and there were spaces outside the bunks.

I must have pulled out of those spaces 400 or 500 classified patrol reports, which should never have been taken to sea. They'd been kept aboard to read during the war. And I must have pulled out 20-some-odd bottles of liquor that had been cached away, because back in the war I'm not saying they drank aboard, but they'd carry it out to wherever they were going because maybe you couldn't get liquor out there. And so we cleaned up all those things.

Then we got under way, and I took each one of those officers who really could have done it except they didn't know where they were. Took them up on the bridge in Long Island Sound and said, "Determine your position," and not one of them could do it. Not that they didn't know how to plot and take a fix, but they didn't recognize Little Gull or Race Rock or whatnot. They'd come from the city and hadn't done anything since. So we lost all those officers as the Navy was cutting down, and we got new ones. And we shipped in a lot of new crew members, and the *Raton* became probably in our opinion the best ship in New London. Might not have been, but we thought it was. And the way the West Coasters would come and enlist on our boat was some sort of an indicator. We had a good reputation.

Paul Stillwell: Well, you must have acquired it very quickly.

Admiral Wilkinson: Nobody was operating, and we started operating again. We acquired it quickly.

Paul Stillwell: Well, please tell me about the PCOs that you took out.

Admiral Wilkinson: Janney was a very good ship handler, a very good approach officer, and a very experienced guy. And some way or other with a reputation with the Sub School, they chose us to be the boat that would take the prospective commanding officers out whom you had to put in charge and let run approaches. But the captain was still responsible for the ship, and just because he had some PCO trainee out didn't mean he could let his periscope be run down by a destroyer or something.

I really admired Fred Janney. He would wait till the last possible minute or seconds before he would take it away from a PCO who was doing wrong. And the instances of their doing wrong were very infrequent. But then we had an interesting time. The PCO class was filled with all the released prisoners of war, submarine guys who had all worked up to be senior enough to become commanding officers, but they hadn't gotten the experience.

And everybody wanted to be nice to prisoners of war. They didn't want to deprive them of professional advancement because they'd been prisoners, so they put these guys in the prospective commanding officers' class, and I'm talking good guys, sharp guys. There was nothing they couldn't do mentally, except the interesting phenomenon was they were slow in reaction. They would have to think about it. And you can't waste time thinking about it when you're in a closing situation with a guy that may run into you.

I don't know how many times Fred Janney at the last minute would say, "Eighty feet," and so we'd dip under to keep our periscope from getting hit. But that happened more times in that one PCO class with the prisoners of war than it did with all the others we ever took. But some way or other we seemed to be the one the Sub School wanted to use as a PCO boat all the time, because Fred Janney would let the people do it to the utmost and would only interfere when the final moment of safety came.

Paul Stillwell: Did their reactions get quicker as they got more practice at doing that?

Admiral Wilkinson: Not in the time that I saw them, which was maybe three weeks. I'm sure it must have over the years. But it didn't change instantly.

Paul Stillwell: Do you remember any of the individuals in that group?

Admiral Wilkinson: Yes, but I'm not going to talk names.

Paul Stillwell: Okay. What else was involved in that tour of duty?

Admiral Wilkinson: That was all we did. We were one of the boats that operated out of New London giving services. Other ships were going out of commission. There was great turmoil and transfer of people. A large part of the Navy that had been in for the war, a large part of the military got out, so maybe only a quarter of your people would be left. You had to get new people. They had to be brought up to speed in your boat. It was a time of turmoil. It was easier for us because we had all these guys come and reenlist on board, and they were all permanent guys. But some of the boats had a hectic time being undermanned in strength.

Paul Stillwell: Many ships had a really difficult time and couldn't spend much time under way.

Admiral Wilkinson: I came aboard just before a few ships were going to go to sea and start doing their functions again. Sub School had to have some services. But there was a period right at the end of the war when all the people were getting out that many ships were at very low state of readiness. I reached the ship when it was at that state, and we went through the turnaround.

Paul Stillwell: How long was that tour of duty for you?

Admiral Wilkinson: Oh, not long. I think less than a year.

Paul Stillwell: Did you have any other roles besides being the PCO boat?

Admiral Wilkinson: New London training boat, Sub School, and PCO. But we seemed to get most of the PCO duty. The reason I didn't stay on the *Raton* as long as a normal tour was because I was a reserve that had shifted to regular Navy, and they sent most of us that they could to the General Line School. That was maybe a six months' course. And I went from there to be exec of the *Cusk*.

Paul Stillwell: Well, it's 9:00 o'clock. I wonder if this is a convenient breaking point.

Admiral Wilkinson: All right.

Interview Number 2 with Vice Admiral Eugene P. Wilkinson, U.S. Navy (Retired)
Place: Admiral Wilkinson's home in Del Mar, California
Date: Sunday, 18 January 1998
Interviewer: Paul Stillwell

Paul Stillwell: Admiral, yesterday you described working for Commander Janney in the *Raton*. After that you went to the General Line School. What are you recollections of that?

Admiral Wilkinson: Sort of hazy. Since we had a lot of reserves that shifted to regular Navy, we were in this indoctrination that was given to us. All I remember was that we took the General Line Course up at Newport, Rhode Island, and my family and I lived in Newport. I don't remember as much about it as I should, except I'm sure we learned a lot.

Paul Stillwell: Was it useful in giving you a broader prospective on the Navy as a whole?

Admiral Wilkinson: Undoubtedly it was, but I don't remember it that way. Years later I went to Newport again to the senior course at the Naval War College. Looking back, the General Line Course at Newport impresses me more than the Armed Forces Staff College did. But, anyway, that's what took me off the *Menhaden* before a longer tour as exec of the *Raton*. And since I hadn't had that much time as exec, when I left General Line School at Newport I had orders as exec of the *Cusk*, SSG-348, which was the first submarine that fired guided missiles.*

---

* USS *Cusk* (SS-348) was a *Gato*-class submarine commissioned 5 February 1946. She had a displacement of 1,525 tons on the surface and 2,410 tons submerged. She was 312 feet long, 27 feet in the beam, and had a draft of 15 feet. Her top speed was 20 knots surfaced and 9 knots submerged. She was initially armed with ten 21-inch torpedo tubes and a 5-inch deck gun. She was redesignated SSG-348 on 20 January 1948 to reflect her new mission of firing guided missiles.

Paul Stillwell: Well, that's an exciting story. Please tell me about that. Who was the skipper?

Admiral Wilkinson: We had a very capable officer as skipper, superbly capable and competent, Pete Summers.* But Pete had a hard time delegating responsibility to others. He was so good and so capable that he did a lot of things himself as CO rather than trust other people to do it. He had been unhappy with the performance of his former executive officers and in fact had had two of them fired. Then I went as his third executive officer, and the only defense I had was BuPers telling him as they sent me that, "Pete, we're sending you an executive officer that we know will be okay."† That may be fine in the broader sense, but in the day-to-day context of things it was not completely so.

Paul Stillwell: How well did the relationship work out in practice?

Admiral Wilkinson: It changed over time. Pete was a tough taskmaster. With leave en route I was contacted by the ship and told to report in early. So I reported aboard late Sunday afternoon in San Diego and the next morning took over as the exec and navigator. The ship was due to sail that morning for Hunters Point in San Francisco.‡ We had quarters, stationed the maneuvering watch, made preparation to get under way, sailed out of the harbor, and passed the sea buoy. As the maneuvering watch was secured and the regular section set, the word was passed for me to report to the captain. And this was my first minute on board not at quarters and maneuvering station.

    I went in the captain's room, and Captain Summers said to me, "What time are we going to pass under the Golden Gate Bridge?"

    As good luck would have it, when I had reported aboard on Sunday, the afternoon before, because I was going to be navigator I had checked out our track and schedule on up. So I happened to have done it, but certainly I hadn't had any time that morning, and I was asked just as the maneuvering watch was secured. I said, "Well, Captain, what time would you like to pass under the Golden Gate Bridge?"

---

* Commander Paul E. Summers, USN, was the first commanding officer of the *Cusk*.
† BuPers – Bureau of Naval Personnel.
‡ Hunters Point Naval Shipyard, San Francisco, California.

That slowed Pete down for, oh, 15-20 seconds, and he thought about that he said, "What time should we pass under the Golden Gate Bridge?"

I said, "Well, 1011, sir." By the time we passed under the Golden Gate Bridge I was on the bridge navigating, and the captain was there, and I said, "Conning tower, mark the time."

They said, "1011, sir." I'm sure they would have done that if we'd been a couple of minutes off, [laughter] because the troops were pleased to have a new exec and navigator aboard, and by that time were on my side.

Paul Stillwell: How soon did it take him to get confidence in you?

Admiral Wilkinson: Well, I don't know if he ever got full confidence in me, because Pete had great confidence in himself, which he merited, and he liked to check up on everything. But he did everything exactly by the book. He kept a list every day of everything that he didn't like, and he'd call me in every morning and go over the items with me one by one. I guess that reached the high point one day of more than 90 items. "I saw the mess cook topside without a hat on, and you know that's against my policy," or, "I saw the fireman in the engine room that had a torn sleeve on his dungarees, and you know that's against my policy." And that's the right way for the chain of command to work, the captain to go through his exec. On the other hand, there is a timeliness to tell a guy to get down and get his hat on when he's supposed to have a hat on.

I happened to have access to Captain Summers's safe, so I would open it each night. I guess through my entire tour as exec he was never on board that I wasn't there. I met him every morning when he came aboard and saw him off every evening, and so afterwards I would get out his list and take care of all the items that I could. So the next morning, when he'd go through the list, I'd say, "Well, Captain, that was Jones, and he's gotten rid of that jumper, and he'll never wear it again. That dungaree shirt will never go again," or, "That was such-and-such, and he'll always wear his hat topside." And this went on item by item.

Or if it was a more important item like, "I think we ought to write a letter to the Bureau of Ships asking about this," I'd say, "Well, gee, Fred Berry was talking about that, and there might be a draft in your basket." [Laughter] And so after about four or five months Pete stopped keeping a list, but I'm sure he never did get complete confidence. [Laughter] That sounds wrong. Pete Summers was very capable, did a tremendous job as the skipper of the *Cusk* in evaluations of the guided missiles we had, which were V-1 rockets that had come from the Germans.[*] The *Cusk*'s and *Carbonero*'s performance in that program led on to the Regulus program, which led on to Polaris. So Pete Summers deserves his place in history and did it very well. But he was a tough guy to be exec for.

Paul Stillwell: Please tell me about some of those tests and your work with Point Mugu.[†]

Admiral Wilkinson: We were test firing the Loons, as we called them; they actually were V-1 rockets. Some 483 of them were captured from the Germans at Peenemünde, and we got them to the submarine force.[‡] They fired them from Point Mugu, and we fired them off the after deck of the *Cusk*.[§] Eventually we had a big watertight hangar built on the *Cusk*. We could open it up so we could dive with a Loon in there, surface, open it up, pull the Loon out on the launcher, and fire it. Then we would secure the hangar, dive again, and track this bird we had fired, which was a pulse-jet rocket. We had a transponder in it so we could get a good echo on it with our radar, and we would track it.

The controls were very rudimentary in that we could give it a signal to put on right rudder or left rudder, or we could cut the engine so it had no more power and would drop into the sea. And just like a crew race making so many strokes, we had a really superior plotting party on the *Cusk*. We would track this bird that we had put in the air; it also was being followed by a jet plane that was for aircraft safety, to shoot it down if the course was erratic.

---

[*] The V-1 was a pulse-jet flying bomb, also known as a "doodlebug" and "buzz bomb." It was 25 feet long and had a 16-foot wingspan. It carried a one-ton warhead some 150 miles (later increased to 250) at a speed of about 400 miles per hour. It was first successfully flown in December 1943. The Germans fired more than 13,000 V-1s during the course of World War II.
[†] Pacific Missile Test Range, Point Mugu, California. For more on missile testing in the late 1940s see the Naval Institute oral history of Captain Grayson Merrill, USN (Ret.).
[‡] Peenemünde is a German town on the Baltic Sea's Pomeranian Bay. During World War II it was the site of a German rocket complex where the V-weapons were developed.
[§] The first submarine launch of a missile was a Loon fired from the *Cusk* off Point Mugu 12 February 1947.

We would fire this Loon at a target called Bird Rock, maybe some 60, 70, 80, 90 miles away. We would track it with our superior plotting party, and we would be taking range and bearing and plotting it every minute. And then, just like a stroke, we would shift the plots every 30 seconds and every 20 seconds and every 15 seconds and every 10 seconds. If it wasn't going toward target, we would apply right rudder for two seconds and then back to amidships, and then we'd plot and see what had happened, and that way we would correct the course toward the target. When we thought it was at the right point, we'd cut the power. Then its engines would cut off, and naturally it would go down into the sea. I don't think we ever hit Bird Rock, but we came really close. [Laughter]

Paul Stillwell: Could you vary the altitude on it?

Admiral Wilkinson: No. You know, I don't remember what determined the altitude. We didn't. We steered it right or left, and we cut off its engine. They also did shots from the beach. And the *Carbonero*, which didn't have the capability to launch, would also track it. It seems pretty elementary now, but that really was the beginning that led into the Regulus program, which was a 500-mile missile that had better control than that.[*] And that led on to Polaris and our strategic weapons capability.[†]

Paul Stillwell: The Loon had a launcher that looked like rails at an angle. Could you vary that angle?

Admiral Wilkinson: No.

Paul Stillwell: So that's probably what established the trajectory right there.

---

[*] Two Regulus missiles were designed to be fired from surface ships or surfaced submarines. Regulus I, which entered the fleet in 1952, was 34 feet long, weighed 12,000 pounds, and had a speed of Mach 0.9 and range of 500 miles; Regulus II, which had its first flight test in 1958, was 57 feet long, weighed 22,000 pounds, and had a speed of Mach 2.0 and range of 1,000 miles. Regulus II was tested, but the program was terminated for budgetary reasons and did not become operational in the fleet.
[†] Polaris was the name for the U.S. Navy's first submarine-launched ballistic missile, which became operational in the early 1960s. Its more-capable follow-on was the Poseidon missile, which entered the fleet in 1970.

Admiral Wilkinson: Yes, and what altitude that went to I just don't remember.

Paul Stillwell: How many Loons could you carry at a time?

Admiral Wilkinson: One if we submerged. Now that I think about it, we could have put one in a hangar, one on the launcher and run around on the surface. But one was what we took.

Paul Stillwell: How often did you make these shots?

Admiral Wilkinson: Well, that was one of the things that was tough on the crew. We gave the services week after week, and we left San Diego Sunday evening to be up at Point Mugu Monday morning to start work at 8:00 o'clock.* So when the other submarines were getting under way on Monday, week after week we were getting under way Sunday. Eventually, from a home and liberty aspect, that was tough on our crew. Also our crew for other reasons wasn't the happiest in the world. Now, they didn't get as much liberty. Had some pretty stringent things.

On the other hand, morale was high, because morale is not really chow and liberty. Morale is pride in unit, and there isn't any doubt that the officers and crew on the *Cusk* had great pride in unit. I could have gone down to the control room as exec and said, "The *Squatfish* thinks they can defeat us playing Parcheesi, and I'd like to bet $500.00." I would have had $500.00 instantly, because there wasn't any submarine in our crew's opinion could beat us at anything. An awful lot of people would pay the same $500.00 to get off the ship. [Laughter] But morale in that key essential of pride in unit was there. I've had people on the *Cusk* say to me, "Commander, there isn't any ship I would rather be on in wartime, but it's not wartime." So I had a lot of people on that ship that weren't completely happy, and part of it had to do with our operations of getting under way every Sunday evening instead of Monday morning like the other submarines.

Paul Stillwell: Who directed the tests? Who gave you the specifications?

---

* Point Mugu is located on the California coast, approximately 65 miles northwest of Los Angeles.

Admiral Wilkinson: It wasn't us, and it wasn't our submarine commanders. We the submarine were giving services to support the program, so although we did the operations and fired the missiles, the actual laying out of the program and the control of it were from authority that was based at Point Mugu, not us. We were in fact only providing services of support. But we worked hard at that and did it well. I had a really good plotting party and a very capable fire control group, and they did their jobs well.

Paul Stillwell: Was it one of the submarine's people that gave these orders, left rudder, right rudder, and so forth?

Admiral Wilkinson: Oh, yes, that was us. That was part of our services. After all, we were the ones tracking it, aiming it to hit this target and tracking it along its way and controlling it from our plotting and tracking.

Paul Stillwell: I would think that maybe after a while the novelty would wear off and cause some of this disgruntlement, but at the very first it must have been exciting.

Admiral Wilkinson: Oh, for me it was exciting all the time, but it didn't bother me as much to get under way Sunday night as it did some of the troops. And it only bothered them because it was week after week after week with no end in sight. As I've said, at other times on another submarine, "How long can you stay out there operating, a year, two years?" You can if it's necessary, but not one weekend if it's not. I mean, people will do what is necessary, but if they don't see it as necessary then it can be a bad morale thing.

Paul Stillwell: How long did the tests go on?

Admiral Wilkinson: As long as I was on the *Cusk*. And then finally I was chosen for another program, and I was transferred from the *Cusk* to a two-year assignment to work on this nuclear propulsion plant for submarines, a new concept. So I went from the *Cusk* to Oak Ridge National Laboratory to work on that.*

Paul Stillwell: Did the *Cusk* do any regular submarine things while you were on board? Shoot torpedoes?

Admiral Wilkinson: Oh, yes. We didn't go to Point Mugu every week. We did all the other kinds of operations that submarines ought to do. Did our exercises, fired torpedoes and whatnot, and all that we did well. Pete Summers was very capable, a capable fire control officer, a capable approach officer, professionally competent. He just had a little bit of a problem of delegating and depending on people.

Paul Stillwell: Did that hangar on the after deck cause handling problems?

Admiral Wilkinson: It made a difference in our maneuverability submerged, yes. It didn't seem to give us any trouble in surface operations, making landings and whatnot. I wasn't aware of it. It did slow us down submerged.

Paul Stillwell: Anything else about that boat to mention?

Admiral Wilkinson: No. It was a different tour for me, something new and very interesting. In retrospect it was a tour I'm glad I had, because it was at the very beginning of missiles for the submarine Navy. I didn't envision at that time such a thing as Polaris, but in retrospect the Loon, the Regulus all were part of the trail that led on to Polaris when the missile technology, combined with the nuclear propulsion technology, gave us a fantastic weapon system.

Paul Stillwell: Well, and you could argue another outcome of it was that submarines now

---

* Oak Ridge National Laboratory, Oak Ridge, Tennessee, which has long been involved in research and development in the field of nuclear energy.

fire Tomahawks.*

Admiral Wilkinson: Yes and that was much later. By that time I was in a controlling position in what happened in the submarine force.

Paul Stillwell: Well, you talked about being in on a new thing. Going to Oak Ridge was certainly that. How did you get picked to go into that program?

Admiral Wilkinson: Well, I didn't know it at the time, but looking back Captain Rickover had got himself a group of very capable engineering duty only officers such as Lou Roddis who had stood number one in the class of '39 and some other very, very capable young engineering duty officers.†

Paul Stillwell: Miles Libbey was with him for a while.‡

Admiral Wilkinson: Yes, and Lou Roddis and Jim Dunford and a really capable group.§ Rickover had taken them down and looked into things at Oak Ridge and had managed to get the group that was there working on nuclear propulsion for a ship, and then because of the capability it would be a nuclear propulsion plant for submarines. They had the concept, and they had done that sort of work. In his infinite wisdom, Captain Rickover decided about that time that they should get an officer that was submarine experienced to augment his group. So he'd asked BuPers to pick such an officer and have him sent there. As it happened by the submarine group's system and the submarine opinion and submarine detailing at BuPers, I happened to be standing number one in my age group.

---

* Tomahawk is a long-range cruise missile that entered the fleet in the early 1980s, capable of delivering either conventional or nuclear warheads. Originally conceived to have both antiship and land-attack versions, the antiship type is no longer in service.
† Then-Captain Hyman G. Rickover, USN, was considered the father of the nuclear Navy. He ran the Navy's nuclear-power program for many years, eventually leaving active duty in 1982 with the rank of four-star admiral on the retired list. Lieutenant Commander Louis H. Roddis, Jr., USN (Ret.). As a Naval Academy midshipman, Roddis stood number one of the 581 graduates in the class of 1939.
‡ Lieutenant Commander Miles A. Libbey, Jr., USN.
§ Lieutenant Commander James M. Dunford, USN.

They picked a couple of us, and one of us was ordered to Oak Ridge, and the other one was ordered to the Office of the CNO in Washington.

Paul Stillwell: Who was he?

Admiral Wilkinson: I don't want to say. His daddy was an admiral. At the end of the year, he didn't want to leave Washington and go to Oak Ridge or Argonne, and so arrangements were made that he stayed there in OpNav, and I did the two years of field duty. That made him happy, and that made me happy, and that made Captain Rickover happy, so I never got my year of duty in the Office of Chief of Naval Operations. Instead, I had the tour in Oak Ridge, and then the group I was working with was moved from Oak Ridge National Laboratory to Argonne National Laboratory, and so I moved with it to Argonne.*

About that time, Captain Rickover made arrangements for Westinghouse to get their contract, and there was a Pittsburgh area office of the Atomic Energy Commission, set up to support Westinghouse at Bettis Field.† Rickover sent me there as his representative. So in my two years in that program I was with the group at Oak Ridge National Laboratory and then with the same group now transferred to Argonne National Laboratory under Dr. Zinn.‡ Finally I was the operations officer in the Pittsburgh area office of the Atomic Energy Commission, which was overseeing the work of Westinghouse, which now had a contract to support the program.

I thought at the time that Captain Rickover made a mistake arranging for me to go and be the Navy member of the Pittsburgh area office, because my tour of duty with that development was only two years. And then in 10 or 11 months I would get new orders and go back to sea, hopefully to get command of a submarine, which in fact did happen.

---

* In 1942 physicist Enrico Fermi's team produced the first sustained nuclear reaction at the University of Chicago. His reactor was later moved and reassembled in the Argonne Forest outside Chicago, thus leading to the name Argonne National Laboratory when the facility was officially established in DuPage County, Illinois.
† Bettis is the name of a nuclear laboratory in West Mifflin, Pennsylvania. The Pittsburgh-McKeesport Airport was named Bettis Field in honor of an Army Air Corps pilot, Lieutenant Cyrus Bettis, who died in 1926 after being injured in a crash in the Allegheny Mountains.
‡ Dr. Walter H. Zinn served as the first director of Argonne National Laboratory; he held that job from 1946 to 1956.

That was an important job, and so I recommended to Captain Rickover that he not choose me but rather that he should take one of his very capable and experienced EDOs such as Roddis or Dunford or Turnbaugh or somebody like that and send him to Pittsburgh.[*] They could stay in the job for the several years of continuity that would be required to do the job purposely.

But Rickover was not one to listen to my recommendation and told me, "Listen, don't tell me what to do. I'll run my program, and I'm sending you. And, besides, you will shift to EDO, and then you can stay there." But when the time came, I did not shift to EDO and went back to sea. I had to be replaced by Turnbaugh, who then was there for many years, because the job was important and required continuity. But it was a fun job for me.

In one report at Argonne I had more than 50% of the pages in the report of the whole organization, because I was doing the nuclear physics calculations. Besides the thermal energy neutron water-cooled reactor, the power pile division group had studied a gas-cooled reactor, and they'd studied an intermediate energy neutron liquid-metal cooled reactor. For various reasons they had settled on the most desirable being a thermal energy neutron water-cooled reactor, which was the one that was finally designed and built in *Nautilus*.

In those studies they had not taken into consideration some of the perturbations you would have in the neutron flux distribution when the core was fully loaded and the rods were inserted. So in the original calculations that they had made, they had not allowed enough surface for heat transfer, and the size that they had chosen for the water-cooled reactor was wrong. The people working for me were young ladies that were running the Marchant calculators or the Friden calculators, because that's the way we did it in those days. These young ladies came out with the data from some formulas I had set up, and they showed that the calculations that had been made previously were in error and the size was wrong. I had to change the dimensions of the core. What we came up with turned out to be right, and what was after more intensive study by Westinghouse in the design was right. And that was the size and the uranium loading and the number of

---

[*] Lieutenant Commander Marshall E. Turnbaugh, USN, stood ninth among the 581 graduates in the Naval Academy class of 1939. EDO – an officer designated for engineering duty only.

control rods and whatnot that were finally built into the prototype and then into the *Nautilus*.

Rickover was very eager to get a contract let with industry instead of having a national laboratory work on something. Rickover realized that no national laboratory would ever actually be the one to build hardware. So he got the Electric Boat Company involved, the Westinghouse Company, the General Electric Company, Portsmouth Naval Shipyard. The Electric Boat Company and the naval shipyard would be the ship constructors, and General Electric and Westinghouse as component and nuclear reactor developers. General Electric followed after Westinghouse. Westinghouse was first.

Westinghouse had the responsibility of developing the thermal energy neutron water-cooled reactor, which was what was built in the prototype at Idaho and in the *Nautilus*. But Rickover used an arguing point when talking to Congress. Referring to me, he said, "Listen, this poor dumb line officer has shown that the work the national laboratory did was wrong." That wasn't really quite fair. I had just continued on and found out some of the things they did were wrong [laughter] and corrected them. But Rickover used that to make his point that he needed to get industry involved. He had his way, and Westinghouse was given a contract.

The Pittsburgh area office was set up, and Rickover sent me there as the operations officer. I wrote my own job code description: "As the operations officer of the Pittsburgh area office, you are responsible for the technical program." So that gave me a lot of insight in dealings with Westinghouse in the development that was to follow during the rest of time at Pittsburgh.

Paul Stillwell: Wasn't it also a matter of practicality to have commercial outfits do the manufacturing part of it?

Admiral Wilkinson: Oh, yes. In fact, Rickover was absolutely right. You never could have built ships and built reactors and all the components, pumps and turbo-generator sets and valves. You wouldn't build those with a national laboratory; industry had to be involved. Rickover was wise, and he got industry as fast as he could in contracts and in on the development.

Westinghouse did a superb job, and it all worked out just as Admiral Rickover wanted it to. I keep saying Admiral Rickover because he was admiral later. At that time, understand, Rickover was still a captain. During that time period and working on that program, I made several contributions. One, I did do the calculations that changed the core size and uranium loading and whatnot, the first cut, but it was close enough that's the way it actually turned out. After it was refined, it was a right circular cylinder. It was still the same dimension in diameter and the same height as what I had worked out in my calculations. It had the same number of control rods. So I contributed in the primary design of what was built.

I also made two more contributions. I conceived of the idea of the chemical poison system, wherein as an extra safety measure to the control rods you could inject a solution of some neutron-absorbent material like Borax or something. And for 30 years we carried bags of this stuff on our submarines and never ever used it, of course. And for years I tried to get rid of that chemical poison system, but safety is a powerful word, and I never could get rid of it. As a matter of fact, our larger power commercial reactors that will run and generate power much longer do effect control by having a variable amount of poison in solution.

The other contribution I made, I did for the wrong reason. Before my work the concept had been to have control rods. And a rod was what you think of as a rod, a circular cylinder. But in doing my physics calculations, since the purpose of a rod was to put poison in, something to depress the neutron pumps, I said, "Gee, I could get a bigger surface area if I would have an X-shape instead of having a circular rod where the outer circumference is the very minimum. And so I'll change this to an X-shaped control rod."

Now, if you think about it, building flat things is much simpler and driving it simpler than driving a cylinder. So although I didn't do it for that purpose I conceived it from my limited view of the maximum surface area for poisoning, I made the X-shaped control rod. But from a manufacturing thing that's easy to build, and that's the way all control rods have been built since the very beginning.

Paul Stillwell: You must have taken a crash course in nuclear physics, because this was much different from firing torpedoes and firing missiles.

Admiral Wilkinson: Well, yes, but I took technical courses in college, and I majored in chemistry with a minor in physics and math. And then I did graduate work at the University of Southern California, where I completed all the course work for a doctor's degree. And I did have courses in nuclear physics in my graduate work at the University of California. And then, once I went to Oak Ridge, I studied.

I can talk glibly about Besel functions and two-group theory and flux densities and a lot of those kinds of things. As a matter of fact, when Rickover got his contract with Westinghouse and with Electric Boat Company and was also trying to get Portsmouth Naval Shipyard into the act, Rickover had a lecture for the executives of those places every week. I gave the nuclear physics lectures to the Westinghouse Electric Company management and to the Electric Boat Company management. I guess after a couple of years' work on it I was as knowledgeable on the exact thing we were doing as anybody.

Paul Stillwell: It's interesting that not being a Naval Academy graduate had been held against you before, but now maybe it helped.

Admiral Wilkinson: I was probably the first submarine officer in the program. Over the years, one of Admiral Rickover's strengths was to ensure that very capable people were sent to that program. He got in the position of interviewing and selecting every officer that went into the nuclear program. He also got the power to ensure no really capable people could be hidden from the possibility to go to that program. Some admiral couldn't corner a guy as his aide and see that that guy never had a chance of being selected. So all the officers were scrutinized, and the most capable or those with the highest class standings were sent down to Rickover for interview. And Rickover didn't do it alone; he did it with a group of his people.

I guess I was the first such one. I'd already been picked by BuPers for that program as a matter of the token. I didn't know who Captain Rickover was. A group interviewed me. Rickover asked me what math courses I'd had. I enumerated as many as I could remember, and I said, "Well, there might have been more, but I don't remember them all."

Rickover said to his people, "That can't be true. He'd know as much math as Roddis here." Well, I didn't know who Roddis was either. I didn't know who these people were interviewing me.

I said, "Well, that's probably true. He only went to the Naval Academy." [Laughter] I did not realize that I was talking about one of the brightest guys that ever came out of the Naval Academy. Lou Roddis stood number one in his class at the trade school and had the highest mark anybody had ever had up to that time. I can remember saying that, and afterwards it turned out I was embarrassed I'd said it. But I had had probably as much academic background as any of the highly specialized engineering duty officers that Rickover took with him to Oak Ridge.

Then, once I got to Oak Ridge, I got into working in the nuclear physics for months and months and months with six girls on Friden and Marchant calculators punching out numbers according to equations and formulas I made up for them. I had studied that. So by the time I was lecturing nuclear physics to Gwilym Price and the other executives at Westinghouse, I probably knew more on what I was lecturing about than anybody else.*

Paul Stillwell: The fact that Captain Rickover suggested you become an EDO implies that he did not at that point expect you to be the first skipper of the first submarine.

Admiral Wilkinson: No, he expected me to shift to EDO and stay there in the Pittsburgh area office. When he told me that, I told him, "No, I understand you have to sign something to be EDO, and I'm very careful about what I sign. I read what I sign, and so I don't think I'll ever do that." And that turned out to be the way it was. So when I left, for a period of time there was a certain amount of animosity, because nobody left Rickover's outfit without leaving in disrepute. I guess I'm probably the only guy that ever did. But by the time it rolled around to them building that submarine, Rickover's memory had dimmed, and the unhappiness about me not being an EDO had gone away.

---

* Gwilym A. Price, a lawyer, had served in the Army in World War II. He joined Westinghouse in 1943 and subsequently held a number of posts, including president, chairman of the board, and chief executive officer.

Paul Stillwell: Why did you not want to limit yourself to engineering duty only?

Admiral Wilkinson: Well, I'm an operator. I didn't stay in the Navy to be a technical engineer. I stayed in the Navy for the fun of being in command and being in charge and running ships and whatnot. I could have got out of the Navy and been a technical guy.

Paul Stillwell: What was your role in establishing the plan of action and milestones, sort of a forerunner of PERT?[*]

Admiral Wilkinson: Well, it's sort of interesting. I was up at the Pittsburgh area office of the Atomic Energy Commission as the operations officer. As I said, I wrote my own job code description. After I'd been working up there a short time at Westinghouse, I got hold of Captain Rickover and said, "We have to have a schedule for this program."

He told me, as he did many times, "You're young and immature, and you don't understand. You can't schedule R&D."[†]

I said, "Well, why the hell not? We've got a whole lot of tasks to do, and we've got to develop these very important sealed rotor pumps, and we have to develop this and that, and we'll put resources to it and so many people working on it. There's a date by which it ought to be done, and if it's falling behind schedule, we'll double the number of people and put more resources in it. If that isn't enough, we'll double it again. And the different things that go into getting this done, we'll put the resources to them, and we'll modify these resources over time to make sure we meet a schedule."

He said, "All right. Now, let's you go make me a schedule?"

Well, of course, it was not within my capability to make him a schedule, but I did have control of what Westinghouse did, and there was the capability to make the schedule there. So Westinghouse probably did all of what was the equivalent of the first PERT schedule that SP used later, in that we made and laid out the schedule with me

---

[*] PERT – Program Evaluation Review Technique, a system of milestones for tracking the progress of a program against its schedule.
[†] R&D – research and development.

overseeing and encouraging them and keeping on their backs to get a schedule.* Even with that effort, it took four months to make the schedule.

That schedule was not as simple as that sounds, because it had such things in it as getting authority and building the prototype plant at the Naval Test Station in Arco, Idaho, of getting authority and then building a nuclear reactor for a submarine, and getting authority for a ship and building the ship. And there were all the little development things that had to be done to support a prototype and a ship and a reactor. Remember, the reactor involved the Atomic Energy Commission, so it had to get approval from the Atomic Energy Commission. The ship involved the CNO and the Bureau of Ships. And the work involved the contractors, the Electric Boat Company and Westinghouse.

We finally came up with that schedule, and that schedule was finished in late '49. Rickover took that and over the years changed it one way or another, but that original schedule was to go to sea 1 January 1955. We didn't make that. We went the 17th of January, '55, which is close enough for government work.

Paul Stillwell: Well, anticipating six years in advance, I would say so.

Admiral Wilkinson: We missed our schedule. [Laughter] When I was ComSubLant and we took over the work and schedules for all the nuclear-powered missile submarines, we never missed a schedule, not once.† But that's another chapter in a later interview. But it all tied together and came out just about on time. That was only because Admiral Rickover was on everybody's back all the way and saw that when something fell behind it was recognized and identified, and the resources were more than doubled. Whatever resources were required were put into it, and he got it done. Making a schedule is easier than getting it done.

---

* SP – Special Projects Office, which over the years has managed the U.S. Navy's submarine-launched ballistic missile programs.
† When he was a vice admiral, Wilkinson served as Commander Submarine Force Atlantic Fleet from 12 February 1970 to 28 June 1972.

Paul Stillwell: Of course. Well, part of those steps you've enumerated included getting approval from Congress. How did Captain Rickover go about getting that approval?

Admiral Wilkinson: Well, he got CNO to support it very strongly, and that was through contacts. Some of the original letters that the CNO signed were drafted in Captain Rickover's office. Rickover got himself in the two-hatted position of working both for the Navy and the Atomic Energy Commission and got the Atomic Energy Commission to support this and got the Navy to support it. He told the Atomic Energy Commission, "It'll be embarrassing if just the Navy was doing this if we fall behind schedule," and told the Navy, "It'll be embarrassing if the Atomic Energy Commission is doing this and we fall behind schedule." Rickover worked one side against the other side and both sides against the middle and very cleverly got it all done.

But getting those things done had to be done on schedule. So I was helpful in the beginning of getting the concept of a schedule and in working the first rough cut, but then the refinement of that over the years and the making it happen were Rickover and his people all the way. By making it sound like I made the schedule, that's an awful lot more credit than I deserve. I conceptually said we needed a schedule, and with Westinghouse's help, after four months I came up with the first cut, which is also the way it ended up.

Paul Stillwell: How eager were the industrial representatives to cooperate in this?

Admiral Wilkinson: Admiral Rickover was a very demanding person, and he was on their backs all the way. For example, weekend after weekend he would come up on Saturday night to Pittsburgh and have a meeting with all the Westinghouse executives Sunday morning and throw his weight around and fuss with them all. Then he would leave and catch a train and ride back to Washington and be at work in his office Monday morning. I don't know how many weekends he did that at Westinghouse, because he wasn't there every weekend. He was there a lot, but the weekends he wasn't there he was probably up doing the same the thing with General Electric or the Electric Boat Company. So for Rickover it was total commitment. I talk sometimes about my own commitment. I was fairly well committed when I was awake, but Rickover was committed 24 hours a day.

Paul Stillwell: So he probably worked harder than anybody.

Admiral Wilkinson: Oh, there isn't any doubt about that.

Paul Stillwell: How soon did he start developing contacts directly with congressmen?

Admiral Wilkinson: I can't remember the exact date, but it's an interesting thing. The first contact he ever made, I gave him a ride over to the Congress and that little old man, I let him out there on the steps, and he walked up those steps into Congress. He made his first contact with Senator McMahon from Connecticut and said, "There's potential work here for a company in your area."[*] That was his first contact, but later on Rickover recognized the importance of the Congress.

At least to my knowledge, the most important congressional committee they ever had was the Joint Committee on Atomic Energy, which was senators and representatives, Republicans and Democrats. When the Joint Congressional Committee on Atomic Energy agreed with something, there wasn't any doubt that that was going to pass the Congress. For many years Rickover worked very closely with that committee. I rode them all at sea on the *Nautilus*. We had the deepest-thinking committee meeting they ever had when they had a committee meeting at test depth, and they all thought that was great. [Laughter] Rickover had a lot of contact with those people and had various ones of us talk to them on limited subjects. But in addition to them, Rickover made contacts with many other congressmen, but his real strength area was the relations he developed with the Joint Congressional Committee on Atomic Energy.

---

[*] Brien McMahon, a Democrat from Connecticut, served in the United States Senate from 3 January 1945 until his death in Washington, D.C., on 28 July 1952. He was co-chairman, Joint Committee on Atomic Energy from 1949 until his death.

Paul Stillwell: Well, I think especially Senator Jackson and Senator Pastore were two of the prominent ones.*

Admiral Wilkinson: Yes, Senator Jackson was very important and very influential and thought very, very highly of Rickover and was a good supporter of the *Nautilus*. And I rode him at sea on the *Nautilus*. As far as I could see, Senator Jackson always did what he thought was right.

Paul Stillwell: Well, in your AEC days and setting up this schedule, is it your opinion that Rickover is the only one who could have achieved that schedule as soon as he did?

Admiral Wilkinson: I'd say I don't know anybody else. There was total dedication on Rickover's part, absolutely, and when I think back to the days of the *Nautilus*, if I had a problem I could call at midnight, and at 3:00 AM the trucks would roll. I could get a spare part. I certainly couldn't get support like that out of Mechanicsburg or the Bureau of Ships, but from Rickover's group there was absolute and total and complete and immediate support of anything that was required.† It was the same as he followed and made the program happen. As I've said sometime in my description, if you put Rickover in charge of bedsprings there'd be plenty of bedsprings if the jet planes wouldn't fly, because he would have the material that was required. Rickover got it done.

Paul Stillwell: Well, he did that in World War II I guess on electrical power cabling.

Admiral Wilkinson: Yes, he did.

---

* Henry M. Jackson, a Democrat from the state of Washington, served in the House of Representatives from 1941 to 1953 and then in the Senate from 1953 until his death in 1983. He was chairman of the Senate Armed Services Committee and a strong proponent of nuclear-powered warships. The ballistic missile submarine *Henry M. Jackson* (SSBN-730) is named in his honor. John O. Pastore, a Democrat from Rhode Island, served in the U.S. Senate from 7 November 1950 until his resignation 28 December 1976. He was co-chairman, Joint Committee on Atomic Energy, 1963-64, 1967-68, 1971-72, and 1975-76.
† Navy Ships Parts Control Center, Mechanicsburg, Pennsylvania.

Paul Stillwell: There were just mounds and mounds of it. In Ted Rockwell's book he describes going to Oak Ridge and rather primitive conditions.* What was it like when you got there?

Admiral Wilkinson: There was a group under Harold Etherington.† Rickover and his people were gone. But Rickover had got them oriented to working on a propulsion plant to go in a submarine, and Rickover had laid out some of the things. Like it had to fit into a 16-foot hull. As a matter of fact, that was because submarines then had 16-foot hulls. It couldn't be done, but Rickover put the pressure on to make it fit in and laid out some of the design requirements that they worked at. But the work under Etherington was a group of loanies from different places. There were some guys that were top people at Westinghouse and General Electric and other companies that were working there, but by the time I got there some of those people were gone. I replaced a guy that later on became a very high-level guy at Westinghouse.

I think unless Rickover had given them an objective they wouldn't have accomplished development. Rickover recognized that the difference in performance you could get would be so much greater with a submarine than it could be with some other type thing. For example, there was a development down there, nothing to do with Rickover, called NEPA, Nuclear Energy Propulsion of Aircraft. That really never got anywhere, although they spent a lot of money and did a lot of studies, because they were competing against jet airplanes with very high performance. It was really tough to come up with a nuclear plant to put in an airplane that would outperform a jet airplane. It was easy to come up with something that you could put in a submarine that would outperform a submarine that could run submerged on its battery for one hour at top speed or maybe 72 hours at a minimum speed. Rickover recognized if he could get something in a submarine it would make a major difference in performance of the vehicle. And besides, Rickover had background in submarines, and that's what he got them working on.

---

* Theodore Rockwell, *The Rickover Effect: How One Man Made a Difference* (Annapolis: Naval Institute Press, 1992).
† Harold Etherington was an engineer who had been with the Allis-Chalmers Company and then joined the Oak Ridge lab as head of the reactors division.

Rockwell was right. After Rickover and his people were gone, the people that were left down there weren't completely organized.

Paul Stillwell: Well, I was thinking more about the way Rickover depicted the living conditions as almost rustic. Were you able to take your family down there?

Admiral Wilkinson: God, you've opened up a whole new vista. That is probably one of the reasons again that Rickover thought of me as a little different than some of the other people. When I was transferred from *Cusk*, Oak Ridge in those days was a closed community. When I went to Oak Ridge, I took my family with me. I looked around the whole perimeter of that damn place, and I could not find any housing for my wife. I looked at Clinton, and I went as far as Knoxville, but I just could not find a place to live. My wife was in a hotel over in Clinton. I looked at the situation. In Oak Ridge there was a lot of housing, and as far as the record showed, I looked just like any other damn civilian. So I went and signed up for a minimum two-bedroom house, which I got but unfurnished.

There had been military down there during World War II, and in those days they had furnished housing to the military that were in working on the nuclear weapon development, and there was a provision to give them furniture. So I went over and saw that place and said, "Hey, I'd like to draw some furniture." The girl laughed, and she said, "We haven't had a military person come in here and ask for furniture for over three years, but the provision has never been cancelled." So I got a set of brand-new furniture and put it in the house that I had signed up for. I've forgotten for sure, but I think it was $38.00 a month. I moved my family in and quietly was living and working there.

All the other people that came down in the officer program couldn't get housing for their families and couldn't find a place to live. They looked, and there was Dennis Wilkinson, happily ensconced in a house and still collecting $2.00 a day per diem. And so they all went back and fussed with Rickover so that he had to get them housing. Well, Rickover didn't want to create any waves or any problem with the military being down there checking on the program. And they said, "Wilkinson's got a house."

"If Wilkinson went down there and got a house, he did it without in any way talking to me. And he did it very quietly, and I'm happy for Wilkinson, but I'm damned if I'm going to try to get housing for the rest of you people." [Laughter] So I had a nice house in Ogden Lane at the top of the hill. My number-three child, my daughter Mary Lynn, was born there, and I had nice place to live. But the other people that came down mostly rented houses two weeks at a time from somebody in there that was going on vacation. Then they'd have to hunt around and find somebody else that wanted to rent their house during two weeks' vacation.

Paul Stillwell: That's a tough way to live.

Admiral Wilkinson: Yes.

I'll tell you a sea story. Janice was pregnant when I was at Oak Ridge, and that's when Mary Lynn was born. We like to play bridge. We were playing bridge the night before and came and turned in after midnight surely and maybe closer toward 2:00. At 4:00 o'clock my wife punched me and said, "It's time to go."

I said, "Go back to sleep. It's 4:00 o'clock."

She said, "Dennis, it's time for me to go. Get up." So that got me up, and I took my wife off to the hospital. I left her there, and as I came back it was first light. As I was driving along, there was a tortoise, a land turtle, walking across the road, so I stopped and put him in the back seat. I got home and it was lighter now, and I was getting around trying to get some things straightened away. My two little boys, Skipper and Stephen, got up, and they came in, and they said, "Where's Mother?"

I said, "She's gone, but I brought you a turtle."

They said, "Okay." [Laughter] I got them squared away and off to school, and then I hunted around to get somebody to come and take care of the kids while I was working, because I was on a tight schedule. I didn't get back over to the hospital till about noon, and Mary Lynn was born about 12:30. So I didn't have very much of an anguish, chewing my nails waiting, sitting out there just a few minutes. But I was there. And Janice was so pleased with me for being there waiting, and I felt a little guilty. I never did tell her I'd only been there about 15 minutes.

Paul Stillwell: You said that you were treated like any other civilian. Did you wear civilian clothes on that job?

Admiral Wilkinson: Oh, yes.

Paul Stillwell: How stringent were the security precautions?

Admiral Wilkinson: Oak Ridge itself was a closed community. You didn't get into the whole geographical area without going through a gate. Then, of course, there were other security gates out at Y-12 or X-10, the different places where the electric magnetic separation of the uranium that had been done, the cascades for the separation of uranium 235 and 238. All those areas were very controlled access. So was our area at X-10, where we worked. Everything was secret, and searches were made, and desks were locked. Each different facility had its own little area with access control. There were stringent security requirements.

Paul Stillwell: How much of a concern was there about nuclear radiation and protecting people from that?

Admiral Wilkinson: We were only doing paper studies. There wasn't any radiation there, but there were radiation worries over at the gaseous diffusion plant and whatnot. One of the things Rickover did was he ensured in our design that there was great concern for the amount of radiation and protection of personnel from it. Ted Rockwell was an expert on radiation control and the effect different materials would have on cutting exposure to neutron or gamma ray fields. So we were very aware of the problem and considered it in our design and studies, but we ourselves didn't have any radiation activity in our study group.

Paul Stillwell: Radiation shielding was also a factor in making the atomic-powered aircraft not so feasible because of the weight that would have added to the plane.

Admiral Wilkinson: Yes, and, as I said, it was really harder to develop something that would outperform what a jet aircraft could do. As a matter of fact, probably the only way they could have done it would have been unmanned. And then also there's the safety worry if the thing crashes somewhere with radioactivity. Submarines, after all, can be operated pretty safely and can be kept out of populated areas and so on.

Paul Stillwell: Anything else to mention about your time at Oak Ridge?

Admiral Wilkinson: Well it's sort of interesting. I had forgotten that business about getting housing. I think Rickover in a sense wasn't unhappy with me that I had gotten my family taken care of, but he was unhappy with a lot of other people that came that wanted him to take care of their families. Rickover thought it would put him in a bad light with authority if he was making too many demands to provide this or that support for this or that.

Paul Stillwell: How frequent was your communication with Captain Rickover while you were in that position?

Admiral Wilkinson: Not very often at all. I guess he was aware of the results that came from my nuclear physics design work. After all, they were important to him in putting pressure on to get the contract let with Westinghouse. And then when I went to Argonne there were more. I still worked in the nuclear physics, and finally I became the number-two person in the nuclear physics department with the number-one guy a titular head. And so people working for me did all the nuclear physics calculations that the group did, and Rickover was aware of the results.

It wasn't until after he sent me to Pittsburgh and he wanted to be kept advised as to how Westinghouse was doing on the development that I had very frequent communications with him. There was a period there of a long time that Captain Rickover would call me and talk about things every night and read a draft letter and ask me what I thought of it and tell me that I didn't know what I was talking about. He said I was young and immature when I would differ with it, but he'd change it. [Laughter] So I had an awful lot of contact with him during my time at Pittsburgh.

Then when I wouldn't become EDO and stay but got detached instead, Rickover, in his way, said "Damn Wilkinson. He's screwing things up." Well, he didn't really mean it. But in any organization the guy that's the boss has to be careful in what his people will do, because suddenly all the hatchet men types that worked for Rickover thought they could curry favor if Rickover was unhappy with me by rending and tearing. So during my last six weeks there, for a short time I had a lot of pressure put on me by various people in Rickover's organization.

But I had at my disposal, one, the whole Westinghouse organization, two, the awareness of all the problems. So anytime anybody would call me up with some complaint, I'd say, "I'm glad you called. I was going to call you. Listen, here's what I need. Zip-zip-zip." And then as soon as I'd finish I'd dictate, and I had a super secretary, a memo to file, copy to the guy, copy to Captain Rickover with these, "Discussed this with Panoff today, and these commitments were made."[*] After about two weeks there, everybody backed away from putting any pressure on me. And so finally, as I mentioned earlier, I was giving the nuclear physics lectures to Gwilym Price and the other executives at Westinghouse and to the executives up at Electric Boat Company.

In the last three or four days before I was detached to go out and be commanding officer of the submarine *Volador* in San Diego, I caught the train from Pittsburgh to Penn Station in New York. Then I walked to Grand Central rather than try to hunt around for a cab and caught the train on up to New London. Rickover met me at Penn Station and walked with me to Grand Central; he told me I'd done a good job and wished me well. As I said, I was the only person that ever left that organization without being damned forever.

Paul Stillwell: Why were you going to New London if the *Volador* was in San Diego?

---

[*] Robert Panoff was a civilian engineer who had met Rickover while both were with the Bureau of Ships during World War II. Panoff specialized in submarine design issues.

Admiral Wilkinson: I wasn't going to be detached for another three or four days, and I was going up to New London to give my last lecture on nuclear physics to the executives of the Electric Boat Company.

Paul Stillwell: I see. Well, please tell me about the *Volador*. You'd been aiming for command your whole commissioned career.

Admiral Wilkinson: I had been the exec of *Menhaden*. I'd been the exec of *Raton*. I'd been exec of *Cusk*. I thought that I was ready to be a commanding officer, although I was still a lieutenant commander in rank. And by the good fortune and wisdom of the submarine detail shop, I did get my orders to be skipper of a submarine, and it was the *Volador*, which was a fast attack submarine based in San Diego.*

I went from Pittsburgh and reported in to be skipper of the *Volador*. It was a great ship, and morale was high, and it had great operational capabilities compared to the other submarines, and we had very, very successful operations. We thought we were the best operating submarine in San Diego, and we might have been. We certainly thought we were better than any operating submarine in Honolulu, where they stayed in port more.

Every once in a while, submarines were deployed to the Western Pacific, and so finally *Volador* was scheduled for a six-month deployment to the area around Japan. We were probably the best operating submarine at that time in the Pacific—at least we thought we were. I had a little group that played basketball, seven guys off the boat. For example, when we were up getting a refit up in San Francisco, we had played in the basketball tournament. In the finals we met a cruiser, which was a good-sized ship, and we beat them. I didn't have any real tall guys, but they had guys that liked to play basketball and they were pretty good.

As we went through Honolulu, I was the fat, dumb, and happy captain. In my lack of knowledge and ignorance, my whole basketball group went up and played a basketball game with the big blue team, the SubPac basketball squad that competed every

---

* USS *Volador* (SS-490) was a *Balao*-class submarine commissioned 1 October 1948. She had a displacement of 1,570 tons on the surface and 2,415 tons submerged. She was 306 feet long, 27 feet in the beam, and had a draft of 15 feet. Her top speed was 20 knots surfaced and 9 knots submerged. She was armed with ten 21-inch torpedo tubes and a 5-inch gun.

year for the All-Navy basketball championship. My guys made the mistake of beating them. [Laughter]

SubPac at that time was an all-American, and he thought quite highly of his basketball team.* The next morning, at a quarter of 8:00, I was up at rigid attention in the SubPac office. I was being accused of disloyalty by the admiral, and I really didn't know what he was talking about. Finally, when I got the word during that condemnation of what was happening, I told him right back, "Admiral, we're the most loyal submarine you've got in the whole force, and what are you talking about?" And when he explained, I said, "Gee, Admiral, they're really not that good. They must have been playing over their heads." [Laughter]

We were only there for a day or two before being deployed on out to WestPac. And that afternoon the captain, Lockwood, came down. They contacted each one of my guys and offered him a change of duty to not go to the Western Pacific for a six-month deployment. They could stay there in Honolulu and become part of the SubPac Force basketball team if they volunteered for that, and none of them volunteered. [Laughter]

Paul Stillwell: That says something about loyalty.

Admiral Wilkinson: Yes. So, again, I didn't know about this either. So the next morning, again at a quarter to 8:00 [laughter] I was up at the admiral's office at rigid attention. This story was disclosed, and the admiral said, "What did you do with your people? What did you say to your people?"

I said, "Admiral, I didn't say anything to them, but let me tell you I'm proud of them."

And he said, "Get the hell out of here." [Laughter] Then we sailed for WestPac, but I had got in trouble, absolutely innocently.

Paul Stillwell: Well, did he expect your team to lose on purpose?

---

* Rear Admiral John H. Brown, USN, served as Commander Submarine Force Pacific Fleet from 1949 to 1951. Brown, who graduated from the Naval Academy in 1914, had been an all-America football player as a midshipman.

Admiral Wilkinson: I don't know, but ComSubPac was pretty rabid about his team. With a tough operating schedule, I guess we didn't send as many people to the SubPac team from the San Diego area as they did from out in Hawaii. So as we passed through there, I really perfectly innocently got in great trouble. I was shorthanded too. Later, as we were finishing our six months and getting ready to come back from the Pacific, some of my guys' time was up. They could get transportation and go back, or they could ride back with the ship. I told them all, "Hey, we're shorthanded, and we really need you. If you guys need to get home right now, I'll go up there and help and see what I can do to get you on priority for transportation. If not, if you'd like to extend here until we get back to the States and ride your ship home, it would help us all out."

Again, every man volunteered and decided they would do the right thing and ride. So I really had a crackerjack bunch on the *Volador*, and they were extremely loyal to the ship. They referred to her as, "She's not much for chow or liberty, but she's a seagoing son-of-a-bitch.". Like I've said about morale, "Morale really isn't chow or liberty. Morale is pride in unit." The guys on the *Volador* did have pride in their ship and its performance, and they thought they could do better than anybody in anything, and they probably could have.

I remember a funny story from when I was CO of the *Volador*. I got a requirement from the Bureau of Medicine, that they wanted to know about my anti-venereal disease program. They wanted a copy of all my lesson plans for the year and how many people had been to this lecture and who gave the lecture and what the subject matter was for the year and a hell of a lot of information on our training. That letter came to me, commanding officer of *Volador*, directly from the Chief of Bureau of Medicine and Surgery. I looked at that and I said, "Gee, that is a hell of a lot of work. I'll tell you what." And so I wrote the thing. I said, paragraph (1), "Your thing is returned herewith. We can be of no value to you. We have no anti-venereal program on the *Volador*, so I have nothing to submit." Paragraph (2). "There has never been a case of venereal disease in this command." Then I signed it and sent it back. I said, "You know, they won't be completely happy with that, but let them check that performance against some ship that has a real good anti-venereal disease program." [Laughter]

Paul Stillwell: You told me an interesting *Volador* story last night. That was about the flying fish. If you could put that on tape, please.

Admiral Wilkinson: Oh, dear. I'd forgotten that. Well, if the ship is cruising through an area that has flying fish in it and the ship is approaching the flying fish, you'll notice that the flying fish will come out of the water and fly away from the ship. That's because the fish really can see it. But if you're on a submarine, black hull, at night, and don't have any lights on and the fish is scared and comes out of the water, he can't see what scared him, and he's apt to fly in any which direction. So running an exercise, darkened ship at night in an area where there were flying fish, we'd scare them up. Some of them would fly over the submarine and hit into our sail, our conning tower, and that would knock them down on deck.

Being as I was the captain and up at that time of day, I would ease down on deck just before light and pick up three of four of these flying fish and take them down and have flying fish and scrambled eggs for breakfast. A flying fish is a good eating fish, but it is to trout as horsemeat is to beef. It's just as good a meat, but it's sweeter, and I enjoyed my flying fish and scrambled eggs.

But the young man that was cleaning them every morning was our colored steward named Wilson. I kept this up for a week, and finally he said to me, "Captain, this nonsense has got to stop." [Laughter] He wasn't for cleaning fish every morning. [Laughter]

Paul Stillwell: Well, it's a coincidence. When I was interviewing Admiral King this past week he also talked about flying fish.* He said there's a Navy tradition that it's the captain's privilege to get any flying fish that land on board. I had never heard that.

Admiral Wilkinson: Well, they were there in abundance every morning because we were darken ship.

The *Volador*, in her six-month deployment in the Pacific, it was the time of the Korean War, and we made patrols north to Korea. But we also gave services to the

---

* See the Naval Institute oral history of Vice Admiral Jerome H. King, Jr., USN (Ret.).

hunter-killer task group that operated between Yokosuka and down to Taiwan and back. We gave services to that hunter-killer task group coming and going, and did it quite a bit. We were highly regarded by the hunter-killer force commander.

One time for diversity purposes they had on board a visitor, Charlotte Knight, who was the Far Eastern bureau chief of *Collier's* magazine. They were giving her quite a rundown and pitch on the capabilities of their ASW forces and doing quite well at it and transporting her around from place to place.[*] In transporting her around by helicopter, the helicopter crashed, and she was in the water and needed to be rescued.[†] Although four destroyers aimed to pick her up, we were closer and beat them there. Of course, we'd done our man-overboard drill and all that. As we called away man overboard, I said, "This is the captain speaking. This is not a drill. There are really people in the water. Bear a hand." And so my people did and went through all the evolution of preparing to rescue somebody that was overboard, which consists among other things of having some strong swimmers that go into the water help them out, and in our man-overboard forward party we had four strong swimmers.

After you give the first command, be it "Man overboard" or "Emergency this" or "Back that" or "Right full rudder" or something, there really isn't much to do. So on the bridge with the conn, I said, "Conning tower, Lee," who was my chief quartermaster, "Bring your camera up here."[‡] So he came up and filmed our whole evolution as we were attempting this rescue of Charlotte Knight. This showed my man-overboard party out on deck, me giving the signal to the OOD that the swimmers could go in the water, the three of them diving off, arching as one into the water, and swimming over toward this lady and the other crew people that were in the water.[§]

The first one that reached her was an electrician named Slaton. He grabbed her as she was about to sink and said, "My name is Slaton, S-L-A-T-O-N." So my people were aware of who was involved. We got her on board and had her aboard for three or four hours before we got her transferred back to the carrier, and in that time we were able to

---

[*] ASW – antisubmarine warfare.
[†] This incident occurred on 3 December 1951 as Ms. Knight was being transferred by helo from the escort carrier *Badoeng Strait* (CVE-116) to the *Volador*.
[‡] The individual with the conn—normally an officer—directs the ship's movements in course and speed.
[§] OOD – officer of the deck. The swimmers were Engineman Second Class Frank E. Slaton, Seaman Richard N. Norton, and Commissaryman Third Class Ernest S. McMullen.

give her I guess a fairly good low-key pitch on submarine capabilities. As she came aboard, wet and bedraggled, I was younger and slimmer then, so I gave her some of my clothes to put on. We dried her clothes in the engine room, and as she left she was still wearing my underwear.

Some weeks later I got a package from her with a nice little note. As a matter of fact, in getting ready for this talk with you, I happened to find it, and it started out, "I've looked all through Emily Post for a paragraph on the proper procedure for returning a submarine skipper's borrowed underwear. Unfortunately, the subject isn't covered. I can't find the answer anywhere. My experts in the Navy have told me I should send it back to you by the chain of command, but that might give a wrong impression, so I'm just sending it directly. Hope I can do the same for you sometime." It was a fun, fun business.

Paul Stillwell: Her letter to you was dated December 7, 1951, the tenth anniversary of Pearl Harbor.

Admiral Wilkinson: Yes, that's just a coincidence. As a matter of fact, I got a letter of commendation out of rescuing them, I think, so I profited thereby also.

Paul Stillwell: Did you pick up the other people that had been in the helicopter crash?

Admiral Wilkinson: Oh, yes. We got them all.[*]

Paul Stillwell: And did her write-up in the magazine then mention Slaton and his efforts?

Admiral Wilkinson: Remember I told you that I'd said, "Lee, bring your camera up here." I don't know the answer to your question, but when we got back into Yokosuka I thought of it, and I said, "Lee, how did that film turn out?" He hadn't sent it up yet, so he took it right up, and although we weren't that public relations conscious, somebody up

---

[*] The helicopter crew included Lieutenant Y. J. Dyson, the pilot, and Aviation Machinist's Mate First Class Dewey B. Sanders, plane captain.

there was. They were really impressed with that camera tape and flew it right back to the States. We had five minutes on the Fox Movietone news, and it showed all my people with their identification and different names. Let me tell you, a lot of wives at home saw their husbands being heroes on Fox Movietone news. That didn't hurt morale on my ship a bit, so we had a lot of profit out of that.

Paul Stillwell: Who sent that back, Commander Naval Forces Far East?

Admiral Wilkinson: Probably the submarine commander in Yokosuka.

Paul Stillwell: Did you take part in any patrols that were directly connected with the Korean War?

Admiral Wilkinson: Yes, we made some operations north of Korea.

Paul Stillwell: I interviewed Captain Schratz, who commanded the *Pickerel* then, and he talked about reconnaissance/surveillance-type patrols.* Was that generally it?

Admiral Wilkinson: Yes. I did the same kind of operation that Paul did in *Pickerel*

Paul Stillwell: How would you describe the increase in capability from that generation of submarine with the Guppy improvements compared with the World War II fleet boat?†

Admiral Wilkinson: Oh, the Guppy was far superior to the World War II fleet boat. It had extra battery, and it was streamlined so we could make a much higher speed submerged. It could make it for a longer period of time. It had a snorkel system, so it could charge its batteries without being fully on the surface. By only sticking its snorkel tube up, it was less apt to be detected. It could recharge its battery without ever actually surfacing. And it had really superior radar. We didn't even have an effective radar in

---

* See the Naval Institute oral history of Captain Paul R. Schratz, USN (Ret.).
† The term "Guppy" grew out of the initials for the postwar modification fitted to World War II fleet boats to give them greater underwater propulsion power (GUPP).

World War II. And it had superior sonar. The combination of the ability to avoid detection, to do detection at longer ranges both by radar and sonar, to avoid detection by being able to charge batteries without surfacing or avoid as great a probability of detection, and to operate at higher speed for longer time gave it a much greater capability. It had the same torpedoes and the same number of them. It was just the same there.

Paul Stillwell: What do you remember about the satisfactions of being in command as opposed to XO roles you'd had earlier?

Admiral Wilkinson: I have a certain amount of self-confidence, and I was the exec of three submarines. They were good submarines, and I really thought that I knew everything I needed to know. But it was sort of interesting when I got to be captain. When a submarine dives, the captain is in there overseeing it, and then when it surfaces the captain is the first one to go to the bridge and all. The first time I surfaced as the captain in real rough weather, where it was tough to get to the bridge and all, I had a little trepidation, and that surprised me. It is different being the ultimate responsibility and accountability with nobody backing you up, nobody to fall back on. Of course, I was commanding officer of naval ships for 11½ years, and I had command of four submarines, so eventually I got over that.

Paul Stillwell: I would think so.

Admiral Wilkinson: But it was surprising to me to have a moment of doubt, because after having been exec of three good submarines for a long time, I had absolute confidence in myself. Funny you should bring that up.

Paul Stillwell: [Laughter] You talked about the massive exodus of personnel after the war. Had that shaken down by 1950? How stable was the personnel picture?

Admiral Wilkinson: By then it had shaken down. I became skipper of the *Volador* in 1950. Certainly we had no problems then. That's a long time. When I was exec of the

Raton right after the end of the war that wasn't so. They were putting ships out of commission. The reserves that were in during the war were being sent out of service as fast as they could. The submarines that were tied up in New London hadn't operated for a long time. They were all shorthanded. Things were a mess in the state of readiness for a certain period of time. I happened to come to be exec of the *Raton* just at the peak of that. Nobody had done anything since they'd tied up there when they got back to New London after the war. A lot of the personnel had been transferred. It was really at a low state of readiness, and *Raton* was one example. The same was true of every boat tied up and down the river.

Paul Stillwell: Did you start getting some reservists in after the Korean War started, people who'd been recalled from the reserve?

Admiral Wilkinson: Yes, the Navy did, but we didn't get very many in submarines. Submarines are a different breed and a different group.

Paul Stillwell: How much opportunity did you give your junior officers for ship handling and making approaches?

Admiral Wilkinson: Oh, when I was skipper I did that all the time. We never came in to make a landing that I didn't give my officer of the deck the chance to make the landing. I did that on the *Volador*. I did that on the *Wahoo*. Didn't make very many landings on the *Sea Robin*, and I only had command of that for a short period of time, so I guess I didn't do it much, but I did that on the *Volador* and the *Wahoo* and the *Nautilus* all the time.

Paul Stillwell: Anything else to say about the *Volador*?

Admiral Wilkinson: *Volador* was a very capable Guppy submarine at the time, and I had a really competent crew that was very loyal to the ship. The story I told you about my basketball team refusing to volunteer to stay in Honolulu instead of going to a WestPac deployment to the man, and probably that was just those seven, but they probably couldn't have got a volunteer out of the whole ship. It was a ship's company that thought very highly of themselves and were loyal to the ship and to one another. I was proud of the ship and her operations and the prowess of my people. I had some good officers and men on there.

I had one interesting young officer that reported, a junior officer, that was very capable. That was Jim Watkins, who later became CNO, so I must have had some pretty good people working for me.[*]

Paul Stillwell: What do you remember about him as a junior officer?

Admiral Wilkinson: Very capable and very dependable and stood a superb watch on the bridge. He was forthright and would tell you when things were screwed up and what he thought. He was a crackerjack. He was as good a young officer as I ever saw, and it doesn't surprise me, from my opinion of him then, that he progressed on and became the CNO. Now, if you have a ship that you're fortunate enough to get that kind of people working for you, it has a tendency to do well.

Paul Stillwell: Yes. Was *Volador* the boat that had the voice call sign "Pokeweed?"

Admiral Wilkinson: Yes, Pokeweed. I hated that call sign, but that was the call sign. Every ship is assigned a call sign, and that's the one we got. We made that call sign well known with the hunter-killer group in our Western Pacific deployment. They recognized we had lots of capability.

Paul Stillwell: Well, you told a story last night that involved a voice transmission. I think it was with a carrier. What was that incident?

---

[*] Ensign James D. Watkins, USN. As a four-star admiral, Watkins served as Chief of Naval Operations from 1982 to 1986.

Admiral Wilkinson: We gave the services to those people from Yokosuka down to Taiwan or the Pescadores and back, and so that's a lot of exercises. One time they scheduled a hunter-killer exercise, a four-day hunt to exhaustion. Supposedly, with all the ASW capabilities and the aircraft over you, they keep the submarine submerged so it can't charge its batteries. Eventually its resources are exhausted, and it's got to surface and give up, but with the *Volador* that's not the way it really was.

To us a hunt to exhaustion was just a time to break contact and have a four-day rest period. But the poor carrier over there—to keep planes in the air all the time, it was twisting and turning, running into the wind, launching and recovering planes day and night. Eventually those guys were apt to get pretty exhausted. So we were providing services in a hunt-to-exhaustion, and after a couple of days had gone by no contacts had been made on us. When we had to charge our battery, we would snorkel a little, and if a plane came near we'd pull it down. No contacts had been made in nearly 48 hours, and I got to thinking, "You know, those people are over there going through all this evolution, and they're supposed to be learning something and making submarine contacts and taking action and four days will go by, and they'll never make a contact, and that's not right."

So I called in and got the hunter-killer commander. I called him about 8:00 o'clock at night and said, "King Post, this is Pokeweed."

He said, "This is King Post himself."

I said, "This is Pokeweed himself, sir."

He said, "Pokeweed, where are you?"

I said, "Well, we're bearing such-and-such, 84,000 yards from King Post."

He said, "Yeah, but how good is your navigation? When were you last able to get a fix?" That showed he had a little bit of thinking that they'd probably been giving us a little more trouble than we'd really had, because we hadn't any trouble navigating.

But we were able to say back, "Well, that's actual range and bearing," because I really held them on a sweep of the radar at that range and bearing. So I said to him, "Sir, would you like me to join up with your force and give you some contact and a little excitement?"

"Yes," he said. And understand this isn't quite that easy, because they were not steaming on a steady course. They were going to change course from time to time to launch planes, and to get airspeed over the deck they turn into the wind and one thing and another. But, after all, I, too, could look up and see which way the wind was blowing, so I figured 42 miles away. So I gambled a little and told him, "Well, look to port for flares at 0400."

As fate would have it and luck would have it, we managed to close in. At 0400 I was 700 yards broad on the bow and told my two signal ejectors, "Fire for effect." We sent up a lot of green flares exactly at 0400 and stirred them up a little.[*] The hunt-to-exhaustion didn't bother us much.

Paul Stillwell: Was this one of those escort carriers, a CVE?

Admiral Wilkinson: Yes, it wasn't a great big carrier. It was just a hunter-killer task group.

Paul Stillwell: So it sounds like despite what they were preaching to the magazine correspondent, the submarines were ahead at that point.

Admiral Wilkinson: That's as variable as the sea itself. Where we were at that time the sonar conditions were lousy. We could hide beneath the layer.[†] We had great capabilities ourselves. It was tough for them. In fact, in that time frame with our ship, that hunter-killer group, good as they were in that area, they didn't have a chance. [Laughter] And we were able to demonstrate that to Charlotte Knight during the three or four hours that she was aboard.

Paul Stillwell: And you demonstrated it to the admiral during that episode.

Admiral Wilkinson: Yes.

---

[*] In an exercise such as this, the firing of green flares by the submarine signifies a successful simulated attack.
[†] In some cases the signals from a hull-mounted sonar bounce off when they hit a layer of temperature differential and thus cannot detect the submarine beneath the layer.

Another time when we were giving services, we were involved with the carrier and, due to a change of forces coming back, 16 destroyers. During hunter-killer exercise weeks, I tried—in addition to giving services—to make an approach and attack on those ships. In the six weeks involved, I managed to attack the carrier and the tanker, of course, many times and the 16 destroyers also. As a matter of fact, I shot each one of the 16 destroyers on both port and starboard except one destroyer I made three attacks on them, but they were always to starboard. I never got a port shot on him, but every other destroyer I had port and starboard attacks on with pictures taken to show it.

I went to the hunter-killer debrief afterwards, and it was cold, so I was in my blues. Both of the side pockets of my blues were filled with pictures. I probably had a couple of hundred pictures. They asked me to make a report, and I got up and said it had been a very valuable exercise. We'd had a great amount of pleasure providing services and hoped we had been satisfactory. And also we'd had the ability to get a lot of training ourselves. We had managed to make approaches on all the ships in the task force.

The commanding officer of some destroyer suckered and said, "Never made an approach on my ship."

I said, "Well, I guess I'm sure we did, because we made an approach on all of them." And I said, "You know, we always send a sonar attack signal, and we fire a green flare, and maybe the lookouts don't see the flare."

So he said, "Maybe from 10,000 yards."

I said, "No, no, our torpedoes don't run that far. We were always quite a bit closer than that." I said, "What's the number of your ship?" And I was hoping it wasn't the one that we'd never been able to get on both sides. Well, it wasn't. That was out of 16.

So he told me, and then I reached down into my two pockets and pulled out a couple of hundred pictures and said, "Here's some nice ones of your ship." And we had one picture of his ship from so close that it took two pictures to get the full ship's length in the picture. And I said, "Here, here. Here are souvenirs for all of you. You can show all those to your lookouts." I laid those 200 pictures out on the table, and so we were highly regarded by the flag. The next cycle, again the admiral called on me first and said, "Pokeweed, what have you got to say?"

I said, "We don't have anything to say, but we've got pictures." [Laughter] In those sonar conditions at that time we had an easy task in looking superior.

When Charlotte Knight was aboard, they sent out the group to find us, and I said, "As long as they're coming, we might as well penetrate these destroyers and simulate an attack on the carrier," and so it was. And we explained to her that, "There's a group of ships coming here, and what we should do to keep from getting detected is slip between two destroyers and get up close to the carrier. Then we can attack it if we manage to get through them successfully. And normally I'm the captain and keep the conn and look through the periscope, but just because you're aboard we're going to let you do that."

I said, "We look every three minutes, and then it's easier to compute how far they've traveled, what speed they're making, and what the bearing means. Now, when you look through this periscope what we're really focusing on is the carrier over there. Move it just as much as you have to, and when the line is right on the carrier say 'Mark.' Then we'll pull the scope down." I had her looking through the number-one scope, which had a radar in it. So, unknown to her, I also would get a range, and she would say "Mark."

Three minutes would go by, and, of course, we were getting information from our sonars on the destroyers, etc. We eased over to where we were between two destroyers and the sonar conditions were poor. And she did her function of saying "Mark, Mark" every three minutes. In between, we were laughing and scratching and telling her stories.

Finally, after we'd penetrated the screen and were approaching the carrier, I said, "We're really giving you a wrong impression of how easy it is to be a submarine skipper. It's really a lot harder than that. It's just not as simple as picking up that periscope and saying 'Mark'. Now we're at that final point, and this time when we stick it up and you've got the line there, you've got to say 'Fire.'"

So we eased up, and we were close, maybe 700 or 800 yards from the carrier. It looked big, and she said, "Fire." Then we took the scope, and I had a superb camera party. We took some pictures of the carrier before we went down and broke contact. Then we pulled away, surfaced, and approached, and they transferred her back to the carrier. In the few minutes that that took, my guys developed the pictures and made prints. We gave her pictures of this carrier, which again took more than one picture to put it in from about 700 yards. I said, "Show them on the carrier your approach."

Well, I got my story out of time. Earlier than that, when she was first aboard and getting her clothes dried, we were having lunch. She really dug in and said, "Why are you people in submarines, when if a war came you wouldn't survive?"

We said, "Well, you know, it's independent duty, and we stop and have swimming call anytime we want, and they pay us 25% extra pay, and there's not a war going on, and so there's a lot of advantages to us from our lifestyle and all."

"Yeah, but why would you be here if you'd be destroyed if there was a war going on?" And so after we had had her make the approach and penetrated and fired at the carrier and given her the pictures, she said, "This is not what they told me over on the carrier."

We said, "Well, it's all in your perspective." [Laughter] So she went back with a little bit of a different picture of the submarine capability. As a matter of fact, in some of the stuff she wrote she became quite a submarine proponent—all in four hours. [Laughter]

Paul Stillwell: Did you have to have some kind of special camera arrangement to take pictures through the periscope?

Admiral Wilkinson: Yes and no. You just fasten the camera right to the eyepiece, just where you look through, and you just looked and lined up and put the camera there and snapped. We could do that very quickly, and we could develop our film on board very quickly, and we did it. I had a really good camera-taking and film-developing picture group. That's how I had those hundreds of pictures of all those destroyers that I was talking about.

Paul Stillwell: Did you physically attach the camera to the periscope or just hold it up to the lens?

Admiral Wilkinson: Physically snapped it on. There were some clips that snapped it right on.

Paul Stillwell: Ernie Schwab told me about taking pictures. I guess this may have been even in a submarine before he got to the *Darter*, and I guess it had not been done much before that.

Admiral Wilkinson: No, because of the stress in wartime. In peacetime, the operations I'm talking about, I just shot a simulated attack at a destroyer and sent a "Baker-baker-baker" and fired a green flare.* The guy was 700 yards away, and I could take 15 seconds to take a picture and then go down deep, and my ship was safe. I didn't do anything that imperiled its safety by taking an extra few seconds to take a picture.

Now, it was different in wartime when the guys were shooting real torpedoes at the real enemy with guns to shoot at the periscope and depth charges to come and drop on them after they had fired their torpedoes. If the ship was 1,000 yards away, the torpedoes would take some time to get there, two-thirds of a minute. That meant waiting two-thirds of a minute to see the torpedo hit, and during that time somebody could come and drop depth charges on you. So there was a tendency for the people to fire and get out of there as fast as they could, so there were an awful lot of very marvelous and successful attacks made that there was no pictorial record of them, naturally.

We had a crackerjack bunch of cameramen on the *Darter*, and each time we had a chance to make an approach, old Captain McClintock would say, "You know, the war's almost over, and we ought to get some pictures of some of these ships. You people be ready after we've fired our torpedoes to take pictures of the explosions. Is the camera ready?"

"Absolutely, Captain, absolutely." It was my line up there in the approach party to be the one that as soon as we'd fire to say, "Captain, we're not going to sink any ship with that damn camera. Let's get the hell out of here."

---

* At the time "Baker" was the word used for the letter B in the phonetic alphabet. It was signaled to simulate the firing of a gun or torpedo.

At which time the captain would say, "Yeah, let's get the hell out. Take her deep." So we never did take a picture, but we were certainly prepared to. Well, now some ships were probably braver, and so at the end of the war there were a few ships that got pictures but not very many. There is a difference in feeling toward taking a picture where somebody's shooting at you than when it's just to be cute over at an ASW conference.

Paul Stillwell: That's a very understandable difference.

Admiral Wilkinson: Yes.

Paul Stillwell: Well, anything more about the *Volador* before you move on to the *Wahoo*?

Admiral Wilkinson: It was a good ship and a good crew, and they performed superbly. I was a lieutenant commander in my first command, and I probably enjoyed that tour of command as much as any.

I'll tell you a sea story. Happened to be in port, but I was lieutenant commander, and it was the time of the Korean War and, eventually I reached that point that I was senior enough and my record was good enough to make commander. We were in a division in San Diego. We thought we were the best submarine in the division, and probably some of the other submarines in the division thought they were best.

One of them that was pretty damn good was the *Pomodon*. The skipper was Al Bergner, who was an all-American football player at the trade school and ran his ship a little different than mine.* Abrupt "If you won't f---, you-won't fight" attitude, I mean, and they were good. They had pride in unit, and they were pleased with themselves. So they were competitors of ours in the division. We both thought we were the best, and really the *Volador* was. [Laughter]

But it came up that Al and I were both going to make commander. It was the Korean War, and the promotion exams were scheduled. So I said, "There's a war going

---

* Lieutenant Commander Allen A. Bergner, USN, graduated from the Naval Academy in the class of 1940.

on. They'll never have promotion exams. It's just that the people haven't had a chance to study. They're out there in the war zone. Those will be cancelled." But they didn't cancel them, and that time was coming when promotion exams were scheduled. I am sort of book smart, and there were 26 books that were going to be covered on the promotion exam. And the wardroom in the forward battery on the *Pomodon* was deathly silent for three months. Al Bergner was over there boning every day on his promotion exams, but I thought surely those things would be cancelled.

So I collected the 26 books and said, "I can do one book a day. I'll wait till 26 days before they're scheduled, and I'll do a book, and the next day I'll do another book. When the thing comes, I will just review these 26 books. I can pass any exam easily." So I didn't really worry much about it, except I did make the provision and collect the information. I had the 26 books stacked up. Well, they didn't cancel the exam, and the 26th day came, and I did a book. And the 25th day came, and I did a book. And the 24th day came, and on the 22nd day they cancelled the exam. [Laughter] And so I didn't do those other 22 books.

We were in port in San Diego, and Al Bergner was agonizing over these exams for three months. He was in his room, and the curtain was pulled, and his people were keeping out of the forward battery. I eased up off the *Volador* and over into the *Pomodon*, and there was Al Bergner. And understand he was a big guy, an All-American football player, and a crackerjack guy and a strong skipper. I eased in and said, "Where's your captain?"

"Well, he's in his room studying."

So I banged into there, drew the curtain back, and I said, "Al, what the hell are you doing?"

"I'm studying for these exams."

I said, "Listen, Al. Either you're qualified to be a commander or you're not. If you're qualified, you'll pass any exam and make commander, and if you can't pass it you shouldn't be a commander anyway. It's just ridiculous for you to be down here at the last minute trying to prove to somebody that you're qualified to be a commander."

He looked at me like I was out of my mind, and finally I said, "You know, if you can't pass an exam to be a commander, you shouldn't be a commander. I hope you don't." By now he was starting to get madder and madder. Finally, when he was just at the point of hitting me, I said, "And besides, Al, those exams have been cancelled. Why don't we go ashore and have a beer?" [Laughter]

Well, suddenly he wasn't mad at me anymore. There was really intense relief, because he really was worried about those exams. But now suddenly, he asked, "How do you know?"

"Well, we got a communication about it a while ago, and they've been cancelled. It's AlNav such-and-such." Well, now he was really mad, so he went and got his communicator and booted him in the ass for the fact that my communicator told me faster than his communicator told him. [Laughter] And we went ashore and got a beer. But we made commander in 1951 without promotion exams. Funny story.

Paul Stillwell: Yes, it is.

Admiral Wilkinson: I'll tell you one more story about the *Volador*. I was detached in Yokosuka, Japan, and flown back to go to my new duty assignment. I didn't get to bring the *Volador* back home after I'd been on that six-month deployment; I left just before she started home. As I passed through San Diego, I did call up the wives of every married man on my ship. I talked to them about their husbands and that they were on their way home and that I was passing through first. I told each one that her husband had done a fine job and enjoyed his tour in Japan. There'd just been the big exposés about the steam baths in Japan, the hotsi baths, and told them their husbands had a great time out there and had been spending lots of time up at the hotsi bath. [Laughter] I had fun talking to all of my troops' wives.

But improperly, I guess, we used to play poker on the *Volador* for limited stakes. We had a poker game in the wardroom, and they had a poker game back in the crew's mess. When I was captain of a ship, I always made a walk through the boat as I got up in the morning and certainly just before I turned in at night. So when I'd walk through the crew's mess and there was a poker game going on, I'd watch a minute and I'd shake my head and say, "It's just a shame that I can't take your money, but it just wouldn't be right, but it looks so easy." And I'd make some snide comment like that and be on my way through the boat. Well, I got my orders and was leaving the ship.

The night before I was going to be transferred the next morning, change of command and leave, a delegation came up from the crew and said, "Captain, now you're leaving and you've made a lot of disparaging remarks over time about our poker. And so this last night aboard when you're leaving and it's not the same anymore, we challenge you to come back and put your money where your mouth is."

Paul Stillwell: You had been hustling them.

Admiral Wilkinson: So I went back, praying that I would get some cards. As luck would have it, I did, and I quickly got quite a bit ahead. And I said, "Please cash me in. You know, it would really hurt my conscience to take any more." [Laughter] So I left, and I left that ship in good order with my troops and had fun talking to all their wives as I passed through San Diego en route *Wahoo*, which was a new-construction submarine being built in Portsmouth Naval Shipyard.[*]

Paul Stillwell: Well, with the *Wahoo* you got yet another new experience. You certainly had never put a boat into commission as the skipper before. What was involved in that?

Admiral Wilkinson: During the war, when they were building submarines as fast as they could to join the force and go out and fight the war, they put 25% experienced guys, qualified submarine enlisted men, on each ship. They augmented them with additional people, and then they trained them as quickly as they could. But after the war we got a much higher percentage of qualified submarine people, so I had some good people came

---

[*] USS *Wahoo* (SS-565), a *Tang*-class fast attack submarine, was commissioned 30 May 1952. She had a displacement of 1,560 tons on the surface and 2,260 tons submerged. She was 269 feet long, 27 feet in the beam, and had a draft of 17 feet. Her top speed was 15 knots surfaced and 18 knots submerged. She was armed with eight 21-inch torpedo tubes.

to *Wahoo* and some good officers including Harry Train that you and I have mentioned as one of the junior officers and Harvey Lyon and Reuben Woodall.*

Paul Stillwell: And Dave Johnson, who later became a vice admiral.†

Admiral Wilkinson: Yes, and a crackerjack guy, Dave Johnson. Hadn't thought of him. Why don't I tell you a story about Dave Johnson? There was a sweet old guy who was a rather ineffective shipyard commander, whose name I won't mention, it's a long time ago. But Dave Johnson, that made me think of it. Harvey Lyon, Reuben Woodall, Harry Train, so on. Good people, good troops, and our job was to get a ship's organization written, the people trained to operate, get ourselves qualified in this new design submarine different from anything any of us had been on before with a high-pressure system, with the high-speed diesels, a different kind of diesel engine, high-pressure hydraulic systems. A lot of things gave trouble, but we were getting checked out and making sure the yard took care of deficiencies and doing us a good job and people getting trained and getting the spare parts and ship's organization and all the things you do. We also were trying to make our ship pretty, and I got an agreement from the shipyard commander once when he was aboard that we could get a certain kind of special pretty tile put in.

Paul Stillwell: Terrazzo?

Admiral Wilkinson: No. A certain coating on our bulkhead in the wardroom and in the crew's mess and it didn't happen. And finally he was down, and I said, "Hey, Captain, you agreed you would do thus and so, and it hasn't happened."

He said, "I know, but my people have not been able to get the material."

I said, "Captain, is the only thing that's keeping you from doing it is being able to get the material?"

---

* Lieutenant (junior grade) Harry D. Train II, USN; Lieutenant (junior grade) Harvey E. Lyon, USN; Lieutenant Reuben F. Woodall, USN. The oral history of Train, who retired as a four-star admiral, is in the Naval Institute collection.
† Lieutenant John David Johnson, Jr., USN.

He said, "Yeah."

I said, "Captain, I'll get one of my junior officers. Mr. Johnson, go out of this ship and get that material and bring it back and don't come back till you do." [Laughter] Four hours later, having gone to Boston, he was back with the material, and we called up and said, "Captain, the material is here." And we got our ship gussied up pretty. But Dave Johnson, it's a good thing he came back. [Laughter] Crackerjack.

After the *Wahoo* was built, it was going to go through qualification training at SubLant, and then it was going to deploy from SubLant around to the Pacific. We were going to be assigned to Honolulu, which we were all pleased with. As we came down to the wire, it was harder and harder to get everything done and meet the schedule. Finally we were loading our stuff on board at the last minute. A sleepy sonarman came aboard over the brow, came around the conning tower, went toward the after hatch, and dropped the movie machine over the side. We were due to leave in 48 hours. No movie machine. So I said to him, "I can understand how the movie machine can go over the side. I just can't understand why you aren't with it still holding on to it." [Laughter] I guess I was really upset.

So we got the divers. We said, "Right down there is our movie machine. Get it back. We'll see what we can do with it." And so they went over the side down there, 30-40 feet of water, and pretty soon tug-tug-tug, and up came a piece of electronic equipment. That was not our movie machine. The guy went down again. Tug-tug-tug. Up came another piece of electronic equipment, but it wasn't our movie machine. It wasn't till the third time that the item was our movie machine. You know, we took that thing and flushed it out with fresh water and dried it out, and it worked perfectly. Didn't hurt it a bit to be submerged in brackish salt water for must have been an hour before we got it back, which really surprised me.

Paul Stillwell: What were the other two things?

Admiral Wilkinson: It shows you what was going on in that shipyard. [Laughter]

I had a fantastic yeoman on that ship, crackerjack guy. I can show you something from him because he got out of the Navy and became president of some company. He was a crackerjack, smart guy. Name's Patrick McEnroe, really good. There wasn't any time left to do training or anything, and we were supposed to go through the whole training cycle at SubLant and then go deploy to the Pacific. The yard had been late, and we didn't want to miss our deployment date to the Pacific. The time in support in New London got shorter and shorter, and we had to go through Goat Island and do our torpedo shooting and all that stuff.[*]

We did all those things, and we got down to SubLant. SubLant's big team came aboard to give us an administrative inspection. They took all day, and it was flawless. I had a great yeoman. There were absolutely no discrepancies. And, being stupid and brash, I said, "Hey, we've spent all day, and it's pretty crappy that we didn't get a damn bit of good out of it. Pretty crappy you guys come aboard for 24 hours and can't find anything wrong." [Laughter] Well, that antagonized them, so they came back for three more days. Finally they found one card in the dead file that hadn't been initialed right. After three days, except for that one card, we were still flawless. We had the best yeoman you ever saw, and he had done everything perfectly. Now, operationally we also did pretty well for a new boat, and we set sail with high spirits toward the Pacific with these four new high-speed diesel engines.

Paul Stillwell: Harry Train damned those pancake diesels.[†]

Admiral Wilkinson: Pancake diesels. When we were about a few hundred miles out to sea off Norfolk and a little farther south they crapped out one by one, one by one. Finally there was only one left that was running, and I said, "Hey, we'd better shut that down and look at it." Some way in the shutting it down it had a casualty, and so I was at sea with no engines. I said, "It's only machinery. I can't believe you guys can't fix it."

Oh, one thing we had done. We had lied and stolen and beat the system. We knew those diesels were trouble, so we had far more than the full allowance of spare parts for those engines on board. We brought all the other technical people, the torpedomen to help, and we went to work. The guys worked 12 hours on and six off. We took all those

---

[*] Naval Torpedo Station, Goat Island, Newport, Rhode Island.
[†] See the Naval Institute oral history of Admiral Harry D. Train II, USN (Ret.).

engines apart, and by the time we got to Panama we had them all fixed but one. We couldn't fix one, because it needed a new crankshaft, which then was flown to us in Panama. By the time we reached Honolulu we steamed in with all four engines running; we got there on schedule, and we never had a casualty. We had lots of problems with the hydraulic system and the diesels, but we never had anything the rest of my time on there that the guys couldn't fix. But they completely redid those four engines en route from New London to Honolulu. We got there on time, except it was really harrowing looking through the Christmas mail trying to find this crankshaft that was supposed to meet us in Panama, but it finally got there.

Harry Train recognized—and we all recognized—that those diesels shouldn't have been put in the way they were without testing. But because the guys had made advanced preparation in getting the parts, they fixed them. And the hydraulic system with all those O-rings and the alignment required, 2,000-pound system, they'd spring a leak. And we tried to line it up and put all new O-rings and, I said, "Five times, five times on any leak, and the fifth time the hell with it. Weld it up." And so there were a few joints that we were never able to fix except we welded them up so they didn't leak anymore.

And, again, they made the 2,000-pound hydraulic system work. And we had new evaps that were trouble, and we recognized that as the ship was being built.* So we operated those evaps. They were supposed to have a 48-hour test. We probably operated them 30 days and debugged them.

One time I was down in New London, and I visited the *Trigger*.

Paul Stillwell: Ned Beach.

Admiral Wilkinson: Ned Beach in the *Trigger*, the first fast attack being built in New London.† I eased through the boat and shot the breeze with the guys. I got back to the engine room, and I said, "How much trouble are you having with those evaps?"

---

* Evap – an evaporator heats seawater and converts it to fresh water by distillation.
† USS *Trigger* (SS-564) was commissioned 31 March 1952. Commander Edward L. Beach, USN, was the first commanding officer. See the oral history of Admiral Harold E. Shear, USN (Ret.), the first executive officer of the new *Trigger*.

"No trouble," he said.

"How much time you got on them?" say I.

"Well, we've got the 48-hour run."

"Well," I said, "You better run some more than that. You're going to have trouble." Sure enough they took off and went on a grand shakedown cruise, headed down to—

Paul Stillwell: Rio, I thought.

Admiral Wilkinson: Well, they never got to Rio till later because their evaps failed and they didn't have any water and they had to stop in Gitmo first.* But my guys did everything so well in the matter —with all the troubles those new ships had, but we had a crackerjack crew and they fixed it all. They made it run.

We tied up on schedule in Honolulu, and we were a good-looking boat. I had some crackerjack people in Dave Johnson, Harry Train, Harvey Lyon. Harvey Lyon was a competent engineer. There were 10,200 items, and he would follow up after every one. He was a crackerjack guy. He got to the nuclear program, and the only guy that didn't was Harry Train. He could have, but he didn't care for Admiral Rickover.

Paul Stillwell: I understand that Marge Lyon, Harvey Lyon's wife, was also a very interesting person.

Admiral Wilkinson: Well, you knew Harvey Lyon?

Paul Stillwell: I heard of him from Admiral Long.† He said Marge Lyon could walk on her hands and was a very entertaining individual.

Admiral Wilkinson: Well, I don't know what stories to tell you about Harvey, but my exec was fantastic. Reuben Woodall, good old southern boy, and he got to the nuclear

---

* "Gitmo" is the nickname for Guantánamo Bay, Cuba.
† See the Naval Institute oral history of Admiral Robert L. J. Long, USN (Ret.).

program, and later he put the *Robert E. Lee* in commission as skipper down in Newport News. Reuben Woodall with that accent could get whatever he needed for the *Robert E. Lee*. [Laughter] He probably put as good a ship in commission as was ever done. Reuben was a crackerjack guy. Bill Anderson got sent to a fast attack along with Reuben, but he never did get the *Tang* completely squared away.[*] Reuben Woodall really was probably a little bit better operator than Andy but, see, Reuben was my exec on the *Wahoo*. Anderson was Enders's exec on the *Tang*, and Andy came over to relieve me, and Reuben went over and relieved Enders.[†]

As soon as that happened, Anderson was the captain of a better submarine and better trained crew with better people, better operating, so the *Wahoo* being second had more chance for debugs, outperformed the *Tang* hands down. So Anderson on his tour on *Wahoo* did very well and got selected by Rickover and came on and got to be skipper of the *Nautilus* and did a good job.[‡] Third skipper of the *Nautilus* probably did better, and that was Lando Zech.[§] Downhill they got some pretty sorry people, and *Nautilus* went through a nadir, but then at the end they came up again. Let me think a little bit more about the *Wahoo*.

Paul Stillwell: What do you remember about Woodall in his role as your executive officer?

Admiral Wilkinson: Crackerjack, absolutely superb, got everything done, low key, easy for the crew to deal with. The crew really liked him. The tough, feisty guy was Harvey Lyon, who also was a crackerjack guy. Reuben Woodall's personality was that you would love Reuben, and everybody did, and he did a super job. Now that I think back, Reuben Woodall, Harry Train, we had some really good people on there. A lot of those guys made admiral too. And then you think back in the *Volador*. I had some really good people in there. So I've been blessed with exceptional people working for me. I was the

---

[*] Lieutenant Commander William R. Anderson, USN.
[†] Commander Enders P. Huey, USN, was the first commanding officer of the *Tang* (SS-563), commissioned 25 October 1951.
[‡] Commander William R. Anderson, USN, commanded the *Nautilus* from June 1957 to June 1959.
[§] Commander Lando W. Zech, Jr., USN, commanded the *Nautilus* from June 1959 to April 1962.

first nuclear guy that was selected for admiral, and then as time went by there was a multitude of them and then faster and faster. When they got to 43 that had made admiral I was checking down a list, and 41 of them had worked directly for me.

Paul Stillwell: That's remarkable.

Admiral Wilkinson: Yes. So remember, guys working for you are the guys that carry you. So I had people that never gave me a chance to not succeed. Looking back, I was really lucky. I had some fantastic people that worked for me.

Paul Stillwell: And there's the possibility that you helped them too.

Admiral Wilkinson: I tried if they asked me to, yes. I still hear from people all the time going back 30, 40 years ago or more, including a lot of guys now from INPO.* An awful lot of my INPO guys have gone out, and they're executives in the nuclear utility industry just because they were in a good outfit and they got the right standards and knowledge. It's catching. If an outfit is started right and gets a good reputation, it's gratifying how long it will carry on. How long the people will do right just because that's the way it is.

Paul Stillwell: It becomes a tradition.

Admiral Wilkinson: I think back all the time in my life when things have gone to pieces it was my fault in that I let down what was expected, and it's sort of interesting. If you expect your people to do 100% percent they'll never quite do 100%, but if you expect them to get 90% done they won't do 90. People have a tendency to live up to your expectations.

Paul Stillwell: What do you recall about the caliber of the enlisted personnel in the *Wahoo*? Was that as high level as the officers?

---

* The nuclear electric utility industry created the Institute of Nuclear Power Operations (INPO) in 1979. As he relates later in the oral history, Wilkinson headed INPO after retiring from the Navy.

Admiral Wilkinson: I said that ships that were put in commission after the war had a higher percentage of experienced submariners, and it was still a plum to get new construction. So the force detailers probably gave us picked people. We had good leadership, and I really believe people will live up to your expectations. Remember my story of the four diesels crapping out en route Pearl and those guys fixed them at sea. That would be a big shipyard overhaul now, but they did it because we believed they could. They worked 12 on and six off for about 16 days. I sat in the engine room a lot of those hours, and so did my people, and the guys just fixed it. When guys have done something like that, then they're really better, and they know that they're better and they know they can do it again.

There was a guy that wide on the *Gudgeon*, and the *Gudgeon* came along. That was the next submarine. It was Don Whitmire. You know Don Whitmire?

Paul Stillwell: I saw pictures of him. I think his call sign was Big Boy.

Admiral Wilkinson: He was an All-American football player.[*] He was a yard wide, and he was the gunnery officer on the *Gudgeon*.

Paul Stillwell: And a good submariner from what I've heard.

Admiral Wilkinson: He was a good submariner, and I'm really high on Don Whitmire. One of the things you did, as a ship was going in commission, in addition to the torpedo reload with all the automatic equipment, was a hand torpedo reload to show that you could. It was a timed reload, and you had to meet a certain time requirement. With Dave Johnson and some of my guys we did that once. Then we said, "Hey, there's a mark for you guys on *Gudgeon* to shoot at. We challenge you to ever beat our time for a hand reload." Well, Whitmire was in charge as the gunnery officer on the *Gudgeon*, and so they did their timed reload. They didn't beat our time, and they did it again and they didn't beat it. They probably did it 50 times with Don Whitmire before they finally beat

---

[*] Midshipman Donald B. Whitmire, USN, graduated from the Naval Academy in the class of 1947. He eventually became a submariner and still later a rear admiral. He was a lieutenant (junior grade) when the USS *Gudgeon* (SS-567) was commissioned on 11 June 1952.

our time. But they only did it that fast because there was a challenge. Guys will do better if it's expected of them and under pressure, and they kept up till they did. But when our people fixed those engines, when they fixed the hydraulic system, when they fixed the evaporators, other things and made them work, the crew gained in something thereby.

So when I left *Wahoo* I thought I had a fantastic crew and I did. And that's why Andy on *Wahoo* did better than *Tang*. I mean, I'm telling you, he had a crackerjack outfit. Andy's a good man, too, but he had some awfully good people. You take guys like Harry Train. They're good guys. I told you the troops referred to the *Volador* as "Not much for chow or liberty, but she's a seagoing son-of-a-bitch." Well, for a shorter time I was commanding officer of a submarine called the *Sea Robin*, which is a story in itself, and my troops referred to her as "A speeder, a feeder, a flotilla leader." But all my troops on the *Wahoo* referred to her as "Lucky you came *Wahoo*." So there was a certain high performance and morale of the troops on that ship.

Paul Stillwell: Wasn't there one individual who originated that slogan of, "Lucky you came to *Wahoo*?"

Admiral Wilkinson: I don't know who did that. Like I always do, even on the *Long Beach*, I interviewed every new man that came aboard. I interviewed everybody before he was transferred. I wrote a letter to his folks or his wife telling them they were glad he was there and he was lucky to be on her. I'd talk to a new guy coming to the *Wahoo*, and they were getting kids out of Sub School and I would say to them absolutely seriously, "You just came from Sub School. Were you first in the class?"

The guy would say, "Well, no, sir."

"Well, how did you ever get assigned to the *Wahoo*?" Finally with the right approach the guy would always say, "I guess I was just lucky." [Laughter] And not me, but I guess that became a little bit of a joke and I don't know who, some of the troops started the saying, "Lucky you came *Wahoo*." And pretty soon that's the way everybody on the ship referred to it. I don't know who started that. But after they did and after a while they also all felt that in their heart. And that does make a difference in the morale and well-being of a ship's company. They all felt that they were lucky that they were on that ship.

Paul Stillwell: What do you remember about handling the *Wahoo* in those currents around the State Pier in New London?

Admiral Wilkinson: I was commanding officer a long, long time. I got my first command as a lieutenant commander and except for going to General Line School and the senior course at the war college, I really was a commanding officer until I made admiral. So I had 11½ years of command, and I've seen an awful lot of landings come and go, and so mostly I didn't make landings. I had my young officers make landings. The *Wahoo* and the *Nautilus* both have two screws. It's not like the *Skipjack* class with a single screw, although the trouble we had was with our main cubicle on *Wahoo*. I made 19 one-screw landings with *Wahoo* in Honolulu in not much current. So I made a lot of landings, and it didn't give me any trouble making landings at State Pier, which is easy because you're coming in parallel to the current. It's really harder to make a landing up at the Submarine Base, but I didn't have any trouble. But I've seen other people plow into that dock and the timbers fly in the air, but we didn't have any trouble. Now, the *Skate* did.

Paul Stillwell: What was that?

Admiral Wilkinson: Crackerjack guy as he was, Jim Calvert wasn't the best ship handler in the world.* After four submarine commands and when I got to be skipper of the *Long Beach* I was the only captain of a capital ship that made his own landings in Norfolk. Other ships would come in, and they'd get a pilot and tugs and all. Sometimes we had to have tugs, but I ran them. Tying up at State Pier was no problem at all.

Paul Stillwell: Why did you make so many single-screw landings in Hawaii?

---

* USS *Skate* (SSN-578), commissioned 23 December 1957, was the first ship of her class. Commander James F. Calvert, USN, was her first commanding officer.

Admiral Wilkinson: Because just like we had trouble with the engines and just like we had trouble with the hydraulic system and the evaporators, we had trouble with our cubicle, lots of failures.

Paul Stillwell: What's the cubicle?

Admiral Wilkinson: That's the electrical distribution panel back at the maneuvering room. And so we'd come in, and one engine with one screw would be out of commission. And so in *Wahoo* the cubicle they had actually used was the same one that they used on the so-many-thousand-hour test and just a lot of things wore out till it finally got fixed.

Paul Stillwell: That Portsmouth Naval Shipyard has a long-time reputation for building and repairing submarines.

Admiral Wilkinson: Yes.

Paul Stillwell: How good a job did they do building the *Wahoo*?

Admiral Wilkinson: They did a pretty good job. The problems weren't in the construction. They were in the design of new pieces of equipment like those pancake diesels that weren't really debugged. Each part had to be tuned to that engine, and that hadn't always been done. It was possible eventually to make those pancake diesels run, and eventually we got all ours fixed and ran. But the problem we had with them wasn't really Portsmouth Naval Shipyard's part. I don't know whether Portsmouth Naval Shipyard or the Bureau of Ships or who designed the 2,000-pound hydraulic system with all its O-rings. That was a mess, and probably it was not obtaining a perfect lineup of all the pipes and O-rings that caused trouble. But, by and large, I think Portsmouth Naval Shipyard was a good shipyard. They didn't have real control of their people, in that there was a lot of theft in the yard. People in the surrounding community would steal stuff from the shipyard and take it home, and they just felt it was their right to have a piece of pipe if they needed it. And so just as the *Wahoo* was finishing up we lost the chains to hold the crew's bunks up and some stuff like that.

Paul Stillwell: Well, we didn't really talk about the checkout and training by SubLant. What did that involve?

Admiral Wilkinson: Well, because the ship had trouble getting finished on time by the yard we were real tight. And there was a commitment to us to deploy to the Pacific, so there wasn't enough time to leisurely go through the kind of shakedown training that you would normally do. We had to go to Newport to Goat Island and do our torpedo test firing and some other things. And we had to have an administrative inspection and an operational inspection and probably a supply inspection and some of those things from SubLant and all those were done on a rush basis. And because I had exceptional people and a good crew we came through them all with flying colors. But it was a really rushed schedule to get us ready to sail on the scheduled date for the Pacific to report to our new reporting senior, Commander Submarine Force Pacific Fleet.

Paul Stillwell: What sort of operations did you have once you got out to Hawaii?

Admiral Wilkinson: Oh, things were a little more leisurely there, and we did the normal operations that all submarines do. Going out and giving services for ASW forces and getting to do our own exercises and practice torpedo firings and those kinds of things.

Paul Stillwell: Well, this is a more capable submarine than they'd had to deal with before. How did the ASW forces do against you?

Admiral Wilkinson: Although this was a new class, I'm not really sure that it was a more capable submarine. It could dive deeper, but it really didn't have any more submerged speed than the *Volador* had had. Certainly it didn't have as reliable engines. Probably in Pearl in those days in our training we weren't up against the most crackerjack capable ASW forces, so we did all right, but I don't have any dramatic stories to recount of it.

Paul Stillwell: Those pancake diesels got replaced later in her career, and that improved the situation.

Admiral Wilkinson: Yes, that did. But, as I said, our people when ours broke down that first time had repaired them, and we continued to have lots of casualties, but it wasn't ever anything that we had any doubt that our people could fix. We never had to go to the shipyard to get it done. When we had a casualty on our submarine our people fixed it, and we always seemed to have everything in commission. That was really because we had a capable crew and good support in spare parts. There still was a lot of trouble with those engines till they were finally, as you say, replaced. That was years later.

Paul Stillwell: Last summer I was on board the USS *Maine*, and one of the senior petty officers in her crew had put the *Wahoo* out of commission, so you were in the first crew and he was in the last.*

Admiral Wilkinson: That was a good ship, exceptional officers and crew. The spirit was good and the morale was high. It was a happy tour for me. It was the first time I'd had my family to Hawaii. We weren't there long enough to feel rock happy, and I was transferred to the next job before I was ready to go. I was replaced by a very capable officer, Bill Anderson, and I had confidence that the ship would continue to run well and it did.

Paul Stillwell: How did you get the short tour in the *Sea Robin*?

Admiral Wilkinson: During the construction period for *Wahoo* I was up in Portsmouth; the *Wahoo* was being built, but it was not yet in commission. The commanding officer of the *Sea Robin* went down to New York for the weekend, and the *Sea Robin* was supposed to get under way Monday morning for extensive operations. His first day in New York the knee on one leg locked up, and he couldn't bend his leg. The ship needed to go to sea

---

* The *Wahoo* was decommissioned and struck from the Navy list on 31 March 1980 and sold for scrapping in 1994.

on Monday, and the captain, who now was incapacitated, said his exec was not competent to do it. So I got a call on Sunday evening that they wanted me to come down and be the CO of the *Sea Robin* for some period of time until they could get a proper CO on it and that they were due to go to sea at 8:00 o'clock in the morning.

I had that call about 6:00 in the evening on a Sunday, and it was wintertime, and it was bitter cold. I lived in an old farmhouse with a coal furnace, and I showed my wife how to work it and got out of there about 9:00 o'clock and got down to New London at 2:00 or 3:00 in the morning. I walked through the ship and scanned the ship's orders and organization and turned in and got up at 5:00 or 6:00 o'clock, an hour or so later. It was freezing, drizzling rain topside, and so instead of mustering the crew at quarters I read my orders over the 1MC and said, "Station the maneuvering watch, make preparations to get under way."* At 8:00 o'clock we sailed out on what ended up to be three or four weeks of very intensive and interesting operations that included photo reconnaissance off Watch Hill, made a full-capacity mine plant and some other operations like that, and I had a lot of fun. Finally they got the captain's leg repaired. He came back and was CO again, and I was replaced. But for about a month of intensive operations at sea I was the captain of the *Sea Robin*. It was a short tour, but it was a command tour. That was in February 1952.

Paul Stillwell: Where is Watch Hill that you did this?

Admiral Wilkinson: Oh, that's on the coastline off New London.

Paul Stillwell: What's involved in mine-laying by a submarine?

Admiral Wilkinson: Unless the submarine does it all the time it's different. All the torpedoes are taken out and mines are put in, and the mines are fired one by one as the submarine moves along. Depending on the pattern of the minefield you may be laying out—I think we laid some 56 mines in a field. It's quite an evolution before you're finished, and things can get screwed up. You could have an interruption in the rate that

---

* 1MC – the submarine's general announcing system.

you're putting one out every so many seconds. To do a full-capacity mine plant for a submarine that hadn't done it for a long time—with those people probably ever—was quite an evolution. So it was fun to get prepared and do that.

Paul Stillwell: And presumably you had to chart the location very carefully.

Admiral Wilkinson: Oh, yes. Of course these were all dummy mines. It was just a training exercise. Photo recon is an interesting thing where you either move along a shoreline taking pictures that are superimposed over one another, so you have a continuous picture, or you stay in one spot and take the radial circular sweep and you're supposed to do this undetected. So we went in and did a photo recon off the beach against some air search, and all those things are fun. They're not things that submarines do every day. It just happened that in the year's training cycle *Sea Robin* hadn't done any of these things that you're supposed to do once every cycle or once every two cycles or something. I had the fun of going down and being skipper as we did all those. We were at sea most of the time, and, of course, I had no desire to be in port and go ashore. My family was up in Portsmouth, and so my entire time on the ship was operational time until finally they got somebody to relieve me as captain and I went back to my primary job of putting the *Wahoo* in commission.

Paul Stillwell: How much contact did you have with Admiral Rickover during this period when you were in the *Wahoo*?

Admiral Wilkinson: Practically none. While I was in the pre-commissioning detail up at Portsmouth—I'm thinking back now—work in the nuclear program had progressed, and the prototype was being built. Finally this to-be-nuclear submarine was authorized, and the keel was laid in New London, and President Truman came and put his initials in the keel as it was laid.* I did get an invitation to attend that. I watched from way in the back and thought that was terrific that they were laying the keel on schedule. I don't know

---

* The keel for the world's first nuclear-powered submarine, *Nautilus* (SSN-571), was laid by President Harry S. Truman at the Electric Boat Shipyard in Groton, Connecticut on 14 June 1952.

whether Admiral Rickover asked somebody to send me that invitation or whether I got it because I was a CO of a submarine, but it was pleasing to me to go watch the keel laying. But as for any day-to-day contact I didn't have any. I wasn't in the program yet.

Paul Stillwell: Did you find out what was involved in the selection process that chose you to be the prospective commanding officer?

Admiral Wilkinson: I guess Rickover knew me and was pleased to see me and helped me get to be selected to be skipper of the *Nautilus*. By that time I had been commanding officer of some pretty capable submarines with pretty good records. Afterwards Admiral Tyree told me about the selection process.[*] I believe he was in BuPers at the time; I'm not sure. Tyree later showed me a book a couple of inches thick where they had considered ten different people as potential first skippers. They had gone back even and looked at an older gentleman with the Congressional Medal of Honor from World War II. That has a lot of stature. And they looked at some other people. Ned Beach had stood second in his class at the Naval Academy and was aide to the President and a famous writer and a known name and some other things.[†]

It just worked out that, in fact, for a submarine commanding officer I was the right experience, the right age. Finally they went the normal course of events instead of going back and taking a Congressional Medal of Honor guy. The submarine detail desk keeps a running list of the officers for submarine detailing in each age group, and for quite some time I had stood number one in my age group in the opinion of the submarine detailers, what we call the fry. And I had had the background of having worked on the nuclear development, so I was knowledgeable. And there isn't any doubt Captain Rickover was very strongly on my side. He really controlled that in years later for other ships. But although that wasn't an absolute factor in my time, it certainly didn't hurt. [Laughter] Rickover was happy for me, somebody he knew, to get the job rather than

---

[*] Vice Admiral John A. Tyree, Jr., USN (Ret.). In the mid-1950s he was a captain.
[†] Commander Edward Latimer "Ned" Beach, Jr., USN, Naval Academy class of 1939, wrote a number of books, most notably the submarine novel *Run Silent, Run Deep*. Beach, who had compiled a notable record as a submariner during and after World War II, served as naval aide to President Dwight D. Eisenhower. For a profile of Beach, see *Naval History*, Summer 1988, pages 62-64.

somebody they'd have to start all over with. I had really sat there quite some time before and watched them lay that keel and itched to someday be on that ship, so I was really pleased.

Paul Stillwell: What were the circumstances when you went out to visit the prototype?

Admiral Wilkinson: After the *Wahoo* was finished construction and quick shakedown and checkout in the Atlantic, we sailed for the Pacific and reported to our boss in Honolulu. We operated for the rest of my time on board out of Pearl Harbor. Finally, as good fortune would have it, I got my orders to be the prospective commanding officer of *Nautilus*. That was great to me, but my orders provided for me to stop by the Naval Reactor Test Station near Arco, Idaho, and visit the prototype for a period of time en route to New London. So I got to the prototype, and it by now was already running.

    The reactor was critical, and Rickover did a brilliant thing as he laid out the prototype. The screws came out the end and turned a water brake, but the total plant was built in the exact dimensions in a submarine hull just like it would be when it was put into a ship. So the access and everything were just as they would be on the ship. The people that later became my engineering force on the *Nautilus* were out as the engineers operating the prototype. My chief engineer, Les Kelly, and Bus Cobean and the other two officers that were my engineering officers were there running things.[*] I stopped by, and the plant was running, and it was terrific.

Paul Stillwell: Do you want to mention the story about the pumps?

Admiral Wilkinson: It was terrific, but they weren't doing everything exactly as they should. They were operating the plant, but they weren't keeping the records that they should. Rickover back in Washington was really pleased. After I had been there a short time he got me on the phone and said, "What do you think?" I told him how great it was and how impressed I was and how marvelous it was the thing was running and whatnot. And finally I said the word, "But."

---

[*] Lieutenant Leslie D. Kelly, Jr., USN; Lieutenant Warren R. Cobean, Jr., USN.

That triggered, "But? But? But? But what? What are you talking about, Wilkinson? But what?"

I said, "Well, the great development here in the sealed rotor pumps was one of our biggest developments, and it would be nice if they were keeping hours of time on the hours they were in use. I don't care if they all run identical hours or if you run two ahead of the other so you can overhaul them first or how you do it. But the young engineering rating on watch at midnight shouldn't make that decision, and it would be nice if they had real intensive machinery and history records of all the parts that were used and whatnot."

Rickover had quit calling me Dennis. He said, "Wilkinson, you stay right there. You stay right there. Don't you leave till I get there." There weren't the jet planes then, and time took a little longer. It was almost 24 hours before he was there in Idaho. We set up the administrative procedures for who controlled what equipment was run and when and how and what records were kept, etc. Rickover really respected the opinion of an operator, and if something was wrong and it was brought to Rickover's attention he recognized it, and, by God, he did something about it. And think of that. That man was out there in less than 24 hours, and heroic action was taken—much to everybody's distress. [Laughter]

Paul Stillwell: Why distress?

Admiral Wilkinson: I mean, anybody would be shocked if he was turned around and told they he wasn't doing right and made to do different instantly. Rickover was not easy to get along with.

Paul Stillwell: I've heard that.

Admiral Wilkinson: I had the greatest admiration for him.

Paul Stillwell: I've heard both of those things from other people.

Admiral Wilkinson: I knew the young officers that were in training and had gone through the long period at Bettis and then during the construction of the prototype and then during its operation. My engineering officers and crew when they came to the ship surely were more qualified than any engineering crew that ever went to any subsequent submarine because they had been involved in the design, they'd been involved in the construction of the prototype, they had written the operating procedures for running the plant. They now came to the *Nautilus* to a plant identical to the prototype. They knew it would work, and they knew they could do it, and they knew more about it operationally than anybody.

Whereas if you look downstream at the others, I sent ten engineers and an officer to be part of the engineering detail on the *Skate*, and Jim Calvert selected an augmenting force of really good people, but they hadn't as one unit operated a *Skate* plant before. So I probably had the best qualified engineering crew that any submarine had then or since as it started. Similarly the submarine force in their detailing system selected very, very good people for the rest of the ship. I had those four engineers as my engineering gang, and I had four select submarine officers who were not engineering qualified. For example, in my time on *Nautilus* I had four young officers out of the class of 1950 of the trade school and the junior one of the four had stood tenth in his class. All the others were higher, including Dave Boyd.[*] Dave Boyd had been valedictorian in high school, number three in his class at the Naval Academy, number one in his class at Sub School. And then qualified in submarines and came to the *Nautilus*. Now, that's a crackerjack young officer. And I had three similar ones in my non-engineering qualified. My exec, Dean Axene, was tremendously capable.[†]

Paul Stillwell: What was his background?

Admiral Wilkinson: High performance, first in his age group, submarine qualified, qualified for command submariner. Crackerjack guy. Troops, I needed a chief of the boat. Chief of the boat is a really important person on the crew of a submarine. And the

---

[*] Lieutenant (junior grade) David S. Boyd, USN.
[†] Lieutenant Commander Dean L. Axene, USN.

SubLant detailer said, "Well, now, the *Squatfish* here [and I won't name the submarine] won the big fleet E and their skipper's about normal, but the reason they won it is because of that chief of the boat."[*]

I said, "Gee, that sounds good to me. I'll take him." And that was Chief Ingles.[†] So I really had selected people on the *Nautilus*. It's a good thing I did, because from the ship's company standpoint putting the *Nautilus* in commission was a tough job because there were an awful lot of organizations with strong character individuals involved. There was my operational commander, the Commander Submarine Force. There was the Chief of the Bureau of Ships. There was the other part of the Bureau of Ships, Captain Rickover. There was the supervisor of shipbuilding, who thought he was in charge of ship construction, and he was. And there was the company that was building it, the Electric Boat Company. Always before new ships were tested out at sea by an EB trial crew. But because there was a nuclear reactor and we were responsible for its safety for the first time, there wasn't an EB trial crew. The *Nautilus* ship's company became the trial crew, and that didn't set completely right with all the trial crew type people at Electric Boat Company.

Then there was Westinghouse, which had built the reactor. And then there was the Atomic Energy Commission. And then-Captain Rickover wasn't fully as powerful as he became later. So it got down to a lot of pressure and conflict because Captain Rickover did generate pressure and conflict. It became a question of pressure and conflict among a lot of the involved organizations, but ultimately it couldn't get done until my guys threw the switch or turned a valve or ran the pump, and we had an awful lot of pressure on us in what we did. I had really good people, and they lived through that very tough period and did it well and didn't lose their cool, and I was proud of them.

Paul Stillwell: Was that the top group of officers and enlisted men you have served with any time in your Navy career?

---

[*] An "E," for excellence, is generally awarded to a ship or component of a ship as a result of top performance in competition with other ships during a given time period.
[†] Chief Torpedoman Leroy Ingles, USN.

Admiral Wilkinson: Let me tell you, I had some awfully good people on some awfully good ships. There were no flies on the *Volador*. There were no flies on the *Wahoo*. I had an awful lot of my officers that became admirals from all those ships. And I had crews that performed superbly, but in truth in totality the best group that I ever had was the group on the *Nautilus*. You could look at some of the statistics of how many of my troops in the Navy competitive exam made commissions. When we went in commission we had 10 officers and 85 troops. There was a turnover over the time. I was on the pre-commissioning detail or commanding officer of *Nautilus* for four years, so with turnover I'm probably talking a little over 200 troops instead of 85, and out of those I had over 40 that made commissions in the Navy competitive exams. One time there were more people off the *Nautilus* that made commissions than there were in the rest of the Atlantic Submarine Force, and you've got to be proud of those guys.

Another time I remember there were tough times for promotion. There were eight guys in the Navy that, on a promotion exam, made first class machinist's mate from second class. I had three guys went up, three made it, and there were only five spots for the rest of the Navy. [Laughter] So I had some pretty crackerjack guys, and they performed like that kind of people. That was in a real tough maelstrom of pressure and activity, and they didn't lose their cool and did their jobs, and we met our commitments.

Anything that went wrong wasn't from any member of the *Nautilus*. There were other things that went wrong for one cause or another. With the technology in America there wasn't the same quality control, marking of pipes and equipment, but on 16 September 1954, we had what I referred to as the steam pipe incident. I was the prospective commanding officer of the *Nautilus*, and this was the first nuclear reactor to go into a ship. We set up the organization and the ship's orders and organization to take care of ours and the Navy's responsibility in that regard. But my orders were modified and on July 31, 1954, the *Nautilus* was placed in service, and I shifted from PCO to officer in charge of the *Nautilus*. That was so Navy personnel could be responsible before the reactor was installed. I don't think they did that on subsequent ships, but from July 31 I was the officer in charge. And to get ready to run the reactor critical and operate the ship at sea with Navy personnel instead of an EB trial crew, it was decided to place the ship in commission on 30 September. There was a lot of politics involved.

After all, it had been Truman with his initials in the keel, and Mamie Eisenhower had christened the ship.*

Paul Stillwell: Had you been present for the launching and christening?

Admiral Wilkinson: Yes. I had already reported aboard as the prospective commanding officer. I was on the bridge and rode the ship down the ways as it was launched. Mamie Eisenhower was a military-background wife, and she realized that that was important to me and my wife, and she very graciously invited my wife, Janice, to be her matron of honor. And so when Mamie Eisenhower christened the ship and broke the bottle of champagne my wife was there holding the flowers. That meant a lot to me and to her, so, yes, I was there when the ship was christened.

Paul Stillwell: You showed me a letter yesterday in which Admiral Rickover asked you to apply for command of the *Nautilus*. What was the outcome of that?

Admiral Wilkinson: He really wanted me to be chosen as the commander, and he thought it would help if I wrote a letter requesting the duty, but actually I never did that. I was fortunate enough to be chosen without asking for the job. My wife was a doll and she still is. There's the christening. There's Mamie Eisenhower swinging the champagne. I'm showing you a picture.

Paul Stillwell: Right.

Admiral Wilkinson: There's my wife holding the flowers right there. That's Hopkins.† That's Ned Beach.‡ That's Janice. Look at this. "Carried aboard launching of the world's first atomic submarine, the USS *Nautilus*, launched by Mamie Eisenhower,

---

* The *Nautilus* was launched on 21 January 1954 with First Lady Mamie Eisenhower breaking a bottle of champagne across the bow as the submarine slid down the ways into the Thames River. She was the wife of President Dwight D. Eisenhower, who succeeded Truman. Her husband had been an Army general.
† John Jay Hopkins was chairman of General Dynamics, the parent company of Electric Boat.
‡ Commander Edward L. Beach, USN, was President Eisenhower's naval aide.

January 21, 1954." Signed and attested to by E. P. Wilkinson. Signed and attested to by the executive officer, Dean Axene. And you can see there's Richard Nixon, Dwight Eisenhower.*

Paul Stillwell: Why did you not take the step of applying for the job?

Admiral Wilkinson: It didn't seem the thing to do to me.

Paul Stillwell: You alluded to the steam pipe incident. What did that involve?

Admiral Wilkinson: With the political considerations for us to go to sea, the date of September 30, 1954, was picked for us to go in commission. I would just change from officer in charge, responsible for this ship in service, to commanding officer, responsible for this ship in commission to operate it as a ship of the United States Navy at sea. Our speaker at the commissioning ceremonies was going to be Commander in Chief Atlantic Fleet, Jerauld Wright, and there was a certain political interest.† At the same time we were doing our part with ship's company as the trial crew and the operators testing out pumps and valves and whatnot.

Finally the plant had been put together in the ship, and we were at the point of heating it up and bringing up temperature and pressure and testing out all the systems. As we brought it up to temperature and pressure, a 2-inch line ruptured in the engine room, and it ruptured because of a lack of quality control in the construction. And in that section of 2-inch line, instead of being seamless, stainless steel tubing was lap welded. And in those days there wasn't the marking system on pipe that there is today. And, as it turned out, there wasn't a way of telling one piece of pipe from another unless you cut it open and looked at it. There wasn't a way of testing it short of a destructive-type testing.

That was disclosed in some days to follow, but I could see the magnitude of the problem, and so I was worried about us going in commission on 30 September. Now it was 16 September, and from a political aspect did the Navy still want us to put us in

---

* Richard M. Nixon was Vice President from 1953 to 1961.
† Admiral Jerauld Wright, USN, served as Supreme Allied Commander Atlantic, Commander in Chief Atlantic Command, and Commander in Chief Atlantic Fleet from 12 April 1954 to 28 February 1960.

commission? This involved the President and Mamie Eisenhower and the Commander in Chief of the Atlantic Fleet and then us not make our schedule in any way. So I quickly sent off a dispatch to the CNO and said, "We've had the scheduling, and in my personal opinion the ship will be delayed in delivery and won't deliver [that's with trials and everything completed] to the Navy till about 15 April." Well, the next day all the experts in the world were there from the Bureau of the Ships and from the Westinghouse Steam Division and from the Atomic Energy Commission. There was a general conference that went on, the first hour of which was spent in castigating me for sending this dramatic dispatch off to the CNO.

The thrust and tenor of all their comments was that I didn't know what the hell I was talking about, which was true in some aspects. But as I pointed out to them, "That's not really true, gentlemen. If you'll read that dispatch you'll see that I'm the world's leading expert on what I told the CNO."

They said, "How can you send that off?"

I said, "Because I don't have to be right. It's just order of magnitude. The CNO should know quickly. Politically they may want to make a decision not to have the commissioning on 30 September, and I want to give them as quick a warning as I can."

"But you don't know what you're talking about."

"Well, no," I said, "but if you read that dispatch again you'll see that I'm the world's leading expert. It starts out 'In my personal opinion'." [Laughter] "Now, I gather from the thrust of your comments that you think I've overestimated the problem and that the delay won't be anywhere near that much."

"Absolutely," they said.

"Well," I said, "Let me tell you." And I pulled out my wallet, as I've done a couple of other times in my life. "Twenty dollars a day, each and every one of you. If it delivers any day before 15 April I'll pay you $20.00. If it delivers any day after 15 April you pay me $20.00." Silence in the room. Not one guy said, "You're on."

Finally Captain Rickover's representative—I was proud of him, Saltwater Willie, S. W. Shor, who was an EDO, too—spoke up and he said, "Dennis, I'm ashamed of my corps."* He said, "I can't afford $20.00 a day. I'll take you for 10 cents a day."

---

* Lieutenant Commander Samuel W. W. Shor, USN.

I said, "Willie, you're on. The rest of you gentlemen $20.00 a day, any one of you." And nobody took that up, and I said, "Well, if you won't back your opinion up with your own personal money, then don't tell me I don't know what I'm talking about." As events transpired my estimate wasn't too far off, because when all was done the ship completed and delivered to the Navy on 22 April, and Saltwater Willie paid me 70 cents. [Laughter]

Paul Stillwell: That's a great story. Was the commissioning date in fact changed?

Admiral Wilkinson: No. They held to the 30 September, and Admiral Wright came and gave the speech, and we had a good commissioning. And it turned out that in fact it wasn't a great deal too early, because finally we got the reactor critical. They had to rip out all the 2-inch pipe and replace it, because they couldn't test and find out. That was done, and that took some time. Then we had to retest all the systems, but some way with people working around the clock the reactor was finally made critical just before New Year's. On New Year's Eve we blew the ship's whistle on nuclear steam and kept an intensive training program going and were able to go to sea on schedule on 17 January. They all leak a little at first. The sea trials, which lasted four days, tested a lot of things that showed some deficiencies and discrepancies. Lists were made, and more tests were done. We operated more before delivery, and finally everything was completed, and the ship was finished and delivered to the Navy on the 22nd of April. I was now the commanding officer of a naval ship in full commission at sea.

But it was a hectic period going through the construction period. There was a lot of tension and a lot of pressure, and we're talking 24 hours a day, day after day after day. The last ten months before the ship was finished I never missed a change of shift. I was there every time the Electric Boat Company workmen's shift was changed. Now, that sounds more impressive than it is, because the shift was changed at 8:00 in the morning, and naturally you're aboard at 8:00 and then 4:00 in the afternoon. And naturally you're at work at 4:00, and so the only extra time I came in was at midnight every night, but I did that for ten months, because problems happen as the watch changes and new people come on and take over what the old people were doing; there's frequently a lack of proper turnover and whatnot. It seemed that you would have most of your problems at time of change of shift, so I and my leading people were always there watching that. It was a tough time. Obviously my engineering people worked a lot harder, spent a lot more time than that. I'm one to delegate. But my guys were watching them hard.

That reminds of me of a very interesting story concerning the sealed-rotor pumps; all of them had been. Then they had trouble in one of the ones at Arco, and there was a question of whether the people in the installation had put a cotter pin in right. Rickover was one to make sure that things were done right, and he said, "We don't know that that was done right. We're going to open all those things up and check them." And I said, "Not necessary, Admiral. Undoubtedly I had one of my crew members watching those guys. Let's get 'em in here."

So we got them in there, and it was a first class petty officer, machinist's mate, and Admiral Rickover said, "Did you watch that?"

"Yes, sir."

"Did they do the thing right?"

"Yes, sir."

"Well, how can I be sure?" said Admiral Rickover.

"Because my guy doesn't just watch. He keeps notes."

"Get your book." And he came, and there was observation of all that work, and in every pump there was a little note that the cotter key was installed, and Rickover said, "That's good enough for me." That probably saved us a couple of weeks.

But my guys were there observing the work that was done, and they were there many, many, many, many hours. And I really did have a fantastic crew with a great sense of responsibility. They knew more about that plant from an operational aspect than anybody, because they had written the operating procedures, they'd operated the prototype. We knew that the *Nautilus* was going to work when we took it to sea. There wasn't any doubt in any of our minds that this nuclear-powered ship was going to work and work well. And sometimes when President Eisenhower would talk about atoms for peace and energy for the power-hungry countries of Europe I'd say to my people, "Hey, that's us, fellows. We're the only nuclear power they got." So there was really an awful lot of pride and confidence in our ship.

Paul Stillwell: What do you recall about the incident when you had a discussion with Carl Shugg?*

Admiral Wilkinson: God, what a mind you have. I can't mention anything to you that you don't remember it. There was an awful lot of pressure and friction. Shugg was the dominant guy in charge of the Electric Boat Company, and every morning we had a meeting. We had a meeting that talked about all the problems and what was going to happen in the next 24 hours and the next day. One morning there was bitter castigation of my personnel for a problem they'd had the night before by the EB people who were covering their numbers.

When they all got through I made a little speech and said, "Gentlemen, I'm the commanding officer of the *Nautilus*, and my people are the operators. We have this responsibility, and we feel it very strongly, and if ever we in any way do anything wrong don't worry about our feelings. You just lay in on the line just like you've done and say we screwed up and we did wrong. And the fact that we're here working with you and working hard doesn't mean a damn thing. Gentlemen, now you've heard a statement of policy from the *Nautilus* that I wish you'd adhere to in future. But, as to this incident that we're talking about, that happened at a quarter of 2:00 this morning. Mr. Shugg, were you there?"

He said, "Well, no."

I said, "Well, Mr. Shugg, I was there, and that's not exactly the way it was." [Laughter] And that puts you in quite a strong position, you know. This goes back to my statement that I never missed a change of shift because that's when problems happen. I had stayed on a little later, and it was a quarter to 2:00. And about three days later there was another flare-up and complaint and I said, "I'll cut through all the chippapa and tell you that was at a quarter to 1:00 this morning. Mr. Shugg, were you there?"

"No."

"Well, I was there and that's not the way it was." [Laughter] And let me tell you. The next night and several nights to follow Mr. Shugg was there at midnight and every

---

* Carleton Shugg was president of the Electric Boat Division of the General Dynamics Corporation. His recollections are in the Naval Institute oral history volume on the Polaris program.

change of shift, and it made a dramatic change in some of the things that happened, so it was of value to put it on the line. I had great admiration for Shugg. He was really a good man. You only had to tell him twice that he ought to be there, and he was, and it made a big difference. But that also was another example of the friction and stress that we were under all the time.

It wasn't easy, because there were a lot of conflicting organizations and goals and objectives and forces and strong people. During an operation we had a spill of slightly radioactive fluid, and Les Kelly, my engineer, got on the 1MC and said, "Now attention everyone on board. This is Les Kelly speaking. Don't anybody move. Now let me tell you we've had a little spill of radioactivity, and we know exactly what to do about it. We're going to square it away, but we don't want anybody getting into it or tracking it around. Just stay where you are, and a ship's company man will come to you and tell you what to do." From that moment forward we were really in charge of the ship.

Paul Stillwell: What were the types of issues that the complaints were coming about that led to those meetings with the shipyard people?

Admiral Wilkinson: We were on a real tight schedule of checkout, and tests, and integrated with that had to be the completion of systems, actual physical construction work. At the same time when a new valve was installed it had to be tested, and that meant operation of systems. Those were my guys that were the operators, so there had to be a coordination between the work and the testing. This was done at a very tight schedule, 24 hours a day, around the clock, seven days a week, trying to make a schedule. We did this with lots of advice and opinions and requirements and suggestions from many parties, such as representatives of the Bureau of Ships, certainly representatives of the supervisor of shipbuilding office, representatives of the Atomic Energy Commission, representatives of Westinghouse—all of them had representatives there. Every morning there was a coordination meeting of what was going to happen in the next watch, the next eight hours, and the next 24 hours, and it was a schedule that we tried to make.

For example, I mentioned a while ago that just before New Year's we finally put the plant critical, and then we were doing the testing. And let me tell you that we were up to full power in four days, which was a lot faster than the week that was on the schedule for that.

The prototype was the world's first nuclear plant, but this was the first plant in the ship and a reactor. And reactors have to be tested and operated safely, and all your systems checked out before that's so. This was done meticulously and on a very intensive schedule to get a ship completed, and for every one of those operations the ultimate actual operation of a valve or something was done by one of the crew members on the *Nautilus*. And that was around the clock, 24 hours a day, day after day, so my guys were on regular watch just as though they were at sea. Certainly for the last seven months before the ship was finished my guys stood just as many watches as though we'd been seven months continuously at sea. And so the ship's company did have a considerable part in the process.

Then we'd get lots of people who would come and say, "You have to do thus and so."

I would say arbitrarily, "We won't do that."

They'd go away, and maybe 24 hours later they'd come back and say, "Hey, you, this has to be done. Such and such and such and such."

I'd say, "I'm sorry. I apologize. I didn't understand. We'll be pleased to work that into the schedule."

My engineers would say, "Captain, how can you tell the people just like that that we're just not going to do that?"

I'd say, to my chief engineer, for example, "Les, you just keep track. You notice how many times they don't come back." We got an awful lot more guidance and instruction than we needed.

As we came down to the wire to put the ship to sea on sea trials, an awful lot of people wanted to go. So a list was made up of the experts that we had to take to sea on our initial sea trials, and that included physicists from Westinghouse and from the Atomic Energy Commission and such and so from here and there. The mandatory list that we had to take from sea trials was 122 people. Well, now understand, I had 10 officers and 85 men. That's more than one expert per man.

Paul Stillwell: That's right.

Admiral Wilkinson: I said, "Now, we're not going to do that to my people." So we talked about it and said, "We're just not going to take that many people." We decided we'd tell them we could take 30. And I said, "You know, if we tell them we'll take 30 we'll back away from that. I'll tell you what. We'll be just as reasonable as we can, and we'll tell them 50 and we'll never, never back down from that number." So I told them, "I can't take 122 people to sea, and in my opinion it's not operationally safe to have that many extra people on board. The maximum number I consider operationally safe to take is 50, and that's all I'm going to take."

Then there was a lot of pressure on me, such as, "You've got to have this rod control expert, you've got to have this."

I said, "Gentlemen, don't push me. Don't push me. We're only going to take 50, and we don't care what 50 it is. If you really push me, let me tell you how many people we need. Zero." [Laughter] Well, that caused a flap, and let me tell you higher authority can be quite effective. I had sent a dispatch to the effect that I didn't consider it operationally safe to carry more than 50 and I had sent that to CNO, CinCLantFlt, ComSubLant, BuShips, supervisor of shipbuilding, and I'd laid it on the line that that was my opinion, and that's the way it was.

Finally, with less than a week to go, I was called up by the supervisor of shipbuilding to his office. The Chief of the Bureau of Ships was on the phone, and he wanted to get me on the phone.[*] They were clever, and the Chief of the Bureau of Ships said to the supervisor of shipbuilding, "Where did this ridiculous figure of 50 come from?"

The supervisor knew where it came from, and he said, "Well, that's the commanding officer's opinion, and that's what he has said, and he's on the phone."

"Well, do you agree with that?" the Chief of BuShips asked.

"Oh, no. I think we need to take the people that are required to do those trials properly."

---

[*] Rear Admiral Wilson D. Leggett, Jr., USN, served as Chief of the Bureau of Ships from 1953 to 1955.

So the Chief of BuShips said to me, "Wilkinson, how do you justify that figure? Your experience is in a different kind of submarine. There's never been a submarine like this before. How do you justify that figure?"

I said, "Well, Admiral, in my opinion that's all I consider it's safe to carry."

He said, "Is that something you picked out of the air, something within 10 or 20%?"

Well, I'm as quick at figures as anybody. I said, "Admiral, I don't mean 55 or 60. I mean 50."

Well, that made him mad, and he said, "Well, this is ridiculous." And he said to his supervisor of shipbuilding, "You send us down a list of whom you consider we need, and we'll take it over to the CNO and get the commanding officer ordered to take the people that are required to do these trials properly."

I said, "Well, excuse me, Admiral, but when you're making that list up to take over to the CNO I'd suggest you make one list with 50 on it, because, let me tell you, I don't think the CNO will order me to carry more people at sea than I consider safe to carry. And let me tell you, if he does it won't be me." But evidently they went over and talked to the CNO, because pretty soon there was a dispatch from the CNO to me, info everybody, that the CNO was quite concerned about the success of the *Nautilus* operations. They'd thought about it, and they considered it was only safe to carry 50. I was ordered to only carry 50 people to sea trials, info Chief of BuShips and everybody. Well, that's the way it actually happened. So that was a certain amount of pressure, and for years and years none of us ever carried more than 50 people. [Laughter] Policy was set.

As we were writing the ship's orders and organization, there'd never been a nuclear ship before. So as we set up the reactor control division, including responsibility and accountability for the reactor, one of the young officers came back and said, "Hey, we can't do this, Captain."

"Why not?" I said.

"Well, it doesn't comply with Navy Regulations," he said.

"Well," I said, "then we'll change Navy regulations." And in fact Navy Regulations later were changed to the way we were doing it. Just the advent of this new technology in this ship caused a lot of things to change. The steam pipe incident and then with the force from Rickover changed the whole system of the marking of pipes and equipment in the whole of industry, the whole of America. They don't do it that way anymore. You no longer cannot tell the difference between a piece of seamless tubing and a piece of lap-welded pipe. And those things came out of the *Nautilus*. And, by God, we didn't take more than 50 to sea. That was the number we gave them, and we never backed down. [Laughter]

Paul Stillwell: Where did the sense of urgency come from that dictated the 24 hours a day work and seven days a week?

Admiral Wilkinson: Well, it wouldn't look very good if our schedule kept slipping, so there was a lot of pressure. Like I said a minute ago, the President had talked Atoms for Peace, Energy for the power-hungry countries of Europe. We were the only nuclear energy there was. There was no doubt that there was tremendous pressure to not fall behind in schedule. After all, we'd established that schedule back in '49. We were going to make it. [Laughter]

Interview Number 3 with Vice Admiral Eugene P. Wilkinson, U.S. Navy (Retired)
Place: Admiral Wilkinson's home in Del Mar, California
Date: Monday, 19 January 1998
Interviewer: Paul Stillwell

Paul Stillwell: How good a job overall would you say that Electric Boat did in building the *Nautilus*?

Admiral Wilkinson: We've talked about the steam pipe incident and the fact that due to a lack of quality control we were held up for a time in that lap-welded, hand-rolled stanchion pipe that had been put in instead of seamless tubing in part of our steam system, and obviously that was a poor thing to do. But actually in overall performance they really did a great job in building the *Nautilus*. They did a great job in putting the people in to solve problems to meet schedules, and the problem with the steam pipe wasn't all theirs. It was a problem in America. The pipe wasn't marked. That and Rickover caused a change in many things in America in the way pipes and valves and electrical things are marked, and so it's easier to make sure that those kind of things don't happen today than it was then. I have a theory and it's true. It works out pretty close that if people are really busting their tails and trying, they can do about four and a half times as much as they normally do. Time after time my people and the Boat Company people were really trying in order to get stuff done.

Paul Stillwell: What do you remember about the first time under way in the *Nautilus*? That was 43 years and two days ago.*

Admiral Wilkinson: We were scheduled to get under way at 11:00 A.M. on 17 January 1955, and in order to prepare for that we had what we called the fast cruise where we were tied fast to the dock. To make sure our guys were checked out and all the systems were checked out, we got the Boat Company workers and everybody else off the ship

---
* The event was on 17 January 1955.

four days before we were getting under way and put our people on watch and ran all equipment. We rotated the watch and went through emergency drills, battle stations and collision and man overboard and manned all the parties and did all the communications.

I had an interesting call from the Vice Chief of Naval Operations, telling us it was important and wishing us well and asking how things were going.[*] I told him, "Well, we're halfway through our fast cruise and things are going fine, sir."

"Oh, fast cruise?" I explained it to him, and he said, "Oh, yeah. Oh, yeah." As we hung up, I grinned at my guys and said, "You gentlemen just heard Navy policy being set." And, sure enough, ever after that's the way it's done. All the ships now have a fast cruise and a checkout before they go to sea. But that was one of the things we did on the *Nautilus* to make sure we had everything checked out. So we were in our fast cruise period, all was going well, and we resolved—and also this was part I guess of the call from the VCNO—the problem of how many technical experts we were going to have on board to help us with the sea trials. I told you how it went from 122 to 50, which was all we considered were safe to carry. And again Navy policy was set, because we were backed up by that dispatch from the CNO, and after that we never carried more than 50.

People from Chinfo, the Chief of Naval Information, came down about two days before we were due to get under way. Of course, they were all senior to me, and so they came aboard and said, "This is a historic event. And when you get under way you should send a historic message."

I agreed with that by nodding my head, and then I said, "Let me tell you, we're in our fast cruise period. We're really busy checking out our ship. You guys are expert at that stuff. You go write me a historic message and bring it back here, and we'll send it." That got rid of them for a day and a half. [Laughter] And they came back and they had a fabulous message that was a page and a half typewritten. And you've got to understand that as we were getting under way we were going to communicate with a rescue vessel by flashing light, and I didn't really have a signalman. We could all send and receive flashing light, but we had lots of other things to do. I had a quartermaster who operated

---

[*] Admiral Donald B. Duncan, USN, served as Vice Chief of Naval Operations from 10 August 1951 to 1 September 1956.

the flashing light. He was good, and he could have done it, but I wasn't really sure how good that receiver was over on the *Tringa*.

So I said, "You know, that could get screwed up." [Laughter] So I just wrote a short dispatch, "Under way on nuclear power."* That's what my guy sent over, and they were able to send that and get it receipted for really quickly. So that's part of the story related to what really turned out to be an historic message. But there was a lot of interest in our getting under way, and there were a lot of news people there to see us off, and, of course, there was Fox Movietone News. I think there were a couple of helicopters with newspaper people taking pictures. They made a terrible racket so that I couldn't—loud-voiced as I am—send my orders down to my people on the lines. I can remember having to use hand signals for orders to the linesmen to single up and take in the lines and whatnot.

We breasted the stern out, took in the number-one line, and backed clear. But just as we backed away from the pier, we had a terrible thing happen, and the maneuvering watch blared up at me, "Bridge, this is maneuvering, we got a noise in the starboard shaft." I was under way now, and there were an awful lot of press and all watching us, so I decided not to tie back up. I shifted propulsion from the main shafts to the creep motors. Aft of the clutch we had some electric motors that would drive the ship at about five to six knots. And it was still nuclear power, because the reactor was running turbo-generators, which were making the electricity that was powering the creep motors. But it was not nuclear power to drive the steam shaft. I didn't want to ask for help, so I just twisted around slowly. Once I got headed right, I could go ahead at any speed I wanted to just on the steam-driven port shaft, because the port shaft would drive the ship faster than I wanted to go in the channel anyway. But it was an agonizing few minutes while we twisted around on the creep motor.

In the meantime, Admiral Rickover left the bridge and went below to see what the problem was. I had a first class named Reece who was there.† Admiral Rickover was overseeing the work, and my guy Reece opened up access to see why we had this noise in

---

* Wilkinson provided a detailed account of getting under way for the first time in the *Saturday Evening Post*. Originally the first message was to have included the time the ship got under way, but that was omitted when she was slightly delayed from the original plan.
† Engineman First Class Thomas C. Reece, Jr., USN.

the starboard shaft. Rickover was handing him the tools. [Laughter] Things went along at a rapid pace, and Reece performed admirably and quickly had everything disassembled and looked at it. The problem was just a piece of sheet metal hitting. That was pulled aside, and by that time we were turned around on the creep motors, and we shifted propulsion back to the main propulsion. Rickover wanted me to give a spot promotion to Reece. [Laughter] But I told him, "No, he was just doing his job." [Laughter]

We steamed on out, and our sea trials were extensive operations. We had a lot of evolutions to do, observed by the 50 experts that were helping us, and data to be recorded and readings to be taken and first dive to make. We were conducting operations and recording data and doing all the checkouts on a 24-hour-a-day basis. We had very successful four days' worth of sea trials, during which time I was younger, and I did not sleep during those four days because I was up getting reports all the time. All submarines leak a little at first, so we checked for leaks, and this now had to be on the deficiency list. So we went back in with a big work list for EB to start working on before we did the next trial. And then more work and then the next trial finally to complete the ship. It was completed on the 22nd of April and turned over to the Navy. We had made our underway schedule, and the dispatch, "Under way on nuclear power," was absolutely true.

We accomplished a lot during the first sea trials. And, remember, this was the first nuclear-powered ship. The tests and things were a lot more extensive than if you were putting out a diesel. With the first nuclear reactor, there was a multitude of data to collect and trials to do. And it was the ship's force instead of an EB trial crew, and not everybody at EB was happy about that. They would have liked to see us stumble, but we didn't.

Paul Stillwell: Were the 50 people in fact helpful?

Admiral Wilkinson: Sure. We could have gotten along without them [laughter], but they were good people. They did their function and did it well, and they were probably wise in the selection of the 50 they took. After all, there were other organizations with responsibility. The General Dynamics Company was forced to build that ship, and we were to develop deficiencies and information, and they liked to have senior people there look at them. And the supervisor of shipbuilding had a responsibility, and certainly Admiral Rickover had responsibility and the Atomic Energy Commission. It was right and proper for them to have authority and representation on board, and they did. It was just that I was appalled when we were told originally to carry 122 people.

I will say that in all the pressure that was put on me by the supervisor of shipbuilding and the Chief of the Bureau of Ships in that regard, there was never any pressure from Admiral Rickover to carry more than 50, because that was an operational matter. Admiral Rickover wasn't going to differ with those words from the commanding officer of his ship. Now, Rickover fully understood the difference between a design engineer and an operating engineer. It might feel different to some of the engineering duty only officers like the Chief of the Bureau of Ships.

Let me just jump back a minute to the *Wahoo*. The boat ahead of us up at Portsmouth, the *Tang*, had ruptured their fuel tanks from over-pressurizing a tank. As a matter of fact my quartermaster, Teixeira, on the *Nautilus* had been on the *Tang* at the time, and I can remember talking to my officers and talking about the importance of absolutely proper lineups.[*] I said, "Now, when it comes to, for example, the fuel lineups all I ask is that you be able to say to me, 'Captain, with that hand I checked the valve myself.'" [Laughter]

After the *Nautilus* was delivered and we'd been out operating, we went into dry dock for the first time. They were pumping down, and there were Ralph Kissinger and a couple of BuShips admirals. Kissinger was a brilliant EDO captain.[†] As we started to pump down, there was a bulge in the expansion tank, in the fuel oil system. Ralph pointed down and said, "You people have lined up wrong and over-pressured your expansion tank." And clear across the dock was my main propulsion assistant, Lieutenant Nicholson, whom that was under.[‡] He could see where Captain Kissinger was pointing, and he knew that he was pointing down toward the expansion tank.

We all knew our ship totally. I was qualified enough on the *Nautilus* that I could have stood on the dock blindfolded and gone aboard and gone somewhere and turned on

---

[*] Quartermaster First Class John P. Teixeira, USN.
[†] Captain Ralph Kissinger, Jr., USN.
[‡] Lieutenant John H. Nicholson, USN, later a vice admiral.

a switch and said, "This light bulb will be warm." [Laughter] I mean, I was thoroughly qualified in that ship. I personally could stand any watch. So when Ralph Kissinger pointed down clear across the dock, Lieutenant Nicholson knew exactly what he was pointing at. He held up his hand and put his other hand around his wrist, which said to me, "Captain, with that hand I checked those valves myself."

So when Ralph said, "You're guys have screwed up," I said, "Bullshit. [Laughter] There isn't anybody on *Nautilus* that has lined up any fuel system wrong. You've got a design problem. We are going faster than ships did before. We're making 20 knots. We're going up and down with 30-degree angles. You probably don't have a big enough vent line."

Ralph said, "What an insidious attack!" But when they went back and computed, that's what it was. [Laughter] They didn't have a big enough vent line to handle that rate of change in depth and a concurrent rate of change in sea pressure, so it had caused just a little bit of overpressure because it wasn't venting fast enough. But I can remember I was so proud of Nicholson because clear across the dry dock he held that hand up, one arm up with his fist doubled and the other hand around his wrist, which said my own words back to me, "Captain, with that hand I checked it myself."

Paul Stillwell: Did you operate out of New London once the Navy accepted the ship?

Admiral Wilkinson: Yes, we had to tie up somewhere, and we moored over at State Pier where the squadron, Submarine Squadron Ten, and their tender were. The skipper of tender then was a pretty good guy, smart guy named Pinky Baer.* He wasn't a friendly guy, loved by all his people, but he was very capable. And *Nautilus* after delivery was still under the operational control of ComSubLant.

Forward of the tender where there was a long, narrow part of the pier, maybe eight feet wide. And inboard of that was a big building, but where the tender was moored there wasn't the building inboard, so there were acres of pier space. The *Nautilus*'s design was such that if you went aft from the sail structure, there was a gap between the

---

* Captain Donald G. Baer, USN.

last deck and the rudder, which stuck up out of the water. We used to burn a light on that rudder so nobody would run into it and damage it when we were at anchor or in port.

We came in one day and tied up at State Pier, forward of the tender, at the place where the dock is maybe eight feet wide, which I'll get to with another story in a minute. My duty officer, who was Bill Layman, one of my four original engineers, wanted to get a light up on the rudder.[*] He tried to get a boat from the tender to come over and carry our people back to do that. The boat didn't come right away, and he tried again. When the boat still didn't come, he got mad and swam back there and put the light up.

All was well, except the next morning I guess Pinky Baer was a little bit incensed at us and my duty officer. So I was called up to the squadron commander's office on the tender, and Pinky launched into a diatribe. It probably lasted about 30 minutes about how my officer had misbehaved and endangered his own safety. Then there wouldn't have been a duty officer on board to look out for the safety of the ship and the reactor, and some disciplinary action ought to be taken against him.

All that was embellished with quite a few other allegations. Finally Pinky ran down, and I said, "Captain, I could spend a long time talking to every one of those things you've mentioned, but let me just sum it up by saying you're not always right." I paused for tick-tock, tick-tock, a couple of seconds on the metronome, and then I said, "And what's more, your jack's upside down."[†] [Laughter] I had observed it coming up the pier to go aboard the tender and talk to the squadron commander, who was Ozzie Lynch.[‡] What I said appealed to Lynch, because he'd just heard 30 minutes of diatribe and 30 seconds of response.

Paul Stillwell: And Lynch was senior to Baer.

Admiral Wilkinson: Oh, yes, he was Baer's boss. Baer was flying Lynch's flag, and his

---

[*] Lieutenant William H. Layman, USN.
[†] The union jack is a small flag that amounts to a portion of a U.S. national flag--the part with white stars on a blue background. It is typically flown from a jackstaff on the bow of a Navy ship when she is moored or anchored.
[‡] Captain Richard B. Lynch, USN.

squadron was berthed on the tender. Well, Ozzie said, "What an insidious attack, Pinky. Do you think he's bluffing you?" With that, Pinky grabbed his cap and went out there from his stateroom, which was nearby. And, of course, the jack was upside down or I wouldn't have said that I'd seen it on the way up the pier. Suddenly we could just hear the blasphemy and cursing and his voice raised and hell being raised getting that jack squared away. A little while later Pinky Baer came back in and took his hat off and threw it down. Then he went into his stateroom and slammed the door without another word. [Laughter] A really humorous incident.

Paul Stillwell: And you didn't even mention that the tender refused to provide a boat.

Admiral Wilkinson: Oh, no. No, no. I was not going to go into all that crap. I just said, "Let me sum it up by saying you're not always right, and what's more your jack's upside down." [Laughter] I can understand Pinky Baer being upset with us, because we had a lot of important visitors coming to us, and I used to fuss with him all the time that they ought to clean up that goddamn area where all their garbage cans were out there. It was embarrassing to me to have senior officers walking by and them having sailors out on the dock that were out of uniform and it smelled bad. And I guess the commanding officer of a tender didn't like to be bitched at by a much junior skipper of the *Nautilus* about how fouled up it looked out there.

One time I was going to have the Secretary of the Navy Thomas come and ride the *Nautilus*.[*] We were tied up at State Pier, and that was where we were going to take him aboard. And so I especially wanted to have things looking nice. Really in retrospect they couldn't have made it look perfect. But I went to the city authority and got permission to do a little improvement of the part of the State Pier that I tied up to, which was just forward of the tender and was somewhere between six and eight feet wide. So just the day before the Secretary of the Navy was going to come down, I had my sailors paint that with white enamel, and all the bollards that we tied up to were painted a jet black. When the Secretary of the Navy came down, the *Nautilus* itself was a jet shiny black and the wind blowing and the colors flapping and our lines looked marvelous, and

---

[*] Charles S. Thomas served as Secretary of the Navy from 3 May 1954 to 1 April 1957.

our brow undoubtedly was to perfection. So he came down this dirty old pier and passed the tender and turned the corner, and there the dock is pristine white and the bollards were black, and the *Nautilus* looked great and he came aboard. I can see that might have annoyed the tender skipper, but I had told him he should straighten things out over there. [Laughter] We had a real good trip taking Secretary Thomas out, and things like that are important. When you take the Secretary of the Navy out and he's making very commendatory comments to all that he comes in contact with, it's really good for the morale of your ship.

Besides the things we were doing in the nuclear field, we had some impact on other programs than our own. The submarine force really needed a new and better torpedo. We were still carrying Mark 14s and Mark 23s and Mark 18s, the torpedoes from World War II. When you have a torpedo, every three months you give it some routines and tests. You have a torpedo book, and you open it up, and the senior torpedoman who did that signs the book that all the routines and tests were properly done. The leading torpedoman up in my forward torpedo room was a first class torpedoman named Fields.[*] And Fields was quite knowledgeable, being the first man on the ship to qualify in the *Nautilus* and also being a very competent torpedoman.

When we would get congressional people aboard and I would tell them that our torpedoes were antiquated and we needed new torpedoes they'd say, "Oh, yes." And if my young torpedo officer, a lieutenant, said it, the visitor said, "Is that so? Oh, is that so?" But if Fields said it, it was gospel; had been a torpedoman in World War II. So we got so all the important congressional people that came, we talked to them about the problem with the torpedoes. So we hunted out around the submarine force and got some torpedoes that had been on Fields's ship in World War II. They'd never fired, and they were still in the inventory of torpedoes that the submarine force had. In Fields's speech he'd say, "These are the same torpedoes that we had during World War II." And then he'd say, "Sir, I don't mean the same kind of torpedo. I mean the same torpedoes." [Laughter] Then he'd pull out the record book with his name in it where he'd put the routines in back in '44. And, let me tell you, people's mouths would drop, and the

---

[*] Torpedoman First Class George W. Fields, USN.

submarine force didn't have any trouble getting the Mark 48 torpedo program through. I gave Fields a lot of credit for that.

The noise in the starboard shaft when we first got under way was sheet metal touching. That wasn't us. That was an installation error. There was nothing during my time on *Nautilus* where something went wrong because one of our guys made an error. As a matter of fact, our guys were fantastically good. They carried out their orders admirably. There's little I ever told them to do they didn't do.

I had one fine example one day. The telephone rang, and it was the Marine lieutenant at the base saying, "We've caught one of your troops stealing government material."

I said, "I find that hard to believe, but what's his name?" They told me his name, and it was one of my electricians. I said, "I know him very well. I find it even harder to believe. What did he steal?"

He said, "A Navy flashlight."

I was able to reach up and pull down the book and said, "Was it number 47?"

"Yes."

I said, "Every man on the *Nautilus* carries a flashlight, and I've ordered them to always have that flashlight available. [Laughter] He's doing just what he's been told to do, and I'd like it if you'd apologize to him and let him go and keep his flashlight." [Laughter] Silly story. But just like everybody did have a flashlight, and everybody was signed for it, and we had it in the book. It's just like we could have reached up and pulled out another book that listed all our ship's company, every man, whether he was married and where he came from, what state. I've had a congressman call me up and say, "Do you have anybody on board from the state of Ohio?"

We were able to reach and pull down the book and say, "Would you like to have his folk's name and their address?"

Paul Stillwell: Well, you talked about Rickover's people, and there's another story that I think is useful and that's how you got them to appoint a delegate so you didn't have to deal with all seven trying to run your people.

Admiral Wilkinson: Well, Rickover's people were good, and they probably weren't as experienced then as they became later because they were learning too. But they were crackerjack people, and they wanted to do things. We had different experts, and so we happened to have seven of them out at sea with us on the trials. Rickover himself wasn't there on this one. Each one of these experts was going around talking to my people, telling them what they ought to be doing and what needed to be done, and that was a lot of pressure. Finally my chief engineer, Les Kelly, who was no sissy, came up to me and said, "Captain; I can't take this anymore. Man that's bothering me, I'll break his leg in a watertight door."

I said, "Les, those are my kind of problems. You go back there and do your job, and I'll take care of that." Then I got all seven of them in a room and told them I was pleased to have them on board and pleased with the support, and we wanted to be responsive as we could be. But it was hard for us because there were so many of them, and if they would just pick out the one that was their representative, and anything he wanted if he'd come and talk to me they'd just be amazed at how responsive we were. So I went away and they were in a room by themselves, and I guess they decided.

The one they picked really wasn't the dominant person in their organization, but they decided for the protocol reason that the person that would speak should be their representative in New London. So they picked Willie Shor, whom I mentioned earlier. They said, "Commander Shor is our spokesman, and we want you to bleed and feed." It took two hours and 40 minutes for them to make a decision it was Shor, during which time my people were undisturbed doing their tests and whatnot.

Bleeding and feeding means taking some of the pure water that's in the core out and replacing it with other pure water, but unfortunately that other pure water is apt to have dissolved oxygen in it, and oxygenated water is not good in a core. As a matter of fact, we keep hydrogen in it to depress any oxygen content. With my background as a chemist, there was just no way that I was going to do that to a nuclear core. So I said, "Willie, I want to compliment you on being the representative, and if there's anything else we'd just love to do it, but if it comes to bleeding and feeding water in our core, by God, we're not going to do it. You go back and talk to the chemical experts and come back." So that didn't work out. "But anything else you'll be amazed how responsive we'll be." It's too bad they picked that item. We never did. After they talked to the chemists they never came back. [Laughter]

Paul Stillwell: But I think the point was that both sides were sort of feeling their way, and much later they had more authority than they did at that time.

Admiral Wilkinson: Yes. I don't want this to sound wrong. Superbly competent people, totally motivated, totally dedicated, and gaining more knowledge all the time. And by the time you got down to the 20th submarine, there wasn't any doubt they knew more about what needed to be done and what we were doing than the people on the submarine. But the *Nautilus* was different. We had been in on it since the beginning. Nobody knew more about it than our people did. Oh, in some individual area I'm sure that expert would in the design or something, but when it came to the overall business of operating that plant and its problems our people were really the best qualified.

Again, there's the little bit of the phenomenon that I've mentioned before. Sometimes the people that work for a man will mistakenly take actions that he would not himself. Rickover would have probably been appalled if we were bleeding and feeding oxygenated water into our core. It's just like when the *Nautilus* was being built. I'll give an example. *Nautilus* had the primary reactor system with water on the core that was under 2,000 pounds of pressure, and the yard was always doing something to that. A 2,000-pound pressure system happened to be tested to a pressure of 3,750 pounds, and every time as the construction was going on they seemed to work on some piece of pipe or something in that system time and time again. After each time when they finished the job they wanted to put a 3,750-pound pressure test on it. I was afraid that somewhere that might damage something else. So after doing that a couple of times one day I said, "No more, no more. We'll do one more 3,750-pound pressure test. I don't care where it is, when it is. I'll do it right now or I'll do it the last day, whenever you want. But let me tell you as the operators we're only going to do it one more time."

Well, of course, that antagonized all of them, so they went and complained to Admiral Rickover that Wilkinson wouldn't put on the requisite pressure test. He told them, "You people must be out of your minds risking damage in the system like that.

There'll be no more pressure tests." [Laughter] Rickover, too, was an operator. But, as I say, sometimes people mistakenly will do things that supreme authority himself wouldn't do. I've seen that time and time again in life where people do for a boss what they think he wants when it's not what he wants at all and he wouldn't do it himself. And you have to fight against that. You've got to be especially careful of that with the people that are working for you. I guess in my entire career I have tried my utmost to make sure that doesn't happen to me, because I've been the head guy in lots of organizations where the people were eager to do well.

Paul Stillwell: Over eager sometimes.

Admiral Wilkinson: Yes.

Paul Stillwell: What's the story involved with the *Saturday Evening Post*?

Admiral Wilkinson: I don't know whether I can tell that properly. Right over there in that pile of stuff I got prepared for your coming I've got all the correspondence from Hugh Morrow, the guy that wrote the articles for the *Saturday Evening Post* after listening to me talk. I've got copies of the two articles, too, right there which go back to '55.* And I've got letters over here from the Navy Department and the press handout and my speech at a press conference that was given. But, without going through all of those things accurately just as a sort of an overview, let me say that as the *Nautilus* was getting ready to go to sea, the Navy wanted for the story to be told. Different magazines approached me, and the best one seemed to be the *Saturday Evening Post*. Arrangements were made for the *Saturday Evening Post* to hear my story and put it into words and publish it, giving the story of those first sea trials of *Nautilus*.

    This was done after I talked to the guy and he wrote it up and I reviewed it and corrected it. I have the first draft copy and the corrected copy in that file over there and the final thing that was issued, which matches the corrected copy, and the corrected copy

---

* Commander E. P. Wilkinson, USN, as told to Hugh Morrow, "We Took the Atom Sub to Sea," *Saturday Evening Post*, 9 April 1955, pages 17-19, plus continuation; 16 April 1955, pages 38-39 plus continuation.

that after I had reworded a little what he wrote from listening to me on tape. The corrected copy was authorized by the Navy Department, processed through the Navy Department for security review, all properly done. And all the authorities that be, senior officers in the office of the CNO, the head of Chinfo, everybody had given their blessing. The Navy had reviewed it. It was properly handled. The only thing that wasn't done was nobody bothered to brief the Secretary of Defense, Engine Charlie Wilson, on it.[*] But then a rival news person complained to him at a press conference about privilege being given to *Saturday Evening Post*, and incidentally for my work in the article, *Saturday Evening Post* paid $7,500, which was a lot of money in 1955.

Paul Stillwell: Probably more than your salary.

Admiral Wilkinson: Yes, but I earned it. I worked hard on helping write that article, although I probably didn't work that hard. But in the ensuing discussion Secretary Wilson was sort of sandbagged into saying he wouldn't have an officer like that that would do something for his own profit and not properly authorized in the service. That was me, but I hadn't done anything that hadn't been properly cleared and properly authorized and properly handled. And so the senior officers—and I could show you some of the correspondence over here—in fact that authorized and reviewed and stood behind me said, "But the one thing, Dennis, you have to hold a press briefing for everybody so that one place won't have a benefited thing." That had been planned already, and so we held a press briefing on the 30th of March 1955. I briefed all the news people that were interested, and there were many, about the initial trials and operations of the *Nautilus*. Here's a copy of my press briefing right there. But it was sticky for a couple of days.

Paul Stillwell: Who got you off the hook with the Secretary of Defense?

Admiral Wilkinson: Senior people in the Navy Department stood behind me.

---

[*] Charles E. Wilson served as Secretary of Defense from 28 January 1953 to 8 October 1957. He was nicknamed "Engine Charlie" because he had previously been chairman of the board of General Motors.

Paul Stillwell: What factors had led you to choose the *Post* in particular?

Admiral Wilkinson: I can't remember except Hugh Morrow had talked to me, and he was an impressive guy, and he's the guy that wrote it for me or corrected my words. And it was well done. A lot of my people were mentioned by name and the jobs they'd done, and that wasn't bad for the morale of the ship. In the articles, if you look at them, there's a considerable amount of credit given for the performance of various of my people, and I was pleased to see that happen. And it was a good account. This is the account of that first four days that we've talked about, and it went well, and it was well done. I don't know why I picked *Saturday Evening Post*. Maybe they offered me more money than anybody else, $7,500. [Laughter] But also it was one of the better magazines at the time. The *Saturday Evening Post* did have the right coverage, and it was respectable, and it was a good magazine at the time, and it had a good reputation. There were other magazines. I don't know whether *Collier's* was still printing. I think it was.

Paul Stillwell: Yes.

Admiral Wilkinson: But *Saturday Evening Post* probably had the best reputation and it was a good place to run it, and they wrote good articles.

One of the best men we had on the *Nautilus* was a fire control chief named Al Crossick. Crossick was a bachelor, and he was really a superb photographer. That was his hobby. He had a fantastic amount of his personal funds sunk into photographic equipment. Many times Crossick was of great value to us on the ship in taking pictures. We had the ability to schedule family cruises where we took all our wives to sea and our ex-wives. By that I mean the wives of people that had been crew members of the *Nautilus* and then been transferred. And we took all the *Seawolf* wives and we took all the SubLant wives and we really exhausted ourselves.* In three days we made eight trips carrying out our wives and *Seawolf* and SubLant wives.

---

* USS *Seawolf* (SSN-575), commissioned 30 March 1957, was the Navy's second nuclear-powered submarine.

Paul Stillwell: Taking them on dives?

Admiral Wilkinson: Took them out to sea and took them on a dive. My wife made five of those trips. And every one of those wives looked through the periscope, and Crossick took a picture of every one. We developed them and gave every wife a picture of herself conning the ship looking through the scope and some other pictures too. In many ways Crossick was of great value to us, and he took an awful lot of pictures and a lot of pictures of us making torpedo approaches and one thing and another.

Sometime later we had the misfortune of having a helicopter drop a helicopter pilot on afterdeck of *Nautilus* visiting the ship and break his back. Then he got well, and a year or so later we were back in Bermuda and happened to visit him and his family. Crossick shot so much film he didn't always print it all, but when we got to Bermuda he pulled out his negatives of the time and darned if he didn't have a picture of the guy in the air, which was quite a memento when we gave it to him and his wife. Crossick was fantastic, and I have a letter from him right over there, because I hear from him to this day.

Paul Stillwell: Well, please tell me the story about the man with the broken back.

Admiral Wilkinson: When the *Nautilus* went into commission, it was big stuff, and we had a lot of good publicity. The word went out from many sources that now the other submarines were obsolete. Let me tell you, we had a lot of really good, proud submarines, and they didn't feel obsolete. We operated in company with and sometimes in opposition to some of those submarines. The other word was that now the ASW forces couldn't hack it anymore. They were obsolete. And let me tell you they didn't feel obsolete. And we operated time and time again in exercises against them. And every man's hand was turned against us. They did their very utmost to outperform us in exercises.

For example, I would operate against our very silent hunter-killer submarines, and there isn't any doubt that they didn't make the noise that we did. When *Nautilus* was cruising along, without the sound isolation that propulsion systems have today, she would shake, rattle, and roll. *Nautilus* was noisy when she was moving at speed, and an SSK silenced is very silent.* So I would be pitted in exercises against them, and I'd do my utmost to win. If we were in an area with one of them, immediately I rang up all stop, and I did not move at all. If some other submarine wanted to shoot me, they had to come to me. I'd just lie there doggo. That SSK's battery would run low, and eventually he'd have to light off his diesel and charge his batteries. Now he made noise. I'd hear him, and I'd creep toward him, and if he secured his diesel I stopped again. It might take three or four days, but finally I'd creep up on him and plug him.

I don't think any one of them ever defeated us in an exercise, but we did it with a different kind of operational patience. Now with the ASW forces on the surface it wasn't that same way. We could crank up to speed and whistle under the layer and maneuver around and use that capability. But anytime we were working against the ASW forces the surface of the sea was forbidden. If you stuck anything above the surface, all the radar search that was being done by the aircraft forces, by the poopy baggers, by the surface ships, so when I operated against the ASW forces I never stuck anything above the surface.† I did it all by sonar. So it was a question of using what capability you had. And it's really true that the forces were against us. Among the things that were done to us by the ASW forces in evaluations were literally hundreds of ASW weapons without explosives in them, but ASW weapons were fired at us in an effort to make a successful attack on us and have them hit the hull. Conservatively we estimated it at about the time I left that we had had 5,500 ASW weapons fired at us, and of those 5,500 the hits were zero. It's improper for us to joke that way, but jokingly the only thing that they ever hit us with was a visitor that was dropped out of a helicopter and fell and hit our deck.

Paul Stillwell: How did the mishap happen?

Admiral Wilkinson: Visitors were being transferred to us, and the hatch was open when the helicopter was up and the normal procedure was to let a ladder out, and the guy would climb down. We were holding the ladder at the bottom, and he stepped up on deck, and

---

* SSK was the designation for the hunter-killer, a type of diesel submarine specialized for operations against other submarines.
† Poopy bag is a reference to a Navy blimp, a non-rigid, helium-filled airship.

the next visitor up there climbed down the ladder. As they opened the hatch there was some kind of a screw-up. Instead of getting the ladder out, the first person fell out. I don't know exactly, but he fell maybe 20-25 feet, hit the deck and bounced, and started to slide over the side, which would have been into our screws. One of my electricians that was in the party there to receive the people aboard leaned over and grabbed him as he was slipping down the side and pulled him back.

We had on board a doctor who was our health physics expert. They don't carry doctors now, but in the beginning we did. Doctor Ebersole recognized that the man was injured and sent for a stretcher.* They put him in the stretcher and back to the helicopter and back to the carrier. My doctor was concerned; he came up to me an hour or so later and, "Captain, how's our injured man doing?" So I called the carrier and asked, and they said he was doing fine. And my doctor said, "Captain, tell them he's got a broken back."

So I told them, "Hey, my doctor says your man has a broken back. Now, what are you doing?" They checked, and, sure enough, he did have a broken back, which had not been identified over there. He also had a damaged spleen and some other things. I'm showing you the "Well Done" file, which is a big file of letters and messages from higher authority telling the *Nautilus* what a fine job she'd been doing. One of my prized letters in that file is a letter from the wife of this injured flier that says that her husband had fallen on my ship and been injured with his back broken and his spleen damaged. But that he was on the road to recovery and was going to get well. She said she understood that if it hadn't been for the fast action of one my troops that grabbed him as he was going over the side, that he might not be recovering this day. And she didn't even know the man's name and asked if I would say "Thank you" to him for her? And that was a real nice letter. And I did.

A year or so later we went back to Bermuda again, and the guy was completely recovered. The electrician that had kept him from falling over the side was still aboard. And Crossick, my photographer, got down in his files and got a picture of him in the air and we were all invited out to dinner and went out and just had a marvelous time. The guy himself was a super cook and we had fish and we had a great time visiting them. The wife got to say "Thank you" to the troop that had rescued her husband, and we were

---

* Lieutenant John H. Ebersole, Medical Corps, USN.

happy to see all was well. So later on we had no trepidation in telling the story that the only thing they ever hit us with was a visitor they dropped on deck. [Laughter]

Paul Stillwell: That's remarkable.

Please tell the story about the ship's oxygen supply, because this is a new thing for a submarine to be submerged for long periods.

Admiral Wilkinson: Heretofore submarines, even the snorkel submarines, had a tube open in which fresh air was coming down to run the engines. When submarines were submerged without that open, just on a battery for extended periods of time, eventually they surfaced and got fresh air. If they didn't, they carried candles that would make oxygen and absorbent that would pick up the carbon dioxide so they could purify their air for 72 hours. But here was a new design ship that you would like to be able to submerge for long periods of time. The longest period of time that *Nautilus* was submerged while I was on it was 30 days independent of the earth's atmosphere. But although we had 72 hours' worth of candles and CO_2 absorbent, certainly we couldn't carry enough oxygen that way to stay submerged indefinitely, not the length of time, for example, that the *Triton* did when she followed Magellan's course around the world.*

So we had systems installed to purify our air. We had an oxygen generator that by electrolysis separated oxygen and hydrogen from water, and the hydrogen was pumped overboard and the oxygen was distributed throughout the ship. With a lot of effort and maintenance and whatnot we were able to make it run. But also when you breathe you make carbon dioxide, and if you smoke or sometimes from other things, cooking, you make carbon monoxide. I don't get a headache. I'm a very good indicator. My head aches just at 24 parts per million carbon monoxide.

Now, we had dryer kits to measure carbon dioxide and carbon monoxide and whatnot, but the system that we had with the methyl-ethylamine and whatnot we were able to keep our carbon dioxide, the highest level it got to was 1.25%. But that's more than you would like and perhaps to put to that concentration of carbon dioxide for

---

* In the spring of 1960, the USS *Triton* (SSN-586), commanded by Captain Edward L. Beach, USN, made the first submerged circumnavigation of the world. Commissioned in November 1959, she was ostensibly a radar-picket submarine but actually a test ship for a two-reactor propulsion plant.

extended periods of time you could even have some formative brain damage. So we fussed quite strongly about some of the problems with our air purification system, and finally we were given a hydrogen burner with a certain catalyst that we could eliminate the carbon monoxide. Processing the air through there changed any carbon monoxide to carbon dioxide, and then our system with the methyl-ethylamine and a regenerative cycle that we took out the carbon dioxide. But there was a long struggle with lots of effort from that section of Bureau of Ships to make our air purification systems work. And over time that was done, and eventually before I left *Nautilus* did make a continuous 30-day submergence.

Now our Trident submarines can go out and be independent of the earth's atmosphere for 75 days.* The limit of endurance is how much food they carry. With *Nautilus* the limit of endurance certainly wasn't the nuclear plant. Eventually we got the air purification system fixed enough that that wasn't the limit of endurance. When I left the *Nautilus* the limit of endurance was the factor of how much lube oil we carried because you used a certain amount of lube oil as you're lubricating your equipment. Other than food, that was the limit, and food you were able to carry 90 days' worth. Once for some other reason we loaded up to where we had a 120-day supply of food.

But back to your question, we had real troubles with our air purification system, and we got quite a bit of support from the responsible people in the Bureau of Ships, Red Gates and people like that. Eventually, with that heroic effort, they improved our system so as I said we were finally able to make a 30-day submergence. In the process at the time, though, we were quite vocal in our complaints in telephone calls and in correspondence. Do you want me to tell you about our canary?

Paul Stillwell: I'd be disappointed if you didn't.

Admiral Wilkinson: We were operating down off Florida out of Key West one day and maybe 10-15 miles offshore. We had been submerged. We'd surface. Beautiful blue sky. Blue sea. As a submarine surfaces the first person who hits the bridge is the

---

* USS *Ohio* (SSBN-726), the first of a class of nuclear powered submarines armed with the Trident ballistic missile, was approved in the early 1970s. She was laid down 10 April 1976, launched 7 April 1979, and commissioned 11 November 1981. The ship is 560 feet long and displaces 18,750 tons submerged.

captain. After the hatch cleared the water, we opened the hatch, and I went up, and so I was the first person up on the bridge. And, lo and behold, a poor wild canary, which had been fluttering around up there 10-15 miles from land for I don't know how long, landed on the bridge right three feet in front of me. It was so tired that it couldn't move. I was able to reach out and pick it up in my hand. Now, as it happened we had in the wardroom a tame canary suspended in a cage that was on gimbals. As the *Nautilus* would go up and down and sometimes maneuver at a 30-degree angle, the cage with gravity would spin out 30, and the canary would go "Peep, peep, peep." So I went down from the bridge and opened that cage and stuck the wild canary in there. But I guess he'd had a really hard time, because shortly thereafter he died.

So I said, "Gee, now's a good time to write another letter to the Bureau of Ships complaining about our air." So we wrote a nice letter that said, "We've been having trouble with our air, and so like some miners we had a pet canary that we watched and the problem is that recently our canary had died." Actually it wasn't our pet, but it was this wild canary. And we needed some more work done on our air purification system. So we made a nice little sealed Lucite box, with cotton in it and put this poor dead canary in there on his back, feet up in the air. He looked so pitiful. And that was one of the enclosures to the letter. We had a lot of fun on the *Nautilus*.

Paul Stillwell: Did you get an answer to your letter?

Admiral Wilkinson: Everybody enjoyed that letter when we wrote it, and we got some more action out of the Bureau of Ships. Eventually they even got our system fixed. I talk about the Trident submarines now going out, and they're totally independent of the earth's atmosphere for as long as they want to stay and the systems in all the submarines work superbly well. But that wasn't under the jurisdiction of Rickover, and in the beginning we had a lot of problems getting our air purification debugged.

Paul Stillwell: Were there any psychological difficulties for being under water that long a period of time? That's certainly longer than submariners were used to being under.

Admiral Wilkinson: No, I don't think so. This is not quite the answer to your question, but it's apropos in another way. I've been asked at times how long you could stay at sea, and my answer is as long as it's necessary. I could stay for a year and keep the morale high if there was a reason. But let me tell you, if it was one weekend that there wasn't a reason, morale would be bad. [Laughter] So psychologically a submarine, whether it's surfaced or submerged, all the people are down in that pipe. The only people that are topside are the OOD and a couple of lookouts, and so it really is no different to most of the people whether they're surfaced or submerged as long as the air is good. As a matter of fact, if the weather's at all rough and you're rocking and rolling around, it's a lot more comfortable to be submerged. So I wouldn't say there was any psychological problem at all. Now, there are people that have a psychological problem with being enclosed and being in a small space. But we don't have any of those kinds of people in submarines to start with.

Paul Stillwell: They've been weeded out already.

Admiral Wilkinson: They've been weeded out before they go to submarines by psychological tests and psychiatric tests. Also remember especially in those days—I don't know if it's still the case—everybody who went through submarines went up and escaped through an escape trainer, came up from 100 feet of water in a training escape tank. And for the period just before that a guy was in a small container put to 50 pounds pressure. It's true that once in a while at that place they'd have a guy whose ears would hurt. Sometimes that was psychological, but certainly in the submarine itself we never had any of those kinds of people. So being submerged was only a relief in being out of rough weather.

Paul Stillwell: You told me a story when the tape wasn't running that had to do with the sail and some vibrations.

Admiral Wilkinson: That part of the ship design and construction not under Rickover was maybe not done as carefully and certainly with not as much checkout as the nuclear part. After all there wasn't the rest of a hull built somewhere getting checked like the space from the forward reactor compartment to the end of the engine room had been at the prototype. So we had many other new things and new characteristics. We had a shape going through the water that was going much faster than any submarine had ever done before. And with water flow past the ballast tank openings and water flow past the ship's structure, as it turned out we had what's called the Von Karman vortices or disturbances in the water at the tail end of our sail structure.* And we had a Helm-Holtz resonator effect, which is like whistling over an open hole, over the open flood openings.

Those things exerted a force on the ship that made the ship actually vibrate. I could take a cup of coffee and set it carefully on the wardroom table, and it would get a standing wave in it from the ship vibrating. Not only did this make a certain amount of noise and have interference with the sonar, I'm sure the energy slowed our speed a little bit, maybe a hundredth of a knot, but also the ship vibrated, and I was worried that it would in fact do damage to physical structure. I complained to the Bureau of Ships, and I was told, "No," that it was safe enough. But I was able to say back, "What about these places that the structure is breaking apart up here in the forward part of my ship?"

That terrified everybody, and experts came and we put covers over our ballast tank openings that we could open and shut, and they changed the shape of the trailing edge of the sail. That eliminated the Von Karman vortices. The ship quit vibrating and got a little bit quieter and maybe went a hundredth of a knot faster, and the vibration went away. Undoubtedly we had some other things that were squared away. For example, we had some trouble with some periscopes, and that wasn't as hard a problem. It was straightened out. Not everything was perfect when the *Nautilus* first went to sea, but it was good enough that we could have operated it as a vehicle of war and been better than anything they ever had before. It's fantastic that everything was done so well and the *Nautilus* operated as well as it did. And put into very extensive operations against the best the Navy had at that time, we were able to turn back all comers. And that's in spite of a few little problems that weren't minor, but they weren't major enough to cause us to tie up and not operate the ship.

---

* Theodore von Karman (1881-1963) was an engineer and physicist who did important work in the area of aerodynamics. The principle of the von Karman vortex is applicable in both air and water, in that flow over a surface that is not streamlined produces turbulence.

Paul Stillwell: How soon did you get those structural things squared away after you started operating?

Admiral Wilkinson: That was a long time ago; and it's all a little hazy in my mind; I don't know exactly. But it wasn't very damn long because it was a bad thing. I mean, if you're the captain of a ship operating submerged and you're getting a standing wave in a cup of coffee sitting on your wardroom table, it worries you. And so that one we screamed fast on. The hull shaking and vibrating thing was identified, and an effective solution decided on and accomplished in really a quite short time. That must have been done within the first two or three months of operation when we came in from sea. And when we came in we got heroic effort on the part of the Boat Company to come and do this or that and great support.

We also had a problem with some pipes. Admiral Rickover brought a group of 12 congressmen down to Key West. We had had a problem the night before, and we freeze-sealed some stainless steel piping on both sides of the problem because we didn't have valves in the system. The guys went in and did it, and the next morning we couldn't get under way on time with normal heat up. And I told them, "Hell, heat up with the reactor." And they did and we met our operational commitment like we always did.

Paul Stillwell: By freeze sealing you meant you froze the contents of the pipe on each side of the problem?

Admiral Wilkinson: Right, so it was stopped with ice, solid. And so we could cut into a system that had hot water under pressure on the other side of it and do our work and melt the free seal. And the job was done and we isolated a place where there was a problem and fixed it without any valves to isolate it. You understand?

Paul Stillwell: I understand what you're saying.

Admiral Wilkinson: You understand what I'm saying. As the *Nautilus* was being built and as we were training and getting prepared, we knew that there was going to be problems, and that one was a special stainless steel piping and that we could have to weld it. And maybe in some cases the piping would be radioactive because the fluid we were looking at happened to be water that was used to cool the core and became radioactive. You had to see how long a guy could work on that piece of pipe, because you wanted to keep exposure to a minimum. So how many people should we have that were qualified stainless steel welders? Well, how much work are you going to have? How much radiation? How many guys should we really qualify as stainless steel welders? So we qualified them all. [Laughter]

All 40-odd guys and the four officers that were in our engineering department qualified as stainless steel welders. Not all of them were that good, but years later we still had five or six guys that were really fantastically good stainless steel welders. Rickover had done his job so well that one would have been enough, but in the beginning the entire engineering force qualified as stainless steel welders. Now, unless you have a little bit of an engineering background, that might not impress you as much as it impresses me. It's not easy to be a qualified stainless steel welder.

A couple of years later, when I no longer had the ship, they were under the Arctic icecap. This wasn't on their polar transit trip, but they came up in a polynya and ran into ice and bent over their number-one periscope, split the pipe, and ruined that periscope. If that periscope had been in the optical shop in the tender they would have thrown it away. But, gee, they really wanted a periscope up there. So they took hydraulic jacks and they straightened it out, and they brought up their best stainless steel welders and they welded it up and they turned it down to the right dimensions. And they brought a lead up from the engine room and took a vacuum on it with the vacuum in the main condenser. And then they purged it with nitrogen and they took a vacuum again and then put nitrogen in it. And they made it work again. The couple of guys that did that were pretty damn good stainless steel welders.

Paul Stillwell: Please tell me about Admiral Burke's visit to the *Nautilus*.

Admiral Wilkinson: One time we had the pleasure of taking the CNO, Admiral Arleigh Burke, to sea.* We were supposed to get under way at 0800. I was tied up at the pier at Electric Boat Company, and the admiral came aboard at about three minutes of 8:00. I carried a lot of senior officers. I had ten foul weather parkas reserved for that with wool gloves in one pocket and a wool watch cap in the other pocket. And it was really nice sometimes to see some old sea dog that maybe was now on duty in Washington and hadn't been to sea for a while to reach down there and pull out that watch cap and put it on his head and really, really feel great again. Not that that happened that morning with Admiral Burke; it was a bad day. It was foggy, the visibility was zero. When he came aboard, I met him and said, "Ready to get under way, Admiral. Shall we go up to the bridge?"

We went up to the bridge, and the speaker blared with a message from our operational commander. It said, "Permission not granted to get under way." And so I said, "Excuse me a minute, Admiral."

I left the bridge and went down and I got the sub base operational command on the phone. I said, "Hey, I've got the CNO that just came aboard to take him out on operations. What is this crap? No permission to get under way?"

The base said, "The visibility is zero here at the base."

I said, "Well, the visibility is zero here too."

They thought about that for a few seconds, and they said, "Permission granted." [Laughter] So I went back up to the bridge, and we got under way a minute or two late after 8:00 o'clock. We were supposed to rendezvous at 11:00 o'clock down off Newport to join up with four destroyers to have them operate with us so they could see the capability and track us, and the Chief of Naval Operations could observe. Remember, this was 31-knot Burke, who had run the small boys at 31 knots in World War II.†

With the efficacy of our people and our radars and whatnot, we proceeded and in spite of the fog we were at our 11:00 o'clock rendezvous on time. But the four destroyers that were supposed to come down there from Newport weren't there. This rendezvous point was in water that was between 150 and 200 feet deep, and in shallow water our

---

* Admiral Arleigh A. Burke, USN, served as Chief of Naval Operations from 17 August 1955 to 1 August 1961. His oral history is in the Naval Institute collection.
† During the war Burke commanded Destroyer Squadron 23.

ability to maneuver was a little bit restricted. We couldn't take advantage of going under layers. So I said to Admiral Burke, "We're at our rendezvous point, and the other ships aren't here. It must be awfully foggy in Newport." [Laughter] And he and I both knew that it couldn't be any foggier than it was where we were. We couldn't see the stern. [Laughter] I said, "I suggest I give them another rendezvous down here at 1:00 o'clock another 30 miles down. After all they can make 31 knots." [Laughter] Admiral Burke concurred that that was a good plan. We proceeded south toward deeper water, and the destroyers were worrying. At 1:00 o'clock they were not there yet, but they were closing fast. I said, "They should be here shortly and I suggest I give them another rendezvous another five miles down here, and we'll dive."

So I did do that, and we crossed over the 100-fathom line where we got deep water, and the world was ours as far as sonar conditions and all those little things. By now we had also come out of the fog, and it was bright and beautiful. And with bones in their teeth, we could see four destroyers making 31 knots, let me tell you, coming to join up. I was steaming along submerged with lots of periscope and masts up and, zoom, they came up and formed an immediate square, right around us, 1,000 yards on a side with *Nautilus* in the middle.

We steamed along, and we submerged down to 150 feet, and we cranked up speed to 15 knots. Now they were above the layer. We were making good speed and a good wake, and they could get an echo range. Admiral Burke was watching that intently, and he said, "They're tracking you. They're right on you."

"Yes, sir, Admiral," I said. Then we eased down a little deeper, and we still hadn't gone under the sonar layer. We cranked it up to 20 knots, and they were hanging onto us.

He said, "Hey, they're tracking you."

I said, "Admiral, would you like to see us disappear?" [Laughter] He allowed he would, so we eased on down deeper and went under the layer and went into some turns and evasive things, and the world was ours. Suddenly all the destroyers were gone. [Laughter] But anyway we had a great deal of fun taking him along, and my people enjoyed it. That wasn't the only time we rode Admiral Burke or the only CNO we had aboard.

I had some crackerjack young officers. Young Lieutenant Nicholson, who was my engineer officer, had the deck when we took Admiral Carney.[*] We were operating in the area there up by Hen and Chickens lightship, and Admiral Carney told my Lieutenant Nicholson that he'd been the officer of the deck of a ship when they ran aground over there.[†] Lieutenant Nicholson said, "Admiral, you mean to tell me that you were the officer of the deck of a ship that ran aground. How did you ever get to be the CNO?" [Laughter]

Admiral Carney said, "I warned the captain that we were standing into danger, and I wrote it in the log." [Laughter]

Paul Stillwell: What do you recall about the time that Slade Cutter was on board on behalf of ComSubLant?[‡]

Admiral Wilkinson: When the *Nautilus* was built and went in commission, because of our nature we did not report into the normal force structure of a division and a squadron. The *Nautilus* reported directly to the force commander, ComSubLant, and as such the admiral was my boss and signed my fitness report.

Paul Stillwell: Was this Admiral Wilkins?

Admiral Wilkinson: I was on there four years, so I went through more than one ComSubLant, and Admiral Wilkins was one of those.[§] I had a certain amount of contact with the admiral himself. But that's not the administrative way that things are run. So the ComSubLant operations guy, who happened to be Captain Slade Cutter, a fabulous submarine operator and probably has more Navy Crosses for performance in World War

---

[*] Admiral Robert B. Carney, USN, served as Chief of Naval Operations, 17 August 1953-17 August 1955.
[†] Hen and Chickens lightship was near Buzzards Bay, Massachusetts.
[‡] See the Naval Institute oral history of Captain Slade D. Cutter, USN (Ret.). During World War II he was commanding officer of the submarine *Seahorse* (SS-304). In the 1950s he was on the staff of Commander Submarine Force Atlantic Fleet.
[§] Rear Admiral George C. Crawford, USN, served as Commander Submarine Force Atlantic Fleet from 6 November 1952 to 13 November 1954; Rear Admiral Frank T. Watkins, USN, held the billet from 13 November 1954 to 2 March 1957, and Rear Admiral Charles W. Wilkins, USN, from 2 March 1957 to 3 September 1957

II than any other, was my guy that I did business with.* I have great respect for him and thought highly of him. He at an earlier time had been in Chinfo, the office of the Chief of Naval Information office, and certainly from time to time *Nautilus* had worries and concerns in that area. Captain Cutter's expertise as a submarine operator and his knowledge of Navy public relations problems were of value to the ship. He was my nominal boss, although my formal fitness report boss was the admiral himself.

Acting for the admiral, Slade Cutter would ride me from time to time, and he was an impatient "get-it-done" guy. The time you're thinking about, Captain Cutter was riding me, but so was the admiral himself. We were out on a fleet evaluation exercise; there was a group of ships hunting us, and conversely we would hunt them. And you've got to understand when they were out operating against the *Nautilus* they did the best they could. And sometimes they didn't like us to shoot the carriers, so no carrier would come into the big operation area, but it would come up toward the edge, and the area would be covered with air search planes. They had blimps, poopy baggers, conducting search and shore-based air conducting search and all the surface ships up there with their radars rotating looking for us to break the surface.

I was out on what happened to be a four-day evaluation exercise with a load of torpedoes. Twelve hours went by, and we'd made no contact. Slade is an aggressive guy, and he said, "You've got to get up there and take a radar search and find those people." But I knew that if I stuck anything above the surface that we would be detected, and in the evaluation that would be a black mark and look bad. I don't like to be detected or get a black mark so I said, "No, I don't believe I'll do that. I'm doing a sonar search." That didn't appeal to Slade Cutter. More time went by, 24 hours, and we still hadn't made any contact, and he was becoming more and more impatient. But we held the line and didn't show ourselves. After all, I was the guy running the submarine. So I held firm, and we never came to periscope depth for anything and weren't detected.

Eventually we made a sonar contact and managed to find and penetrate a group of ships and we attacked them. One time we put real torpedoes under nine different ships in 51 minutes [Laughter], and that's not hay. Finally we fired most of our torpedoes, but I

---

* Slade D. Cutter, who by 1955 was a captain, had earned four Navy Crosses as commanding officer of the submarine *Seahorse* (SS-304) during World War II.

had four left. And I didn't want to shoot them at night when maybe they wouldn't be seen, and I didn't want to throw them away and waste them. I'd like to put them under some ships, and I'd like the people for evaluation purposes to know they were there. So I found the group of ships that had a bent-line screen of destroyers out in front of it and a screen of destroyers behind it. I eased into their formation, and I took up station behind the destroyer all the way to port in the bent-line screen. I crept up behind him to about 200 or 300 yards. I was totally shielded by his wake.

I got there about 2:30 in the morning. And this exercise happened to be scheduled to last until 6:00 A.M., which was just about sunrise. So I could get off a shot of my last four torpedoes when it was light just before the end of the exercise. So, as they maneuvered around during the night and zigged and zagged, I'd always stay 200 or 300 yards behind the port screen. Finally, at a quarter to 6:00, I peeled off and headed into the formation. We were tremendously successful in our attacks with the *Nautilus* when we were firing, but in a way we used our capability to make sure we didn't miss. Normally I would drive up till I had a broadside shot at 500 to 700 yards, and then I'd punch a torpedo out, and it's hard to miss from there. So we always made all hits with the torpedoes we fired, which looked good in your evaluations. What's more we took pictures to prove it.

So we peeled into the formation, and at four minutes of 6:00 I plugged one of them. Then I shifted over to the next target, and at three minutes to 6:00 I plugged another one. At two minutes to 6:00 I plugged another one. I had one torpedo left, and at one minute of 6:00 I plugged it under the flagship with the admiral and his staff aboard with said admiral happening to be a classmate of my boss, Admiral Watkins. At 6:00 o'clock I surfaced 500 yards abeam of the carrier and said, "Finis, King's X." [Laughter] Admiral Watkins followed me to the bridge and said to his classmate, "Charlie, how do you like them apples?" [Laughter] The fact that Slade hadn't been happy with us back in the beginning for not coming to periscope and radar depth and finding those guys faster had all evaporated away. We really had a very successful operation with the admiral aboard, and he was pleased with it.

ComSubLant was always for us and wanted us to show well. *Nautilus* could carry 24 full-sized torpedoes. We've gone out with 24 torpedoes that we could shoot in the evaluation exercise. And once SubLant stationed a tender down at Bermuda, and in the middle of the exercise after we'd shot all 24 torpedoes we just surfaced right off Bermuda and tied up to that tender and took another load and went back. They opposition never detected us or missed us, and we fired those 24. And it was an astronomical number. "How could you shoot that many?"

"Oh, we have plenty." [Laughter]

Paul Stillwell: When was the time that you were prohibited from firing at a carrier and you asked to have the picture drawn?

Admiral Wilkinson: As I said, after the *Nautilus* had been so successful in her early evaluations there was a certain competition for performance of different elements of the Navy, the black shoes and the fliers and the carriers and the cruisers and the submarines and whatnot. And you can't blame any one outfit for looking out for themselves, so finally it was decided that maybe it didn't look good for a submarine to be pushing fish under a carrier. So after that when they'd schedule an exercise the exercise area would be such that the carrier didn't enter it. But it did its functions by coming into an adjacent area and launching its planes and having the planes search for us across our area with the carrier safe geographically, which is a sort of a little bit of a fake situation. And, besides, I couldn't shoot back at airplanes, so that used to annoy me a little bit. I felt that if there were going to be carrier planes looking for me, the carrier ought to be there too. We were having a preparatory conference for another evaluation exercise, and the carrier was not going to be in my area. So I said, "Why don't you let us have the total area here so we can try to get some training ourselves in approaching and shooting torpedoes at the carrier?"

They said, "Well, we don't want to hit the carrier with a torpedo."

I said, "Gee, our torpedoes run deep. We can shoot them to run under the carrier."

They said, "Well, that depth control doesn't always work that well, and we have tanks here with jet fuel in them, and we would hate to have a torpedo hit it and start a fire and jet fuel could be dangerous."

So I leaped up on the platform and blackboard and whacked out a carrier and said, "Gee, that's no problem. Just show me where the jet fuel tanks are, and we'll shoot under another part of the ship." [Laughter] And I, of course, said that poker faced, absolutely deadpan and sincere, but tongue in cheek just to have a little fun. They didn't schedule it so the carrier came into our area. We would have plugged them, and if necessary we could have shot under a different part of the ship. [Laughter]

Paul Stillwell: Please tell me about your competition with Commander Laning who had the *Seawolf*, the second nuclear submarine.*

Admiral Wilkinson: *Nautilus* was the first nuclear-powered submarine, and the civilian contractor was Westinghouse Electric Company. And Captain Rickover had been successful in his effort to get industry involved, not just the National Laboratory. A contract had been let with Westinghouse for this design plant, and we had a water-cooled thermal energy neutron pressurized water-cooled plant. General Electric was also given a contract, and they were to develop an intermediate energy neutron liquid-metal-cooled reactor. Both design efforts had to meet the same performance specifications. Both were successful, and a prototype was built. And a nuclear plant was built and installed in the submarine.

It just happened that *Nautilus* and Westinghouse finished first. The *Seawolf* was the second, and their plant also worked. The skipper of the *Seawolf* was a gentleman named Dick Laning out of the Naval Academy class of '40. He was a fantastically smart, superb submarine operator, and he really had a fetish. He was really oriented toward fire control, and he probably had the best fire control party you can imagine. I started to say the best you ever saw, but that's not so because we really had that on the *Darter*. [Laughter] But certainly they paid more attention to it than we did on the *Nautilus* because we did many things. Now, there was nothing wrong with our fire control on the

---

* USS *Seawolf* (SSN-575), commissioned 30 March 1957, was the Navy's second nuclear-powered submarine. Her first commanding officer was Commander Richard B. Laning, USN. The *Seawolf* served as a test bed for a reactor cooled by liquid sodium. It was not deemed a success, so the *Seawolf* was later equipped with the pressurized water type. For Laning's recollections, see, "The *Seawolf*'s Sodium-Cooled Power Plant, *Naval History*, Spring 1992, pages 45-48.

Nautilus. All the torpedoes we fired, we always hit. But also we didn't take a lot of bad shots. We drove up to 600 yards abeam and plugged them, and we used our capabilities to ensure that we hit. But I guess Dick Laning really did have a better fire control party than I did. [Laughter] It's hard for me to say that.

Paul Stillwell: I can understand that.

Admiral Wilkinson: So he had a good fire control party, and they worked hard at it. One time we were going from New London to Bermuda, and unfortunately because of the high radioactivity in the liquid sodium plant poor *Seawolf* was not able to go into Bermuda and the *Nautilus* was. But we were proceeding in company and actually leapfrogging ahead of each other and operating restricted to different depths so there was no possibility of us having a collision with one another. One would go out ahead and slow down and wait for the other to come by and make a contact on them and make an approach on them, and then the next one would leapfrog down and so on. So *Seawolf* was out ahead of us, and we were moving along at a respectable speed, which meant we were making noise, and they were up there probably not moving, quiet. They had contact on us, and we didn't have the slightest idea where they are.

With their really good fire control system, their tracking party was at battle stations. They were tracking us, and they were going to plug us when we reached where they were. I had a habit on the *Nautilus* that whenever I got up in the morning I made a complete turn through the ship, and always before I turned in at night I walked through the ship and looked at everything and talked to people. It was a quarter of 2:00 in the morning, and I was in my bunk and doing what a captain ought to do, being rested so that I could be ready for any emergency. I woke up at a quarter to 2:00, and I thought, "Gee, I might as well take a little turn through the ship." So I got up out of my bunk, and I was as far as the control room, just passing through our darkened attack center at 2:00 A.M., when the Gertrude, the underwater phone, blared out and it said, "Aggravate." That was the *Nautilus*'s voice call. "This is Broke." That was the *Seawolf*'s voice call. I really liked mine. I really liked Aggravate better than Broke, but they said, "Aggravate, this is Broke." And there I was. I reached and picked up the Gertrude phone, which was right by my hand, and I said back, "Broke, this is Aggravate. Bravo, Bravo, Bravo." That meant I had just launched an attack on the *Seawolf*. Well, the fact that it was my voice, which everybody recognized, the fact that the response was instantaneous at 2:00 in the morning, lent a certain credibility to our answer.

Still and all, there was a cry of anguish over the phone, "No, we want to attack you." [Laughter] With their very superior fire control party they had probably been tracking us for an hour. But I said, "Broke, this is Aggravate. We have already attacked you. Please give us your course and speed and quit whining about it." [Laughter] See, without even a fire control party we defeated them. [Laughter] It was over a year before I admitted it to them. We didn't have the slightest idea in the world where they were. [Laughter]

Since I thought of it, let me tell you one other thing we did. It was on that same trip that *Nautilus* lived life to the full. As it happened, the individual customs authorities have a tremendous amount of personal authority, and if you go overseas and are gone for a certain length of time every 30 days you can bring back into the States with you, tax free, a gallon of liquor. Actually the regulations as written aren't quite that restrictive, so we were not one to carry liquor improperly. I didn't have a bonded warehouse. There was no way we were going to carry liquor improperly on the *Nautilus*. *Nautilus* tried to do most things reasonably, according to regulations. But it would be nice if when we went somewhere we could ship back through commercial shipment our tax-free liquor.

So I went down and saw the authority in New Haven; it happened to be a charming lady. I took her to lunch, and we talked over the problem, and the real regulations say that you can bring back a quart plus a reasonable amount. So we talked about that. The quart is tax free, state and national. The reasonable amount is tax free nationally but taxable by the state. To bring a bottle of liquor into the state of Connecticut was 10 cents of duty. So when we talked it over at lunch she decided that a reasonable amount was two cases. So we could now bring back a quart plus two cases, the reasonable amount, and pay the state tax, 10 cents a bottle, on the two cases $2.40. So I said, "Well, we go to sea and we're outside the territorial limits and we're gone for the requisite 30 days or more and we do this. It's been 30 days since we've done it before. And sometimes we reach other countries, but we don't always go in port. Is that all right?"

"Oh, yes," she said. "That doesn't make any difference."

I said, "Sometimes we just make landfall on them."

She said, "That's all right."

I said, "You know sometimes we can make landfall at 90 miles."

She said, "That's all right." [Laughter]

So we reached very good relations, and it was possible for us when we went to sea for an extended period and made landfall on other countries to order liquor and have it shipped back to the Unites States. Of course, we didn't carry it on board. Well, that trip going down to Bermuda was a historic trip in that we broke the price of liquor in Bermuda, because always before that when the ships would go in they'd be entertained, taken up and given a free lunch and maybe a dice cup or two and their liquor order filled and shipped back. I remember well that the ships were paying for Canadian Club tax free $28.00 a case. And so when we went into Bermuda that time, having gone down with the *Seawolf*, we carried our orders, two cases per man, the *Seawolf*'s orders at two cases a man, and we had a little over 400 cases of Canadian Club that we wanted.

I said, "Don't give us any lunch. Don't give us any dice cups. Don't give us any of that. You just give us a bid on how much you want for"—I've forgotten the exact number, 380 cases of Canadian Club or whatever it was. And we'd gone to London, Canada, and we were getting a bid from there, and that day the price of Canadian Club for the Navy ships in Bermuda dropped from $28.00 to $19.00 a case. [Laughter] So with the *Seawolf*'s additional muscle we were able to break the price of liquor. Silly story.

Paul Stillwell: But it required some imagination.

Admiral Wilkinson: It really is amazing the authority that an individual local customs person has.

Paul Stillwell: Well, please tell me the story behind that call sign you mentioned, "Aggravate." How did that come about?

Admiral Wilkinson: When a Navy ship went into commission it was assigned a voice call. That voice call came out of a book, and obviously it was one of the calls in the book that wasn't already assigned. You weren't given a voice call of somebody that already had one. For example, my voice call on the *Volador* was Pokeweed, which we made a known name in the Western Pacific with the antisubmarine forces, but it was not as grand as my voice call was on the *Wahoo*, which was Old Ace. [Laughter] When I got to the *Nautilus* and looked at what voice call had in mind for us, it was Club Moss. And that didn't appeal to me. I didn't want to keep referring to myself as Club Moss, so I decided what the hell. I wanted to get it changed before we ever went into commission.

So we looked through the book at all the voice calls that were there that were not assigned, and one of my officers was Lieutenant Carr, whose wife's name is Molly.* She really wanted me to put in for Molly Moe, but I didn't do that. I looked through and the one that appealed to me was Aggravate. So I wrote a letter to the CNO, which is where voice calls come under, and requested that my voice call be changed from "Club Moss" to "Aggravate" and sent it via the chain of command, so it went by CinCLantFlt. When it went by the Commander in Chief Atlantic Fleet—and I don't know what his voice call was, but it obviously was one that was annoying to him because in his forwarding endorsement he said, "Forwarded, Recommended, and what's more I don't like my voice call either. I want it changed to such and so." [Laughter] So before the *Nautilus* was built we got our voice call changed, and over the years that "Aggravate" was a good call. We probably aggravated quite a few of the ships that we were in contact, the evaluation forces that we operated against. [Laughter] At least we tried our hardest to.

One of the interesting experiences we had during that time was we had Edward R. Murrow come to the ship and do a program, and he was a remarkable character.† I really enjoyed him, because he was so human and so sincere, and he did so superbly well. He observed different evolutions on the *Nautilus* and took pictures of them and saw us going

---

* Lieutenant Kenneth M. Carr, USN, later a vice admiral.
† Edward R. Murrow was a highly respected newsman for CBS. He had a hand in the downfall of Senator Joseph R. McCarthy, who alleged to have found many Communists in the U.S. Government.

to battle stations and tracking stations, which we did so fast you can't imagine it with all the right words. And saw us make a dive with all the right words and phraseology and all so perfectly. And in making some pictures of the diving we pumped some water in the trim tank, and when the order was given my guy spun that valve so fast it looked like it was going backwards in the thing and my people were observing that and they said, "Hey, that's not nuclear. That's the same old valve that's on every submarine."

I can remember him saying, "And everybody will recognize that that's not nuclear. That's just plain conventional submarine."

I said, "Yeah, but also everyone of them will realize he couldn't do it any faster." [Laughter] And that's the way everything went that our guys did on the Edward R. Murrow program. Our guys just looked terrific, and he gave us a real good plug. And then that program was shown, and again there were countless numbers of our people's faces and many names and seeing them doing their job. Their wives watched that, and let me tell you, having that program done on board was not only fun but a big boost to the ship's morale.

Another time Disney came and took a program on board with a couple of our kids, young children looking like mouseketeers and wandering through, and that was a real nice program. I had them put all the names of all our ship's company in a hat and draw a boy and draw a girl. They drew a nice little girl, and the boy they drew by good fortune happened to be mine. So I still have that film here, and as a matter of fact a year or so ago we had it made into a videocassette and gave it to our son Rodney, who's now in his 40s, showing him as a mouseketeer going through the *Nautilus*. As I said, I tried to be fair and have them put all the names in the hat, but now I sort of wish I'd have had my boy and my girl. [Laughter] But at the time I didn't do it that way.

Paul Stillwell: You had a telephone call a couple of days ago from your chief of the boat from 1955 congratulating you on the 43rd anniversary of the first time under way on nuclear power.

Admiral Wilkinson: Ingles was a crackerjack chief of the boat, and, yes, he did.* He had quite a note in his Christmas card this year. The 17th of January he called up and remembered that that was the day that we got under way on nuclear power in 1955 and that is 43 years ago. I really had a good crew. They were really for the ship, and they've stayed loyal to it till this day. If they're still alive, they're still on our side.

Paul Stillwell: What was his role in dealing with all these talented people you had in the crew?

Admiral Wilkinson: Chief of the boat of a submarine is really important. He is really *the* guy on a submarine. He is the controller of all the other troops on board and such things as the plan of the day and a lot of things like that. And oversight of training and qualification and just the sort of father daddy to the young seamen and firemen. He is an older, more mature guy and is really valuable to a ship. He helps ensure that all the troops on the ship perform well. And I had a selected bunch of people who had been going through the prototype. My engineers were especially trained and selected and had run the plant we were going to have. But also I had selected troops for the rest of the ship.

I can remember when I was getting my chief of the boat the SubLant personnel officer came up and talked to me. He said, "Well, now, Dennis, the *Squatfish* [and I won't tell you the ship] won the big fleet E last year, and it's not that their skipper's all that good. It was really the chief of the boat."

I said, "Gee, I'd like to have him." As you can see from the fact that 43 years later he called me up to see how my knee is, and sick as he is, and can remember that we went to sea 43 years ago, he was really a pro-*Nautilus* man. And he isn't the only guy I've heard from or will get communication from. I've had people from World War II come back and say, "Hey, my son is doing this. Would you talk to him and tell him how it is?" And I've even had the experience of one of my old shipmates coming up to say, "Captain, would you talk to my grandson?" [Laughter] Not that I'm that good at talking, but it shows a certain rapport between me and my own guys.

---

* Chief Torpedoman Leroy Ingles, USN.

Paul Stillwell: Do you have examples of what Chief Ingles did as an intermediary with the rest of the sailors?

Admiral Wilkinson: As I say, a chief of the boat really is the intermediary between the officers on the ship and the enlisted people, and he ensures that, by golly, things are done well. Also, at battle stations he probably is the chief of the watch in the control room, which is important to the diving. But if there was unrest or a problem he'd come up and talk to the exec or the captain about it. If there was a morale problem he would identify it. If somebody brought liquor aboard, anything, you would probably hear from the chief of the boat. He is really a key individual in the hierarchy. And it's different, doesn't quite match the organizational diagram on the wall, which is captain and the exec and departments and divisions, the chiefs and the troops. But in between that there's the chief of the boat who worries about it all. He probably talks most with the other chiefs, but he also talks a lot with the captain and the exec. There's a lot of communication back and forth.

A really good chief of the boat can be a great contributor to the morale and well-being of the people on board the ship. Let me see if I can think of some examples of things that were done. As I said, I made these arrangements for the crew to be able to buy liquor and have it shipped to New London tax-free once we were down in Bermuda. Then it was almost unbelievable to me, but one of the chiefs brought a case of liquor on board, and I don't believe in that baloney. We lived by the book, and we lived by the law, and we didn't do that kind of thing. Sure enough, the chief of the boat came up to me and said, "Captain, I'm ashamed to tell you that one of the chiefs has brought a case of liquor aboard, and I would appreciate it if we could take care of the matter ourselves."

That meant for me not to get involved in a disciplinary way with the matter. I said, "Chief, be my guest." [Laughter] And I never heard any more about that problem. On the other hand, you have a sort of a feeling that things are going okay and they're under control.

Paul Stillwell: And I'll bet that problem never happened again.

Admiral Wilkinson: No, no. Maybe I didn't do it exactly by the book either, but let me tell you, we had the kind of a ship that I'm sure that never happened again.

Paul Stillwell: But I think in the Navy as a whole, chiefs were more likely to handle things that way back then.

Admiral Wilkinson: But when it's the chief of the boat he's going to see that things are done right. See, he also cut me in. And dumb little things. When we came into port and laundry had to go off, money had to be collected and laundry paid when it got back. The chief of the boat wouldn't collect it all himself, but he'd see that it happened. And the officers on the ship didn't have to be involved. That sounds like a dumb example, but it's really not, because some of the little administrative things like that happened. And if somebody made off with his foul weather jacket or if we were low on some rain gear or something, someway or other the word would come from the chief of the boat. After all, we didn't have a supply officer on the thing, so for individual spare parts, the chief of the boat and the petty officers made those things work.

I had two supply officers on the *Long Beach*, and I had all these spare parts for the missile systems and some spare parts for the nuclear systems, and it was really frustrating to me to try to make sure they all ran right. I'd get up in the morning, and there'd been a priority dispatch put out for an emergency spare for a part for a missile system, and so when I was awake and I looked into that, I'd say, "Here, what's the problem? Were we not smart enough to get that put into our spares, or is it on allowance and we're not up to allowance and we don't have it on board, or what's the problem?"

"Oh, none of those, Captain. We're smart enough to get it on our things, and we have it on board, but we can't find it. It's easier for us to order emergency than try to find that part." Gee, that used to frustrate me. Later on, when I was the division commander, I gave an operational readiness inspection to the *Nautilus,* and understand they were good. Among other things during the inspection, I asked them for ten spare parts. And I identified them in different ways. I'd say, "I want the line item, page number spare part," or "I want a good one of these," or "I want the diaphragm that does thus and so." I asked for those things in the wardroom, and they brought the ten parts back and put them on the wardroom table in front of me. For the ten they had an average time of 52 seconds. And they wouldn't have been that good except three of them were fire control parts and Crossick, the fire controlman, the bachelor, his locker was right by the wardroom, and he reached in there and got his three in ten seconds. But the average for all ten was 52 seconds. It really used to frustrate me when in four days they didn't come up with a part on the *Long Beach* and I had two supply officers. I even had a crackerjack one. I had Dick Laning's brother.[*] Eventually we got that squared away on the *Long Beach*, but it was hard.

Paul Stillwell: What do you remember about the role of Lieutenant Commander Axene as the exec?

Admiral Wilkinson: Axene hadn't gone through the nuclear training, although he went on the nuclear course after the *Nautilus*.[†] And he stood high in the submarine evaluation of his age group, was a crackerjack guy, had a crackerjack wife, and I was lucky to have him as the exec on the *Nautilus*. Did a super job. I've got some nice pictures of the two of us there. Eventually he got transferred and in sequence I had my next senior officers as the execs. I had Les Kelly.[‡] I had Jack Nicholson, and finally when I was transferred Bus Cobean was my exec.[§] They all did good jobs, but Dean was super.

We used to talk about the *Nautilus*, and we had a little line of patter that went through everything. You know, more hours under way, and we steamed more miles surfaced and more miles submerged and made more dives and did more of this and fired more torpedoes and made more hits and a higher percentage. And we had more reenlistments and more people rated and more of this and more of that. [Laughter] And our wives were prettier than those in any other submarine. [Laughter] Oh, I'll tell you, that Dean Axene's wife, Liz, was a doll.

---

[*] Lieutenant Commander George H. Laning, Supply Corps, USN.
[†] Lieutenant Commander Dean L. Axene, USN.
[‡] Lieutenant Commander Leslie D. Kelly, Jr., USN.
[§] Lieutenant Commander John H. Nicholson, USN; Lieutenant Commander Warren R. Cobean, Jr., USN.

Paul Stillwell: What do you remember about evasive tactics when you were handicapped by the fact that you had a noisy propulsion plant?

Admiral Wilkinson: The only time we were handicapped by a noisy propulsion plant was if we were working against SSK submarines. When we were working against ASW surface forces, the noise didn't bother us, because we were moving at high speed when they were moving at high speed. They were noisy too. We really had the capability if we used it right to handle that. Our noise didn't bother us. To be good in evasive maneuvers against ASW forces you should never stick anything above the surface because radars could detect it, and you could be localized. You should never radiate something, because electronic devices would detect that radiation and vector the people towards you. So you stayed beneath the surface, and used your own sonar for your detection.

If you were detected and they were going to shoot weapons at you, you wanted to take advantage of your maximum depth which takes longer for a weapon to get down there than if you're closer to the surface. Perhaps by going deep you have passed through some thermal sonar layers that make it tougher for them to use their sonars. If you're up to speed it's harder for them to keep up with you and solve the fire control problem and shoot a weapon out in front of where you're going to be by the time it gets down to your depth. If you're turning, then it's even a harder thing to figure out exactly where you're going to be. And if you don't turn continuously but turn one way and then change your mind and turn another. And if your sonarman is so good that he's told you people are coming in for approach. And they're about to shoot, and then you can turn, and you do that and then break contact so they don't have you anymore so that your evasive maneuver doesn't have to last forever. The only worry that I had in evasive maneuvers was not in keeping from getting hit or breaking contact when I was up to speed in that depth. But my worries were that in different exercises they would start them out with us being at a slow speed, at a smaller depth, and the question was when the exercise started to get the hell out of there before you got shot at. [Laughter]

Paul Stillwell: What was the episode where the man wanted you to go six knots at 150 feet and your objection to that?

Admiral Wilkinson: Well, there were a couple of episodes. One, I was giving services in deep water with no restrictions on our evasion once the exercise started. But before it started I was at 150 feet making five knots, and the force commander of his four destroyers up there was going to do operations against us with us at full capability. But at the start I was at 150 feet making only five knots. As it happened, there was a submarine rescue vessel, happened to be the *Skylark*, in the area. Over the radio he heard the force commander of those four destroyers who was doing this evaluation exercise say to his people, "I am about to give execute. Make sure your weapons are in the air." Well, that meant for the destroyers to shoot us before we could get the hell out of there.

Just by good luck, as it happened, this was just in the neighborhood of chow time in the evening. I happened, thinking it didn't make any difference, to have gradually slipped down to test depth while making my five knots. So instead of 150 feet I was a lot deeper than that, because I hadn't wanted to start out just a mealtime by tipping over 30 degrees and spilling the chow. So as it happened because things had been delayed a little chow was finished, and so when execute went we squirted ahead at top speed and turned and disappeared.

I broke contact, went out about 8,000 yards, four miles away, and came to periscope depth and stuck up my communication mast. I checked in and said, "Here we are."

I got the nastiest toned comment. "Well, how many rockets did you feel?" because one of them had peeled off 22 weapon A's.[*] They were not supposed to shoot even three without communicating with you. Twenty-two weapon A's, and I was able to say back with my poker voice, "Gee, did you shoot?" [Laughter] So I guess it was luck with the people being a little crooked that we didn't get hit that time.

Another time I was giving services to a group not in deep water, and I was 150 feet making six knots, not five knots. Then the gent said he wanted us to do evasive maneuvers and to shoot at us, and I said, "No." I came up and talked to him, and I said, "You know, it's been a couple of years, and there have been a lot of weapons fired at the

---

[*] Weapon A, known at different times as Weapon Able and Weapon Alfa, was a trainable launcher that fired antisubmarine rockets that contained explosive charges. The range was 400-800 yards. Weapon A entered the fleet in the early 1950s

Nautilus, and none of them have hit yet. And if you guys are good enough, if you hit us we'd like you to get the credit for being that good. But if you shoot as us when we're making six knots at 150 feet with evasion 45 degrees either side of course the restrictions, the depth and the speed and 45 degrees have all disappeared. It'll be just that this force plugged the *Nautilus*. And let me tell you if you're those guys we'd like to sing your praises and give you credit, just so we're really trying. But we don't go for this." So he said, "All right. We won't shoot." That was that. But what he meant by that was that he'd rather get the experience of the exercises, something he could track and follow 45 degrees, 150 feet and six knots, because if we go out to deep water and down deep and they tell us to evade we'd just disappear. They wouldn't have any contact anymore.

Paul Stillwell: Well, you made a good observation when the machine wasn't running that one of these ASW people would do better to shoot his weapons at random than where he actually thought you were.

Admiral Wilkinson: I probably had the best sonar operators in the Navy. I had an active echo-ranging sonar that was the latest and very good. And I had Chief Michaud, two pounds of crap in a one-pound bag, but he was the best listening sonarman that the Navy had by far. And those people were superb as they were tracking something in telling exactly in relative movement and they, just as well as I did, knew how far away that ship was and what he was doing. They'd say, "His range and his bearing's steady. He's speeding up. He's turning. He's starting to turn right. He's getting ready to launch an attack." And with that chatter, chatter, chatter, chatter coming from the best sonar guys in the Navy it was easy for me to know when, "Now's the time to turn." If you're at test depth, with the time that it takes the weapon to get down there and you're making speed over 20 knots, the surface ship has got to lead you, and they have to know what course you're on to lead you. Then if you change course just as they shoot—with the help of my sonarmen—they were always trying to shoot where we would have been. In some ways they might have done better if they hadn't tried to aim at all but had at just fired at random. Fifty-five hundred weapons is a lot. Just shooting them at random they might have made a hit, but trying they never were able to manage it.

Paul Stillwell: What do you mean about putting two pounds of crap in a one-pound bag?

Admiral Wilkinson: That means a certain amount of baloney, and it's an expression.

Paul Stillwell: I wondered how it applied in this situation.

Admiral Wilkinson: It really didn't. Michaud was in some ways a bullshitter [Laughter] but on the other hand he also was the best passive sonar operator in the Navy, probably in the world. Surely in the world if he was the best in our Navy. We had him, and he was of tremendous value to us. And I had a first class that was as good an active sonar operator as there was, and I had a really good well-tuned-up active sonar, and obviously Michaud kept our passive sonars in superb condition. If people were going to shoot at us, they were on those sonars, and they were the very best. Those sonarmen didn't want to get hit any more than I did.

Paul Stillwell: My guess is that you used passive far more than active.

Admiral Wilkinson: Yes, yes. In talking with the guys chasing me, shooting at me, if I was putting out active, I was putting out a beacon of where I was. The time I used active was when I was going to attack them. Passively I got into position off their beam or something, and then just before I shot I might take an active range. I'd have a bearing and a range, and when I had the exact solution, then I'd plug them. I didn't shoot to miss. I made sure of hitting not by the greatest fire control in the world, which we couldn't have come close to, but because I drove into the position that was damned hard for a guy to keep from getting hit once the torpedo was in the water. As a matter of fact, if you were out just forward of the beam of a guy and shot at him from 500 yards on a 90 track, he could not evade. It was different if you fired a sharp track angle on the bow for a couple of thousand yards. The guy could thread the needle and maybe make you miss. But if you shoot from 500 or 600 yards on a 90-degree track on the beam and if your bearing is good and your range is good, and that's why I'd light off my echo ranger, my active sonar, just before I shot and punch a fish at him.

Then I'd keep it running as the fish went under him. And then on your screen you'd see the ship, you'd see the fish, and as the track of the torpedo would go right under him we'd take a picture of it. I mean, so here was this attack and show the time and the range and the track and we didn't miss. And we didn't miss thinking back partly because we didn't shoot to miss. We shot to hit. And we had the other capabilities that could cause us to get into the position where we had an easy shot.

Paul Stillwell: So when you made an approach you probably used the periscope only to take the picture.

Admiral Wilkinson: No. When I said I took the picture I took the picture on the sonar.

Paul Stillwell: Oh, I see. So you didn't use the periscope.

Paul Stillwell: Oh, no. No, no. Took the picture on the active sonar when I was down below periscope depth. There was nothing up to be detected.

Paul Stillwell: So you had gotten away from the business of taking the pictures that showed the hull numbers of the targets.

Admiral Wilkinson: That was a little bit *Wahoo*, mostly *Volador*. Didn't do it that way on the *Nautilus*. Oh, we might have done it just for practice once or twice, but when you have intensive radar and air search against you there's no sense in sticking something up where some airplane might drop a flare and say, "I made an attack on a periscope." We didn't ever want anything to show that the *Nautilus* had been successfully attacked.

Paul Stillwell: How good was the logistic support for that ship?

Admiral Wilkinson: Really it was superb. The propulsion plant, of course especially when we were being built, let me tell if you could call up at midnight and a truck would move at 2:00 or 3:00 A.M., you couldn't have had better support. But in the rest of the ship, too, our operational commander, Commander Submarine Force Atlantic Fleet, was eager for us to do well. And so we were given the best of sonar and the best of people, and if we had a problem, heroic effort was taken to do something about it. We never had a logistic problem in any part of the ship except sometimes you might get far away from where it was. Like I'd have hated to bang up a screw in passing through the Panama Canal, because the nearest screw was probably in Norfolk. But if we had done it, I'm sure they would have flown one down there. We had great logistic support, but that would have been embarrassing to us.

Paul Stillwell: Well, you talked about the two groups of junior officers you had in the *Nautilus*. You had four who were the nuclear-qualified engineers and the four who were not. What did you do about getting the other four into the nuclear program?

Admiral Wilkinson: When ship's company was first set up I had the four young officers that had been selected for the nuclear program and had gone through Bettis and had gone through the construction and test of the prototype plant in Arco, Idaho. They came and were my four engineers on the ship. I also had four submarine-qualified crackerjack young officers, and there was myself and my exec, Dean Axene.

The four young deck officers, my weapons officer and so on, had not been nuclear trained or qualified. They were some pretty good officers. Those officers did a great job on the *Nautilus*, and they worked hard for me. Professionally it would mean something to them to be nuclear qualified, so I wanted to see them selected into the nuclear program.

One of the most important things Rickover did for the nuclear program, by God, the nuclear program was important, and he was the Navy's conscience. He ensured that there was nobody of talent that was withheld from the chance to be selected to go into the nuclear program. No admiral could keep his flag lieutenant from getting assigned by BuPers to the nuclear program, so the Bureau of Personnel would search the records, and they would send people over to Admiral Rickover for interview and screening. And

Admiral Rickover would have a group of his officers interview them, and then he would be the last one that would interview each officer that went into the program.

It was Admiral Rickover's nature to demand that he get the people that had stood high academically. He had a great bent to try to pick the top of the class. And he was probably right, because these people were young enough for potential over a lifetime. I also like to apply a lot of attention to performance. But we're talking young ones, and Rickover was going for potential, so he focused on the top half of the class. Then he had a tendency when he interviewed them to only take half of all that he interviewed. So he got an awful lot of good people in the nuclear program and he acted as the Navy's conscience to see that no crackerjack person was hidden. But he probably passed over, for one reason or another, some pretty capable people.

I wanted, of course, all four of my people that were officers on the *Nautilus* to have the opportunity to get into the nuclear program. Rickover explained to me that, by God, he wasn't just going to take a whole lot of people just because they were on the *Nautilus*. And so we had a difference of opinion on that. Ultimately Rickover came around, and all four of my people were selected. The methodology differed over time. The first one was easy. I sent Dave Boyd, who stood number three in his class, and said, "There are two operating reactors in the world, the prototype in Idaho or the one on the *Nautilus*, and I'm going to qualify this officer, and I'm going to do it personally. And if you'd like we'll give him an exam against any graduate of the Nuclear Training Program at the prototype in Idaho, we'll see who does the best." [Laughter]

So Rickover interviewed him and decided he was a good man. And I said it would be nicer if he were selected for the program, and he was selected for the program. He went through the nuclear power training, where he did stand number one, the best, and went through training at the prototype and so on. And in sequence my next two were also selected and I came down to the fourth one, who was Ken Carr, from the class of '49. By that time Rickover was more and more powerful, and so now it wasn't, "I'm going to qualify this guy or other." It was, "Admiral, would you please, as a personal favor to me, select this man for training?" [Laughter]

I explained to Admiral Rickover that he'd been of great value to the ship and that I had no officer that had ever been more loyal to the program. He was extremely loyal to nuclear power, and I sent him down to be interviewed. Rickover didn't say a damn word to me or write me a note in answer to my plea or anything. He just sent me back this tract in an envelope with my name, Commander Wilkinson, on it and this is an old story from literature called "A Message to Garcia."* The funny thing about this tract is if you turn it over on the last page there's written, "When put to the test an ounce of loyalty is worth a pound of cleverness."† He initialed it. That was my answer from Admiral Rickover. Ken had always been loyal to the program, and, sure enough, he was selected and went off to Nuclear Power School. My obligation to my four officers had been discharged; all of them were selected in nuclear power and training did well. Ken Carr did exceptionally well and many years later was a vice admiral and chairman of the Nuclear Regulatory Commission.

Paul Stillwell: And ComSubLant.

Admiral Wilkinson: And ComSubLant and a few other things like that. But Rickover's sending me "A Message to Garcia" was a goddamn clever answer, and I was grateful. Ken Carr left the ship. He was one officer that had broken service in the *Nautilus*. He left the ship and went through nuclear training and went through Idaho and qualified on the prototype plant and then, lo and behold, received orders back to the *Nautilus*. When we were in port we frequently had quite a few visitors. In fact, during my entire tour on *Nautilus* we averaged 36 important visitors a day. And I'm not counting when we had our wives down or something. I mean the kind of visitors that you talked to and toured and tried to explain about your ship to.

The day Ken Carr came back from Idaho and reported in I was busy with the visitors. We processed them at 50 an hour. We would get 50 aboard and lecture to them

---

* In 1899 Elbert Hubbard wrote the essay "A Message to Garcia" about an incident in the 1898 Spanish-American War in which a messenger named Rowan demonstrated heroism in the face of danger by carrying a message to Garcia, the leader of insurgent forces in Cuba. The essay has been widely reprinted and quoted over the years.

† The quotation from the essay that Wilkinson has summarized reads as follows: "There is a man whose form should be cast in deathless bronze and the statue placed in every college in the land. It is not book-learning young men need, nor instruction about this or that, but a stiffening of the vertebrae which will cause them to be loyal to a trust, to act promptly, concentrate their energies; do the thing–'carry a message to Garcia!'"

for an hour, and then guides would tour them through the ship with description and explanation while if we had that many we'd have the next 50 and be talking to them. I didn't talk the whole hour, but I talked part of it. So I was in the crew's mess, and I was talking to the 50 people. Down the hatch came Lieutenant Carr. I'd just reached that point in my spiel that I could say, "And now Lieutenant Carr will tell you about the propulsion plant in the next ten minutes." [Laughter] And Ken Carr was still getting the sun out of his eyes, but he looked at me and said, "Captain, things haven't changed a bit." He stepped forward to the lecture area and started talking and explained the propulsion plant for the next ten minutes. [Laughter] It was fun for me to do that with Ken. He was one of my very best officers.

Paul Stillwell: Well, you commanded that ship for a considerable period of time. Were the replacements as good as the people whose places they were taking when you had turnover?

Admiral Wilkinson: When *Nautilus* was commissioned I had 10 officers and 85 troops. And I was on there, counting the pre-commissioning time, for four years. And I had men transferred, and so I'm probably looking at a little over 200 troops in the time, including some replacement people in the forward part of the ship and torpedomen and fire controlmen. The new two sonarmen I got were better than the first ones, because that was awfully important to us, and the two of them were the best two in the whole Navy. The replacements that I had in engineering might have been crackerjack guys, but they didn't have quite as much experience as my guys had had that were there on the building and checkout of the prototype. So that varied a little bit with individuals. Some were better. Some were not quite as good. But regardless of whether they were better or not quite as good, they were all very, very good. Very good for *Nautilus* and better than the *Nautilus* are two different things. [Laughter]

Paul Stillwell: Would you please tell the story that goes with that?

Admiral Wilkinson: I will later.

Paul Stillwell: Okay.

Admiral Wilkinson: So I'm looking during my time on there at probably a little over 200 troops, 205, 210 troops. I could look up the exact number. And I had 40-some odd that made commissions in the Navy competitive exam. One time in the Navy competitive exam I had more men off the *Nautilus* make commissions than the rest of the Atlantic Fleet Submarine Force put together. And partly that's because they were good and partly that's because we helped them. [Laughter] We worked at it. We taught them mathematics. We taught them English. We held classes. We made them not feel shy to volunteer in the first place. One time I had 30 people up for the Navy competitive exam for a commission.

It was not just commissions. One time it was tough to get rated, and there were eight people that there were vacancies for first class machinist's mate. And in the Navy exam on that I had three guys go up, and they was three of the eight, and there were the other five for the rest of the Navy that were vacancies at that moment. That's because within what we did on the ship, those guys, we knew they were going up and we knew it was going to be tough but, by God, they had studied. We knew they had studied, and their bosses had helped them study. And we'd gone over their courses with them, and so it was in lots of things. So our guys did super well, one, because they were damned good in the first place, two, because it was expected they would and people have a tendency to live up to expectations. And third, because they worked hard to try to do well. It wasn't just chance that we had all those guys make commissions.

Paul Stillwell: What was that story about something, the performance was not very good for *Nautilus*?

Admiral Wilkinson: I wasn't trying to be cute, but I was down on an exercise with some ASW forces. Sonar conditions sometimes are as variable as the sea itself, and we certainly didn't make the detection ranges that I had expected to make. I had expected that we'd be making detection 25,000-30,000 yards, and we just made our detection at 14,000 yards. I was disappointed and said, "No, we didn't do very well." You've got to be careful what you say. To my surprise, when we went to the critique some destroyer skipper stepped up and said that they had done better than the *Nautilus*. I was shocked to hear that statement and jumped up and said, "What are you talking about?"

He said, "Well, you told me yourself you didn't do very well."

I said, "Friend, not very well for the *Nautilus* and better than the *Nautilus* are two damned different things. What range did you make detection at?" And he said, "Four thousand yards." And I said, "Well, we didn't do very well. We got them at 14,000. We expected to do 30," which was a crappy thing to say, but I was mortified at someone saying they were better than the *Nautilus*. That just rubbed salt in my wound, because they really weren't.

Paul Stillwell: You had so much to accomplish in those years. I wonder when you ever slept. What did that long period in command do to your stamina?

Admiral Wilkinson: I had no trouble with that because we spent a lot of time at sea. And except for the first underway trials when I was up for the full four days I had really good people, and I had confidence in them. My bunk was right next to control, submerged information. I was captain a long, long time, and if I was sound asleep and you changed speed or turned I'd wake up. And if anything happened I would maybe get 30-40 reports to me during the night and I can listen and understand them and take the right action asleep or awake. [Laughter] It is the commanding officer's responsibility to always be rested and ready for emergency, so I probably spent as much time in my bunk as I could. [Laughter] And so at sea, other than the first operation, I had no trouble getting all the rest I needed. You were just trying to get me to talk.

Paul Stillwell: Yes.

Admiral Wilkinson: Now, in port there was an awful lot of mail. We averaged 42 official letters a day, 14 of which as an average required an answer. We read our mail, and so that was a strain. And so sometimes I'd take a bundle of stuff home to read. But, by and large, I was young, and I didn't sleep all that much and I still don't to this day. I only sleep five or six hours a night. We operated hard, and it was no problem to me in relation to your question, and partly it was because I had such crackerjack people. And I'm not afraid to delegate. I have confidence in my people.

Navy seniority and all that business never did impress my wife very much, and although I did a lot of business with Slade Cutter my actual boss was Admiral Watkins or whoever the admiral was at ComSubLant. One day we had had extensive operations, and I came home real pooped and went home, and actually I crapped out at 7:00 P.M. and went to sleep. When my wife came to bed about 11:00, that woke me up. [Laughter] So I was aroused in more ways than one. [Laughter] My wife said, "You know, Admiral Watkins called and wanted to talk to you, but I told him you were really tired and asleep, and so he asked you to call him first thing in the morning."

I said, "Honey, you what?" [Laughter] So I guess I wasn't always quite as wide awake and alert as I thought, as I started to tell you, because now I remember that.

I had one time that I complained. I had tried to make my boss really happy and things go well. One time I did complain to my boss, the admiral, and it was an interesting story, which I'll tell you. I've just thought of it now. Morale was really good. It didn't matter that we worked harder than the other boats and whatnot. Morale really was awfully high on the *Nautilus*, and we had it in reenlistment and any other way you wanted to measure it. Our guys were good, and they performed well. The admiral rode us often enough to know that, and he was proud of us. He was bragging about us to his contemporaries in Washington, and this was a time of good morale not being totally true across the Navy.

So it was arranged for a team of people to come down from BuPers and interrogate our people as to why their morale was so good. And damned if they didn't make the damnedest questionnaire you ever saw, and it had question after question like, "You operate more than the other boats. How come your morale is good?" And "You don't see your wives anywhere near as often. How come your morale is good?" and so on. And these people came aboard, and these questions started to be distributed to my people. I saw the first one, and I said, "Pick all those up and get them back here." I grabbed one in hand and hotfooted it up to SubLant and went in to see the admiral, and I said, "Admiral, what are you trying to do to me?"

He said, "What are you talking about, Dennis?"

I said, "There's a group that's come from BuPers, and they say that it's because the admiral there talked to you and they're checking on my morale. Look at these damned questions. I mean, 'You people don't get as much time with your wives. How can you have good morale?'" [Laughter] I said, "I've collected all these questionnaires and put them off the ship and, Admiral, let me put it like this. Our morale on the *Nautilus* is real bad and we like it that way. Please don't try to help us." [Laughter] And he didn't throw me out of his office. He agreed that it was a lousy questionnaire. The people went away.

The organization of the Navy is such that ships in many ways are a little bit defenseless. An awful lot of senior commands can impose requirements on individual ships, and normally that averages out so you don't get everything. But now you take the *Nautilus*, that attracted people's attention. Maybe everybody will ask the *Nautilus*, "Does this ship do this or that?"

I looked ahead, and I recognized that there were going to be a lot of requirements. I was reporting to SubLant, so I made a deal with SubLant. A letter went out to all the commands in the Navy that they could not request anything from the *Nautilus*. If they wanted anything from the *Nautilus*, they should send it to the *Nautilus* via ComSubLant. And so it was. Then SubLant let me process all those letters, and if it was intelligent I put an endorsement on, forwarded for action, and if it wasn't I put an endorsement, return to sender. And SubLant let me for him make the decision of whether we answered it or not. One time from the Bureau of Ships I had a request to send them three copies of all our engineering logs since we had started operating, and this was after about a year and a half. I've forgotten the exact number now, but we probably had 30 engineering logs and three copies and a year and a half, that was a hell of a lot of reproduction. And you didn't have Xerox machines then.

Paul Stillwell: That's right.

Admiral Wilkinson: And so we didn't forward that one for action. We returned that one to sender, and months later I was talking to those people down in BuShips and asking them, "Sorry we couldn't get you all that information on the engineering logs. But what did you guys want to know?"

They said, "We wanted to know how much water you were using."

I said, "Jesus, why didn't you just ask us that? We'd have told you." [Laughter] So that advance defense turned out to be very valuable to the ship.

Actually ComSubLant helped us another way, because he was worried about our morale. After we'd been working so hard and been at sea so much and all that, the admiral scheduled us for a four-day visit to New Orleans for R&R, rest and relaxation. We had trouble going up the Mississippi, because we threw up a terrible wake, and we had to make sure that we didn't put water over the levees, but other than that we didn't have a problem of port entry. We reached New Orleans and we tied up at the foot of Bourbon Street.

Congressmen Hebert, who owned New Orleans, came aboard, and he had his very pretty secretary with him.* They sat down in our wardroom, and they wrote us 19 letters of introduction. She wrote half and he wrote half, and he signed them all. And let me tell you, when you went to one of those establishments, one of the letters, the least it was good for was a free round of drinks on the house. But for most of them it was everything on the house as long as you stayed and the entertainers at your table. And let me tell you, four days there, if it wasn't on fire we didn't even fool with it. [Laughter]

Paul Stillwell: You mean the food?

Admiral Wilkinson: Yes, and it was tough because we were only there four days and four nights, but we managed to get it all done, and so by the end of the fourth night we had used those 19 letters. And, Jesus, we were glad to get back to sea again where we could rest and relax a little. [Laughter]

Paul Stillwell: You had to recover from all that relaxation you'd had.

---

* F. Edward Hébert, a Democrat from Louisiana, served in the House of Representatives from 3 January 1941 to 3 January 1977. He was chairman of the House Armed Services Committee, 1971-74.

Admiral Wilkinson: We really were glad to get to sea and get some rest. [Laughter]

Paul Stillwell: How much of an issue was access to various ports for nuclear-powered ships during that time?

Admiral Wilkinson: Now you've got to go back to an earlier time. Admiral Rickover wanted to make sure that we weren't criticized, so he tried to minimize the access of ships into ports. Certainly we wouldn't send a nuclear ship into New York Harbor today. On the other hand, in 1958 the *Nautilus* went into a triumphal return to New York Harbor after we went under the Pole. So the access of ships was in a controlled manner, and studies were made before the *Nautilus* even went into New London. And certainly with the Reactor Safeguard Committee before we went into dry dock. The dry dock might tip over and would your control rods and safety systems work and so on and so on? So there were a lot of back-up studies by Rickover's people and the Reactor Safeguard Committee.

Paul Stillwell: Did you get a fair amount of correspondence from the general public wanting autographs or souvenirs or what have you?

Admiral Wilkinson: No, we didn't get that many. Sometimes we'd get requests from very important people for first day covers and whatnot. Here right over there is the one of the *Nautilus* going under the North Pole. Some of the others when I was involved we made that many and we destroyed the thing. If it was numbered to 100, that's all there were. And so later for some congressman or something we might get a request, but in direct letters, no, we didn't get so many, which is interesting because since, even last week I got a letter from somebody asking me to endorse this thing and send it back to them. I get those requests all the time, but we didn't get too many on the *Nautilus* at that time. I don't know why. Maybe they weren't as first day cover conscious just then as they are now.

Paul Stillwell: You mentioned the TV coverage of the ship. What about newspaper people?

Admiral Wilkinson: The newspaper business seemed to go with big events. There were a hell of a lot of them there when the *Nautilus* got under way. There were a hell of a lot of them there when the keel was laid. When Mamie Eisenhower launched it, when we first got under way, and later when we came into Seattle with Senator Jackson aboard, and so on. But day by day, no, we weren't approached by the newspapers.

Paul Stillwell: Where else did your travels take you?

Admiral Wilkinson: In 1956 we went into Bermuda, tied up at the pier, and across the pier was a cruiser, the *Boston*. A cruiser is a big capital ship, over 1,000 people and pretty formal. It was Saturday morning, and we could hear them making preparations for the captain to go ashore. The dock had been cleaned up, and attention was called on the dock. I was in the wardroom in the *Nautilus*. There was a hatch out of the wardroom, and the brow was right there. And I was younger and more agile in those days. Certainly I could be up and on the pier in less than ten seconds. So we heard the bells go, "Dong, dong. Dong, dong. *Boston*, departing," which is, of course, the way you refer to your commanding officer of the ship.

So I said, "Hey, let's have some fun," as was my wont. So I was onto the dock before the skipper got down his brow. And it was very formal. Everybody was at attention on the dock, all his sailors and quite a few of mine and a couple of officers that had come up with me. But I was a commanding officer, too, so I said, "Captain," and his eyes swiveled around to look at me. I said, "Captain, as long as our two ships are here, why don't we engage in some athletic competition, loser to buy beer for the other crew?"

He said, "Well that wouldn't be fair. I have a lot more people."

I said, "Well, I don't know, Captain. You have more people to choose a team from. More people to buy beer for. It comes out even." Which, if you think about it, is a little bit stupid.

Paul Stillwell: That's right.

Admiral Wilkinson: But it sounded good, and my people liked it and it's your own people that you want to have fun.

The captain said, "Well, what did you have in mind?"

I said, "Captain, whatever your people are especially good at." And that was a cute answer, wise-ass answer.

He said, "Well, how about softball?"

When I heard that, I really went poker-faced, because we probably had on board the *Nautilus* the best softball pitcher in the Navy, and a pitcher is the dominant person on a softball team. I can't remember how many no-hitters he'd pitched, and every once in a while he'd pitch a perfect game of nobody getting to first base. You know, 21 batters up, 21 batters out. [Laughter] So I went deadpan and said, "Gee, that's good. We'll get a softball team together, and we'll play you for beer for the crew, all they can drink." And my guys liked that. We got our softball teams, and we got our pitcher, and we went up to play softball. There wasn't any doubt in our minds who was going to be the losers, so 30 or 40 of my guys went up and probably 200 or 300 people off the *Boston*. On my team each player took a bottle of beer with him as he went to the field, and as he came in he got another bottle of beer. By the time the seven innings were, over my guys had drunk a lot of beer. But not the pitcher.

We started off with a flurry, and pretty soon we were ahead, 8-0, and I said to my guys, "Hey, take it easy. Don't make it look so bad." So they took the pitcher out. Not out of the game where he couldn't come back but out of the pitching and put him in center field and put a guy in to pitch that had never pitched in his life before. And so we played on, drinking beer and playing softball. It came to the sixth inning with two out with *Boston* up at bat, and the score was 8-5. We were not there to lose, so my guys moved the pitcher back in, and he struck out the third guy and then in the seventh inning he struck out the side. But with a lot of beer the *Boston* people were saying, "You guys got off to a big start, but if we'd a played longer we'd have beat you." But it wasn't really so. [Laughter] It was a sandbag to see who bought the beer.

Paul Stillwell: After all the beer your men had drunk already, I don't know how they could take any more.

Admiral Wilkinson: No. But that was a good morale thing, because it's just like if you go to a restaurant where you eat all you can for a fee, here was all the beer you could drink, and I'd hear my guys saying, "Yeah, how many beers? Oh, I drink that for practice. I could have drunk one more."

So it was a silly, dumb thing, but morale on the *Nautilus* was high, and an evolution like that was important to that. We were in intensive operations all the time with the *Nautilus* where other submarines, if they were on weekly ops they'd get under way on Monday morning and come in Thursday afternoon. *Nautilus* would get under way Monday, and we probably operated and came in Saturday a week. When other ships came in, they would get a couple of line handlers from the ship next door to where they were going to tie up, and those were the people that met them on the dock.

When the *Nautilus* was coming in, you'd look at that dock, and it would be covered with people. There might not be any line handlers, but as you got your lines over and were breasting in, the people would start talking to us before we were even tied up. "What problems you got?" Well, we had just had two weeks of fabulous operations. We didn't have any problem. Our problem was we wanted to go home and see our wives. And so the first time that happened I said, "Gee, no problems." Let me tell you. If the people have been out there waiting for you on Saturday morning, that won't sell. I'd say to my exec, "Get these people some problems." [Laughter]

My problems were people and the mail. I told you about all the official letters we got. Forty-two a day may not sound like so much, but it is if you've been gone to sea for a month and come in, that was 1,260 letters saved up. Four hundred and twenty of them require an answer. And that's the official mail. We had 23 Girl Scout troops that named themselves Nautilus, and they sent us letters and sent us pictures and cookies and let me tell you, you answer those letters if the official mail waits.

In all my time on *Nautilus* we averaged 36 visitors a day. And I don't mean casual visitors. I mean the kind of visitors that were important people that you talked to and toured. And, again, 36 may not sound like so much, but we were a small ship. And remember, again, these were people we were talking to personally. And remember again that's on the average. If we had been at sea 30 days, that was 1,080 saved up. So sometimes we did a lot of them because we could handle 50 an hour, and so we would dig into that backlog. But we had a lot of visitors so we had many, many, many important people, including congressmen.

We had close to maybe 150 admirals, most of the admirals in the Navy. Finally we got the jump on that, because we'd take the new selectee group each year, knock off 30 at once. So we had an awful lot of important people that came and saw and talked to and were toured on the *Nautilus*, and other ones many of them that rode the ship at sea and saw her performance in exercises. And that wasn't all bad. We were young. If you're a young fellow and you have really important people come and Nobel Prize winners, the leading scientists, senior admirals, Secretary of the Navy coming and are really interested in what you're doing, that's heady stuff. My people loved that, and so did I. So we didn't in any way ever resent the tempo of our operations or the visitors we had. We did refer to U.S.S. as "Underway Saturday and Sunday," because frequently we did carry congressional parties to sea on the weekends.

We had a slush fund—that's not quite the way you're supposed to do it—that took care of certain things, helped with ship's parties. I had a Coke machine, and it cost a nickel to get a Coke out of that machine. I had it mounted in the crew's battery, and they liked to get a Coke and put a nickel in and we made a little profit out of that. A Coke out of the machine didn't cost us a nickel to do, although we bought coke syrup and all. And we had a record player machine where instead of a quarter you could put in a nickel and get six plays for a nickel, and my people liked to run the record machine. The Secretary of the Navy was aboard and saw that and asked about that, and I said, "Well, you know we do make a little profit out of that and then on the Coke machine, and so on field day we set it so Cokes were free. And we do make a little bit of profit out of this six plays for a nickel and we do that to buy some more records."

"Gee, that sounds good," he said. [Laughter] Although that's not quite the legal way to handle money, nobody ever objected to it because the Secretary of the Navy had more or less blessed it. [Laughter]

There was one time when I was so embarrassed during a visit. One of our passengers was really a rabid antisubmarine warfare black-shoe officer, and inadvertently the head had blown back on him when he was using it.*

I got my people together and really was upset and raised hell. Then the chief of the boat said, "Captain, you said yourself he was against us." [Laughter]

I can remember saying, "Goddamn it, that gentleman is our guest." But time and time and time again in life I've seen situations where the people that work in an organization mistakenly carry out what they think their boss would like to see done whereas he himself would never have the lack of judgment to do such a thing. It was appalling to me for a guest to end up having pressure in the head when he used it because that's not the way it ought to be. But in my time at least *Nautilus* never had any problem in holding its own against all comers. We probably shouldn't have, but for recreational purposes we played a little poker, and sometimes our visitors would play poker with us. I will say that during my tour on *Nautilus* no visitor ever went away as a winner. [Laughter] That's a lot of luck.

Everybody on the *Nautilus* was pleased and happy to be there. As another nuclear submarine came along, I sent one engineering officer and ten troops to be a nucleus of the engineering force on the *Skate*, and they weren't all eager to go.† Morale was high on the *Nautilus*, as you would imagine it would be, because we were doing well. Some of our fleet operation exercises were intensive operations against all the ASW forces that could be put against us. We still triumphed time after time after time, and the records were there to show it. And SubLant gave us all the torpedoes we wanted to fire, and we fired them. They were all hits, and we had pictures to prove it, and that'll sell.

Sometimes we would come in from sea with a major problem after we were operating, and we would get a refit at the Electric Boat Company. Instead of two weeks to do something, they might it do it from Friday to Monday. I could think back for a moment and cite some examples in the actual jobs that were done in fantastic time. One of the times was after we ran our first nuclear core out in 1956. Cores now last the life of the ship, but our first one didn't last that long. We were eager to keep operating, and we

---

* In this context a black-shoe was a term for a surface warfare officer.
† USS *Skate* (SSN-578), commissioned 23 December 1957, was the first ship of her class.

needed a new reactor core. We came in and hit the dock at a quarter of 5:00 one evening, and the reactor was shut down. The EB people came and started their work, and as fast as possible we had new controls, new reactor, all that and back at sea again. Admiral Rickover came to ride us as we went out to sea again, as was his wont. He was pleased to see how the things were operating, and after he got over that for a few minutes he said we did a lousy job.

I said, "Gee, "Admiral, I don't know. We were out at sea making full power and we've come in. We got new controls, new reactor. We're out making full power again, and they couldn't have done that much better."

He said, "Oh, you're young and immature, and you don't understand. We'll do a lot better next time."

I said, "No, seriously. The engine room's a little dirty, but we'll clean that up, and we're out here making full power, and everything's working and we're doing well. We really couldn't have done much better."

He said, "You don't understand. You're young and immature. We'll do a lot better next time."

I said, "Yeah? Just what can you do better?"

He said, "We'll do it faster."

I can remember saying, "Admiral, someday like you always do, you'll do it faster, but let me tell you, when they do they'll be working their asses off." That was in 1956, and maybe they'll do it faster someday, but let me tell you, they haven't yet. [Laughter]

Paul Stillwell: Was that the time you came in at a 106% power?

Admiral Wilkinson: Yes.

Paul Stillwell: How did you do that?

Admiral Wilkinson: We ran the first core out further than any core will be run out again. They're a different design now, and they're built to last longer, but then our first reactor was good for 900 equivalent full-power hours, and it had that much uranium in it. When uranium fissions and all the host of fission products, it breaks apart into sufficient products that one of them decays into xenon. Xenon has a very high radioactive cross section, so if there is xenon in there it will poison any neutron flux, and you can't start the reactor again. If you wait, that xenon will decay into something else and go away and after a few days you can start again. [Laughter]

So when you build it we had 900 equivalent full-power hours and another 1,500 hours' worth of uranium to overcome decayed xenon. And depending on how much of that was left, you could decay a little bit of xenon when you had it all at its peak. And so we ran out the 900 equivalent full-power hours, and we kept running into the amount to override xenon, which is all right as long as you didn't scram.* As we were coming in that last day, having run our reactor out to the utmost, we were making 100% power. We were not putting that much to the screw, but we were dumping the excess in steam to the steam dumps. Finally all our control rods were topped out, and equilibrium xenon was about to shut us down. My guys said, "Hey, we're going to shut down, and we won't be able to get to port then. You'd better send for tugs."

I said, "Well, of course, you can. Just increase the power above 100%, and the additional flux will burn that xenon back." And so it was. But as we got closer to port and used up more uranium, again at a little over 100% power, at 101 or 102, equilibrium xenon built up and the rods were all the way out and equilibrium xenon was going to shut us down again. So we boosted the power up a little higher and dumped the excess steam, and eventually we get to a 106%. We arrived at New London and tied up at a quarter of 5:00 and just kept dumping the steam and left it at 106% power. Finally, at 5:05, with all the rods out, equilibrium xenon shut them down, and the reactor died away. There'll never, never be another reactor run that far out again. It was tricky at the end to make sure you didn't have a scram and get shut down at sea and have to wait there for three or four days or be towed in. *Nautilus* wasn't ever towed in or didn't ever miss an operational commitment, so we weren't about to get shut down at sea.

Paul Stillwell: So you used every bit of that original core.

---

* A scram is a shutting down of the reactor.

Admiral Wilkinson: Every bit, including all that was left over to make sure you could go critical when you had decayed xenon products.

Paul Stillwell: How did the borax fit into this?

Admiral Wilkinson: It didn't. When I was working on the design I had to do with the calculations that determined the size and configuration of our core, but I also came in with a couple of suggestions. One of them was to change the control rod from a circular rod to an X-shape, which I mentioned. Also, I came up with the concept of the chemical poison system where as an emergency we would be able to shut down by injecting borax, which had the high cross section into the core. Of course, we never had to do that. We never had such a problem with a submarine. But all my submarines carried that for 30 years. Safety's a powerful word. I tried to get rid of it for 30 years and never could. Interestingly enough, with the much higher loading, in all the commercial reactors in addition to the control rods chemical poison is put in and then removed. So that's used as a control system on the higher power commercial reactors, but it was an idea of mine that I was sorry for years that I'd ever had. [Laughter]

On another subject, I'll tell you about my wagers on the World Series. What month does that come?

Paul Stillwell: October.

October. This was in '56. I was a Yankee fan, and they were playing the Brooklyn Dodgers. The Brooklyn Dodgers had won three games, and the Yankees had won two. There was an old expression I used. I said, "I've learned not to bet against Joe Louis, Notre Dame, or the New York Yankees."

Paul Stillwell: Right. I've heard that one.

Admiral Wilkinson: So my crew said, "Captain, if you're a Yankee supporter put your money where you mouth is."

I said, "Let me tell you. The real odds are 8-1. Give me 5-1 and I'll take a dollar with every one of you on the Yankees." So a whole lot of crew members put up 5-1 against my buck and they did and I did and you know what the Yankees did. They won those last two games, and they beat the Brooklyn Dodgers and everybody paid me off.

Now let me tell you a sea story from that year. It was Christmastime of 1956. We had had a very successful and very spectacular year, and we were having the ship's Christmas party. I'd had a few drinks and was a fat captain feeling pretty happy about the ship and its performance and my crew. Suddenly a young voice behind me said, "Captain," and I turned around. This pretty young thing said, "Captain, Deane and I want to get married. We want to have a big wedding, and we don't care exactly when it is, just so it's a date we can count on." Deane was a second class cook aboard.*

I said, "Well, what date would you like to count on?"

She said, "June the 15th."

I said, "Well, you can count on that," I said, being full of Christmas cheer. From about that moment on things went to pot. It was decided that since the Atlantic Fleet had had a taste of the potential of this new weapon system, there should be operations to show the *Nautilus*'s capability to the Pacific. And so a decision was made for the *Nautilus* to deploy for a period to the Pacific Fleet and conduct exercises with them. And there was a lot to do to get ready to go from the Atlantic to the Pacific with the first nuclear submarine. I wanted to get some extra spare parts, and obviously we needed completely new charts.

As we were making all the preparations, I said to my people, "How about Deane? I promised that young lady she could count on June 15, and a commitment is a commitment."

The guys laid out, "Well, here's the date we're going to sail. We can fly him back from Panama, and he'll make it."

I said, "You know, that could get screwed up. Let's send him to a course here in the States and give him a month leave. That can't get fouled up." And so it was, but again fate played its hand. We were due to sail at noon on a Sunday, and Saturday

---

* Commissaryman Second Class Thomas J. Deane, Jr., USN.

afternoon my leading cook, Mother Baird, was playing softball.* We had some pretty good softball players on the *Nautilus*, and he played too hard and he broke his leg. Now I was down to two cooks.

Well, the *Nautilus* had the type priority that on Saturday night I could have had a cook turned out of SubLant, but that's not very nice to somebody, and it wouldn't look too good, especially since I had a cook on leave. So I decided to sail with two cooks. The next day, as the maneuvering watch was stationed and we were due to get under way at noon, about 11:40 down the dock trundling his seabag came Deane. He came aboard, and I said, "Deane, what are you doing here?"

He said, "Didn't Baird break his leg?"

"Yes," I said.

"Did you get a replacement?"

"No."

"Well, then you need another cook, and here I am."

I said, "Deane, if something screwed up so you didn't make the date for that wedding, I'd never be able to look that girl in the eye again, and besides your cooking's not that good. Get the hell out of here." [Laughter]

He said, "Thank you, Captain," and took his seabag and left. So we sailed with two cooks. The funny sequel to that is that here a few years ago I had the pleasure of having a building named after me in New London.† It was a building to be used for training, and they asked me to come. There was a full ceremony with a band and honors and side boys and they asked me to speak, and I said, "How long?"‡

They said, "Fifteen minutes." You know, 15 minutes is a long time to talk, and after you get up and say, "Nobody knows what the future will bring, but whatever it is people will be important, and so I'm really pleased that this building named after me is to be used for the training of people." That took about a minute, and that left 14 minutes to go. I said, "I've told you my message, but I'm supposed to talk for 15 minutes, so the

---

* Commissaryman First Class Jack L. Baird, USN.
† The dedication was on 9 July 1993.
‡ Side boys are crew members stationed in two ranks at a ship's gangway on the arrival or departure of officers or officials for whom side honors are rendered. The number of side boys varies from two to eight, depending on the rank of the individual.

rest of the time I'm going to tell you some sea stories." So I told some stories to make up the 15-minute speech, which was a lot better than if I'd tried to talk seriously.

At the end of it, as the side boys were manned and I was going over to get a look at this building named after me, a gent stepped up and said, "Captain." I swiveled around, and damned if it wasn't Deane. This was 40-odd years later, and he said, "Captain, I want you to meet my grandson. If it wasn't for that story you just told, he wouldn't be here." [Laughter] As I was going through this ceremony where the honors were given, they said, "This is an official thing. You can wear a uniform if you want."

Even though I'd been retired a long time, I said, "No, I don't think so, because I'm not quite as thin as I was." [Laughter]

So we sailed from New London without our cook to deploy to the Pacific and show the capability of the nuclear submarines and exercises in the Pacific Fleet. We had an interesting run from New London to Panama, and we made it submerged. In going through all those islands in the Caribbean I came to periscope depth only five times to take a bearing on some island or other. There are lots of islands down there if you look at the chart, but we reached Panama, of course, on time. And that was interesting, because when you go through the Panama Canal there's a Panama pilot that conns the ship.*

Paul Stillwell: He takes over responsibility from the captain.

Admiral Wilkinson: He takes over responsibility, so as we were going through the Panama Canal I explained to him that this nuclear power was great. There was total power available and immediate response in anything. As a matter of fact, it was interesting. You could be stopped and ring up all ahead flank and flip the throttle open as fast as you could, and the reactor actually was self controlled and the steam was there. Conversely, you could ring up all stop and spin the throttle shut and the reactor would self-control and the steam was gone. It was totally responsive over the entire speed range, as I explained to the pilot as we were going through. But as we were coming in to the landing after having made the transit I said, "Let me tell you that the screws back there stick out about eight and a half inches. Don't get the stern in, because I don't have

---

* The individual with the conn—normally an officer—directs the ship's movements in course and speed.

a spare screw, and I'd hate to be immobilized down here with a damaged screw." The pilot nodded, and I said, "And you may not be able to tell by looking, but that black-looking bow up there is really a fiberglass bow with our sonar behind it. Don't touch the bow."

The pilot said to me, "Captain, would you like to make the landing?"

I said, "I sure would." [Laughter]

He said, "Be my guest." So the Panama pilot turned the conn back over to me, and I drove it up and made the landing. I was respectful and proud of that Panama pilot, because he could see my concern and worry.

It happened that a carrier had transited the canal and was there at the same time and was going to proceed the next day up to San Diego. We were at the club the night before having a little cheer, and I was making my manners and talking to this carrier skipper. He said, "What time are you getting under way?"

"Eight o'clock, sir," I said, "And what time are you getting under way?"

He said, "Twelve o'clock." I guess it takes them a little longer to get ready. He said, "We'll be passing you tomorrow afternoon, and we'll see you when we pass you."

I said, "Oh, how fast are you going?"

He said, "Eighteen knots."

I said, "We'll see you when you get to San Diego," which was a shock to him. He didn't conceive of a submarine with an SOA that fast.* There's a new dimension.

Paul Stillwell: What kind of speed could you make in the *Nautilus*?

Admiral Wilkinson: Submarine speeds over 20 knots are classified, but I don't think the *Nautilus*'s is anymore. We could make a greater speed submerged than surfaced. Due to the resistance and all, the top speed we could make on the surface was a little over 17 knots, but submerged I could make 22.78 knots, and that was it. But that was adequate to lay ourselves out for an SOA up there of nearly 20 knots, so no 18-knot carrier was going to pass us that afternoon.

---

* SOA – speed of advance.

We proceeded submerged then from Panama up to San Diego. With our date and time and speed of advance, we were due to get into San Diego on a Sunday morning. The powers that be had laid out a big exercise to intercept us for training on the way up, so there were lines of destroyers stationed out on our track south of San Diego. We were due to reach them Saturday night in order to arrive at San Diego Sunday morning. There's always the possibility of a scram, a reactor shutdown, in which you can't make your high speed, and it takes a certain length of time to get started up again, so I always had a tendency to be out ahead of my movement report.

I've forgotten now what was the maximum you could be ahead, but maybe it was four hours' worth. I was riding on my transit up to San Diego well ahead of the center of my moving haven, up at the front edge of it, like I always did. So we reached the line of destroyers a little earlier than might otherwise have been the case, and this was our tendency. Of course, we detected them and sonar conditions were bad, so we slowed down and slipped through undetected and proceeded on up towards San Diego.

Then I turned in, and I was lying there in my bunk thinking about that. I thought, "Gee, all those people are out there Saturday night steaming back and forth searching and searching for the *Nautilus*, and tomorrow morning they'll get the word we're tied up in San Diego, and they don't really get much out of that. That's really not right." Since we were three or four hours ahead of our SOA, I said, "Well, we've got time. We'll go back." So we turned around and we went back and we slipped under them undetected again back down south of the line.

Then we came up, and instead of slipping through undetected we eased up and made attacks on a couple of the destroyers and fired green flares. And I said, "Fire for effect." That means we fired as many green flares as we could and, "Send baker to everybody, 'We've made an attack on you,' and circle around here under these people for a few minutes." And then we broke contact and disappeared and proceeded on up and tied up in San Diego on time. But in looking back I'm glad I did that, because that would have been a hell of a thing to sit out there all Saturday night and then get the word that you didn't in any way complete your mission.

Paul Stillwell: It's hard to know which made them feel worse, not detecting you at all or seeing all those green flares.

Admiral Wilkinson: Well, but they had a lot of excitement, and they knew the *Nautilus* was there.

I want to mention something about arriving in San Diego. From our start in 1955, we eventually qualified all our officers on the *Nautilus*. I had them all meet the requirements not just for qualification in submarines but qualification for command. In all the time I was the skipper of the *Nautilus* and offered the OOD the chance to make the landing, I only had them refuse twice. Once was the beautiful clear day when the *Nautilus* was coming into San Diego that first time. The pier was straight ahead, an absolutely straight shot, no current, just to drive up and tie up. I asked the OOD, who was Lieutenant Paul Early, "Would you like to make a landing?"*

He said, "Captain, it's your hometown." [Laughter] So I made that landing.

Once we got there, we opened up the ship. The local command had laid on for us a very extensive visitors' schedule. We could handle 50 visitors an hour, and we toured about all we could after first sitting them down in our crew's mess. We'd talk to them and show them diagrams for an hour. Then we would tour them through the ship for an hour while we were talking to another 50. We kept that up from 8:00 A.M. to 11:00 P.M. every day.

We tied up to the submarine tender when we got to San Diego. People from the tender came down and said, "What emergency jobs have you got, and what can we do for you?"

The pride of my guys was fantastic. They said, "Oh, we've only come from New London. We don't have any problems. We don't have any job orders." And really I had some leaks in the hydraulic systems. My guys were up all night welding them. But everything like that that we had, ship's force did it, and we turned in zero job orders.

Then they said, "Well, don't you have anything?"

We said, "Well, you do have an awfully extensive schedule here for us and an awful lot of visitors. If we could get some handouts printed it would help." After our

---
* Lieutenant Paul J. Early, USN.

submerged transit from New London to San Diego the only job order we turned in was to get some handouts printed. [Laughter] And my guys had a certain pride. Also, they didn't like the other people to work on their equipment. There wasn't anything that our guys couldn't fix.

Years later, *Nautilus* was in a state of decline. When I was SubLant I went out on the *Nautilus* and was not really happy with the state of things.[*] A rod drive motor—one of the two rod drive motors—was out of commission, and I said, "Why is this out of commission?"

They said, "Well, we've been trying to get a job order in on it." And it had been that way for six weeks.

I said, "You know, I could sympathize with you on that, except I can remember when my guys fixed that at sea in four hours." [Laughter] So there was a difference from the original commissioning crew of the *Nautilus*. There was an intense desire on their part to make that ship run perfectly, and they were probably more capable than any crew has been since.

Going back in time, I had a young seaman named Breese that we sent to ET school, Electronics Technician School, and that was in Great Lakes.[†] When he completed the course and graduated from school they screwed up, and instead of sending him back to his ship they transferred him to the Pacific. Since he had not yet finished his submarine qualification, although he was a crackerjack young seaman on the *Nautilus*, they mistakenly put him on a destroyer instead of sending him back to his ship. We tried to get him back, and if he'd have been anywhere in the Atlantic I could have got him, but I couldn't get a seaman transferred from the Pacific Fleet across country to the Atlantic Fleet. As we tied up in San Diego, Breese came aboard, tears in his eyes. All my troops, including the chief of the boat, said, "Captain, we've got to get our man back." I mean, Breese loved the ship and was loyal to it. As he was sitting there crying, I said, "Breese, get your gear aboard. I'll square it away someway." [Laughter]

---

[*] Vice Admiral Wilkinson served as Commander Submarine Force Atlantic Fleet from 12 February 1970 to 28 June 1972.
[†] Great Lakes, Illinois, a town on the shore of Lake Michigan, about 30 miles north of downtown Chicago, is the site of a large naval training center.

Paul Stillwell: What did you do then?

Admiral Wilkinson: I'll tell you about that. In addition to those visitors at 50 an hour during the three days over Fourth of July weekend, we also took a considerable number of local military people in the San Diego area to sea. Among others was the three-star admiral that was First Fleet and who was the senior officer in the San Diego area at the time.[*] He was a crusty old seadog, and we were scheduled when he rode us with a group to get under way at 6:00 and come back in at noon. So they came aboard, and we got under way at 6:00, and we went out into the operating area and rendezvoused with a couple of destroyers to give them services. Sonar conditions were pretty poor out there, and so we were working with them but having trouble keeping them in contact with us and giving them services.

When the time came to surface, you were supposed to get communication with the surface ships above you and make sure all was clear to surface. But I could not get a good communication back and forth with them. This wasted 15-20 minutes of fooling around, and finally I broke clear and proceeded to a safe distance and got clear and surfaced. By now we were a little farther from home and it was a little later than we had planned for the day. My navigator, Lieutenant Nicholson, was taking a quick fix.

Com1stFlt, the admiral, was looking over his shoulder and said either to him or to me, "What's your ETA?"[†] Well, when he had originally asked what our ETA was, I said, "Twelve o'clock, sir." And he looked over his shoulder and said, "What's your ETA?" and my guy said, "Twelve o'clock, sir." But when we plotted it out, we couldn't make it on the surface. So I said to myself, "Well, if I submerge I can go much faster." So I submerged and squirted across the op area to the very edge of it and surfaced. My navigator now took another fix, and First Fleet leaned over his shoulder and said, "What's your ETA?"

Now it was going to be tight, but it was possible, and so my navigator said, "Twelve o'clock, sir." But as we come up toward the entrance to the channel it was touch and go, so I was thinking, "All ahead flank," top surface speed. We came up the

---

[*] Vice Admiral Robert L. Dennison, USN, served as Commander First Fleet from 18 June 1956 to 23 July 1958. The oral history of Dennison, who retired as a four-star admiral, is in the Naval Institute collection.
[†] ETA – estimated time of arrival.

channel at that speed, and we were supposed to tie up at the piers there at Point Loma, the fueling piers just beyond the submarine pier.* It's an easy straight-in approach. So I kept ahead at all ahead flank until I said, "All back emergency, all stop, put your lines over, double up, put the brow over." That was the total landing. Then I said, "Admiral, we're ready to disembark you, sir." He'd been on the bridge, and so he went down to the deck, and we came to attention and saluted the admiral.

As he started to leave, he got halfway out on the brow, and he stopped. He reached in and pulled out his watch, which was not a wristwatch but a big watch with a fob. He looked at it, and I stepped out on the brow and looked down with him. As great good fortune would happen, at that instant in time it couldn't have been more 12:00 o'clock. The hour hand was at 12. The minute hand was at 12. The second hand was at 12. He stepped off at exactly to the second 12:00 o'clock. He had been on the bridge, and truly we couldn't have been there any sooner. We couldn't have been there five seconds sooner, because we'd been all flank, all back emergency, double up.

He looked at that watch, and I looked over his shoulder and looked at it with him. He turned to me and he said, "That is outstanding." [Laughter] And he said, "You people have done an outstanding job here. You've made a lot of operations, taken everybody to sea. You've had visitors from 8:00 A.M. till 11:00 P.M. What can we do for you?"

I said, "Admiral, there is one little thing. I would like to get my man back." [Laughter] And so orders were issued, and although Breese was already aboard with his gear it was legalized. [Laughter]

Paul Stillwell: That is a great story.

Admiral Wilkinson: And the chief of the boat and everybody were happy with their shipmate. Just like they'd worked all night to tell the tender we didn't need any job orders, they were pleased to get their man back on board. After all, you should look out for your people. Those are the people that carry you.

---

* Point Loma is a strip of land that juts southward at the western edge of the entrance to San Diego Harbor.

Paul Stillwell: Well, that story about Deane demonstrates both loyalty upward and loyalty downward.

Admiral Wilkinson: Yes, Deane on his own initiative was back there just before sailing with his seabag saying, "You need a cook, and here I am." And I told him his cooking wasn't that good, [Laughter] which wasn't really true, of course. But you've got to be a little bit wiseass at times. And he did say, "Thank you, Captain," and left.

We then went into extensive operations. They scheduled us so that instead of the surface ships hunting us, they gave us the mission to be part of the force that defended the Pacific West Coast from a high-speed carrier attack, which is a little different mission and harder to perform.

I was out somewhere between Los Angeles and San Francisco, and I didn't have complete faith that if they knew where I was they'd come that way. So I disappeared. I submerged, and we didn't communicate with anybody, and so nobody knew where we were except that we were submerged there off the West Coast. I didn't come to periscope depth or radiate or anything, because I didn't want to be detected. I just got into the best layer position with my passive sonar and steamed up and down, and we made no contacts. A couple of days went by, and we had made no contact and my troops would come up to me and say, "Captain, when are we going to get them?"

I said, "Gee, we may not."

They said, "Captain, we always have before," which was true. Finally, as luck would have it, we did make a sonar contact. They happened to be out in the third convergence zone, which was about 90 miles. We were way off the track and the bearing was going fast. The carrier task group was coming in at a nominal 25 knots. Actually, with zigging and all, they weren't making that good a speed of advance. And, as I've said, the *Nautilus* couldn't make 25 knots, even when submerged. But with the bearing drift we went down deep and went to max speed to intercept. We didn't quite make it, but we got almost there. We chased them as they were constant helming, and we finally caught them from behind.

I came up the stern of a carrier. As I remember it was the *Princeton*. And it was really great to see that one big spoke up there on the sonar. As we got closer we could see it diverge into two spokes, and I drove up between the screws. Then we could hold our depth control to the inch, as you understand, especially at high speed, and my guys were awfully good. So I came up to about 10 feet under the carrier and stuck up my number one scope with the big head just a little bit and took pictures of their keel and pictures of their screw. We got quite a bit of evidence that we were really there, and then we eased out to the side and plugged them with one of our torpedoes and fired green flares and put a torpedo right under the carrier.

I only had ten torpedoes. Back when I was in the Atlantic, Commander Submarine Force gave me plenty of torpedoes to fire, but out there I only had ten fish to shoot, and we tried to not miss. In the Atlantic I think we never missed, because we never took a bad shot. We would drive up to maybe 600 yards on a guy's beam and punch a fish under him and take pictures to prove it. These guys were moving fast, and I had ten fish. I put five under carriers and two under cruisers and two under destroyers. But then I missed with the tenth one because I had some rudder on. I was making a turn, and at top speed it touched the shutter going out and I got an erratic run. So I didn't get all hits, I just got nine. But we were lucky to make contact, and they knew we were there.

We got quite a bit of accolades from that and subsequent operations in the Pacific. That was Exercise Home Run, and I could show you a lot of very commendatory dispatches and "Well dones" on our performance there. We had very, very successful operations in our demonstration of nuclear capabilities to the Pacific Fleet. We proceeded into San Francisco, and we did some other operations. Finally we went up to Seattle to show them nuclear power up there. My time in command was now almost gone.

I got ComSubPac aboard, Admiral Grenfell, and my relief, Commander Anderson, had reported aboard, and we were due to proceed into Seattle.* Sometime during our time in Seattle we were going to have the change of command, and I was going to be relieved. Much to my distress, my beautiful tour on the *Nautilus* would be

---

* Rear Admiral Elton W. Grenfell, USN, served as Commander Submarine Force Pacific Fleet from 1956 to 1959.

over. I was gong to be detached to go on to other duties as I had orders to go to the senior class in the Naval War College in Newport.

I had a personal letter that I could show you over there from Admiral Rickover telling me how important Senator Jackson was and to be sure and take good care of Senator Jackson, because we were going to have the pleasure of having Senator Jackson come on board.[*] I'll quote this letter, but you can just read it for your amusement.

Paul Stillwell: This is dated June 13, 1957. It certainly stresses the importance of Senator Jackson to the program.

Admiral Wilkinson: Senator Jackson was a very important individual. He was *the* leading Democrat. If he hadn't had the aneurysm and died later, I'm sure that eventually Senator Jackson would have been President of the United States. So we were going to have him on board the *Nautilus*. We stopped in Everett and picked him up. As we were proceeding into Seattle, the mayor and the city council and the commandant of the naval district and 120 newspaper people and Fox Movietone News, and the band and my sister and her four boys were there waiting for us to arrive.

The *Nautilus* wasn't as impressive on the surface as it was submerged, and I said, "Jesus, as long as I've got the senator aboard I might as well show him the ship submerged." The water in Seattle Harbor is actually 400 feet deep, so we could proceed on in submerged, and we did. We didn't mean to make it quite that dramatic, but, unfortunately, as we came into Seattle Harbor there were a couple of these excursion ships taking people around, and they were in my way. I picked up the pier at which we were going to tie up on my active sonar at 9,200 yards, and so I had no difficulty in telling exactly where I was and exactly where I was going, and I proceeded on up toward our berth.

The press in those days was prone to be very enthusiastic about the *Nautilus*. On the other hand, they do like a story, and they were all waiting. We were due in at 5:00

---

[*] Henry M. Jackson, a Democrat from the state of Washington, served in the House of Representatives from 1941 to 1953 and then in the Senate from 1953 until his death in 1983. He was chairman of the Senate Armed Services Committee and a strong proponent of nuclear-powered warships. The ballistic missile submarine *Henry M. Jackson* (SSBN-730) is named in his honor.

P.M. When it got to be a quarter of 5:00 and there was no *Nautilus* in sight, now the story was that we weren't there. So they started looking around for that story, and they happened to find my sister. They asked her if she thought there'd been an accident. She certainly hoped not. "Well, if not why would your brother be late with all these people waiting?" My sister said that she didn't know what to say.

A little more time went by, and one of my young officers was on leave with his wife to meet the ship in Seattle, Lieutenant Carr. They found him at about five minutes of 5:00 and went through the same query with him, and just like the First Fleet admiral, Ken didn't have a wristwatch. He used the old railroad-type watch with a watch fob. They asked him if there'd been an accident. "No."

"Why would your skipper be late?"

He pulled out his watch and looked at it. It was five minutes of 5:00, and he said, "They're not late yet." [Laughter] And I was proud of him when I heard that later. He said, "You know, I was really worried, Captain, but I wasn't going to put up with any crap until you were really late."

Well, in the meantime we were proceeding toward our berth. I surfaced a little later than I would have normally, but I surfaced right off the end of the pier. And it was a straight-shot, easy landing. I had already rung up all stop on my approach submerged, and I surfaced. The captain's the first one to the bridge, so I hit the bridge and said, "Control, give it a great big blow," which means we blew up as far as we could with high-pressure air, because there wasn't much time with the low-pressure blower. So I said, "Give it a great big blow. Open all deck hatches. Line handlers, put your lines over." As I said, I'd already rung up all stop. I gave two more bells: "All back two-thirds, all stop, double up. Put the brow over. Senator, we're ready to disembark you."[*] Senator Jackson walked off the ship to meet all that press at exactly 5:00 o'clock, exactly 5:00 o'clock. [Laughter]

Paul Stillwell: Did you hear any feedback from Senator Jackson?

---

[*] Each order to the engines is accompanied by a bell sound on the engine order telegraph. Thus, a "bell" is synonymous with an engine order. The fewer the number of bells in a given landing, the better.

Admiral Wilkinson: Oh, yes. Senator Jackson and I had talked quite a bit during his transit down about what a fabulous job Admiral Rickover had done and how much we all appreciated the support that Senator Jackson and the Joint Congressional Committee on Atomic Energy had given toward the decision to build the *Nautilus* and the program. Senator Jackson was always a great supporter of the nuclear program, and so it was a great pleasure to ferry him into Seattle. As it turned out, it was a rather dramatic thing and worked out very well.

As I said, Admiral Grenfell was riding with me as we made our entry into Seattle, and he was quite happy with us. Senator Jackson was quite happy with the way things went and the press interaction that he was able to have. It all fell together. We were in the area another two or three days, and we had lots of visitors there, the local military and whatnot. Then we went down to Tacoma and had more visitors there. Somewhere in this time I was due to be relieved as the captain. We were in Tacoma, and the *Nautilus* was going to go to sea. So we scheduled it to proceed from Tacoma to Seattle and tie up and have a change of command and then the *Nautilus* would get under way again with the new captain and depart, which was a little tight schedule-wise.

We were in Tacoma, and we had quarters at 3:15. I talked to the crew, and we stationed the maneuvering watch. It's a few miles from Tacoma to Seattle, and unfortunately there was a zero-visibility fog. I was still the captain and responsible. So for the three hours from 5:00 to 8:00 under way I was on the bridge all the time ensuring that we were proceeding safely. We did penetrate the fog and arrive in Seattle and tie up at 8:00 o'clock and secured the maneuvering watch and the special sea detail and manned the change of command party. At 9:00 o'clock we had the change of command, and I turned over command to Commander Anderson with tears in my eyes.[*] Then they stationed the maneuvering watch again and took in the lines and sailed away, and I saw my beautiful ship leave.

Paul Stillwell: I can imagine the tears in your eyes.

---

[*] On 18 June 1957, at Seattle, Commander William R. Anderson, USN, relieved Captain Wilkinson, as commanding officer. At the change of command ceremony Wilkinson received the Legion of Merit from Rear Admiral Albert M. Bledsoe, USN, Commandant, 13th Naval District.

Admiral Wilkinson: Yes. Really, that's the way the *Nautilus* operated. There wasn't even a spare day for the change of command. We just fitted that into the thing. Quarters at 3:15, under way at 5:00, tie up at 8:00, change of command at 9:00, sailed away at 10:00. It was a tight schedule.

We had an awful lot of people make commissions on the *Nautilus*, which was pretty impressive. One of them was Fields, the man who showed the congressmen his old torpedoes from World War II. Maybe he wasn't the smartest man on board, but he was the hardest-working man on board. When the *Nautilus* was being built, every man aboard earned nuclear submarine qualifications for that ship. Although I had a lot of brilliant nukey-poos, the first enlisted man that qualified as knowing all the detail about the *Nautilus* was First Class Torpedoman Fields. He had just made his commission as an ensign, and as we were forming up for the change of command my leading chief said we never got to christen Fields. That's the sort of ceremony when a guy got promoted they might throw him in and give him a dunking. And I can remember saying, "I've been on this bucket for four years, and I never thought I'd see the day that we couldn't get it all done." And with that they pitched Fields over the side. As he climbed up, this was 20 minutes of 9:00, and I said, "Fields, I expect to see you up at the change of command ceremony." He went below and got his other new uniform and put it on and was up there at the change of command. And he didn't really resent that.

Paul Stillwell: Gave him a story to tell the rest of his life.

Admiral Wilkinson: Yes.

But we had a very successful operating period demonstrating the potential, the capability of the nuclear submarine, to the Pacific Fleet, and we were quite fortunate that it worked out that way.

Paul Stillwell: Well, I think I've finally run out of questions on the *Nautilus*. Are we ready to talk about your time at the Naval War College?

Admiral Wilkinson: Yes. I sound like a rebel sometimes, and I'm really not. I try to do right, but you can't imagine how full a schedule there was on the *Nautilus*. I keep pointing down at this pile of stuff on the floor. *Nautilus* was total commitment. I was busy all the time. I maybe didn't get my bank balance right. In retrospect I didn't do all the things that I would like to have done at home. But I did my best possible job on the ship. But there was a tremendous amount of correspondence and other things, and I have copies of all the "Well Done" dispatches and a lot of those other things and they're not in very good order there. And when I was transferred from the *Nautilus* I sealed it up in two or three boxes, and I really just opened them in the last few days to look through them before you came.

I got off on a bad foot at the Naval War College. They sent me a questionnaire and a reading list that I got on the *Nautilus*. I had my orders maybe three months before I was going there. But I was in the midst of evaluation exercises out in the Pacific, and really it was more important for that to go well. And if I had any spare time when I was in Seattle my sister was there that I hadn't seen for years. So I got this reading list from the War College and a questionnaire with a bunch of information to fill out, which I should have done, but I didn't get it done. So a month went by, and I got a second notice that they wanted this stuff sent back immediately, and I should start working on this reading list.

That annoyed me, so I wrote an endorsement on it, and I said, "Look, at the present time I don't work for you. I have a job and I'm real busy at it. Later I'm going to be detached and I'm going to come and report to the Naval War College, and then if you want me to fill out these forms I'll do it 24 hours a day. But between now and then don't bother me with this stuff." I sent it all back, and I didn't hear any more from them. [Laughter] So I got to the Naval War College with a little bit of a chip on my shoulder. But everybody there was nice enough to me, and the course was interesting. I thought I was going to have a course in how to fight naval battles and naval war. I didn't have the right idea at all. It was a course in political science with foundations of national power and what was involved.

Paul Stillwell: Planning and strategy.

Admiral Wilkinson: Yes. One of the young instructors there whom I got to know was a fellow named Schlesinger, who later became the Secretary of Defense and a pretty famous guy.* So I had fun at the Naval War College. There were some antisubmarine guys that made a bunch of antisubmarine speeches, so I managed to fit in 15 speeches to the Rotary and the Kiwanis and all those kinds of organizations explaining to them about submarines. But I enjoyed the political science courses; they weren't what I expected, but I did learn a lot. And I had the time to do it. And I wrote a good paper. I've got a copy of it over there. And we had a great place to live out on Black Point Farm, out in Narragansett Bay, and was there with my wife and the kids. It was really a great tour. There was a little letdown in activity after the intense operations on the *Nautilus* but a great tour nonetheless. The course was good and the people were good and I enjoyed it.

I'll tell a couple of more War College stories to fit with that, and one of them was back to the *Nautilus* when I was the captain. *Nautilus* one day went into Newport to have as visitors the people that then were on the staff and attending the senior course at the Naval War College. We went in and did that and were met by the president of the Naval War College. And we took him out for a trip to sea to see the performance of this new type ship, and he was a crusty old seadog. I got one of those ten parkas that I mentioned once before with the mittens in one side and the watch cap in the other and it was cold as hell, it was that time of year, January. And he put that watch cap down over his ears and enjoyed his trip on the *Nautilus* and being a seadog again and spent a lot of time on the bridge.

That day, as I was coming in from sea, it was really cold, and the wind was blowing, and there's a current up there. We were going up and were going to turn 180 degrees. Instead of tying up to a dock, we were going to tie up to a tender where the bitts are in the side. And we really hadn't done that a lot, maybe never. [Laughter] That was one of the only two times that my OOD said he didn't want to make the landing. I told you about the other one, when we were going into San Diego. But this time I said to my OOD, "Would you like to make the landing?"

He said, "No, sir, Captain."

---

* James R. Schlesinger served as Secretary of Defense from 2 July 1973 to 19 November 1975.

The president of the War College was on the bridge, and he laughed and he laughed, and he said, "I wouldn't either. That is a really smart young officer. [Laughter] I wouldn't either." [Laughter] Well, we allowed the 180 degrees and tied up to the tender. That's another *Nautilus* story, see. There's really a million of them.

Paul Stillwell: Evidently.

Admiral Wilkinson: Yes. For one thing I used to have a pile of notes to jog my mind on this or that story, and I was figuring one day writing them up and I could pull that out and probably think of some things I haven't thought of for years.

Paul Stillwell: Was the Naval War College useful in exposing you to other naval officers besides submariners?

Admiral Wilkinson: Undoubtedly it was. I didn't recognize it at the time. I made some good friends there. Captain Dosé, who was a crackerjack flier, was there.[*] Later on I helped him with some programs when I was in that position in the Navy Department. I got acquainted with Mr. Schlesinger. I didn't concentrate on that and making contacts and all. In retrospect maybe I should have. I more studied all the material, wrote the papers, gave the submarine speeches, and spent time with my family. Some ways it was sort of a surprise to have no real responsibility other than to just do a bunch of schoolwork, which has never been much of a problem to me. I'd just been commanding officer for a long, long time. Even before that I'd been exec, and exec has a responsibility too.

Paul Stillwell: Well, it probably broadened your outlook on the Navy as a whole also.

Admiral Wilkinson: Yes, I was really surprised. It wasn't what I expected it to be. The senior course at the Naval War College, I expected a lot of stuff about wars and battles and whatnot. It was totally a course in foundations of national power.

---

[*] Captain Robert G. Dosé, USN.

Paul Stillwell: Did you have a series of guest speakers from outside?

Admiral Wilkinson: No, really not very many.

Paul Stillwell: Was it mostly a lecture type format?

Admiral Wilkinson: Yes, and study material. A lot of reading.

Paul Stillwell: So they finally caught up to you with that reading that they'd sent to the *Nautilus*.

Admiral Wilkinson: Oh, yes. I got it all done, and I ended up reading that entire list, and I filled out all those forms, but I didn't do it until I reported. [Laughter] Again, that endorsement sounds wiseass, and in retrospect it was, and I shouldn't have done it that way, but on the other hand it was true. I really was busy. I didn't have time to read all that stuff. Reading is easy for me, but I didn't have time to read those 30 books. Gee, that would take me 30 days. [Laughter]

Paul Stillwell: In retrospect was that a useful year in the course of your career?

Admiral Wilkinson: Yes. It was useful to have the relaxation and the rest, even though I didn't recognize it at the time. It probably didn't hurt on my record to get promoted, but I'd have probably got promoted without it. I didn't learn anything I had to know, although I made use of some of that information when I was Chief of Staff, U.S. Forces Japan. I'm not like Rickover. Rickover had the ability to somehow make use of anything he read or any information that was given to him. I could show you in the other room a lot of his things that he wrote, "Swiss Schools and Ours" and other things like that and education, and I've had people damn Admiral Rickover. Well, now here I'm looking at 460 pages of *Congressional Record*. You know, I'd have a hard time talking 460 pages about anything. [Laughter]

One time I was riding with Rickover out to Idaho, and he had a book that was about the civil service system in China about the time of 1,000 A.D., and so I read that book en route because I do read fast. It was quite interesting. Years and years and years later I was reading some of Admiral Rickover's congressional testimony, and damned if there isn't all about the civil service system in China at the time of 1,000, and I'm saying to myself, "Somewhere I read that before. Somewhere I read that before. Somewhere." I finally reconstructed that: "By God, it was when Admiral Rickover was reading that book 15 years ago when we were making that trip."

That guy had the ability, if something was worthwhile, to make use of it. Like our training and qualification procedures for people. And, "Hey, we've got to have machinery history." Let me tell you, if there was some idea that was good, Rickover would take it and sometimes make use of it so that it even became odious back to you, the guy that started it. [Laughter] But I did not have that ability, and still I found some of that information of good background and useful for me when I was Chief of Staff, U.S. Forces, Japan. And we're going to talk about that tour later because it was interesting.

Paul Stillwell: How much contact did Admiral Rickover maintain with you after you had left the *Nautilus*?

Admiral Wilkinson: A lot. I kept contact with Rickover for the rest of the time that I was in the Navy, after I was out of the Navy, and up to the day he died.[*] I went down and rode shotgun for him a couple of years before he died when he was down at Birmingham, Alabama, which is the most pro-military place in the United States. And I was consulted when Rickover was finally retired as to who his replacement ought to be. They talked about that with me from the Navy. I never hired anybody out of the Navy, but I hired a lot of people at INPO that were ex-Navy people.[†]

Rickover was a funny guy. For years and years and years, 20 years of performance didn't mean a damn thing. It was, "What have you done today?" [Laughter] When someone's name came up, Rickover would say, "He's no damned

---
[*] Admiral Rickover died on 8 July 1986.
[†] INPO – Institute of Nuclear Power Operations.

good." Rickover would say of another one, "He's no damned good." There are a lot of people Rickover wouldn't give you thumbs up on, really good people. Rickover would not give you a thumbs up on a really good guy, Jim Calvert.* He would say to Jim, "You're saving up your grease. Calvert, all the time you're saving up your grease. When are you going to use some?" [Laughter]

Paul Stillwell: Well, Admiral, we've had a fascinating day today, talking about the *Nautilus*. I look forward to seeing you tomorrow.

---

* Commander James F. Calvert, USN, was the first commanding officer of the USS *Skate* (SSN-578), the U.S. Navy's third nuclear submarine, following the *Nautilus* and *Seawolf*.

Interview Number 4 with Vice Admiral Eugene P. Wilkinson, U.S. Navy (Retired)
Place: Admiral Wilkinson's home in Del Mar, California
Date: Tuesday, 20 January 1998
Interviewer: Paul Stillwell

Paul Stillwell: Admiral, today we're ready to start the discussion of your duty as a submarine division commander.

Admiral Wilkinson: After my tour at the Naval War College was over, I got orders as Commander Submarine Division 102, which was down in New London, not too far a move from Newport. Division 102 was going to get assigned to it all the nuclear ships, and I was pleased at that. I had the *Nautilus*, my old home, and *Seawolf* in my division. Then, as the other nuclear ships were built and delivered in sequence, I had the *Skate*, commanded by Jim Calvert, and *Swordfish* and so on down the line.

It was fun to me to deal with those ships. From time to time I would ride one to sea, and certainly I would spend a lot of time talking to skippers and the officers and also a lot of people in the ships' companies. I was pleased to be able to go aboard and know some of the troops on every ship. It was enjoyable to me to be back in the fleet after the time at the War College and to be associated with what was going on in the nuclear Navy.

At about that time it was decided to give our expertise to the Brits so they would have a nuclear-powered ship. They selected some officers and sent them over to the United States, and I became their mentor. I guess if they had a fitness report written in the United States that went back to the Brits I wrote it, and so I became acquainted with them. I had a lot of respect for the Brits, and one of them that I became acquainted with in that time became the First Sea Lord, and so I enjoyed being a schoolteacher back in the days. I enjoyed being a mentor and giving advice and counsel and guidance to the very select young Brit officers who were over to go into their nuclear program.

Paul Stillwell: Were you giving them guidance from an operational standpoint, as opposed to the technical knowhow to run the plant?

Admiral Wilkinson: A combination of both, but when they were over there in New London it was more related to the technical. We're talking about the business of "Here's what you ought to know" and qualification and whatnot. But in with it was a heavy amount of operational—a large amount of what you ought to do to check up on things in a mechanical sense: "Here's what you ought to do to check up on people in a personnel sense in training and qualification, and here's what you yourself ought to know and be able to do." I talked to young people that were really intense and weren't just kissing off what you were saying. They were interested; they didn't go to sleep while you were talking to them.

Paul Stillwell: Did they initially go through the training at Idaho, or did they have a setup over in England?

Admiral Wilkinson: I don't know. I don't think they went through qualification at Idaho, although they might have. But certainly I had a certain amount of interaction with them. I was surprised in a sense when I discovered that they'd had a considerable briefing before they came over, and one item in the briefing was not to play poker with me, to save their money. So I had gained an international reputation as a poker player, which I did not deserve, although I will say for them they couldn't wait. [Laughter] They discounted that 100%.

Paul Stillwell: Did you clean them out?

Admiral Wilkinson: I don't remember, but I did have one very lucky session that I was really happy about playing poker.

In this time the Canadians decided that they needed to get some more submarine capabilities, because they had British boats and other things providing services for them for training their ASW forces. They didn't have submarines of their own, and they wanted their own, and they figured they might as well build some nuclear. And, gee, they didn't really have the capability to do that, but they wanted to talk to somebody that really knew. So the Navy sent George Morin and me up for a week to Canada, to answer any questions the Canadians might have.* They're a pretty tough, proud outfit and, gee, they worked us hard. Every day I briefed the head of their Navy and the head of their supply and the head of their engineering, and with lots of questions this went on for several days.

At the end of every day, at 4:00 or 5:00 o'clock, they would take me off, and we would party, have cocktails and whatnot, and when that was over they'd give me a big list of questions for the next day. And, God, I might be till 2:00 in the morning going through that and up early and off for the next round. This went on for three or four days, and there was a lot of snide comments about Americans this or Americans that. About the fourth day one guy made a comment, "Americans are lousy poker players."

So I stopped and said, "You know, I've been up here working my tail off for a few days, and there's been comment after comment like that. Each time it was made, just for political reasons, I swallowed my spit and smiled and didn't say anything. But there's nothing political about that. Actually, just like some of the other things, Americans aren't lousy poker players. They're probably the best poker players in the world. And as the only American up here I'd be real pleased to demonstrate that." And, by God, they did set up a poker game, and, as luck would have it, I got good cards.

Paul Stillwell: As luck would have it.

Admiral Wilkinson: As luck would have it. [Laughter] Thank God, because I always throw that comment in. I've had the comment made to me by people, "It all averages out." That is really not so. The winners win, and the losers lose, and it goes on that way forever. But in any one session a lucky player will beat the hell out of a skillful player, and so you always worried that maybe you'd be really unlucky that session. But in the ones that I've really wanted to win, I was really lucky every time.

The tour on 102 was a very pleasant one for me because I was involved with all the new nuclear ships. They had some super people in charge of them, like Jim Calvert and Shannon Cramer and others like that.†

---

* Commander George F. Morin, USN.
† Commander Shannon D. Cramer, USN.

Paul Stillwell: Would you like to comment specifically on those skippers, please?

Admiral Wilkinson: They were crackerjack people, they had superior crews, and they ran crackerjack ships. Witness *Skate*'s getting to the North Pole only just a few days after the *Nautilus* did in '58.* They wanted to be there sooner, but, of course, we wouldn't let them. So it was fun to me to be involved, and they were capable, very good people, and I enjoyed talking to them and associating with them. They performed really well, and I was their boss, and if the people that work for you perform well it makes you look good. And so I had a nice successful tour as Commander Submarine Division 102.

Paul Stillwell: When you were the commanding officer of the *Nautilus* in '57 were there already plans under way for the North Pole transit?

Admiral Wilkinson: No. During my time on the *Nautilus* each one of my young officers did something where he got some kind of a letter of commendation. I had one young officer do a study on going under the Arctic ice. *Nautilus* was up and on the fringes and went under the ice. It wasn't anything we couldn't do. We had sort of a coined phrase, "Under the pack to the Pole and back." [Laughter] I wanted to do that so much but never could get that scheduled, and there was never any concept of us doing that. It wasn't until 1958 that authority was granted for the *Nautilus* to do that, and they didn't do it like I said, "Under the pack to the Pole and back." As a matter of fact, they started in the Pacific and went under the ice and under the North Pole and out into the Atlantic, 1,800 miles.

I wrote the operation order. I had the fun of taking the officers off both the *Nautilus* and the *Skate*, which about ten days later went to the North Pole from the

---

* On 3 August 1958, the *Nautilus* made the first successful submerged transit across the geographic North Pole. She had submerged on 1 August in the Barrow Sea Valley and continued her voyage until surfacing near Greenland. Her total underwater voyage lasted 96 hours and covered 1,830 miles. For firsthand details from her commanding officer see William R. Anderson, with Clay Blair, Jr., *Nautilus 90 North* (Cleveland: World Publishing Company, 1959). On 3 August 1958 the USS *Skate* (SSN-578) became the first submarine to surface at the North Pole. For her skipper's account, see James F. Calvert, *Surface at the Pole: the Extraordinary Voyages of the USS Skate* (Annapolis: Naval Institute Press, 1996).

Atlantic side, and flying up to the pole and coming back and counting up on any track how often there was a hole that was safe enough to get up through. At that time of year on a track, just looking down, there was an opening every seven point something miles. So even if they'd had a power failure, which fortunately they didn't, they would have had a good chance of getting to a polynya and getting to the surface at that time of year. But we had confidence that they wouldn't have a power failure, and they fortunately didn't. They steamed the 1,800 miles nicely and steamed under the pole, and Anderson sent the message, "*Nautilus* 90 North." The *Nautilus* was famous, and I would have liked to make the trip, but it wasn't proper for the division commander to ride along.*

I told you before about Chief Fire Controlman Crossick, who was such a good photographer. He was still in the crew when the *Nautilus* went under the pole, and he had some fantastic pictures. I told him, "Crossick, if you'd like, I can make you a contact where you can sell those pictures to *Time-Life* or something for quite a bit of money."

He said, "Captain, I'm being approached not with money, but I'm being approached by *National Geographic*, and there is something about having your pictures in *National Geographic*." The point I'm trying to make is that the reputation of the magazine meant more to him than the money.

Paul Stillwell: You told me something interesting when the tape recorder wasn't running about how whales operate under the ice pack.

Admiral Wilkinson: As I said, I have been under the ice myself. During that trip, when I flew up before the *Nautilus* made her trip, I had Nicholson and I had a couple of other officers. Nicholson was now on the *Skate*, but he used to be on the *Nautilus*. He used to be my exec and navigator, and we had a close rapport. We boarded this plane that was going to take us to the North Pole so we could fly back down the route. We got out on the end of the runway in this Navy plane, and I was not the pilot or commanding the plane, of course. On the other hand, I was the senior officer on board, and we were going to do an unusual thing, go up to the North Pole and come back, which they'd never done

---

* See the Naval Institute oral history of Dr. Waldo K. Lyon, who was the scientific advisor on board during the *Nautilus*'s voyage under the North Pole.

before. So I asked the aviators if the had a good time check, if their chronometer was right, and they assured me it was. And then I looked, and actually the clock was stopped. [Laughter] And so we didn't take the air.

We turned around and went back and set the chronometer and wound it and had to get more fuel and had a little delay in getting started. This caused me to lose a certain amount of confidence in the plane's navigation. We started up, and we flew over Iceland, and then we turned north and went up toward Thule, Greenland. But as we were going over Iceland, again something happened that made me lose confidence. So then I apologized to the captain for the fact that he had all these extra people to carry and we'd like to help him. Could we take over the navigation for him? [Laughter] And he said, yes, he would like for us to do that.

So for the rest of the way Nicholson was using that bubble octant and taking fixes, and we were the ones that navigated that plane to the North Pole and back to Iceland. En route we landed in Thule to get more fuel. This was a time of national emergency. When we landed at Thule, out came a weapons carrier. Armed troops leaped out as we tried to start to disembark from our airplane, which was out on the runway. Bayonets were thrust in my face, and the word was, "Halt. What's the password?" And I was shaking like that. I didn't know any password. I didn't know what the hell to say. But Lieutenant Nicholson said, "Don't give us any of that crap. We're in the Navy."

The guy said, "Oh, okay." [Laughter] We went into the control tower. Our pilot taxied over. We got the fuel, and we went on with our flight up to the North Pole and back.

The Arctic ice is constantly shifting, and depending on the time of year it freezes over faster or slower. The average depth of the ice is 20 to 30 feet, but as the ice moves it'll split open and you'll have what you call a polynya and for a short time it will be an open lead in the ice. Then it will either move and come back together, or it will freeze over. So if you were looking from below, where you had accurate depth control and the topside sonar showing you just the depth, you'd find places where the ice up there was a foot thick, two feet thick, five feet thick, 10 feet thick.

Our modern submarines can twist their planes vertically, find a place where the ice is thin, and at zero speed come up until they touch the ice and then come on up and break through it without the force of any sheer against structure. One of our modern submarines can break through ice five or six feet thick that way. The picture that I showed you out there is one of my submarines when I was SubLant coming through five or six feet of ice. I've done a lot of study about the Arctic, and from that study it's an interesting thing. A whale is able to sense thickness, and a whale needs to come up and breathe for oxygen. And, depending again on the time of the year, the lead may stay open longer, or it may freeze over. But still, even if it freezes over, there'll be shallow spots, and a whale's sensing systems can find a place that the ice is not thick, and a whale can break through two feet of ice. But it does it differently than the submarine. He gets down and comes up and hits it with a crack and breaks through and then gets fresh air. A submarine doing it properly comes right under at zero speed and comes up slowly till it touches and then shoulders his way on up through to make sure he doesn't get any sheer action against structure.

Paul Stillwell: What else do you recall about that trip by the *Nautilus*?

Admiral Wilkinson: As far as the dependents of the men on the *Nautilus* knew, they didn't know that it was sailing under the North Pole. All they knew was that their husbands were on the *Nautilus*, which had been sent to the Pacific Ocean for a trip. The wife of an enlisted crew member wife might be back in Missouri. After the ship got back to the Atlantic, I as the division commander made arrangements for *Nautilus* to come into New York so the crew could get a heroes' welcome. And I managed to get the wife of every person in the ship's company there—no matter where they were, no matter how hard it was.

In setting up that event, I went down to New York to deal with all the public relations types. And I remember with horror them saying, "Well, here's where we'll board, here at the foot of Broadway, and the *Nautilus* crew can march up Broadway, four abreast." And, gee, I had a great ship and a great crew, but probably any high school Girl Scout band could outmarch them. [Laughter] So I was quick on the uptake and I said, "March, hell. Those guys are heroes. Heroes ride." [Laughter] So we made arrangements and got that many Jeeps and they came up Broadway doing a parade, four

to the Jeep, looking like Mauldin characters, and that was a lot better than marching up.*
I was pretty pleased.

Paul Stillwell: What do you remember about the Boston reception for *Skate*?

Admiral Wilkinson: *Skate* was going to come into Boston, which was not quite as grand as the *Nautilus* coming into New York, but still we should do it as best we could. So I went up to talk with the authorities, with all the PIOs, and whatnot.† In the arrangements I guess there was a little bit of a shortage of funds. The *Nautilus* crew members' wives all saw their husbands come into New York City, and they didn't have to pay. But when arrangements were made for the *Skate* coming into Boston, the city was really going to take care of Captain Calvert and many of the senior people, but not all the functions called to take care of all the troops' wives.

As I went one of the arranging meetings, the mayor of Boston was there. I had started hearing about some of these plans, so I said, "May I have everybody's attention? I have a letter from Captain Calvert at how distressed he was when he went into Netherlands as to how second rate his troops were treated as compared to his officers and how sorry that made him feel." I read that letter word for word with the newsmen and a lot of other people hearing, and then I concluded, "By God, I'm really glad that's not the American way." [Laughter] And, let me tell you, suddenly the plans were changed, and every one of the *Skate* crew's wives was invited to the mayor's breakfast. [Laughter] And they came into Boston in grand style. That in my heart was a little bit of a personal triumph. I felt good about that, glad I'd gone to help with the arrangements.

After the *Nautilus* had gone under the pole it got a lot of national and international attention. The commanding officer, Commander Anderson, was to go to Italy for a celebration of Columbus, I think, and *Nautilus* was an important ship. The question was brought up as to whether the exec should operate the ship while he was gone, because the *Nautilus* had operational commitments. I said, "Well, gee, that's no problem. I'll ride the ship, as is my privilege as the division commander, during that time. I'm sure the

---

* Bill Mauldin was a popular World War II Army cartoonist.
† PIO – public information officer.

exec will do a fine job, and I'll make sure that nothing goes wrong." So it was, and so the *Nautilus* went out on her operation.

About that time Senator Kefauver for political purposes wanted that exec to accompany him on some things down in Tennessee.* And, by God, damned if we didn't transfer the exec at sea to go make Senator Kefauver happy, and I got orders to be the commanding officer of *Nautilus*. So for three or four weeks in late '58 I was the captain of the *Nautilus* again. I had great fun, and the total time was at sea. We had to go investigate a Soviet submarine that was down in the southern part of the Atlantic off the United States and do some other operations.

During that time, in late 1958, about October, I got a letter from Admiral Smith, the Chief of BuPers.† He told me that I was going to be the commanding officer of our country's first nuclear-powered surface ship, the guided missile cruiser *Long Beach*, CGN-9. I enjoyed that, and I was in on a little bit of the dealings related to the *Triton*, which was coming with the famous guy, Ned Beach.‡

Paul Stillwell: Were you involved in the planning for his trip around the world?

Admiral Wilkinson: No, but he got my best man. [Laughter]

Paul Stillwell: What do you mean by that?

Admiral Wilkinson: Admiral Rickover took the best guy I had, my engineer, Les Kelly. He went over and became the first engineer on the *Triton*, which had two reactors and two engine rooms.§ I can remember going over and going aboard the *Triton* and being

---

* Carey Estes Kefauver, a Democrat from Tennessee, served in the House of Representatives from 13 September 1939 to 3 January 1949 and in the Senate from 3 January 1949 until his death in the naval hospital at Bethesda, Maryland, on 10 August 1963. In 1956 he ran unsuccessfully for Vice President as running mate of Adlai Stevenson.
† Vice Admiral Harold Page Smith, USN, served as Chief of Naval Personnel from 31 January 1958 to 12 February 1960.
‡ In the spring of 1960, the USS *Triton* (SSRN-586), commanded by Captain Edward L. Beach, USN, made the first submerged circumnavigation of the world. Commissioned in November 1959, she was ostensibly a radar-picket submarine but actually a test ship for a two-reactor propulsion plant.
§ Lieutenant Commander Leslie D. Kelly, USN, who had been in the crew of the *Nautilus*.

toured through it by Les. We got back to the engine room, and I pointed at something and said, "Les, what the hell is that?"

He said, "Gee, I don't know, Captain, but there's another one just like it in the after engine room." And then we roared with laughter. Roared with laughter. Of course, he knew what it was.

Later Les was skipper of his own submarine, and I was on the *Long Beach*, and we were having a lot of trouble. Les offered to give up his job. He called me up and said, "I'm ready to come, Captain, and be your engineer on the *Long Beach* so we can get that squared away."

I told him, "No, I really appreciate that, Les, but we'll muddle along here with the guys we've got." More than one of the nuclear submarine officers offered to come and be in my engineering force on the *Long Beach*. But the Navy had selected and trained some young surface ship officers for the engineering force on *Long Beach*. So I said I'd get along with these guys, and they turned out well.

I guess I have been enormously fortunate time after time—maybe because of the programs I have been involved with—I have really had a spectacular group of people that were working for me. I mean, you've interviewed some of these guys. One of my junior officers on the *Volador* was Jim Watkins, who became CNO.[*] One of my junior officers on the *Wahoo* was Harry Train.[†] I could name you a multitude of other guys that were pretty damn good and all of them busting their tail to carry me on their backs, and that helps a lot.

Paul Stillwell: But you were giving them the inspiration to do that. That's what Harry Train said.

Admiral Wilkinson: Well, people will live up to your expectations, and my standards were high. Let me tell you about Jim Watkins. What was the word you used? Inspiration? He'd have done well no matter what and where he was. That's the kind of a

---

[*] Admiral James D. Watkins, USN, served as Chief of Naval Operations from 1 July 1982 to 30 June 1986.
[†] Admiral Harry D. Train II, USN, served as Supreme Allied Commander Atlantic, Commander in Chief Atlantic, and Commander in Chief Atlantic Fleet from 30 September 1978 to 30 September 1982. His oral history is in the Naval Institute collection.

guy he was. Yes, it helps if you're a member of a good organization where it's just, "That's the way we do it. We don't accept anything less."

So SubDiv102 was an enjoyable tour to me, associating with really an awful lot of good guys, the guys on the early nuclear boats that were getting built in that time frame, all of them working for me. It's really fun to be in charge if the people under you are all good people, busting their heart doing well. And all my boats were peopled with that kind of people. So it was a very pleasant and enjoyable tour for me, especially being back to the submarine force again.

Paul Stillwell: Did you have any kind of a role in that job as an operational commander?

Admiral Wilkinson: The division commander didn't write and issue an operation order to his people. That was done under an operational command, a refit and training group or something. I wasn't in on the planning or looking at that level. For example, I've said glibly that I wrote the op order for the *Nautilus* going under the North Pole and the *Skate* going up to the Pole. That wasn't signed and delivered by me, but let me tell you I drafted those op orders and gave them to the authority that was supposed to issue them. Actually, the op order that was given to the *Nautilus* to make the polar transit, probably that was a SubPac op order because they were in the Pacific.* But SubPac didn't conceive and plan it. That came from us. So, no, I was not the operational commander, and yet no operations were done by them that I wasn't in on the planning. Do you understand the difference I'm trying to say?

Paul Stillwell: Sure. Absolutely. Did you report directly to SubLant when you were SubDiv102?

Admiral Wilkinson: No. SubDiv102 was one of two divisions in Submarine Squadron Ten.

Paul Stillwell: Who was your boss?

---

* SubPac – Submarine Force Pacific Fleet.

Admiral Wilkinson: It may have been Ozzie Lynch; I'm not sure.* But that time as division commander was a golden, easy time with lots of fun for me.

Paul Stillwell: I've just got a couple more questions on the submarine division. How much contact in New London did you have with the people who were going to be going into the Polaris submarines?

Admiral Wilkinson: I envied the guy, High Gain, who became the first skipper of the *George Washington* and wished I could do that.† What was his name?

Paul Stillwell: James Osborn.

Admiral Wilkinson: Yes. High Gain we called him because he was a loud talker.

And I wished I could do the Trident years later. But I couldn't do them all, and so I was happy with the *Long Beach*, but I felt a little bit, "Say, gee, that's really a good job that guy's going to." But I didn't have anything to do with determining the personnel allowance on the Polaris. It was wrong, of course, and I did have something to do sometime later with straightening it out [laughter] and getting the proper number of people on there to take care of those ships. That was when I was OP-31. But I didn't have anything to do with the first determination where they made it too small, trying to show how cheap it would be to do this strategic missile system that way. I've forgotten what the number was, but we brought it up to 124 later.

Paul Stillwell: Any personal observations on Captain Ward, who was the first ComSubRon 14?‡

---

* Captain Richard B. Lynch, USN.
† When the ballistic missile submarine *George Washington* (SSBN-598) was commissioned on 30 December 1959, Commander James B. Osborn, USN, was commanding officer of the blue crew, and Commander John L. From, Jr., USN, was commanding officer of the gold crew.
‡ Submarine Squadron 14 was established in 1958; the initial members worked in the Pentagon to do planning for the Polaris-armed submarines. Later the squadron received and operated the SSBNs as they went into commission. The first squadron commander was Captain Norvell G. Ward, USN; the oral history of Ward, who retired as a rear admiral, is in the Naval Institute collection.

Admiral Wilkinson: I knew Captain Bub Ward, who later became admiral, of course. I knew him very well and had great admiration for him; he did a fantastic job. I think he was really important in the early success of the submarine strategic weapons system, because you can conceive it and you can design it and you can build it, but in order for it to be a success it also has to operate. Squadron 14 in Holy Loch was on the forefront of empire, and over there there were lots of public relations problems and logistic problems, and Bub Ward was the guy that made it all work.* The early operations of the submarines out of Squadron 14 were very successful. They met their mission, and I give Admiral Ward a lot of credit. He was a crackerjack.

Paul Stillwell: He told me one of his toughest jobs was writing the fitness reports on the skippers, because they were all all-stars to begin with.

Admiral Wilkinson: Well, you know, I can imagine that's so. Also, for each submarine he had a blue and gold skipper.† Also, he didn't have them under observation. They were out at sea patrolling most of the time, and he was reading their patrol reports to see how they did. Some people wrote patrol reports with a little more poetic language than others, and so you've got to extract the real stuff from all that. So I imagine he really did have a problem. It was always easier for me doing fitness reports. That's an important function that you do, and it's hard work. But what I did in every one of my commands, I used to have a file folder for everybody that I was going to write a fitness report on at the end of a reporting period. As any little thing would happen, I'd jot myself a little note and stick it down in that folder. At the end of six months, when I was writing the fitness report, most of it I'd throw away, but on the other hand I was able, when I wrote a fitness report, always to tie character with deeds. If you've been on a selection board, and I've been on many, there's nothing as impressive as tying a characteristic with a deed. "This guy's a great leader, and his reenlistment is 98%." [Laughter] And so on.

---

* When the Polaris program was established, the range of the initial A-1 missile was so short that the submarines had to operate close in to the Soviet Union. To facilitate operations, the submarines and their assigned tender were based in Holy Loch, Scotland. The base was used until the early 1990s, when the advent of the long-range Trident ballistic missile made overseas basing unnecessary.

† In order to get maximum at-sea time for the Polaris submarines, each had two separate crews—designated blue and gold—that alternated taking her on patrol.

That would have been tougher for Bub Ward because the words he used were true. He did have all top-quality people, and he didn't have them under day-to-day observation where he could say, "Joe did this and did that." Let me tell you, when you get to be on a selection board you have a hard time winnowing out. It's easy to pick the bottom, and it's easy to pick a top group. The toughest thing of all is right at the middle, where this guy's going to make commander and this guy isn't. The difference isn't too great, and it's really hard. So you got to be pretty intuitive in reading what was really meant behind the words in a fitness report, and any time there were some facts in there to support it, that was helpful. Some people write an awful lot better than others, you know, and it's tough to separate the facts.

The Navy has tried for years to get different gimmicks to force the reporting senior to differentiate between his people, and it didn't matter how good they are. One gimmick that was put in at one time was to rank people, no matter what, taking into account seniority and everything else. You've got 14 officers you're reporting on. Make one of them one. Two, three, four, five down to 14. Take into account experience and everything else, and that's really tough for you as a reporting senior.

Humorous incident. I was on a selection board where we were considering people for promotion who had many reporters, one of whom was Admiral Zumwalt.* He was quite eloquent with words and quite one to stick up for the people that worked for him. So in one reporting period every officer that worked for him he marked number one of the group. And descriptive language would say, "This officer is one of 100,000." Well, when you get to the selection board and it's something signed by the CNO, you read it very carefully. And that ended up actually not doing any of those guys any good, because every member of that selection board instantly recognized that every one of those guys was marked number one, and there can't be two of them that are number one. And the comment was made, "One of 100,000? There aren't that many officers in the Navy." [Laughter]

So it's hard to be really objective in writing his fitness report. Sometimes through enthusiasm and trying to support the guy, you could go beyond the truth. The Navy has

---

* Admiral Elmo R. Zumwalt, Jr., USN, served as Chief of Naval Operations from 1 July 1970 to 29 June 1974. His oral history is in the Naval Institute collection.

tried hard for years to force reporting seniors to differentiate. It's hard to do that and, as I said, what always tried to do in my write-ups was tie words with deeds. And having been on selection boards, let me tell you, that gets to them. They really like it when they read something solid: "This guy's ship won the Big E and the skipper gives him a lot of credit for it." And all of them wish that their ship had won the Big E and that gets to them. But I'm sure Bub Ward wrote his fitness reports really well. I'm telling you he's a guy of the highest integrity, and he's one of the most crackerjack guys I knew, and he certainly deserves a great deal of credit for the early success of the Polaris missile system.

Paul Stillwell: The *Triton* was officially a radar picket submarine, but I think even more so a test bed for a two-reactor plant. How well did she work out?

Admiral Wilkinson: Her deck configuration was such that she could make high speed on the surface. The *Nautilus* threw a wake up that you can't believe, and due to the surface slowing you down, the *Nautilus* could only make a little over 17 knots. We made considerably more than that submerged, with more hull touching the water, but without making that terrible wake. The *Triton* was so designed that she had more freeboard and could make high speed on the surface, and that went well and she did that. And certainly they made the two-reactor system work. If the Navy had needed her as a radar picket, she could have been long successful. But the Navy didn't really need her as a radar picket, and she wasn't a strategic weapons submarine. If you want to talk about her being a sea-control attack submarine, there was a lot of extra expense for no more torpedoes, not any more performance. So, unfortunately, we didn't have the tactical requirement for her as a radar picket submarine, and she cost more money to be an attack submarine, a sea-control submarine. So as a test bed to show the reactors worked, she did that really well, but we really didn't have the need for more submarines like that.

If you want to take the *Skipjack* class or the next better class, the 688 class, we had requirements for numbers of them.[*] There are very few jobs you do with such talent that one man makes the difference. Maybe to be a Nobel Prize winner or something, but

---

[*] USS *Los Angeles* (SSN-688) was commissioned on 13 November 1976 as the lead ship of a class of 39 nuclear-powered fast-attack submarines. They were followed in 1988 with the commissioning of the USS *San Juan* (SSN-751), lead ship of what is known as the "improved *Los Angeles* class."

there are other jobs it takes numbers to do. And to win the sea-control battle we needed more than just one submarine. We needed quite a few attack submarines. At one time we had over 100 nuclear attack submarines. And it wouldn't have been worth the extra money to build 100 like *Triton* when they couldn't do it as well as the 688, which was cheaper. So she did a good job demonstrating the capability of either one of those two reactors. [Laughter] And Ned Beach got some pretty famous and fantastic performance out of her about following Magellan's route and sailing around the world. But she didn't show we ought to build a lot of them like that.

Paul Stillwell: I think she was the first nuclear submarine to be decommissioned.

Admiral Wilkinson: And that's why. We didn't have a requirement for a fast radar picket in submarines.

Well, as I said, in October of '58 I got the letter from the Chief of BuPers that I was going to be the first captain of the first nuclear-powered surface ship, which was a real nice job to get. I got that letter a year before I reported to the ship. And I had a personal conversation with Admiral Burke.[*] He told me that I got the job because the *Nautilus* worked real well, and they wanted to make sure the surface ships got off to a good start. All that was pleasing to me.

When I got that letter, of course, I didn't say anything to anybody about it. I mean, I might have told my wife, but certainly I didn't discuss it with anyone else. But eventually if you have a letter that a senior guy signed, somebody typed it and somebody saw it, and maybe since the CNO had talked to me somebody over there must have known. Eventually the word got out while I was off making lots of arrangements as SubDiv102 for some of the things these nuclear submarines working for me did. I was not hidden. I was sometimes a public character, and I'd have four-stripe captains that I didn't even know, surface officers, come up and say, "You son-of-a-bitch, what makes you think you're qualified to be skipper of the first nuclear-powered cruiser?"

---

[*] Admiral Arleigh A. Burke, USN, served as Chief of Naval Operations from 17 August 1955 to 1 August 1961. His oral history is in the Naval Institute collection.

I'd go absolutely poker faced and say, "Well, gee, I was born in Long Beach. Where were you born?" And I happened to have been born in Long Beach. But other than that little bit of unpleasantness and fun, time marched on. Eventually I finished my tour at 102, and it was time to assemble the people for the *Long Beach*. Admiral Smith's letter that told me I was going to get the job also said that some engineers would be there first. That wasn't so. I got there first. I was the first officer that reported on the *Long Beach* detail.[*]

I was really quite shocked by the lack of cruiser experience in the officers I got, especially after seeing us put submarines in commission, where even in the war we put 25% really qualified submarine people in a new crew. But here was the country's first nuclear-powered cruiser, and I think it was the 33rd officer that I had report aboard before I had one that had had duty on a cruiser before. The first one that had was a warrant officer named Snowe, who was a crackerjack guy.[†]

Paul Stillwell: What do you recall about the surface officers that came to your crew after having received nuclear training?

Admiral Wilkinson: Before I knew them I had had offers, as I mentioned, from some of my nuclear submarine people to come and help me out. I didn't ever ask for them, and I didn't want to impact their careers in submarines. I had just a polite way of saying, "No," to my guys. I said, "People from the surface ships have been selected to be trained for this, and I'll do it with those guys." Probably if I'd asked for Les Kelly to come and be my chief engineer, I probably could have had him because the squeaky hinge does get the oil, but I didn't. In fact, they were crackerjack people, and they did a great job for me. There are no flies on Bill Spencer, who was my head engineer.[‡]

The *Long Beach* was delayed from original planning. Well, the ship was different

---

[*] USS *Long Beach* (CGN-9), the Navy's first nuclear-powered cruiser, was the only ship of her class. She was commissioned 9 September 1961. She had a standard displacement of 15,540 tons, was 721 feet long, 73 feet in the beam, and had a maximum draft of 31 feet. Her top speed was 30-plus knots. She was armed with two twin launchers for Terrier missiles, one Talos missile launcher, and ASROC. She was eventually decommissioned 3 May 1995.
[†] Chief Ship Repair Technician Marvin L. Snowe, USN.
[‡] Lieutenant Commander William A. Spencer, USN, was the ship's first chief engineer.

than the original planning. Originally it was going to be a 7,500-ton ship, and it ended up 14,000 plus, and so we had to get our personnel allowance changed. But also it slipped in time until it was down to the point that it really worried Rickover whether it was going to beat the *Savannah* to sea, which we did.[*] But the situation was such that one of our officers ran out of his obligated time, and that officer was young Brock Barkley.[†] He was the one that I was training to be my reactor control officer. And so we were still up at Quincy, the ship not yet finished, and he came in with his chit to get out of the Navy.[‡]

I was shocked. I have the good fortune that sometimes I perform better in time of crisis than just normally, but I was shocked and I lost my cool. I said, "How can you possibly do that?"

"What do you mean, Captain? My time is up."

I said, "How can you look at yourself in the mirror if you do something like that?"

"What do you mean?" he said.

I said, "There were dozens of young officers who would have liked to have your opportunity, and the Navy selected a group and you were one. You went out and took all that training time, keeping some other worthwhile young officer from doing it. I don't give a damn about this so many years of obligation—before you discharge your obligation for having filled that training spot, you're leaving before you've done. How could you ever look at yourself in the mirror and not be ashamed of yourself for the rest of your goddamn life?"

He said, "Captain, I don't want you feeling that way."

"Well, goddamn it, that's the way I feel, and that's the way I want it. So I'm telling you right now, as I say, how could you look at yourself in the mirror when you shave?"

He said, "Captain, what would you think I'd have to do to discharge my obligation?"

---

[*] NS *Savannah* was the world's first nuclear-powered passenger-cargo ship as a joint venture of the U.S. Maritime Administration and the Atomic Energy Commission. She was nearly 600 feet long, displaced 22,000 tons, and had a top speed of 24 knots. She was launched 23 March 1962. She carried cargo from 1964 to 1970 after several years of at-sea testing. She was retired in 1971 and later spent several years as a museum at Patriot Points, South Carolina.

[†] Lieutenant Commander Henry Brock Barkley, Jr., USN.

[‡] The keel for the *Long Beach* was laid on 2 December 1957 at Bethlehem Steel Company, Fore River Shipyard, Quincy, Massachusetts; the hull was launched 14 July 1959. She was commissioned in 1961.

"Well, goddamn it, you ought to stay here until the ship is in commission and a year of operation afterwards so we can properly get another guy trained and relieve you."

He said, "Captain, tear it up." [Laughter]

I say, "Brock, you're a good man, and I'm goddamn glad I've got you as one of my engineering officers." And so it was. Except the ship went in commission, and a year's operations were done, and then Brock did put in his chit to get out of the Navy because he wanted to do other things. Unfortunately, the Cuban Missile Crisis had come. People who wanted to get out were held a year before they could leave. So it came back that Brock was told he couldn't get out. He said, "Well, at least I've learned one thing. Boy, for the rest of my life it's what's in it for me. I'm never going to be sucker enough to be talked into something like that again. Okay, when this year's up I'm going to be a different guy."

I said, "Brock, you've got a totally wrong attitude. Let me tell you that. I was absolutely right in everything I said to you a couple of years ago. You were absolutely right in what you did. You can be goddamn proud of what you did, and I don't want you to feel that way. You've done a fantastic job on here." And so forth. I've forgotten the exact words. "That really shouldn't happen to you, because you did a job that was important to the Navy for this ship, and the Navy should take care of you. Let me show you what I mean."

I reached over and picked up the phone and got Washington and said, "I want to talk to the Secretary of the Navy." [Laughter]

"Well, who the hell are you?"

"This is Dennis Wilkinson on the *Long Beach*." Well, *Long Beach* was a pretty important ship, and it was enough so to get me on the phone with the Secretary of the Navy in a couple of minutes. [Laughter] I said, "Mr. Secretary, I want to tell you a story." So maybe not in that many words I ran through that story that he'd stayed beyond his obligation and took care of the ship. And I said, "Now, he did that, and in my opinion the Navy's got an obligation to him, and I'd like to see them let him get out."

"Well, of course," the Secretary said. [Laughter] And so Brock didn't have to wait his year. [Laughter] Silly story.

Paul Stillwell: But he's another one of the many people in the Dennis Wilkinson fan club as a result.

Admiral Wilkinson: Brock Barkley's a goddamn good man, and he got out and made a lot of money and did a good job. And he did do right. He did a really important job and in an important time. He was a reactor control officer when it was important. He looked out for us, and when that moment came it was our obligation to look out for him and, by God, we did, if that's what he wanted.

Paul Stillwell: Who was your executive officer?

Admiral Wilkinson: On the *Long Beach* it was Hal Castle.[*] He's passed away now. And he was a good guy. Red Youman was my operations guy, and you probably saw me drink a cup of coffee this morning with the Wilkinson crest, and that's not my crest.[†] That's the USS *Wilkinson* crest. Red Youman went from *Long Beach* to be the commanding officer of the *Wilkinson*, which was a pretty damn good command. We had lots of problems and controversies sometimes on the *Long Beach*, and Hal Castle was a big guy, and my weapons officer was a big guy, and Red Youman had been a football star down at Georgia Tech or somewhere. He was a 6-foot-5, 270-pound guy. We could go up to somebody in a small room with those guys and say, "We don't really like what's going on here." [Laughter]

Red Youman had a tendency to gain weight and then take it off. During the time he worked for me on the *Long Beach* he probably lost 1,500 pounds. He'd gain 30 or 40 pounds, and I'd fuss with him about his physical condition. This was the time the Navy was fussing. I guess that came from Kennedy, and there was an awful lot of pressure on all ships to keep their people physically fit and be able to meet physical standards of push-ups and chin-ups and whatnot.[‡] I was the captain, and I guess I could fuss with one of my guys, and he couldn't fuss back at me quite as much—or anywhere damn near as

---

[*] Commander Hal. C. Castle, USN.
[†] Commander Harold R. Youman, Jr., USN.
[‡] John F. Kennedy served as President of the United States from 20 January 1961 until he was assassinated on 22 November 1963.

much. [Laughter] But I've seen Red Youman go out on Saturday night and party all night and get in at 5:00 in the morning and shift to his golf clothes and shoulder his golf bags and be off to play golf. So I was fussing at him one time that I couldn't afford to have an officer like that that in poor condition. At this time he was 30 or 40 pounds overweight. Instead of 270 he was probably up to 290.

He said to me, "Captain, let's put it like this. How about you going and getting a couple of those guys that are in really good physical condition and bring them back, and let's see what they can do that I can't do." [Laughter] And he had me there. Nobody could have stood up to Red.

At that time we went through and carried out what higher authority had asked of physical condition very religiously. We put all our ship's company people through all the physical tests that they should do in the push-ups and the chin-ups and all that stuff. In one division the chief was really terribly out of shape. He was 40-50 pounds overweight, and his stomach was hanging out over his belt. He was making these demands on all the young kids that they had got to do this. They had to do only three chin-ups, and you'd be surprised. Some kids couldn't do three chin-ups. But everybody on the *Long Beach* was tested to meet the standards.

Everybody had done it except the chief, and all these people were sitting there. They knew that poor old 50-, 60-pound overweight chief couldn't meet those standards until—just like Red Youman—they finally said to him, "Well, how about you, Chief, chinning yourself three times?"

The chief was able to say, "Which hand?" And he reached up and chinned himself three times with his right hand and three times with his left hand, and he had a lot more respect from his division. Well, Red Youman was like that.

Paul Stillwell: How did you get the crew size increased?

Admiral Wilkinson: As I said, the *Long Beach* was originally conceived as a 7,500-ton ship, and the allowance was 750 people. For one reason or another, over time it grew to over 14,000 tons, but the allowance was kept the same. The ship was going to be built with berthing and showers and storage for food and all that, to take care of 750 enlisted men and a number of officers, which I've forgotten. And there was more and more new equipment going to come on board, weapons systems and radar systems. It didn't take very long to see that 750 people were not adequate to take care of all that.

Certainly Rickover ensured that there was an adequate part of that number to take care of the two nuclear reactors and the two engine rooms. So there was an even lesser number left to navigate and detect and fight and maintain the ship that was twice as big as was originally planned, especially to do it if it was in battle. So that concerned me, and I was there early enough to recognize it would be possible to take a lot of corrective action while the ship was being built. Since it had grown, there was more room. It was possible to have more bunks, and it was possible to have a bigger refrigerator and carry more food and a lot of other things as long as it was recognized.

I requested immediate studies to determine what the proper ship's company size should be. So BuPers with a little reluctance went along with that, and BuPers provided people, and I put in my utmost. [Laughter] We studied that very thoroughly from battle station requirement, section requirement, maintenance requirements, manning requirement, and who would sit on which console, and we came up with a number. I'm not positive of the number, but let's say 970 or a few more. After wrestling a while with it, the Bureau of Personnel in its infinite wisdom cut me down a few, and we settled on 964. CNO approved it, and so it was.

The action started in motion to make some changes in the ship, and part of the pitch was, "Forget that, Dennis. It's important to get this first nuclear-powered ship to sea, and after we've evaluated nuclear power for surface ships we'll go back in and make any changes and corrections that are required." But there's a flaw in that kind of an argument, because while it's being built is when you can lay it out to get the right number of bunks and the right size refrigerators and some other petty little things like that. So it was important from my standpoint to get approximately the right number of people in the allowance and provision to take care of them and the ship at sea.

I was faced with a problem of getting action out of the Ship Characteristics Board. This was the same Ship Characteristics Board, maybe not all the same people, but the same functional command that had approved characteristics that were in it at the time. So we were an annoyance to the Ship Characteristics Board and telling them we wanted everything changed. So I went back to a meeting, and that meeting started off with the chairman of the Ship Characteristics Board, Admiral Speck, picking on me and more or less going into quite a little diatribe of how improper my actions had been and so forth.* Admiral Speck also happened not to be a real fan of Rickover's, and so that probably added to his ire.

After over 50 minutes of that, I finally got carried away and said, "Admiral, the Bureau of Personnel in its infinite wisdom has changed the allowance of this ship to what in my opinion it ought to be, and the CNO has approved it. The job of the Ship Characteristics Board is to change the characteristics to fit, and I'd suggest we get on with it." That caused another little flurry, and after that was over we did get on with it. The characteristics were changed, and the ship was built with that allowance of personnel and crew and other facilities, the bunks and other facilities to take care of them. I'm really glad it was done that way, because we didn't have to go back sometime later for nobody knows how long a period to try to make major structural modifications.

Paul Stillwell: How much contact did you have with Admiral Rickover during the construction period?

Admiral Wilkinson: Oh, a lot. I talked to him on the phone frequently. Not as frequently as I'd talked to him when I was his representative at the Pittsburgh area office of the Atomic Energy Commission when Westinghouse was first starting up at Bettis Field, because by then we didn't have any ships and we only had one really going. But now, by the time of the *Long Beach*, there were a lot of nuclear ships in commission. The Polaris submarines were coming out at the rate of one a month and with two crews of people to talk to, so Rickover had a lot to divert his interest. So I didn't talk to him every day like I did at Pittsburgh. But, still and all, the *Long Beach* was important to him. He wanted to see the Navy build a lot of important capital ships nuclear-powered so they would be independent of fuel supply restrictions.

He felt that carriers should be nuclear powered, and hence the first three surface ships were the *Long Beach*, a guided missile cruiser; the *Bainbridge*, which had to be

---

* Rear Admiral Robert H. Speck, USN.

bigger than a destroyer but it was a destroyer; and the *Enterprise,* a carrier. And after that a lot of nuclear-powered carriers were built. So Rickover wanted the *Long Beach* to do well, and he wanted the plant to work well. He probably paid more attention to us than he paid to any one of all those other ships, but his attention was diverted some. I'd talk to him from time to time or at times of problems one way or another. An awful lot of people, when they're telling about their encounters with Admiral Rickover, they were the heroes. That's not the way it was with me, especially during the time on *Long Beach.* Normally when we had a conversation it was because he was unhappy about something, and he was fussing with me. So I had a lot of bickering at and fussing with me.

Then also Rickover was really eager for *Long Beach* not to fall behind any more but to get out so it could beat the *Savannah* to sea, because he would have really hated for our country's first nuclear-powered surface ship to not be one under his jurisdiction. And we did go to sea quite some time before *Savannah*. As it happened, as geography turned out, I happened to be there in *Long Beach* when the *Savannah* first came out to sea and I was able to send them a little flashing light dispatch, "Welcome." [Laughter]

Paul Stillwell: Just to kind of rub it in that you'd been first?

Admiral Wilkinson: No. No. I really meant well.

Paul Stillwell: Okay. What do you remember about the job that the Bethlehem people did at Quincy in building the ship?

Admiral Wilkinson: It was good and bad.

Paul Stillwell: Did you have a 24-hour-a-day schedule as you'd had with the *Nautilus*?

Admiral Wilkinson: Yes and no. We're talking over a considerable period of time. Right near the end, before we were finished, it was 25 hours a day. It was really an all-out, full-press effort. But in earlier time one the reasons the *Long Beach* had a tough time meeting the schedule was because they had a full 100% shipyard strike.[*] It was in the wintertime and cold. There was mass picketing to keep anybody from going into the yard with hundreds of striking yard employees along the entrance to the yard with oil tins with fires in them to keep warm. There was a time when there wasn't anyone working on the ship. By that time I had some people in the prospective ship's company. I talked to the union people, and they agreed that I could go through their picket lines with my people. So every day we marched up and saluted back and forth and went through the picket lines and went into our ship to be built and looked out for it, because there weren't any yard people aboard to do maintenance or anything like that. It's hazy in my mind. I can't remember for sure now how long that strike lasted, but during that time we looked out for the well-being of the ship. Before that time, when they were to the point when they were going to strike, they had the slow-down where less and less was done. And it was pretty bad.

The manager of the shipyard for Bethlehem was a very nice gentleman named Sam Wakeman, and his wife was quite a tennis player.[†] He had an experienced nuclear-trained, Navy experienced deputy working for him named Bob Laney, a retired captain from Rickover's office.[‡] Bob was class of '39, one of the original guys. Really a good man and really a super good tennis player. Because he'd had a broken arm when he was nine years old and still kept playing tennis, he could play equally well with either his right hand or his left hand. And Sam Wakeman's wife was a really good tennis player. We used to play together. Mrs. Wakeman and I would play Bob Laney and Sam Wakeman. Laney was tough in doubles. If he was serving in the first court he'd serve right-handed, and the ball was way over in the alley that way. And if he went to the second court he served left-handed, and the ball was way out over the alley that way. So we had some really great tennis games, but Mrs. Wakeman was better than her husband so that carried us through.

Just before the strike Sam Wakeman came down one Sunday and started walking through the ship. I saw him come forward, and I trailed after him a compartment or two behind. He spent two and a half hours going through there, and it was pathetic. I mean,

---

[*] The strike began on 22 January 1960, when shipyard workers walked off their jobs.
[†] Samuel Wakeman was general manager of Bethlehem Steel's yard at Quincy.
[‡] Captain Robert V. Laney, USN, resigned from the service in 1959.

60% of the employees were actually sitting on their asses. They really had a slow-down. It was only a short time later that they went out on full strike with mass picketing stopping entry. So as he was leaving the ship I went up and accosted him and said, "Mr. Wakeman." He turned around, and he knew I was the PCO of the *Long Beach*. This was earlier on; we hadn't played that much tennis together yet. That came later before we were finished.

I said, "Mr. Wakeman, here on a Sunday you've come down, and you've spent two and a half hours on this ship that's really important to you and really even more important to me. As a guy that it's important to, I want to really express my thanks and appreciation to you for spending that amount of time down here. And having said that, Mr. Wakeman, let me tell you it didn't do a goddamn bit of good. As the guy in charge of this yard, you must really feel bad to walk through compartment after compartment and see those yard workmen sitting on their ass. You know, I spent two and half hours following you. How about you doing me a favor and just spend five or ten minutes trailing along and follow me because I'm going to walk through the ship? Someday I'm going to be the captain, but right now I have no position and no authority on this ship, but there's one thing I want you to notice as you're following me. There isn't any compartment I go in that everybody won't get off their ass and act like they're doing something." [Laughter]

I said to him, "You know, if you'd have had ten white hats with you and you'd have waved your arm this way and you'd have waved your arm that way, there would have been a flurry of activity. You'd have had some impact here. Just walking through like you did, nobody knows who the hell you are. But if you'll do me the favor of following me five or ten minutes you'll notice one thing. Every space I go into they're get up off their ass. You know why they do? It's because if they don't, I walk right up and talk with them, and I ask them what their problem is and are they held up for lack of material. I'll get hold of their supervisor, and I'll see that it gets down there. They don't like to get into that, so there isn't anyplace I go that they won't get up and act like they're doing something." So I did, and he did, and they did. [Laughter]

You asked me if it was a 24-hour-a-day deal like it was on the *Nautilus*, and I couldn't say yes or I couldn't say no. Certainly it wasn't during that time they were getting ready to strike. That had an impact. During the strike there was nothing. As we were coming down to the wire, it was 25 hours a day. And I'd got permission from the union. I'd gone and talked to the union leadership: "While your guys are having this strike and doing mass picketing, this ship is something important to the country and the Navy. I'd like to be able to go through your picket lines with my people and be on that ship and take care of it."

It was, "Just be our guest."

Then the goddamn supervisor of shipbuilding office asked, "If you guys are going in there all the time, would you bring this out for us?"

I said, "Hey, you guys go to hell." [Laughter] So downstream, when Rickover had his way, the ship was delivered with the propulsion plant totally finished and checked out and in good condition. But the other important things on the ship like the weapons, the directors and all, other stuff came one year late or two years late. The one-year-late stuff they put aboard before we were delivered not checked out, and the two-year-late stuff we had to come back in the yard in Philly later on to get. But as long as it wasn't going to be completely finished at delivery, that is, the ability to fire weapons and fight, we'd better get it finished as much as we could. So several months before the end I asked for permission from the supervisor of shipbuilding for my people to work side by side with the yard employees and try to finish some of those weapons systems.

The supervisor of shipbuilding and the yard management, both of whom that request went to, had said, "No way. We can't afford the risk of antagonizing the unions. We've just got over a bad strike here."

But, just like I'd done before when I got authority to go through the massed picket lines, I went to the union leadership and said, "Hey, if you've got any man that can work the weapon system, there's nobody will keep him from getting a job. Every man that you want to hire, we'll hire. But, in addition to that, I'd like it to be okay with you for my ship's company that's here waiting for the ship to be built, my weapons people, to go down and work on it, too."

They said, "Gee, Captain, be our guest."

So I went back to the yard and the supervisor of shipbuilding and said, "The union leadership says it's fine with them." And that sort of cut the ground out from under them telling me that'd cause a strike. It's a little hazy in my mind whether the strike was three and a half months or four months or four and a half months, but it lasted about four months while my young enlisted people were there, and they were pretty crackerjack selected people. Before they select people to get trained, you probably get a little smarter bunch of guys that are getting trained as electronics technicians. And you really get some pretty damn good guys, potentially good guys, smart guys, trained to be missile techs, and these are guys that were there had ratings for second, third class, chiefs. Those guys came down there and worked for four months like they were yard employees wiring up things, hooking up this, checking out that. So my weapons system people worked hard at the end.

Paul Stillwell: Could you tell me about going to sea for the first time?

Admiral Wilkinson: Of course, Admiral Rickover came and rode me because there wasn't any nuclear-powered ship that went to sea that Rickover wasn't on the first operation.* Rickover was that kind of a guy. That was one thing he didn't delegate. We couldn't include such stuff as the missile systems and all that, because they didn't work yet, but this was to test anything to do with the propulsion of the ship.

On the sea trials we were going to do a four-hour full-power run. That is steam the ship around at full power, and that for *Long Beach* was about 32 knots. Unfortunately, during the course of that full-power run I ran into a very limited-visibility fog. Doing a four-hour full-power run is not in my opinion an adequate reason to run a cruiser around at 32 knots in the fog when it might run into some small spit kit or something. And so I stopped the full-power run in the middle, even though, of course Admiral Rickover would have liked to see it finished, but never a word of complaint or criticism. That was an operational matter, and he respected my ability in that regard. He might differ with me on many other things and did, but he certainly wouldn't differ with me on that.

---

* On the morning of 5 July 1961 the *Long Beach* got under way on nuclear power for the first time. After the ship received further work in the yard at Quincy, she was delivered to the Navy 1 September at the Boston Naval Shipyard, where she was commissioned on 9 September.

For whatever the business we had successful underway trials, and we collected deficiencies with them. We came back in the yard and worked on those things and whatever the lists were. We didn't have our weapon systems finished, but as far as the discrepancies from sea trials they were all accomplished and completed and the ship was delivered on what was then the schedule. The schedule wasn't the schedule it would have been four years earlier. But whatever the schedule was then, we met it and delivered on the ninth of September.

When we came back in, one of the things after the trials was to go in dry dock just before delivery to get our bottom painted. And naturally as the prospective captain, once the ship was in dry dock I was down, too, and inspecting all that. I looked at my screws in horror because they weren't that fine. Submarine screws are very beautiful, and they're really designed and built and honed to make as little noise as possible. I looked at these screws on the *Long Beach*, and there were wrinkles and waves. So I screamed with agony and got Admiral Brockett and complained about those screws.[*] I said, "Let me tell you. If we had a screw like that on a submarine, we'd throw it away." [Laughter] He laughed and told me my standards were too high. He explained to me that they don't have quite the same standards on the surface ships. And I was right, it wasn't perfect, but then they'd do all right. And they'd put better ones in later on. He's a pretty good man; later he became Chief of the Bureau of Ships.[†]

Paul Stillwell: You had a fair amount of topside weight in that ship. Was that a problem at all in terms of stability or sea keeping?

Admiral Wilkinson: No. We had a lot of topside structure. Are you making that synonymous with topside weight? As far as our configuration, we very well met the requirements for center of gravity and all this stuff. Now, the topside structure that was there gave me some problems in wind effect on it, but it didn't give me any problems in pitch and roll or stability at all.

---

[*] Rear Admiral William A. Brockett, USN, was Commander Boston Naval Shipyard.
[†] Admiral Brockett served as Chief of the Bureau of Ships from 1963 to 1966.

Paul Stillwell: I see.

Admiral Wilkinson: It was because I can differentiate between structure and weight as related to centers of gravity and all the curves that go with that. There was a hell of a lot of structure up there with the wind blowing on it.

Paul Stillwell: Could you talk please about the commissioning? That was a dramatic bringing alive of the *Long Beach*.

Admiral Wilkinson: You know, I'm ashamed to say. I can't believe it. I don't even remember who gave the commissioning speech.[*] But that step was pleasing to me after we'd had a long hard time in the shipyard, including the time of the strike. Although the missile systems weren't finished, we finally were going to get out of that shipyard and get to sea, and so I was really happy to have the ship get commissioned. Obviously we looked spiffy and did it well. Suddenly this was a Navy ship, and we were responsible for it, and so for a little bit of show we gave the order to station the watch and people marched on. Then you saw the radar start spinning, and that could be seen by all the spectators, of course. And then suddenly a missile came out on the launcher, and the launcher spun around with a missile pointing forward and same with the other launcher. Colors went up, and people marched up to do that. Then the people marched around, and the brow was manned, and spectators could see something happening.

I happened to be present years later when *Long Beach* was deactivated.[†] In the deactivation, which somebody had thought about, they did it just the opposite of what we did in commissioning the ship. They trained the directors around and took the missiles in and the radar stopped and the colors were taken down. The people marched off the ship and everything that we had done in the things like that for show when we went into commission, when they deactivated they did backwards. As a matter of fact, they even did it better, because while all this is going on they had on dress whites because it was the summer time, all the ship's company manning the rail. After all that was finished, then

---

[*] Secretary of the Navy John B. Connally made the commissioning speech.
[†] The *Long Beach* was decommissioned on 1 May 1995.

one by one they marched off the ship and formed up in formation on the pier facing the ship, and then they all clapped. That tore at my heart.

But going into commission obviously our people were sharp. The ship looked pristine topside as far as paint and spit and polish. But the people looked good, and we went in commission and we were really happy as hell to have finished what had been a long, bitter, dirty time in a shipyard. So there was a joy and happiness.

Paul Stillwell: You talked about it tearing at your heart. There is truly an emotional bond that people develop toward a ship.

Admiral Wilkinson: Oh, yes. And again that's a little bit of a function of involvement. Remember, I was in the pre-commissioning detail and operation; I was on the *Long Beach* for four years and a month. I was very fortunate, because normally in the Navy today and in the Navy then a guy got to be a captain of a cruiser for maybe less than a year. So that's why I became so well versed in the ship and knew my men. At one time I knew the name of every man on the *Long Beach*, nearly 1,000, and that's hard.

Paul Stillwell: It's impressive.

Admiral Wilkinson: That's because I met them all when they came aboard, and I talked to them. And I met them all when they left. I had a picture of each of them in my room, and I looked at them from day to day. Obviously I would slip many times, but I came pretty close to being able to call a man by name. That's easier if you're there four years and see them come and go than it is if a guy's just reported aboard and hit that many new people all at once.

Paul Stillwell: People appreciate that too.

Admiral Wilkinson: Yes. We talked to every man that came aboard and we wrote a letter to his wife or mother and told her, "You don't have to worry anymore. Your son has come to the *Long Beach*, and here's something about the ship and something about him and we're happy to have him aboard." And got a lot of good play out of that.

Paul Stillwell: What were your first operations after the *Long Beach* was commissioned?

Admiral Wilkinson: When a ship has just gone in commission, before they show themselves to their boss, they ought to have a little bit of time to get out there and debug a little, so people man the ship promptly at battle stations and don't have confusion in communications. And the watch goes on and the watch is qualified and knows what the hell they're talking about. So when the ship went in commission we wanted not to have to worry for a couple of weeks anyway, till we could shake down just a little bit. But, son-of-a-gun, our boss was Admiral Cavenagh, CruLant, and he decided the first under way after we were commissioned and sailed away from the Quincy yard in Fore River that he would come and ride the ship.* So that's tough to get the admiral of the force aboard the first time under way. You know you're not quite as good that time as you might be a week from then. Do you understand what I'm saying?

Paul Stillwell: Oh, yes.

Admiral Wilkinson: We were going out to sea. I wanted to do some training. I wanted to scram the reactors and start them up again and lose power and have collision drill and man-overboard drill and put the boats in the water and go ahead and go back. And shift sections and those things I'm talking about, scramming, a lot of things that interrupt power flows and secure equipment and start it up again and a lot of checkout. I had quite the plans for doing that.

At that time I guess because of the system of worrying about surprise attacks and all that stuff they had a system called AltComLant, Alternate Command Atlantic Fleet. In case Atlantic Fleet Command in Norfolk was knocked out, there'd be some commander at sea that would be the alternate commander that would take over. That sack was passed from admiral to admiral at sea from time to time. But there was always

---

* Rear Admiral Robert W. Cavenagh, USN, Commander Cruiser Force Atlantic Fleet.

some admiral under way in a Navy ship steaming around, location not quite known, who was the Alternate Commander Atlantic Fleet. I don't know exactly when that started and how long it lasted, but certainly in September 1961 that was the concept that was in force. When Admiral Cavenagh came aboard, he wasn't scheduled to be Alternate Commander, but something happened. So after a few days CinCLantFlt asked him if he could take over as Alternate Commander Atlantic Fleet, because whoever was supposed to be it couldn't for some reason or other, and they needed one at sea.

Naturally, Admiral Cavenagh wanted to say, "Of course," very much. But here he was riding a brand-new ship that had been at sea less then a week, for the first time ever. He called me in and said he had this request, and he knew I was in the midst of all this, and would it be possible for us for him to be Alternate Command Atlantic Fleet. This included a hell of a lot of communications and communications that they didn't want to lose or have interrupted. And, of course, I was smart enough to know just like when CinCLantFlt asked him if he could be Alternate Command he wanted to say, "Yes." And although I wished I wasn't in the position of being asked, once asked I would like to say, "Of course, sir." So I thought about that a very brief period of time and I said, "Of course, Admiral."

So he happily sent back the dispatch that said, "Why, of course, I'd be more than happy to take over as AltComLant." And so a short time afterwards our admiral riding us became AltComLant. And there was a history of AltComLants for a long period of time, and naturally every time that there had been any interruption, if they lost communications or anything, it was noted. So, let me tell you, we didn't scram the plant. We didn't hold collision drills. Starting the day that we became AltComLant, our guys stayed on the line far longer than anyone ever had before. [Laughter] We did our utmost not to interrupt communications, and it probably hurt some parts of our training a little, but it didn't hurt the training in the communication outfit. And it didn't hurt our reputation with our boss, Admiral Cavenagh, either. So our first three or four weeks at sea we were AltComLant before they passed it on to somebody else.

I can remember that Admiral Cavenagh thought very, very highly of us. He thought we were the greatest ship there was in the Navy and probably the greatest ship there'd ever been. We agreed with that opinion, and those were golden times. He was really happy with us. There was nothing we said we'd do that we didn't do, Commander Cruiser Force Atlantic Fleet knew it, and things were really great.

After that we moved down to Norfolk.* We spent time at sea that fall and had various technical representatives aboard. We were having trouble with our elevator up to the bridge. There were eight levels in the superstructure, but they weren't all equally distanced, so the adjustment in control of that elevator was quite a problem. It had a nameplate on it of Westinghouse. One time I was having trouble and complaining, and I got the Westinghouse elevator expert there working on it. I also happened to have two senior vice presidents from Westinghouse aboard. As luck would have it, the elevator failed again, and they got stuck in the elevator. The Westinghouse elevator technician got them out, and they complained about the elevator. He said, "There's nothing wrong with the elevator. It's the people don't know how to operate it. I'm a Westinghouse elevator expert and I know."

Then one of these guys said, "I'm vice president of Westinghouse, and I want this elevator fixed." So I came by about that time and told them for old friendship's sake that I was so proud of Westinghouse, and we had Westinghouse reactors. I had an awful lot of important people coming to the ship, and I liked to show them and tell them so proudly about my Westinghouse reactors. And lots of times they got a black eye because they rode in that Westinghouse elevator, and it would fail. I said, "It's embarrassing to me, and I'm a real true Westinghouse supporter. If you guys will just give me an Otis nameplate, I'll put it up down here, and we'll end the embarrassment." [Laughter] Actually they didn't get it adjusted right initially for the different distances between levels. They did get it debugged finally, but we went through a hectic time on that. Before I'm through I'll tell you some similar stories about other companies and the fun we had when they had the 120 tech reps aboard.

Now I jump ahead to a little incident in the life of the *Long Beach*. We'd gone into the shipyard at Philly for just three or four days, and I don't remember why. But we were in dry dock, and Sunday morning we were going to flood the dry dock and get her under way on operations on Monday. And, lo and behold, who should have a son in

---

* The ship arrived in her new homeport of Norfolk, Virginia, the first time on 2 October 1961.

Philadelphia Naval Shipyard but Admiral Ricketts?[*] Admiral Ricketts was en route from one duty station to another, he was visiting his son, and there was this really new ship. He decided that as long as he was there and the *Long Beach* was there, he might as well go down and take a look at it. So at 6:00 o'clock on Sunday morning, he called up and asked for the duty officer, who was Warrant Officer Snowe, whom I mentioned earlier. He said he didn't want to have any special attention or anything, but he would like to come down and take a quick walk around the ship.

My warrant officer said, "Yes, sir, Admiral. Excuse me, Admiral, but what's your title?"

Admiral Ricketts said, "You've got me. I don't have one, but in six days it'll be Vice CNO." [Laughter]

Without turning a hair, Snowe said, "Admiral, we'd be real happy to have you." [Laughter] So my guy, my smart cruiser-experienced guy, had the right lines.

About 15-20 minutes later down the pier came Admiral Ricketts. Because the dry dock was being flooded, and because we happened to all be there that Sunday morning, I met him at the brow when he came aboard and toured him through the ship. Instead of a quick tour, he stayed for four hours. [Laughter] As we wandered around I'd say, "I'd like you to meet my navigator; this is Commander Boller.[†] And I'd like you to meet my operations officer; this is Commander Youman. And I'd like you to meet my engineering officer, this is Commander Spencer," and so on. Really, I got the joy of having a multitude of my people meet and speak to him. I didn't do all the talking going around. I'd have my engineer tell him something, and I'd have my navigator tell him something, and I'd have my operations officer. They talked about the NTDS system and the special radar, and that's why he stayed so long.[‡]

An awful lot of my people had a certain amount of enjoyment to be able to talk to the guy that was going to be the Vice Chief of Naval Operations in the Navy in six days and have him really interested in their jobs and what they were doing and their

---

[*] Admiral Claude V. Ricketts, USN, served as Vice Chief of Naval Operations from 1 November 1961 until his death on 6 July 1964.
[†] Lieutenant Commander Jack W. Boller, USN.
[‡] NTDS—Naval Tactical Data System, an electronic system that tracked radar contacts automatically, whereas previous practice had involved manual tracking. NTDS first entered the fleet in 1961.

equipment, and they were all really knowledgeable about that. It was a real nice period.

A few months later, when Ricketts was the Vice CNO, he made arrangements with CinCLantFlt for a group of people that he was really interested in to come down. These were some young people he wanted to apply for the Navy. I've forgotten now exactly how many they were, but there were 20 or 30 people, and they were people at least that were important to Admiral Ricketts. And someway or other that probably got lost a little en route, and CinCLantFlt made arrangements for them to be divided into two groups and taken on a couple of Navy ships. At the last minute the word got back to Admiral Ricketts that this was happening. So he called the Commander in Chief Atlantic Fleet and told him he was really unhappy. He wanted these people to really see something and not just be run around the farm. Instead of what they had in mind, why didn't they just arrange to take them on the *Long Beach*? At that time we were operating. As a matter of fact, about the time this conversation was going on, we were just arriving from sea. The Atlantic Fleet people said, "Well, the *Long Beach* has no word of any of this. They wouldn't be ready for any such visit."

Admiral Ricketts said, "Let me tell you. The *Long Beach* is always ready." [Laughter]

Paul Stillwell: He knew from personal experience. [Laughter]

Admiral Wilkinson: So the schedule was changed at the last minute, and as luck would have it, we had just tied up 15 minutes earlier after a couple of weeks' operations at sea. There was mail and everything else to come aboard. I didn't just bag right out of the ship. We got a call, "Can you handle a group for Admiral Ricketts?"

"Absolutely." [Laughter] I mean, he was the VCNO. About 20 minutes later they come down. Every one of my guys was there. I was there. We took them on a marvelous tour, but the funny thing was back that it went back to that experience with Warrant Officer Snowe.

I told you about our great relationship with Admiral Cavenagh. Unfortunately, as time went by, the powers that be in Washington decided they'd change the organization in the Atlantic Fleet and instead of having a CruLant and a DesLant they'd have a

CruDesLant. This was late in '61. Now, instead of being the golden ship in CruLant, we became one of the ships in CruDesLant. DesLant was a pretty strong antisubmarine outfit, and I was a submarine-reputation guy. The new commander of CruDesLant was a gentleman, Admiral Speck, who was not a great fan of Admiral Rickover's.[*] As a matter of fact, he hated his guts. And so he wasn't a great nuclear-power advocate, and suddenly he had this submariner-commanded nuclear-powered cruiser in his organization. Also, he happened to have been the admiral that was in charge of the Ship Characteristics Board when I'd had the flurry with him over changing all the characteristics of the ship that went with the manning. We'd had a little bit of a flare-up over that, and I had been not quite as polite as I should have been.

I don't mean any wrong comments about Admiral Speck, but he wasn't as wildly enthusiastic about us as Admiral Cavenagh was. Admiral Cavenagh really, truly thought we were the greatest, and he was right, of course. [Laughter] But Admiral Speck had his reservations about that. And undoubtedly he expressed some of those reservations with his people, and Admiral Speck was a strong man and said what he thought rather forcefully, and suddenly all his staff was on our backs. And some of them probably took actions that the admiral himself wouldn't have dreamed of taking. But I had some requests toward the ship that almost seemed incredible.

For example—and this was an actual incident—I had received an order to transfer a second class petty officer whose wife was eight and a half months pregnant. That was a real hardship to the man. I had a first class bachelor that was more capable and who really wanted to go. So I went right back to CruDesLant and asked them if we could please substitute this better qualified first class for this second class for the following reasons. And, of course, we get an answer right back, "Carry out your orders." One or two things like that had a tendency to turn you off.

So we built up many defenses. One of them was the "UNODIR."[†] Thereafter if we'd get an order to do thus and so, on Sunday I'd send them a dispatch, "Your zip, UNODIR." They'd call us on Monday and say, "Carry out your orders."

---

[*] Rear Admiral Robert H. Speck, USN, commanded Cruiser-Destroyer Force Atlantic Fleet from 18 December 1961 to 3 August 1963.
[†] UNODIR is an abbreviation for "unless otherwise directed." It is a useful device by which a commander can say to higher authority, "I'm going to do so-and-so unless you specifically order me not to."

"Hey, too late. Didn't you get my dispatch? It's already done." I don't know how many times we got away with that. But it was tough for us to shift from having been the golden ship to fighting to defend ourselves. But *Long Beach* was a pretty great ship and they managed to take that in stride and did it fairly well. But some of the little things like the second class I just told you about, that's really the wrong way to treat people.

Paul Stillwell: Did you wind up having to transfer the second class?

Admiral Wilkinson: Oh, no. Not when you can say, "UNODIR." [Laughter] No, we didn't.

Paul Stillwell: Well, in that case you had been otherwise directed.

Admiral Wilkinson: Yes, but only verbally between one of my guys and one of their guys. Not on the record.

I'll give you another example. Right after CruDesLant was formed, we got an operational order from ComCruDesLant, ordering us to Newport, which was where CruDesLant headquarters were, so they could look at the ship. And you've got to understand, being captain of a cruiser is big stuff. Captains of cruisers were treated with a certain amount of deference and respect. I was a captain of a cruiser—and a damn good cruiser—and the chief of staff said to me, "We're going to eat you up."

What do you say to somebody who talks to you like that? I said, "Well, have at it, Buster, but you're going to find we're a great big bite, because we only put up with a certain amount of crap and not very much of that." So we went into Newport and had dozens and dozens of visitors. One time we got down to the point where we were down to third class petty officers as guides. We didn't get fully eaten up. [Laughter] To many of the officers and crew from the ships in area we were a spectacular ship and the first nuclear-powered ship, and a lot of people wanted to see us. So, like we always did, we had an awful lot of visitors, and I had the War College classes and so on.

The toughest people to deal with were our own bosses, the CruDesLant thing. I'm maybe exaggerating a little but not very much. For the rest of my time on *Long*

Beach the only personnel I had ordered to me by CruDesLant were the output from the Navy detention barracks. They were seamen or firemen or whatnot. But, gee, it wasn't like on the *Wahoo* where I could say to a guy, "Hey, gee, did you stand first in your class? Well, if not, then how did you get *Wahoo*?"

I interviewed every new guy that came aboard, but it's a little tougher conversation saying, "Are you glad you're out of the detention barracks?" [Laughter] But, as a matter of fact, we had the kind of ship and the kind of leadership—and I don't mean our officers, I mean in our chiefs and petty officers—that we could handle that without any problem at all. We laughed at them at headquarters and said, "Send all you've got. We'll make good sailors out of them or get rid of them." And we really didn't get rid of very many. We made good sailors out of them. But you're working against a little more of a handicap.

Again, it's the old story, the thrust I've put to you many times. People that work for an organization will do things that the actual man in charge with his good judgment wouldn't dream of doing. For example, in that trip to Newport, as I said, we really had a multitude of visitors. I got a call from the flag lieutenant who said, "Captain, Mrs. Speck [the admiral's wife] would like to come down and see the ship."

Well, I was real enthusiastic. I said, "Great. We'd really be happy to have her."

He said, "Mrs. Speck would like to come down at 10:00 o'clock."

I said, "Well, I've got the senior War College class coming aboard at 10:00, and I have to talk to them for about ten minutes before the other people talk to them. How about 10:15?"

He said to me, "Mrs. Speck is counting on 10:00 o'clock."

I said, "Well, young man, would you like to call her up get that changed to 10:15, or would you like me to do it?" But I'm sure that didn't in any way, of course, involve Admiral Speck. He wouldn't have done anything like that, but that's a mistake in carrying out what the guy thinks his boss would like to have. Of course, Mrs. Speck came at 10:15. She was a charming person, and we had a marvelous visit. But it's a silly little example of the indication that as far as the staff of CruDesLant, we had an uphill fight to look out for ourselves. Now, it wasn't always quite as bad as when we were tied up with them in Newport those few days. When we were at sea somewhere like over in the Med or something, operations and distance dim some of those problems. [Laughter]

We did well in sports as a member of CruDesLant. We were champions of everything, and that included softball. We were going to compete in the All-Navy against the other forces. I really wanted to beat the submarine force, and the system was that you could augment your team with the all-stars. That is, if there was some destroyer or other cruiser that had a really crackerjack pitcher or a good hitter, we could take him and put him in to augment our crew. And yet when we went to play in the tournament for All-Navy, zero all-stars showed up, and that's a petty little thing. They should have supported us. We were supporting them. So sometimes it flared back on us a little, but on the other hand it probably helped us become a better team and more resolute. So we managed to survive. "Have at it. We're a great big bite." They really never managed to eat us up.

Paul Stillwell: Did you eventually win Admiral Speck's admiration?

Admiral Wilkinson: Admiral Speck was a strong man, and he really didn't like Admiral Rickover, and he really probably wasn't for the Navy's major capital ships being nuclear powered. It does cost you something for that, and he had some experience in that regard, having had the Ship Characteristics Board. So some of his opinions looking back—now that I'm older and more mature—were that he, I'm sure, was calling them like he saw them. But the activities then generated by his people sometimes made it tough for us. But I will say that after he was detached as CruDesLant and was on his way to a job over in the Netherlands, he came through Norfolk and asked me to meet with him, and off the ship. I did, and he told me, "I didn't always agree with you, Dennis, but you did a good job." And really, looking back, it must have taken a certain amount of guts on his part to say that. So I have no animosity toward Admiral Speck. And in truth I never did. I didn't then. As far as I was concerned, he was just one more guy against us, and we could handle them all. [Laughter]

Paul Stillwell: I think that's an appropriate lead-in to the snake ranch story.

Admiral Wilkinson: Most of the first group of officers that came to the *Long Beach* were destroyer officers, and they had a little bit different attitude. They were on bigger ships, and they turned over faster, and maybe they didn't have the same attitude toward their personnel as we have in submarines, in a small ship. Certainly I didn't have the same detailed interaction between the department head of one of my departments on the *Long Beach* and his division officers with the troops that I had had between my officers and chiefs and more junior troops on the *Nautilus* or any other one of my submarines. So this used to frustrate me because I'd get a report in the morning that Paul Stillwell was absent over leave. And with my background and experience, my first action, after I'd get that report, I'd say, "Well, where is he?"

I'd get the answer, "Captain, he's not here. He's absent without leave."

I'd say, "Well, isn't he married? Does he have a wife? Is he at home? Has anybody called to see if he's injured or hurt? What the hell's the matter with him?" Well, that was a different concept on the part of some of my officers that came from a destroyer background. I'm sure that's not true of all destroyers, but mostly they didn't think that way. If you do think that way, you'll discover pretty soon you don't have as many people over leave. [Laughter] I mean honestly.

I had a lot of young men, and, gee, some of these kids were 18, 19 years old. They were telling their mothers they were lucky they came to our ship now. I used to say, "Hey, those are young guys. We're responsible for them."

But some of my people didn't feel that way. They felt, "Hey, he's in the Navy to fight for his country. If he can do that, he can look out for himself, and we shouldn't enter that much into his personal life." So I had 42, six to an apartment, seven apartments. There were 42 young kids that banded together and pooled their money and rented apartments, which I wise-assly referred to as snake ranches over on the beach, and they could go ashore and have their fun and a place to bed out.

Paul Stillwell: Was this in Norfolk?

Admiral Wilkinson: Yes. And some way or other, just a great preponderance, most everybody I had in trouble was in this place. If I had a kid picked up for drunk driving and somebody had to go over and tell the judge, "Hey, that's our man and if you'll give him back to us we'll take care of him." Or if I had a guy over leave or got back late to quarters in the morning or if I found a kid pooped out sleeping on deck leaning up against a bitt, someway or other, time after time it was one of these kids.[*] And I would grouse about it: "It's just not right for those kids to be over there."

I was told by my commanders from the Cruiser-Destroyer Force, "It's not up to us to wet nurse all those kids. If they can fight for their country, it's their money." But, still and all, I wasn't happy with it, and so one Tuesday morning, sure enough, two kids were not back by the time of quarters. Later on, about 10:00 or 11:00 in the morning, I found a kid in one of the deck divisions asleep out on deck, his head against a bitt, and looking terrible. I had had it, and I sent for all my department heads and said, "Hey, I've just finally reached the level of my patience. We're responsible for those kids, and they're not going to act that way. I want all those snake ranches closed out. I want all those kids to leave those apartments and be sleeping back aboard by Thursday. And let me tell you, if there's any one of them that has any objection about that, you just bring him right up to my cabin, and I'll get his mother on the phone, and we'll talk it over with him and his mother."

There wasn't any youngster that wanted to come fuss with the captain and talk it over with his mother. So all the apartments were closed out, and all the kids came back on board. And I think it was better for the ship and for them that they did. [Laughter] If you did that today, somebody would have you sued.

Paul Stillwell: That's right.

Admiral Wilkinson: But sometimes as captain, trying to do right, you need to be arbitrary, and even today I think sometimes you might get sued more than other times. I was commanding officer of ships for 11½ years. Over that period of time I had a certain

---

[*] Bitts, which come in pairs, are vertical metal cylinders used in the process of mooring a ship with hawsers.

number of people up to mast and took action as I considered appropriate in many cases.* But there was only one time that I had a man up to mast and then had him appeal the action that I took, and that was on the *Long Beach*. It was a second class petty officer in the weapons department. We had a seaman in that department that was restricted, and the second class got him his liberty card and took him ashore and they partied together. When they came back and I had the word, I gave the seaman two more weeks' restriction and busted the second class.

The second class appealed, and at that time *Long Beach* was under CruDesLant. So this mast action with appeal went to CruDesLant, and suddenly they had a complaint from and about the *Long Beach*. There weren't many times they had a case like that, so there was a great deal of, "Hey, look at this ugly thing that the *Long Beach* has done, and this man's appealing." And, lo and behold, if I don't get a call one evening from CruDesLant, and I picked up the phone. It was the CruDesLant chief of staff and the force legal officer, both captains and both on the phone. The first thing that the chief of staff asked me was if I had pencil and paper. I guess that turned me off a little bit. I said, "Well, yes, we have lots of pencil and paper on the *Long Beach*. What is your problem?"

He said, "Well, the admiral has lots of questions, and we'd like you to research the answers and get them back to us."

I said, "About what?"

"Well, it's about this mast case of this man."

I said, "Well I'm fairly familiar with that case. I just might be able to answer any questions you have without writing them down."

So the first question was, "Well, it's not clear from the mast write-up and the appeal as to just how [whatever the name of the second class] got his liberty card." I didn't answer instantly. I didn't answer for five or six seconds, and the jab went in: "Captain, as we're saying, there are a lot of these questions. If you'll just write them down and get us the answers and come on back so we can have the answer for the admiral."

---

* Captain's mast is a sort of court in which the commanding officer of a unit listens to requests, awards non-judicial punishment, or issues commendations. Most often captain's mast is used for punishment of lesser offenses than those that merit courts-martial

I said, "Oh, I haven't hesitated because I can't answer your question. It's just that I was wondering how the chief of staff, CruDesLant, and the force legal officer could go in and explain to Admiral Speck that they don't know that second class don't have liberty cards." [Laughter] Sort of a funny incident, but in a way it also shows you the pressure we, the *Long Beach*, were under from the staff of CruDesLant, because the staff knew that Admiral Speck wasn't completely happy to have one of Admiral Rickover's nuclear-powered ships in his command. [Laughter]

Paul Stillwell: You said you would tell me about the technical reps and then how you got them off the ship.

Admiral Wilkinson: Well, I can't tell you about how happy we were when we got the technical reps off the ship unless I tell you how we got them on there in the first place.

Paul Stillwell: All right.

Admiral Wilkinson: That in itself was an amazing story, and it's one of the greatest things that my people on the *Long Beach* ever did. And they never got full recognition for it. They did from some people, like certainly Admiral Ricketts knew and certainly some senior people in the BuShips and BuWeps knew, but that didn't mean that they were going to get the credit.[*] They really did a great job, and it went something more or less like this. As the *Long Beach* was being finished, the nuclear plant was well done and came on schedule. A lot of the other stuff that went to make it a first-class ship of war was late. Rickover's stuff was on time. I would have liked to seen us wait and get it all so we could have gone to sea as one of the most capable fighting ships in the Navy. But such was not to be when we first went to sea, because Admiral Rickover thought it was very important that the *Long Beach* get to sea as fast as possible and evaluate nuclear-powered surface ships. We were the first nuclear-powered surface ship in the Navy and

---

[*] BuShips – Bureau of Ships; BuWeps – Bureau of Naval Weapons.

Rickover put great pressure on, and he didn't really care whether our weapon systems would work or whether we could shoot anybody or not.*

He was right in a way—that the Navy shift to nuclear propulsion for some of its more important capital ships was important. His people had done their jobs really well, and the nuclear plant was in good shape, and it would be finished and ready to go to sea and drive the ship really well. But that was not true of the weapons, of the missile systems and the weapon control systems and the radar systems and other systems. They were there early enough to be landed on and put on board but not early enough to have all the electrical connections and certainly not the checkouts of the system.

The building yard, Beth Steel Company, had advised the Navy that if we would stay till the next summer they could finish all the checkouts. We left there in September, but if we would stay till the next June or July they could finish all the checkouts of all the systems, and it would only cost some $30 million. But such was not to be. Admiral Rickover had enough power and authority, and nuclear power for surface ships was of enough importance, that he had his way and we were delivered with the propulsion system in fine shape but with our missile batteries on board and not checked out. So we weren't able, of course, to shoot any missiles. We would have been helpless if we'd have tangled with some very small combatant.

Paul Stillwell: Did you have guns?

Admiral Wilkinson: We had two guns. [Laughter] And we had an ASROC, a launcher to shoot weapons at submarines, but they also weren't fully checked out. That didn't make me happy.† So I went down and had meetings with the Chief of BuWeps and the Chief of BuShips about what could be done about that. I was told more or less that nothing could be done about it. In the presence of the then Vice-CNO, who was the one before Admiral Ricketts, I told them that if they would give me the test paper and tech

---

* Lieutenant Lawrence Todd Blades, USN, was the Talos missile battery officer in the first crew of the *Long Beach*. Years later he wrote a lengthy letter to the editor that explained the difference in priorities for the ship's engineering plant versus her weapon systems. See, "Comment and Discussion," *U.S. Naval Institute Proceedings*, December 1978, pages 97-98.

† ASROC -- antisubmarine rocket. It entered the fleet in the early 1960s in new-construction ships and in FRAM I destroyer conversions.

reps and the spare parts that we needed we would check out the missile systems at sea with the ship's force by the first of January instead of the following June or July in the yard. Although that was immediately laughed at by Chief of BuWeps and BuShips, the VCNO took that more seriously, and he said, "Why don't we let Dennis try that?"

Paul Stillwell: Was this Admiral Russell?

Admiral Wilkinson: I think so, yes.* So the agreement was made that that would be the case. I went back to the yard and saw the people in the supship's office and said, "Gee, now I'd like to get my ship's company people on board to help out between now and the completion here in September when we'll sail away, and see if we can get as much done as we can before delivery." I was advised by the superintendent of shipbuilding that that was absolutely impossible. After all, they had just come out of a big labor strike with the union and that that would cause untold problems with the union, and that it would be impossible for my ship's company to go and take work away from a craftsman in the yard. As I told you, though, I was able to talk to the union leaders and got their agreement to let us augment their people with my people and help in the actual construction and hookup of wires and whatnot on the ship. So the last four months at least on the *Long Beach* my missile personnel were on the ship hooking up wires and helping in other things.

As I kept checking on things, I didn't have a commitment for the support technical people that I would require at sea during checkout. As it happened, my people in the weapon systems on the ship really knew people all across America and all the companies involved like Sperry. They really knew those people better than anybody, so it was pretty easy for us to make a list of the best people in America that we would like to have. Our guys made up such a list, and I don't remember the exact number but about 128 tech reps and the very best. As a matter of fact, if *Long Beach* got them all, it would probably hurt some other programs elsewhere, but that wasn't really our concern.

---

* Admiral James S. Russell, USN, served as Vice Chief of Naval Operations from 1 August 1958 to 1 November 1961. His oral history is in the Naval Institute collection.

No arrangements had been made yet following up my meeting in which the commitment had been made by BuWeps that we would have those people. So I went back down to Washington and saw the Chief of BuWeps and the Chief of BuShips and said, "Gentlemen, we had a meeting a while back, and I told you I needed tech reps and spare parts and test paper. The spare parts have not been forthcoming, nor have I a commitment on a list of people by name of tech reps. Were you people sincere? Did you really mean what you were saying, or did you just say it because the VCNO was here?"

That made them mad at me, but they said, "Of course, we meant it, and you can have those things. Now what would you like?"

I said, "Well, I would like these tech reps." I pulled out this list of 128 tech reps, and, of course, they didn't know which were the good ones and which were the bad ones in America like my people did. We didn't get every one of the names on that list, but we got almost all of them, and we had the best group of tech reps to check out Terrier and Talos missile systems that you could have got in America.* Vitro did do a fine job without any prodding in producing all the test paper that was required to check the systems out, so what was left was I didn't have the spare parts to support them if something went wrong with a component.† So I said, "How about the spare parts?"

They said, "Well, what do you want?"

My mouth dropped. I said, "Gee, if you're asking me that now, it's too late. I wanted your people to research all the information on the other Terrier and Talos ships systems and see what the history of parts that they required were and make me such a list and give them to me. But you haven't done that," I said. "What I'd really like is to be the Navy's Secondary Stock Control Point for Terrier and Talos spares."

"What do you mean?" they said.

I said, "Well, all the Terrier and Talos spares in the Navy are up at Mechanicsburg, and those clowns don't do too good a job in filling orders for me.‡ They take a couple of weeks. If you will send all those spares to the *Long Beach* and make us

---

* Terrier was a Navy supersonic surface-to-air, two-stage missile. It was 27 feet long, 12 inches in diameter and weighed 3,000 pounds. It had a range of 15 miles and an operating ceiling of 10 miles. Talos was a long-range ramjet missile used by surface ships in the antiair mission. It was 33 feet long, 28 inches in diameter, and weighed 7,000 pounds. It had a range of about 75 miles.
† Vitro is a defense contractor.
‡ Navy Ships Parts Control Center, Mechanicsburg, Pennsylvania.

the secondary stock control point and with all the spares, we'll be able to have anything we need, and we'll fill anybody's order in the Navy in 24 hours."

They laughed at that and said, "That would be eight freight cars full."

I said, "We've got a great big ship, and I've got the space that's reserved for the vertical ballistic missiles. You just send me those first seven, and I'll put them aboard and the eighth one I'll pick over." After a little rassling back and forth, *Long Beach* actually did become the Navy's secondary stock control point for Terrier and Talos spares. We had them all on board, and we filled anybody's order in 24 hours just like we said we would. Months later we gave all that stuff back to Mechanicsburg, and they became the secondary stock control point again, and I had that burden off my back. But when we turned it all back I only had $42,000 worth of spares I couldn't account for, which is nothing. One component could cost that much. And we really did fill people's orders.

Paul Stillwell: What happened on the ballistic missiles?

Admiral Wilkinson: There was a provision at one time for two spaces that were going to have vertical tubes for ballistic missiles. That was one of the original concepts that never happened.

Paul Stillwell: At what point was the plan changed?

Admiral Wilkinson: Well, I don't know, and now that I think about it I don't know what ultimately happened to that space. But I did have plenty of room for being the secondary stock control point for Terrier and Talos spares, and we did have them all. It wasn't really eight freight carloads, and we didn't have to pick over the last carload. We took them all. [Laughter]

Anyway, now we had the tech reps we needed, we had the test paper we needed, and we had the spares to take care of any casualty we might have during the checkout period. Now we just had to get the job done. And my people really worked awfully hard. It's easy for a big fat captain to say, "We'll do this, and we'll do that." But your people end up then doing it, and sometimes they bleed. At the latter part of construction, when my people were doing the hooking up and wiring up, I can remember walking through the ship and getting down to the 106 computer room, and one of my guys had his feet sticking out from behind a board.[*] It was Thursday evening about 8:00 o'clock. I said to him, "Son, what are you working on?" And he told me. I said, "How long have you been there?"

He said, "Tuesday." And, gee I felt terrible, because my guys did bleed, and they had quite a bit done by the time the ship was delivered and sailed nicely away with this nuclear plant working marvelously. But my people with 120-some odd tech reps were working away day and night checking out those missile systems. We had said grandly, "If you'll give us the tech reps and the test paper and spare parts we need, we'll get it done by ship's force by the first of January instead of staying here in the yard till next June or July." Well, time went by, and when the first of January came we were down off Roos Road, and I could not get the people in charge at Roosevelt Roads to fly drones on a New Year's Day.[†] I couldn't.

But, let me tell you, on the second of January my people made a hit with every missile system.[‡] And they were pretty pleased with themselves, now that that job was done and that we had weapons systems that would work. There was lots of trouble with the missile systems in those days, and my missile systems really would work. When they got a target and fired at it, there was a pretty fair chance they were going to hit it. And years and years later—with me having nothing to do with it, of course—they were on station down in the Gulf of Tonkin in the Vietnamese fracas. *Long Beach* was the first Navy ship to shoot down a MiG, and also the second Navy ship to shoot down a MiG was the *Long Beach*.[§] As far as I know, nobody else ever did it, and they did it with their Talos systems at 60 miles. When I heard about it, I was proud of them.

But back to getting drones on the second of January. After we made the hits with the missiles, then I didn't really need those 120-odd tech reps anymore. So arrangements were made, and a couple of days later I had two big tugs rendezvous with me. Let me

---

[*] Mark 106 was the designation of a missile computer.
[†] U.S. Naval Station Roosevelt Roads was located at the eastern edge of Puerto Rico.
[‡] The tests ran from 2 to 6 January 1962.
[§] MiG was the designation for a number of Soviet-built fighter aircraft.

digress a minute. With all the new systems that capital ships had in that time frame, there wasn't any big carrier or any big ship that wasn't carrying some civilian tech reps to help them make their systems work. But my people had really been involved in this, and so when we were asked what special people we would have to keep, we told them the truth. "Hey, zero. [Laughter] We can handle it with ship's company." So two or three days later, after we'd had our missile systems perform successfully and demonstrated it, we were able to bring two big tugs alongside and off-load those 120-odd tech reps. You just can't imagine the morale uplift we had on our ship when we could look around and the only people there was us. You asked me the question about off-loading the tech reps, and I really had to tell you how we got them in the first place.

Paul Stillwell: Indeed, you did.

Admiral Wilkinson: We still had to get some more stuff, the height-finding radars and the devices to keep track of a lot of targets simultaneously, the weapons control systems and the NTDS system. We had to come back in for a yard availability and get that installed in time, and that's another story. But at least we'd reached the point where we had a ship that could, push come to shove, shoot down the enemy. The people that made it so were a whole lot of hard-working guys in my weapons department, and they probably never got full credit for the fantastic job they'd done. No other ship has ever done anything like that.

Paul Stillwell: What do you remember about going into San Juan prior to that missile shoot?*

Admiral Wilkinson: This was a ship-handling problem; we certainly didn't have any tugs or pilots. We went into San Juan, and I had an admiral aboard. For some reason he said, "Dennis, it would nice if you were able to bring this ship in astern up the channel and bow down pointed out. Can you do that?"

---

* The *Long Beach* left Norfolk on 28 December 1961 and steamed to San Juan, Puerto Rico, where she spent New Year's Day prior to beginning missile tests the following day.

I said, "Well, I could put it in sideways if you wanted, but why would you want to do that?"

It was a time of political unrest, and he said, "In case of emergency we could get under way and get out faster." Which really isn't really true. You can back out just as fast as you can go out forward. But, gee, if my admiral wanted to be in stern up the channel, I'd do it. So I went in and spun around. The *Long Beach* didn't drive quite as well going backwards as it did forward. With that big sail structure we had a tendency to back into the wind. But that day, as luck would have it, the wind was coming exactly down channel, so when I turned around and started backing, the wind and fates combined to make it back up flawlessly straight, right parallel to the docks. We backed up a considerable distance until we were right where we wanted to be, and we were just a short distance off the piers. I had put a utility boat in the water in case I couldn't get close enough to take a line over, but we didn't need that. We were close enough, so we just threw the line over with a heave just like you do on a submarine and put it to the capstan and pushed with the utility boat, and we were alongside just like that, backwards just as easily as forward. But it was fun to handle the ship, and we did it enough so we were quite good at it. I've made lots of landings on the *Long Beach*.

The other capital ships in Norfolk all used a pilot and tugs to make their landings, and you were required by the law to have a pilot on board. So when I came in I also would have a pilot, but the pilot and I dealt so nicely that I was always the one that made my own landings and controlled the tugs. I'd tell him, "Don't let me get in trouble. If I make a mistake with a tug, you tell me." But I got so I could handle the ship quite well and handle tugs, which is not as easy as driving the ship itself.

Paul Stillwell: Were there any restrictions on ports the *Long Beach* could go because of her nuclear power?

Admiral Wilkinson: No. We also went up and made port calls into Germany and Northern France.[*] And we were well received in those places. When we went into

---

[*] The ship's visits to Northern Europe were at the beginning of 1962. She was at Bremerhaven, Germany, 15-19 January and then arrived at Le Havre, France on the 20th. After a six-day visit there, she steamed to Bermuda, where she arrived on 2 February.

Germany we did have the ability to fire gun salutes and gave honors. I had a Marine detachment that paraded an honor guard and looked quite elegant. We had people that had never been given honors come from miles around. Once we fired 289 rounds out of our saluting battery in four days. [Laughter] It was a constant struggle for me. When we had a visiting dignitary that rated honors, as the commanding officer I'd be dressed in a uniform with medals and white gloves and all that stuff. And then I had my business to do, and I don't know how many times I have gone up and down. It was really a problem to make absolutely fast clothes changes. I can remember saying to my people, "Help me get this damned uniform on with all the medals." Then I'd go down to give orders and participate in honors.

One of things we were given when *Long Beach* went in commission was a very elegant set of Gorham silver and some very elegant crystal glasses and so on. I can remember we were having a big reception on board, and we had really knocked ourselves out getting ready with super hors d'oeuvres. Of course, we didn't serve alcoholic beverages, but we had made some pretty nice fruit punch and whatnot and had our wardroom more than full with a multitude of guests. So I heard this sweet young voice behind me say, "Oooh, what filthy punch!" [Laughter] I'll never forget that. But a few little problems like that didn't mean anything to us. We really had a great deal of fun up there visiting ports and giving a lot of honors to visitors, to burgermeisters and whatnot.

As I said, here was a ship with the ability to have an honor guard and fire a saluting battery, and some of these gents had never had that done to them in their lives, so we were overwhelmed with that. That was a worry to my admiral. As a young officer he'd been in charge of a saluting battery giving honors when it failed, and it was quite embarrassing to him that at that time.

Paul Stillwell: Which admiral was this?

Admiral Wilkinson: I'm not going to tell you. [Laughter] He's passed away now. And he really used to worry about that. "Dennis, are you sure that you can keep up firing at the exactly right interval of time between shots?" I used a couple of 40-millimeter guns. I'm not talking to the admiral. I'm talking just to the record here. And we'd fire one round out of one and then one round out of the other. Hey, we could have fired at the proper rate on one gun. We didn't. It wasn't the same anymore. There wasn't any chance of us not being able to. And I'd tell him, "Absolutely, Admiral."

He'd say, "But, Dennis, I want you to make sure and check and make sure that the guns are going to work and all."

"Admiral, I personally guarantee that there will never be any problem with our saluting battery." [Laughter] But I don't know how many times that topic of conversation came up between us. And, of course, as I said, either one of our 40 millimeters could have fired off as saluting guns at the proper rate all day long. [Laughter] We did fire a lot in that trip. It was up in Germany. We fired a lot of rounds out of those saluting batteries and gave a lot of honors.

Paul Stillwell: After that the ship went to Bermuda.

Admiral Wilkinson: I'll tell you one more tennis story. When I was skipper of *Long Beach* I still played tennis. We went in and made courtesy calls on the Governor of Bermuda, who was quite a tennis player.[*]

Paul Stillwell: A British man?

Admiral Wilkinson: Yes. And we scheduled ourselves to play doubles, and when we went out to play, whom did he have as his partner but the club pro. I've always been lucky, and I picked up a gentleman playing at the club who was a pickup player from Boston, and he was better than all three of us put together. The club pro had no chance against him, so with a superior partner we had a successful thing there.

Paul Stillwell: How soon was it before the ship was truly complete?

Admiral Wilkinson: The ship wasn't completed until after it had been into another yard

---

[*] The ship reached Bermuda on 2 February 1962 for a three-day stop, during which she hosted more than 3,000 visitors. She arrived back in Norfolk on 7 February.

period. We were still missing some of the stuff that you'd like to have in weapon control, the height-finding radar, the AN/SPS-32 and the weapons-control consoles, and that had now became available. So we were scheduled to go in the shipyard at Philly to have an installation period to put that other stuff on and complete the NTDS and so on, all the stuff that's supposed to be in the ship.

The Bureau of Ships and the Bureau of Weps and the shipyard came up with a schedule for that of 19 months. I didn't want to spend 19 months in a shipyard in my tour so I said, "Seven months." They didn't know how it could be done in seven months, and this went to the VCNO, Admiral Ricketts, who was by now pretty strongly on our side. And so we compromised with the Bureau of Ships and Bureau of Weapons and they set a period of eight months.

Paul Stillwell: [Laughter] Some compromise.

Admiral Wilkinson: Yes. I hated to give up that month. [Laughter] But we were reasonable people, and we compromised at eight months. During preparations for that yard period I would go up and check up on what the yard was doing to get ready: "How are you doing on getting the material? How are you doing on getting the plans out?" The first time I went up, I asked, "What material is behind schedule."

"Nothing behind schedule."

"Which plans are behind schedule?"

"Zero."

"Well, gee, that's really gratifying to hear." And then I thought again, and that had not been my experience over the years in dealing with shipyards. I said, "That's fantastic. It's hard for me to believe it. Show me. Show me. How can you be zero behind? What's scheduled to be done?" Well, they weren't behind because it wasn't scheduled to be done yet, so we got that changed. We produced a new schedule for material coming into the yard, so now we were behind. Effort could be put on it, and so by the time we went into the yard the plans were available and the parts were available.

We tied up and started our yard availability to put on the fixed-array radar system and the weapons control systems and so on.* And immediately they demonstrated that I was wrong. That it couldn't be done in eight months, that it was going to take longer. I put up with that from Monday till Thursday and then I said, "Hey, we're not going to run it this way anymore. We're going to have a meeting of the shipyard masters every morning at 7:15, Monday through Saturday, and we're going to go over what has to be done in the schedule, and I'm going to run that meeting." And I had no authority in the yard to do that. But the supervisor of shipbuilding and the yard commander decided they didn't want to fight with me, and so that's the way it was. [Laughter]

We had a meeting every morning with all the yard masters, and I'm an honorary yard master now. They did a fantastic job, and we completed the yard period four days before eight months and sailed away. Because of that, I got the rest of my time on *Long Beach* as the commanding officer of a ship at sea instead of being in a damn yard. And it was big stuff that the *Long Beach* got out of there in just a little under eight months. The yard captain made admiral in the next selection, as he should for his good judgment in letting us do that, and everybody was happy. [Laughter] Even the Chiefs of BuShips and BuWeps were happy that they got it done in eight months, and so was the VCNO.

And I guess my weapons people were pleased too. Let me tell you, they did an absolutely fantastic job in getting those weapons systems finished and checked out, and they did it well. And the same thing couldn't be done today. I mean, it was a different pressure. Well, I'm proud of the job that the engineers did, but I'm also even more proud of the job that the deck force people did, the weapon system, in checking out those missile systems. The weapons department people that made those missile systems work did something that as far as I know no other ship has ever done, and I don't think any other ship took charge of the masters in the yard availability and got out on time, not to my knowledge. So *Long Beach* was very good, but they worked hard at it. They worked hard. It didn't come easy.

Well, finally the ship was complete. After that we still had to do underway training in Guantánamo and pass all the tests on ship's equipment and the nuclear weapons tests and all that before we deployed. And the schedule again became very

---

* The *Long Beach* arrived at the Philadelphia Naval Shipyard on 28 April 1962 to begin the yard period.

tight. All ships really get beat around the head and shoulders in Guantánamo. They don't do fantastically well. They've lots of discrepancies. You get a lot of improvement out of that underway training. We wanted to do well, and the representatives of the training department came aboard. These stories were at the same time period but not maybe hour by hour.

The first time we got under way, the representatives came up on the bridge and said, "Captain, do you have a list of your equipment that's out of commission?"

I said, "Well, you know, I would if I had any, but I think right now there isn't anything out of commission."

Well, that was very humorous to the guys, and they said, "Hey, we'll make an inspection in the next couple of days, and we'll come back and find out what there is and give you a list."

I said, "If you find something, I really would appreciate it if you'd let me know." [Laughter] And so they went away.

They came back the next day with a little bit of awe and they said, "Captain, do you know there really isn't anything out of commission?" [Laughter]

I said, "I didn't think there was." [Laughter] So we started out with the underway training element on board to go out and give us this inspection. It was pretty rigorous, and they did a damn good job. They'd done a lot of ships, hundreds of times, and although *Long Beach* was a great big bite they had lots of people. They knew what to check up on, and they did well. But the first morning, when we were going to get under way, one of their chiefs didn't make it. The time to get under way came, and *Long Beach* had a tendency to get under way on time. There was one member of the inspecting party, which was quite a large party, who wasn't aboard. Well, I didn't know why, and that certainly wasn't anything to stop operations for.

So we were breasted out and stern twisted out. We took in the number-one line, the last one, and we started backing out. Then, as the captain up there on bridge with good visibility, I could see a car driving frantically down, a woman driving. A chief was in it as it was heading down the dock. It was the missing chief who didn't make the sailing. It's all fun and you've got to enjoy it, so I kicked ahead and leaned the bow over to the dock. One my guys reached a hand down and pulled the guy aboard. And then we backed out and were under way and went on out on our operations.

The evening of the next day the chief came up to me on the bridge. It was after chow, and he knew it was dark. He said, "Captain, you didn't say anything to anybody about me missing ship."

I said, "Chief, I thought you made it." [Laughter]

He said, "Well, I want to say thanks, Captain." And that was the end of that conversation. But, as it happened, that chief was the E-9 senior chief, the senior enlisted man in the whole inspecting group in Guantánamo, and I didn't know that.[*] They still call it like they see it, but let me tell you. For the rest of that underway training thing, if there was any chance to give us any benefit of the doubt we had it in spades. And it was just luck, just luck. So we came out of the underway training at Guantánamo with flying colors.

The history of new ships taking their first nuclear weapons inspections involves a lot of people—all the Marines and guards and so on. I won't go into the details, but we're talking about involving hundreds of people, and it was meticulous. The examination took three or four days, and the record of ships in failures was very high. I mean, most ships had to try to pass that two or three times. But by now our schedule was so tight we needed to pass, or we wouldn't make our scheduled deployment date to the Med. As good fortune would have it, when we had that exam we passed it the first time, just like we had done with the training at Gitmo. So there was quite an intensive shakedown, get everything checked, pass our weapons test, pass an ORSE board test.[†] That was Rickover's group of people. And again before we operated there was that test, and our guys passed the first time. Rickover's people didn't like to do that either, but we did. That was much earlier, before we went to sea the first time.

In the early days there were lots of problems with the missile systems, and I remember when a demonstration by forces afloat was made to show the President our

---

[*] E-9 is the senior pay grade for Navy enlisted personnel.
[†] ORSE – operational reactor safeguards examination.

missile systems.* Every one of them that was fired was a miss, and it was a really sad day. We sat there just feeling so bad, because this was just after we'd made our missile systems work, and I said, "Gee, we were ready, and they weren't about to use us, but if they had we'd have hit them." [Laughter] After that exercise we went to Yorktown to off-load our missiles before going in the yard.†

Paul Stillwell: What do you recall about taking the Secretary Korth into Yorktown?

Admiral Wilkinson: Since *Long Beach* was the first nuclear-powered surface ship, there was quite a bit of interest in us. We had great fun having Admiral Ricketts aboard and others of that ilk. At another time I was able to take my wife to sea on a trip. This time we had Secretary Korth who came down to ride the ship.‡ Also on that trip to Yorktown was Marian Hosmer, wife of Congressman Hosmer. She had been our sponsor.

When Secretary Korth decided to come down from Washington and ride the ship, that led higher authority to get interested and make sure all the proper arrangements were made, and so they arranged for a river pilot to come up and meet us off Yorktown and for two tugs to be up there ready to help us land, and I was horrified.

I said, "My God, we're taking the Secretary of the Navy aboard. Certainly we should be able to run our own ship and not have some river pilot or some tugs pushing it around. We shouldn't have any trouble in going up and tying up at Yorktown." Actually it's quite an interesting thing, because you go upstream and you tie up facing downstream so you have to make a 180-degree turn before you make your landing. So we took Secretary Korth up toward Yorktown as fast as the law would allow, and as we got there things really worked out well. We turned around at good speed with a flourish. I drove up alongside the pier and made a spectacular landing of "All back two-thirds, all stop, double up." And that's the way it was. It was a flashy landing.

---

* From 10 to 15 April 1962 the *Long Beach* was one of 40-some Atlantic Fleet warships that took part in an exercise to demonstrate naval power. President John F. Kennedy was present for part of the exercise. Admiral Robert L. Dennison, USN, Commander in Chief Atlantic Fleet, used the *Long Beach* as flagship during a portion of the at-sea time.
† Naval Weapons Station, Yorktown, Virginia.
‡ Fred H. Korth served as Secretary of the Navy from 4 January 1962 to 1 November 1963. Marian Hosmer was the ship's sponsor. They went to Yorktown on board the ship on 24 April 1962. The *Long Beach* then entered the Philadelphia Naval Shipyard on 28 April.

About that time a voice yelled up to me from down on the dock, and as the captain conning the ship I was up on the 08 level, which was pretty high in the air. The voice said, "Captain, would you move forward 10 feet so we'll be lined up for handling the missiles?" So, after having made that super-flashy landing, I screwed around for about five minutes and couldn't get that damn thing moved ten feet. Finally I got wiser, and I called my exec, Hal Castle, and I said, "Take the conn here and finish moving this up. I want to take the Secretary around on a trip." [Laughter] But he liked the trip, and we didn't have to have a pilot and two tugs, and we did make a flashy landing.

During the months after that, when we were in the shipyard, it really frustrated me because I'd go through the ship and there'd be a bunch of cigarette butts around. I fussed with my people, and they'd say, "Captain, that's the yard birds." And so the first day out of Philly damned if I didn't find some cigarette butts around. I said, "I thought it was us all the time. I want that stopped immediately." We never had anymore cigarette butts. But it's not fun in a shipyard.

There was an amusing thing at that time. Even though I was skipper of the *Long Beach* here, I was known to be a submariner. In the yard in Philly at the same time we were in there, there was a little Turkish submarine. I think they had 42 people on board. And so the captain of this Turkish submarine came over to my cruiser and made a courtesy call. And he really did it, not that I was a captain of a cruiser in there, but it was because I was a submarine guy. During the course of that call, he challenged me to a soccer game. I allowed as how we might be able to get a little soccer team together. And so we did, and we played. The Turks just kicked the hell out of us. I had almost 1,000 guys. We didn't have a prayer of a chance playing soccer against those guys.

Paul Stillwell: Americans didn't play soccer back then.

Admiral Wilkinson: Well, this was in 1962, I guess. I couldn't imagine that we couldn't win, but we played soccer with that little Turkish submarine and they just kicked the hell out of us. [Laughter]

Now, after coming out of the yard in Philly getting ready to go to the Med, the day-by-day schedule was such that if anything went wrong we were going to miss sailing on time. And it was a really full operational checkout. But whenever it was that we were scheduled to go to the Med, we sailed at that day and that hour, without any absentees, and that's another story.*

In World War II everybody went in the service, and there wasn't any doubt about it. Certainly there was not always enthusiasm, but there certainly was nothing but public support. Now in '63 not everybody was quite as wild about everything the military did. Not every man was always really enthusiastic to go on deployment. The circumstances were such that if a man missed sailing he was over leave. Some of the people would rather be over leave when the ship got under way than sail on a ship that was deploying for six months. They would report in very shortly after it was gone. And maybe they would really only have been absent over leave for six hours, which is not an enormous offense. Yet thereby they've missed the sailing of their ship. And it's pretty expensive to send them airmail from the Atlantic coast to the Mediterranean. So normally disciplinary action would be taken against them, and they'd be transferred to somewhere else—but they'd missed deployment.

The cruiser just before us that was supposed to deploy to the Med had 56 people that missed sailing, and that's pretty bad on a ship. So I talked to my people and told them I really didn't want them to do that, and that maybe there was a little bit of uncertainty. I had them all come aft on the fantail on the *Long Beach* and said, "Sit down. I want to talk to you." I told them this had happened, and perhaps a little bit of it was because of classification and confidentiality, and maybe some of them didn't really know that they were going to sail that day. They knew they were supposed to be at quarters in the morning. But that wasn't going to be true on the *Long Beach*. There wasn't any man on board that didn't know the day and the hour of departure, because I was telling them right then. [Laughter]

I said, "Now, if there's any man on board this ship that has some reason not to go, if he'll just come up and tell us and it's valid and we can, we'll do our utmost to get him a replacement and leave him here. If you've got problems at home or whatnot, you just come and tell us, and we'll do the best we can. But when that day and that hour come, I expect everybody on board this ship to be there. And if you're not, let me tell you my

---

* The *Long Beach* got under way 6 August 1963 to deploy to the Mediterranean.

feelings are going to be hurt." [Laughter] That was a sort of dumb thing to say, but it was sincere. And they would have been. And so that day and that hour came, and as good fortune would have it we didn't have anybody miss sailing.

When the time came, we sailed away down the channel to deploy to the Med, and, bang, we get a snotty dispatch from CruDesLant within three or four hours: "Submit required reports." There's a requirement if a ship goes to sea and somebody missed sailing that they report that absentee back to higher authority. So we sent them a dispatch right back to CruDesLant from *Long Beach*, "All required reports submitted." Well, of course, that stopped them for a few minutes, so they searched through all their files and sent down to radio and sent all that stuff up and finally they sent us another dispatch, "Send date-time group of your absentee report."*

We were able to send right back, "This is the *Long Beach*. We're surprised at such a question of *Long Beach*. No report. No absentees." [Laughter] But dumb little things. But, again, it was just a little bit of the relations that existed between us and CruDesLant, which was too bad, because there for quite some time with Admiral Cavenagh as CruLant we had a type commander that thought we were really great. And probably it cost my ship something.

We went over to the Med and all those operations went well. As I met *Enterprise* and her skipper, Michaelis, off Spain, I sandbagged them because *Enterprise* really would do 34 knots and *Long Beach* would only do 32 knots.† We were in company with *Enterprise*, so I told them there was a lot of comments about which of our ships was the most capable.‡ "I challenge you to a race." We were side by side, making five knots, one-third on the annunciators. And we went through all the signals. "Standby, mark." And then all ahead flank. Well, although at top speed he'd do 34 knots he was looking at an 80,000-ton ship. I had a 14,000-ton ship, but it didn't have as much inertia. We just walked away from them. And before they could absorb that, I said, "I challenge you to a reversal then. I challenge you in going backwards." And we did it in reverse. We

---

* The date-time group indicates the specific time that a particular message was sent and thus serves as an identifier for the message.
† Captain Frederick H. Michaelis, USN, commanded the aircraft carrier *Enterprise* (CVAN-65) from 20 June 1963 to 17 July 1965. The oral history of Michaelis, who became a four-star admiral, is in the Naval Institute collection.
‡ The first meeting of the *Long Beach* and *Enterprise* was 23 August 1963 in the Western Mediterranean.

walked away from them going backwards. Then I said, "You know, it's only fair if we do a longer race. We challenge you in a race from here to Naples," which was where we were going. He was on his way back to the States, so he couldn't do it.* [Laughter] So Mike Michaelis was frustrated as hell. [Laughter]

Paul Stillwell: Another thing that you had mentioned when we weren't recording was about how you brought up the advancement rates for the enlisted men going up in rating. Initially some of their supervisors had been reluctant to recommend them.

Admiral Wilkinson: Well, that comes from the background of the people I had. All my department heads and people were not submarine background people, and maybe submarine people thought differently about that. I know they did. But the way guys got advanced in rating was they took the Navy competitive exams. Before a man could take an exam he had to be recommended by the ship. And before the ship recommended him he was recommended to the ship by the bosses for whom he worked. The first time we worked out the list of people we were going to recommend for taking the competitive exams for promotion, there weren't very many names on it.

That surprised and shocked me, and I said to my personnel people, "I want a list of every man on board that has enough time in to be available for the next rating. And then I want to know from that list who has not been recommended and why." Oh, that generated an uproar from my people.

"Captain, you've come from submarines where you have all super-selected people. We've got a bunch of bums and no-goodniks here. You're not telling us that we should recommend people for advancement in rating that are no damn good."

I said, "Well, of course not, but let's go down these men one by one. Why aren't we recommending this man?"

"Well, he hasn't got any course in. He hasn't done any practical factors. You can't depend on him. He's no damn good. We're not recommending him for rating. He

---

* On 24 August, the day after her first meeting with the *Long Beach*, the *Enterprise* was relieved by the carrier *Independence* (CVA-62) and left for the United States two days later. In 1964, after Wilkinson had been relieved, the *Long Beach*, *Enterprise*, and *Bainbridge* made an around-the-world cruise in company.

doesn't even do a decent job in the rating he is now. We certainly don't want to recommend him."

"Well, I agree with that." And we went down all the people name by name, and when he got all through I said, "Well, I understand that and I concur with the list, and that's what we'll send in. But let me tell you, from now on people really don't have a personal choice. They are working for the Navy, and they're getting paid by the Navy. They ought to do a good job for the Navy, and they can do a better job for the Navy if they're better qualified. So every man has to put in a course, and he has to complete the practical factors and so on. Make it so. I want every man issued a course, and I want him to complete that course in accordance with the schedule. I want a schedule for them completing the practical factors, and I want that done." And so it was.

I got a certain amount of fun out of the next time that the list was generated for people to be recommended for taking the competitive exams for advancement in rating. There was a multitude of names on the list. Again, before we sent it in I went down them, and I said, "Hey, I don't know about that guy. He's no damn good. Why are we recommending him?"

"Well, Captain, he's got his courses done. He's got all his practical factors in. He's one of the best guys I've got. I'd really like to see him promoted in my division." I kept a straight face, and we sent all those names in, and that's the way it was from then on. As I told you, I would talk to every man that came aboard. A lot of these young kids coming aboard hadn't finished high school, and in my interview I'd say, "Well, gee, you didn't finish high school? What was the problem?"

"Oh, I wanted to, Captain, but I had to work or I couldn't do this or something else interfered."

"Well, fortunately none of those problems are here. There's lots of time here and lots of support, and we can get you working on that." And I will say that during my time as captain of the *Long Beach*—and it was a long time—I had 80-odd kids complete their high school diplomas. I was pleased with that, and they were pleased with that. But as time went by almost everyone that had enough time in rating to be eligible to take the competitive exam probably did. One rating time, I remember 252 of our troops were promoted in petty officer promotions. Seaman to third or third to second or second to first I had 252 guys that advanced in petty officer ratings, and every man of them came up to the bridge and gave me a cigar. I smoked cigars in those days. That took four days. [Laughter] But I congratulated them all, and I was happy with them, and they were happy with themselves. The result because of that was that we had a better-qualified group of people of more value to the ship and the Navy and of more value to themselves. And ultimately it really added to the morale on the ship.

Paul Stillwell: You gave their supervisors a little more incentive to get personally involved in the process.

Admiral Wilkinson: Yes, but once you said there isn't any choice, this is the way it's going to be, the system is such that that's apt to happen. [Laughter]

Paul Stillwell: What do you recall about reenlistment rates? Did that go hand in hand with these advancements?

Admiral Wilkinson: You know, I can talk glibly about reenlistment rates on some of my submarines. I really can't remember the figures now on the reenlistment rates on the *Long Beach*. I should be able to, but at the time they were a lot better than the fleet averages. I don't remember exactly what the figures were, but our reenlistment was pretty good. Not like a ship like the *Wahoo* where maybe we would run 100% reenlistment for a long time. I can remember on the *Nautilus* having been told that one of our guys wasn't going to reenlist. "Why not? What's the matter with him?" I said.

"Why, nothing, Captain. He's really a good guy, but his wife doesn't want him to stay in the Navy."

I said, "You just tell him we'll get him a new wife. [Laughter] Maybe you'd get sued for something like that today, but he reenlisted just the same. [Laughter]

Paul Stillwell: What do you recall about the time that the *Long Beach* was accused of having bedbugs on board?

Admiral Wilkinson: I had a new flag that came aboard, and I think they reported aboard on a Thursday. The admiral went away for that weekend and phoned back Saturday and told me he'd slept in his room I think Thursday and Friday night and called back and said he had bedbugs in his bed.

I said, "Why, sir, of course you don't."

He said, "Don't tell me. I had duty on China station, and I know a bedbug bite when I see it. My legs are covered with bedbug bites and I want it squared away right away before I get back." So we squared it away.

Paul Stillwell: A problem that you didn't have in the *Nautilus* was running ship's boats. What do you remember about the *Long Beach* boats?

Admiral Wilkinson: I recognized that I had eight small boats, and that I should be able to put them in the water and pick them up, and we should be able to do that expeditiously and well. As the captain with the conn I had a certain amount of fun in putting a boat in the water and then driving around and getting the boat alongside and picking it up. And we became quite good at it. But then I had a considerable number of problems in that as a new ship my boats kept crapping out. We'd put a boat in the water and tell it to circle around and come up alongside and that we'd pick it up. It would start circling around, its propulsion would die, and it'd be dead in the water out there.

Well, as the conning officer that was even more fun now just having the ship drive around to the point alongside to be picked up. I could drive the great big *Long Beach* around to put this little boat in the same position and then pick it up. So I probably did that about four times until I got more concerned about the fact that the boats weren't running. So the next time one crapped out I sent for my chief engineer to come to the bridge, and I told him, "We're all ahead one third, rudder amidships. That boat of yours over there is broken down and doesn't seem to be able to run. We have to go over and pick it up. Here, you take the conn and pick up your own boat." And some way or other an awful lot of effort was expended, and the small boats became more and more and very reliable. [Laughter]

I had a really good chief engineer, Spencer, and he also was a ship handler. Every one of my department heads and a great number of officers qualified as pretty good ship handlers on the *Long Beach*. I did let them do things like that, although that day it was for a different reason and a different purpose. Later on I transferred that chief engineer over to be Ray Peet's exec on the *Bainbridge*.* I'm sure he was of considerable value to Ray, and I know Ray liked him. Years later Spencer came back and was a CO of the *Long Beach*.† He was a good man.

Paul Stillwell: What do you recall about the time your knowledge of the signal book and the tactical publications helped you in taking control of a formation the *Long Beach* was in?

Admiral Wilkinson: I hadn't run a surface ship before, and I wanted to be sure that in those kinds of things I could do it well, so I really spent a lot of effort and time studying and being thoroughly familiar with the general signal book. If you can use the general signal book quickly, it's surprising how effective you can be in controlling the movement of ships and doing the things you should do in company with other ships as a surface ship. I really became quite proficient at it. It was of value to me in *Long Beach* operations in company with other ships.

Actually, *Long Beach* did a lot of operations, and we were in control of groups of ships many times. I had a lot of interesting experiences. One of them we were going to join up with a big force, and this was international. There was going to be some Brit ships involved, and things were all messed up. The ships were going every which way, and the Brit cruiser came up and found me and came close and communicated and said, "What is my station?"

I said, "Well, things are a little confused over there now. Why don't you just stay here with me until they get straightened out, and then we can go over and fall in easily?"

---

* USS *Bainbridge* (DLGN-25), a nuclear-powered frigate, was the only ship of her class. She was commissioned 6 October 1962. Captain Raymond A. Peet, USN, was the first commanding officer. The oral history of Peet, who retired as a vice admiral, is in the Naval Institute collection.
† Captain William A. Spencer, USN, commanded the *Long Beach* from June 1968 to September 1972.

He said, "Splendid." [Laughter] So I really admired the Brits as operators. They were good. It really used to frustrate me sometimes that my submarine would have better equipment, and they would do better with worse equipment.

But that's not what you're referring to. Another time we had a flag on board, and there were formations of ships. There were some 20-odd ships, and the control of them all was under the flag that was on the *Long Beach*. They were dispersed into three groups, and they happened to all be aiming toward a common point. If you had tracked it ahead, they'd all reach that point at 0800. Like I did at sea a lot, I had a sea cabin, and I have pictures in the other room of me on the bridge in pajamas. I spent some time in that sea cabin, and I spent an awful lot of time sitting in my captain's chair on the bridge.

So I was sitting in my chair about 4:00 o'clock, and all the three big groups of ships were headed toward a common point. At 5:00 o'clock all three big groups of ships were still headed toward the common point. At 5:30 they were still headed toward the common point, and I was getting just a little more nervous. At 6:00 o'clock they were still heading toward the common point. Sometime after 6:00 they were all still heading toward the common point, and I had a little private telephone line between my chair on my bridge and the admiral's chair on his bridge on the 04 level.

Finally I rang the buzzer on the admiral's bridge, and it was picked up instantly. The admiral's voice said, "Dennis, my people are all fouled up," which I was beginning to suspect. [Laughter] And he said, "Would you like to take operational command?" which meant that we would give all the orders to all the ships for a while as to what they were doing and which way they ought to go.

I said, "Why, yes, sir, Admiral."

Then he hit me with the words, "Well, when could you be ready?"

After a very brief of contemplation, I said, "Why, we're ready now, Admiral."

He said, "Well, take operational command." So, with my knowledge and experience of having spent an awful lot of time studying on the general signal book, I was able to reach over and grab the PriTac and send out a message to all ships that said, "*Long Beach* is in operational command.* Stand by. Signals follow."

---

* PriTac – the primary tactical voice radio circuit.

Almost without a break the orders pealed out from us to all the ships in the formations to go this way or go that way. Instead of now all proceeding toward a common point, they were all acting as a group of ships doing something else. But it was fun to me, and by now it had become easy for me because I really had studied a lot and really was proficient in the signal book. It sounds silly, but a real skill in that makes it fairly easy to control groups of ships. It might not lead to you making a right decision of a disposition to stand an attack against air forces or something but for just driving ships around and making sure they didn't run into one another and steaming from here to there and controlling it, signals out of the general signal book are used.

Paul Stillwell: What highlights do you remember from the 1963 deployment to the Mediterranean? Was there a public relations aspect to that cruise?

Admiral Wilkinson: You've just jogged my memory. My guys did some really great things in Naples, but I'm going to talk about that later after I get it all straight in my mind. We got to the Med, and we did operations, and we did them well. Our people got in no trouble at all.

Paul Stillwell: Any port visits other than Naples during the course of that?

Admiral Wilkinson: Yes. We'd been Barcelona. We went to Naples. I got to go to Capri, where the Blue Grotto is. So we did all those things and had some amazing experiences.

Paul Stillwell: You said your sailors did well over there.

Admiral Wilkinson: Yes.

Paul Stillwell: You mean in terms of no disciplinary problems?

Admiral Wilkinson: No disciplinary problems, and that's what I want to talk about, and that's what I'm trying to get in my mind. There were an awful lot of problems on the ships in there in that some sailors would go ashore and be sandbagged and be in trouble. So we had talked to our people and told them they had to go in groups and look out for one another. In all the time we were there we never had any one of our people ever be on report or in trouble of any kind during the time I was in command. Nobody over leave, nothing. And I was trying to jog my memory and think back. There was a real problem at that time, in that ship after ship would have their sailors in trouble. But my guys looked out for one another to the point that that never happened to any of our people.

Paul Stillwell: Did you get into the south of France at all?

Admiral Wilkinson: No.

I was relieved of command at sea in the Med.* I'd been on the *Long Beach* for four years and a month, and I hated to go. But I had the command at sea, and I was relieved and turned over to my relief. As I walked away from the change of command ceremony the little Marine orderly followed me like he always did and I flipped him a little hand signal that he better go to that new skipper. [Laughter] And finally he got the word. He hustled away, and he started to go, and I hated to see him go. [Laughter] But it was right he did.

Paul Stillwell: Was that Frank Price who took over?†

Admiral Wilkinson: Yes. Then a helicopter came over and picked me up and carried me from the *Long Beach* over to the carrier, and they put me on a COD flight and shot me off and sent me to Naples.‡ I was a flag selectee at that point, because I was selected for flag while I was on the *Long Beach*. So they met me with all due friendship and asked me

---

* The change of command was on 11 September 1963.
† Captain Frank H. Price, Jr., USN, commanded the nuclear-powered cruiser *Long Beach* (CGN-9) from September 1963 to August 1966.
‡ COD – carrier on-board delivery, an aircraft configured for carrier takeoffs and landings, dedicated to transporting personnel and cargo between ship and shore.

what they could do for me. I said, "Well, we're going to go back through Paris, and I've never been there, and I'd just like to go to the Lido and have dinner and see the show."

They said, "Well, we'll see what we can arrange." But just about that time my Navy-arranged flight was ready to take me from Naples to Rome, and so they said somebody would meet me in Rome and square that away. So I got to Rome, and we went through the same baloney, that same story, and they said, hey, yeah, they'd see what they could do about that but at about that time it was time to put me on my flight to Orly.* So I didn't quite get squared away. And when I got to Orly I was met, and there they did some checking on it and said they were sorry. I'd have to have female companionship with me to get a table, and they couldn't arrange just for me to have dinner and see the show. About that time my transportation was there to take me in from Orly to the hotel where I was spending that night, and I told them, "Hey, that's fine. I'll arrange it at the hotel." So I got to the hotel and talked to the concierge, and eventually the same story came back that really you needed to have reservations, and so I thought, "Hell, I'll do something else."

So, lo and behold, I was walking down the Champs Elysées, and damned if there wasn't the Lido. So I turned in, and there was a velvet rope and a guy behind it. I went up and told him I'd like to have dinner and see the show, which is what I had wanted all along. And he said, "Monsieur has reservations?"

I said, "No."

He said, well, perhaps he could get me a seat way back at the bar. By now I had had it. I reached down in my pocket, and I pulled out my big roll of greenbacks, and I said, "You don't understand. I'd like to have dinner and see the show, and I'd like to be right down in front."

The guy said, "Yes, sir, monsieur." [Laughter] We went in and there was a little three-legged table that wasn't any bigger around than that, and I'm showing you something about 16 inches across. The waiter put it up over his head and sidled through all the other tables and put it down with two legs out on the dance floor. They set me up there, and all during dinner these girls are dancing right over my head. I was afraid

---

* Orly is one of the Paris airports.

somebody would see me. [Laughter] I really was an ugly American, but I did get to have dinner and see the show at the Lido.

I hotfooted it, caught a flight the next morning back to America and went right to my wife, and I had a month's leave en route to my next duty station which was OpNav. I took my wife, and we went right up to New Jersey, the Air Force base where they had lots of flights going out that you could bum a ride on, and I said, "Gee, I'd like to get a ride to take my wife somewhere."[*]

They said, "Where would you like to go?"

I said, "Jeez, whatever we've got."

Pretty soon they said, "We've got space on a flight to Paris."

I said, "Gee, that'd be fine. We'd like to do that." We got a free flight, so I took my wife over to Europe for a month, and we did a lot of things, saw a lot of places. We didn't go to the Lido.

Paul Stillwell: Please tell me about getting the news of selection for flag rank

Admiral Wilkinson: You know, I don't fully remember that. You've got to go way back in time. I came in the Navy at the beginning of World War II, like everybody came in the service. I had no intention of making a career of the Navy when I came in in the beginning. At the end of the war I was going to get out and go back to being a chemist maybe or teaching school or something. I enjoyed all those things. And some way at the end of the war I never got out. Then I got some really interesting jobs, such as working on the development of the plant that was later put in on the *Nautilus*. Having the fun of being skipper of some submarines. Then being the first skipper of the *Nautilus*. Then being the first skipper of the *Long Beach*. I couldn't have dreamed of getting out.

But now I was getting older, and I had more than 20 years in, and I had enough time for retirement. Really I was planning to get retired from the Navy as Chester Nimitz, Jr., retired, bang, on 20 years. I already had in 23 years, and so I was going to retire. I won't say that I had the letter signed and in the mail, but I did have it drafted, and I was going to retire as soon as I was no longer captain of the *Long Beach*. And so

---

[*] McGuire Air Force Base is adjacent to the Army's Fort Dix near Wrightstown, New Jersey.

when the selection came and I was selected flag, the important thing was that it changed my plans, and it changed my life. Really because of that I didn't get out then. They did me a lot of honor in selecting me. I was selected far, far below the zone. I had ranked with the Naval Academy class of '41 originally. I was selected captain with the class of '38, and I was selected rear admiral with the class of '35. It was awfully nice of them to select me, and also it might be fun being an admiral, so I decided to stay in.

So the important part out of the word of that selection was that it made a decision in the course of action I took and what I did. I was away from my wife an awful lot and my family. And, yes, I have a great wife and really nice kids and smart kids, and I hadn't spent the time with them that I should, and so I would have retired right after *Long Beach* pleased to go back and take up life with the family. And my kids were still young enough I could have done that. It made a major difference in what happened to me the rest of my life.

Interview Number 5 with Vice Admiral Eugene P. Wilkinson, U.S. Navy (Retired)
Place: Admiral Wilkinson's home in Del Mar, California
Date: Wednesday, 21 January 1998
Interviewer: Paul Stillwell

Paul Stillwell: Admiral, it's great to see you again on a sunny morning.

Admiral Wilkinson: Yes, things look nice don't they, Paul?

Paul Stillwell: Indeed, they do. Yesterday we talked about your selection for rear admiral. Please tell me about your first flag job, which was in OpNav.

Admiral Wilkinson: I had a tour as OP-31. This was the first time I was the top submarine guy in OpNav. As OP-31 I was under OP-03, but later on submarines promoted up to 02, and I went back to essentially the same job as a three-star admiral years later.* I'll talk about OP-31. When I went down there, my job was to look out for the interest of submarines. I had good relations with Ed David, who was the President's scientific advisor.† I had good relations with Levering Smith, who headed the ballistic missile program.‡ I had good relations with Ivan Selin, who was McNamara's systems analyst.§ I had good relations with Dr. Brown, who was Assistant SecDef for Research and Development.** I had good relations with Admiral Rickover and with those other people. I really had no relations with McNamara in that job, but Brown, Selin, Ed David, and Levering Smith were important people to the success of our job at OP-31.

---

* Up until 1971 OP-03 was the designation for the Deputy Chief of Naval Operations (Fleet Operations and Readiness). At that time OP-03 became Deputy Chief of Naval Operations (Surface Warfare), and OP-02, also a three-star billet, became a counterpart, Deputy Chief of Naval Operations (Submarine Warfare).
† Dr. Edward E. David, Jr., served as science advisor to President Richard M. Nixon from 1970 to 1973. Previously, he was executive director of Bell Telephone Laboratories from 1950 to 1970.
‡ Rear Admiral Levering Smith, USN, served as director of the Special Projects Office/Strategic Systems Projects Office from 16 February 1965 to 14 November 1977.
§ Ivan Selin served as a systems analyst for the Department of Defense from 1965 to 1967 and as Deputy Assistant Secretary of Defense from 1967 to 1969. Robert S. McNamara served as Secretary of Defense from 21 January 1961 to 29 February 1968.
** Dr. Harold Brown was director of Defense Research and Engineering, 1961-65. He was later Secretary of the Air Force and Secretary of Defense.

I had one urgent requirement on our time in that the *Thresher* had been lost because of problems of depth and emergency flooding.* There was a tremendous amount of correspondence, a tremendous pressure to release all the Navy investigations. I had to process them all and decide what was classified and what wasn't, and also there was the initiation of the SubSafe Program.† That correspondence put a tremendous load on us. And so our people worked real hard at that, and we dug out from under that a little bit. I went up one day to the VCNO, Admiral Rivero, with a letter that enunciated what the Navy wanted done, the CNO wanted done, on SubSafe, and I had had it chopped.‡ The VCNO looked at that, and it was extensive. He said, "We need to ask some more questions on that. Let me think about that."

I said, "Admiral, this is important. We need to take action on it. There isn't anybody in the world that knows any more about it than I do, and I'm right here. I can answer any question you can possibly ask. Have at it. [Laughter] There isn't a question that we can't answer right now." And so he looked at me a long, long time, and his questions went away, and he signed off. [Laughter] He was a smart man, and that's how the SubSafe Program was done.

But it did some things that shouldn't have been done. I can remember going up and going through a submarine that was in the yard in Portsmouth Naval Shipyard. I saw nothing there but an empty hull, feeling sad. But it was a tough time, the aftermath of the *Thresher*, and a tremendous workload on us in OP-31. It probably took the resources of half my people. But we got over that hurdle and got more and more effective in getting submarine programs and money for submarines and whatnot.

In the Navy Department there's always a competition for funds and resources, and so finally that antagonized some of the other branches of the service in the Pentagon who were far senior to me as individuals. One day there was an opportunity to really put me out of action in that the issue was raised for all the offshore ranges. Do you know what I'm talking about?

---

* The nuclear-powered attack submarine *Thresher* (SSN-593) was lost with all hands on 10 April 1963 while operating east of Cape Cod. The presumed cause was a reactor shut-down during a dive.
† SubSafe was a program of inspection of submarines and replacement of components that might potentially cause a recurrence of the *Thresher*'s problems.
‡ Admiral Horacio Rivero, USN, served as Vice Chief of Naval Operations from 31 July 1964 to 17 January 1968. His oral history is in the Naval Institute collection.

Paul Stillwell: The missile ranges?

Admiral Wilkinson: Any installation in the ocean off the United States. Congress had passed a law that any use of the ocean floor needed to be approved, and any area that used more than five acres had to go through an approval process. Unfortunately, at the time that that had been passed, which was a few years before, the military had not been wise enough to take an inventory of what there was, which would have all been grandfathered. We didn't know everything that was out there, and I'm talking the offshore ranges for shooting missiles in the Gulf and in the Atlantic and in the Pacific, and I'm talking such things as SOSUS installations on the ocean bottom.[*] I'm also talking in another sense since this was more than the Defense Department. I'm talking about oilrigs and offshore drilling, and there really hadn't been an inventory of all that made. So we did that in 1963-64.

So the Defense Department ordered the major players, the Air Force and the Navy, to make a joint study of this and come back with recommendations of what should be done. I was the only flag officer in OP-31, and some powers that be decided that, "Gee, if we get that assigned to Dennis, he won't be annoying us with OP-31 getting all our money." [Laughter] And so it was. They appointed a general from the Air Force and me to be the co-chairmen of this study, and I think I only saw him about four times.

We went down in the bowels of the Pentagon, out beyond the E-ring.[†] There's an awful lot underground out there. I had a study group, and I got a bunch of officers, and I had some Air Force officers, and I wanted to get that done as quickly as I could. So we did that. Got an inquiry and decided what ought to be done and made findings and recommendations, and finally it took maybe four months, which was as fast as I could get it done. At the same time I was trying to go by OP-31 and see what Bob Satterford, my

---

[*] SOSUS – sound surveillance system, a seafloor network of listening devices used by the U.S. Navy to detect noises from transiting ships.
[†] The Pentagon has lettered corridors, going from A at the innermost to E at the outermost. E-ring offices, which go around the perimeter of the building, are considered the most prestigious.

deputy, was getting done.* [Laughter] But I figured, "I'll get this done as fast as I can and get it out of my hair."

Finally we got our study done and made our recommendations as to how there should be cooperation between the Department of Defense and the Department of Interior and how we'd move this firing range. We said people would do oil drilling there, and then we'd do this, and then we'd do that, and how this would all work. Finally we laid that all out. I was wise enough to finish the study and get the Navy's draft endorsement, and the Secretary of the Air Force's draft endorsement and the Secretary of Defense's action all in draft and saying this was a marvelous study. The study said that this ought to be concurred in by the Department of the Interior and become national policy. And bang, bang, bang, each one of them signed off on that, and it was concurred in by the Department of Energy and became national policy and that's the way they still do it today.

Admiral Wilkinson: Did it have to be blessed by Congress?

Admiral Wilkinson: Yes, the whole thing. It got through, and the Air Force initiated a Department of Defense Medal for their Air Force general who had done this study, and I got one too. [Laughter] Then I got back to looking out for the interests of OP-31.

We really were quite effective in having support from Ed David, who was the President's scientific advisor. But there really was always a competition for money. Ed David provided technical help, and certainly financial support on our Black Hat programs, the highly classified stuff. And I had support from Dr. Brown, R&D.

Then one day I got the word that one of our programs was going to be cancelled and the money used elsewhere by Dr. Brown in research and development. And, gee, I had talked to him many times, but suddenly I couldn't reach him on the phone. To call him you had to go through the Defense roster of secretaries and assistants of somebody of that importance. After a couple of days of trying, I realized that I wasn't about to get to talk to him. He did have the admirable characteristic of going to work quite early, so the next morning I called him up at a quarter of 7:00, and I got him. [Laughter] I said, "Dr.

---

* Captain Robert B. Satterford, USN.

Brown, I understand that you've made a decision to cancel this program. That's a code-word program. I think before you do, you ought to have a briefing on it so you'll know just what you're doing."

He said, "I've already had that briefing."

I said, "Dr. Brown, I know you haven't, and I'd suggest you have that briefing before you make a decision on it."

He said, "Well, I'm too busy."

I said, "Dr. Brown. This is Dennis Wilkinson. I'm the submarine guy, and you're making a research and development decision on one of our programs. I've called you up and told you that before you do you should have a briefing so you'll know what it's about, and you're telling me you're too busy? You know, that's doesn't sound right to me. That sounds shabby to me. Dr. Brown, that would sound shabby to anybody." Not that I was about to tell anybody, but— [Laughter]

He said, "When should I have that briefing?"

I said, "Any time before you make that decision."

He said, "Well, could you give it to me now?"

I said, "Sir, I'll be right down." [Laughter] I went down and briefed Dr. Brown on the program, and he didn't cancel it. He didn't. But silly story. Later he became Secretary of Defense, you know.*

Paul Stillwell: Yes, he did.

Admiral Wilkinson: He was a good man, and he didn't cancel our program. But it impressed him to say, "That sounds shabby to me. That sounds shabby to anybody." [Laughter] But as OP-31 I was glad to get that special study done on the offshore ranges because it impacted my ability to do my primary job looking out for submarines. And this was in the period that we were trying to clean up after all the problems with *Thresher* that also impacted my job, and after those things were behind us we had an awful lot of relations with Levering Smith.

---

* Harold Brown served as Secretary of Defense from 20 January 1977 to 20 January 1981.

This was also the time of the Boat of the Month Club, the Polaris submarines being built at the rate of one a month, and Levering Smith needed a lot of support, and he got it.[*]

One time I went up to my boss, OP-03, and said, "Admiral, I've got a problem here I'd really like to talk to you about."

He was just coming out of his office, and he said, "I'm just going to the head."

I said, "Well, let me walk along with you. It's that kind of an item."

Paul Stillwell: Who was that?

Admiral Wilkinson: Hell of a good man, Red Ramage.[†]

That was my first time in Washington, and I got there and reported and sat there for nearly a week wondering how the hell was I going to do business. Finally I got that great big chart of the Pentagon and the Office of the Secretary of Defense. It was amazing how many things that revealed; I saw Dr. Brown and Selin and a lot of other important civilians, and every one of them had a military aide. I looked at that whole structure and said, "Gee, that one is really important to us." So I took a grease pencil, and I circled quite a few of those military aide positions, and I called for the submarine detail officer, who was a young commander named Lando Zech.[‡]

Paul Stillwell: He was also a former skipper of the *Nautilus* by then.

Admiral Wilkinson: Yes. And I said, "Lando, capture me all those jobs with good submariners." And there was a lot of competition to put people in those jobs. First there were the other services. Then in the Navy there were the surface officers and the aviators. But with good submariners we had an awful lot of talent. I can remember talking to Lando on one guy, "The guy's a snob. Send him over a Rhodes Scholar."

---

[*] From 1959 to 1967 the U.S. Navy commissioned 41 nuclear-powered submarines armed with either Polaris or Poseidon ballistic missiles.
[†] Vice Admiral Lawson P. Ramage, USN, whose oral history is in the Naval Institute collection.
[‡] Commander Lando W. Zech, later a vice admiral and Chief of Naval Personnel.

[Laughter] And, sure enough, our Rhodes Scholar guy became the aide. At another time one of the most important positions was Clements, important to us surely.*

Paul Stillwell: This was quite a bit later.

Admiral Wilkinson: Yes, the next time around, and I got Ken Carr in that job as his aide, and they fit together like old shoes.

Paul Stillwell: I've heard that from other people, yes.

Admiral Wilkinson: But obviously a lot of people were sent down for him to see and interview, and he took Ken just like that. So back in the OP-31 days Lando did a good job for me. We had some pretty good people in submarines, and it helped to have some of your people in some of those positions.

That stirred my mind to a story I want to tell. One morning, which doesn't happen very often, it snowed. It snowed a tremendous amount. It snowed a foot, and that completely paralyzes Washington. They're really unable to cope with that.

Paul Stillwell: Right.

Admiral Wilkinson: But I lived four blocks off of Route 50, out at Seven Corners. And, Jesus, I got up early that morning, and I got on my boots and my submarine foul weather jacket, and I beat my way out to the main drag. Of course, our streets were totally impassable with a foot of snow. I actually honestly bummed a ride on a snowplow, and I got to the Pentagon before 8:00 o'clock. I got there on time. Weather didn't matter. And there wasn't anybody else there. [Laughter] I puttered around for an hour or an hour and a half, until about 9:30 I got to laughing at myself, and I spent the next few hours beating my way back home. But there was no sense being there, because an admiral by himself is useless. [Laughter] That's a true story, and it's a valid conclusion too. You really don't do things by yourself. It's really the multitude of people that are

---

* William P. Clements, Jr., served as Deputy Secretary of Defense from 1973 to 1977.

working for you and supporting you that get it done. And I've been really fortunate in my Navy career and at INPO afterwards that I had a tremendous group of people working for me.

I had the kind of an organization that would support me to the hilt. In that job I had a big disagreement with Admiral Martell, OP-95, a powerful position, on building an electric drive submarine.* He said, "Let me tell you, you're only one submarine officer. We're not going to do that. There are a lot of submarine officers that don't agree with you. There are lot of your own officers don't agree with you."

I said, "Admiral, I'm going right back down to my office. I'll send every one of my officers up to talk to you. You talk to each and every one of them. If you can find one that doesn't agree with me, you let me know, and I'll get rid of him." [Laughter] He really envied that, because he had an organization that his people would grouse all the time. They'd come up to me and say, "Our crazy admiral's doing this. Would you see if you can put a stop to it?" There wasn't one of my officers would have gone up and said he didn't support me. [Laughter]

As I mentioned, my deputy then was Captain Satterford. Admiral Martell had a meeting of all the different subsidiary activities and all the ASW-related things, and submarines are ASW-related too. So my guy, Captain Satterford, was up there representing the submarine thing because I was out of town. Admiral Martell said, "We're going to do this, and we're going to do that."

Captain Satterford spoke up and said, "Admiral, Dennis won't agree with that, and he'll put a stop to it." [Laughter] It was inconceivable to Vice Admiral Martell that a captain would tell him, "That's not the way it's going to be, and Dennis will see it isn't." [Laughter]

As the ASW czar he was a strong man and really thought that he was going to end up being CNO, which he could have been. He really ran things with an iron hand and wanted to disperse the different assets in the way that he thought best. That meant that at times he wanted to take an awful lot of the submarine assets and apply them to other things, and that wasn't something we would like to see done. So we tried to hold our

---

* Vice Admiral Charles B. Martell, USN, a surface warfare officer, was Director of Antisubmarine Warfare Programs on the OpNav staff.

own as best we could. My people worked hard at that and were loyal, and I guess we were successful because we didn't lose anything.

Paul Stillwell: What do you remember about your discussions with Admiral Rickover on trying to bring about quieter submarines?

Admiral Wilkinson: We talked about that a lot, and I won't go into all the bitter stuff back and forth. But finally when I was OP-31 we decided we'd try to get a really quieter submarine, electric-drive submarine, which turned out to be the *Lipscomb*.* There was rabid opposition to that from Admiral Martell, who said, "We're not going to spend that kind of money. We're really going to put that money into ASW stuff." But as happened more than once in our differences of opinion with Admiral Martell, that's not the way it ended up. We got the extremely quiet *Lipscomb* authorized, and maybe Admiral Martell was right. We didn't ever build any more like that.

But in the ensuing struggle and in the determination to get that done, Admiral Rickover became a real zealot and committed and put the major effort of his people into, by God, sound-isolating everything and doing all the other things and making a quiet submarine. He did the same then for all the steam-driven submarines, total sound isolation of their whole platform on which the steam plants were mounted, every pipe as it touched the hull. Admiral Rickover made that a major objective of his. And, let me tell you, when Admiral Rickover became a zealot about something and would put his total effort on it, something happened. Our submarines became very, very, very quiet, and for decades it was a major advantage of our forces over the Soviet submarines.

The Soviets built more and more nuclear-powered submarines, and in fact they would eventually go faster and dive deeper, and they carried more weapons. They had the advantage of firing unlimited numbers of those weapons at sea for training in exercises, as we know. And they had really great command and control communications. But when push came to shove, we had better detection. That is a combination of the

---

* USS *Glenard P. Lipscomb* (SSN-685), named for a congressman, was the only ship in her class. She was built to test a turbo-electric drive nuclear propulsion plant. Speed was sacrificed in order to reduce noise in comparison with the nuclear submarines that had steam turbines. Construction of the *Glenard P. Lipscomb* began on 5 June 1971, and she was commissioned 21 December 1974.

effectiveness of your sonar and the self-noise you radiate that interferes with your sonar and the noise you radiate that can be detected. Rickover in his efforts had made us so good that we had a detection advantage over them for many, many, many, many years. So we were superior, and it all goes back to Admiral Rickover's effort to quiet our submarines.

Paul Stillwell: Was Admiral Martell reluctant to acknowledge the advantage that would come in ASW from a quiet submarine?

Admiral Wilkinson: No. Really, Admiral Martell was responsible for ASW, and he truly thought that that kind of money could be spent better elsewhere in the modernization of some of our ASW forces.

Paul Stillwell: Like surface ships and aircraft?

Admiral Wilkinson: Yes, and research and development. And he might have been right, since the major thing that *Lipscomb* accomplished really was to get Rickover into the fray that, by God, we're going to make these ships quieter. We never built any more electric-drive, because they really aren't as good as the submarines we've developed with well sound-isolated main propulsion plants. But they were a part of the thing that got Rickover committed, and once Rickover was committed all his people were committed and a lot of resources were committed.

Paul Stillwell: You mentioned that you were almost in the ship-of-the-month pace with the 41 Polaris submarines that were coming out. Was OP-31 involved in the manning and training of crews for those ships?

Admiral Wilkinson: No. OP-31 was the submarine representative in the Office of Chief of Naval Operations, and we weren't involved in operational control or manning. Those kinds of functions are performed by the Bureau of Personnel and personnel commanders in the Submarine Force and its commanders of schools and operational commanders. But certain functions do come back to the Chief of Naval Operations, and when the Polaris submarines were first laid down, for various reasons of trying to look good, they had been authorized with what turned out to be in time inadequate personnel allowances. I don't remember the exact number, but it was maybe 90 and really operations and other things showed they needed more, and we changed the allowance up to 124. If you take 40 boats with two crews, in the Navy end strength you can't just pull out of the air that many billets.

So we did what the CNO was supposed to do in authorizing change, and slowly over time we had provisions in the Navy for 124 on each of our Polaris submarines, and so it was. We didn't get them all changed at once, but as quickly as we could the billet structure was changed, and the personnel allowances were changed on those ships. We didn't do the study to decide it was going to be, but we did what the Office of CNO ought to do to get all that paperwork straightened out. That was a significant number and a shift in billet strengths in the Navy from one place to another.

But what OP-31 did more on involved SP.* I had very close contact and interaction all the time with Levering Smith, who became SP, and we were very close and remained very close ever after until he passed away. That was a great outfit, and they did something really important for the country and the Navy. I gave them every bit of support I could. The Office of CNO does approve this or that, and I was a little potato, a little gun in the Office of CNO. I was a junior admiral. Still and all, I was the submarine guy, and so we started the thing that finally would be signed off maybe by the CNO, but the original draft was mine just the same as the original draft for some aviation program would have started over in OP-05 and so on. And the original draft for an awful lot of ASW stuff would have started in 95. We were small potatoes to some of those great big guns but not when it came to our stuff. We did have more than 20% of the Navy's funds.

Paul Stillwell: What kinds of issues would you discuss with Levering Smith?

---

* SP – The Special Projects Office of the Navy controlled the ballistic missile program for submarines.

Admiral Wilkinson: A lot of issues. Setting up training for people, the provision of numbers of billets. Later on building a new class of submarine, the Trident submarines, and what characteristics they would have and the support for the funding for the development of Trident missiles and Poseidon missiles—a lot to do with the design of the Trident, how many tubes it would carry. But more frequently providing him the support in the Office of the Chief of Naval Operations that he needed to do his job as SP.

Paul Stillwell: Do you remember any policy issues that came under your purview as OP-31?

Admiral Wilkinson: Well, a real load of work in OP-31 was the follow-up on the loss of *Thresher* when I first got there. This is not a policy issue but an awful lot of work in replying to a multitude of questions and people and congressional inquiries, and certainly the review of all the things for classification that were released, the testimony and whatnot. But, see, out of that now a policy issue emerged as to what should happen in the design and characteristics of all of our submarines related to SubSafe. So the SubSafe program that followed the loss of the *Thresher* involved major policy issues and that again in the Office of Chief of Naval Operations came down to OP-31 under 03. I don't care what it was. If it had to do with submarines, it was mine. [Laughter] If anybody fooled with it, we tried to prevent that.

For example, policy issues, I had constant interrelation—just like the frequent, essentially day-to-day contact with Levering Smith, I certainly had day-to-day contact with Admiral Rickover, and there were some policy matters in regard to that. And certainly we dealt all the time with Vice Admiral Rebel Lowrance.[*] My contact seemed to be an awful lot more with ComSubLant than with Commander Pacific Submarine Force.

Paul Stillwell: What kind of policy issues did you discuss in the frequent conversations with Admiral Rickover?

---

[*] Vice Admiral Vernon L. Lowrance, USN, served as Commander Submarine Force Atlantic Fleet from 1 September 1964 to 19 November 1966.

Admiral Wilkinson: Mostly things that had to do with the manning of ships, with the personnel and with the training of people. Leap ahead where you want in time, and certainly we were involved hip and thigh on characteristics of the 688 program of submarines. But back earlier in OP-31 there were forces that be that said these submarines didn't have to be as fast as *Nautilus*. That they didn't need to build that fancy and fast a submarine. The idea was that 18 knots was fast enough, and that's why we built the 18-knot *Skate*-class submarines, *Skate* and *Seadragon* and *Swordfish* and *Sargo*. Admiral Rickover certainly didn't agree with that, and there was a lot of interaction with me. Do whatever was required to go for a higher-speed submarine, of which I believed in emotionally and vehemently from my operational expertise. The Navy had previously gone to higher speed submarines in spite of him.

So we had all the political maneuvering, and otherwise that changed us from the *Skate* class to the 30-knot *Skipjack* class, and certainly I must have had a lot of conversations back and forth with Admiral Rickover on that.* Rickover many times and many ways understood what the Navy needed in characteristics and performance of ships that the Navy didn't understand itself. There really were strong forces that said, "Hey, 18 knots is fast enough. They're cheaper, and you don't have to spend as much money." So, tongue in cheek, maybe a little bit of that was like in the case of Martell they wanted to use that money for something else.

Paul Stillwell: What was the nature of your dealings with Admiral Lowrance?

Admiral Wilkinson: Certainly Admiral Lowrance was very, very interested in the SubSafe program, which impacted all the submarines under his command. And he certainly was interested in Polaris submarines and the missiles and whatnot. He was a wise man and a good counsel to me, and I talked to him all the time about anything that had to do with submarines. I didn't ever just go around making decisions in a vacuum. I didn't do anything without talking it over with my people and studying it and talking with

---

* USS *Skipjack* (SSN-585), commissioned 15 April 1959, was the first ship of her class. She was 252 feet long, 32 feet in the beam, and displaced 3,075 tons surfaced and 3,500 submerged. She had a top speed on the surface around 20 knots and a speed in excess of 30 knots submerged. She was armed with six 21-inch torpedo tubes. She was the first U.S. nuclear-powered submarine with a teardrop-shaped hull.

Admiral Lowrance and talking with Levering Smith and talking with Admiral Rickover. I'm one to do a lot of liaison and get the most facts I can before I go marching off.

Paul Stillwell: Did you have dealings with the investigators who looked into the *Thresher* sinking?

Admiral Wilkinson: No. *Thresher* didn't happen on my watch. I was on the *Long Beach*. And the *Scorpion* was lost when I was later out in Japan.* Nothing ever happened wrong on my watch [Laughter] as luck would have it. But, no, seriously there's a lot of luck, and none of those things happened when I was in charge. I didn't have anything to do with the investigation except for the follow-up, the SubSafe program, but review of all the congressional testimony to tell them what they could print and disclose on the public record and what we had to correct for security. We had to answer a multitude of congressional letters and other things; it's hard for me to remember now, but it was an enormous paperwork load on us.

Paul Stillwell: Could you please put on the tape the cute little story about your parking place?

Admiral Wilkinson: No, that's not worth putting on. [Laughter] To me the interesting part of that story was where it went for decision—up to the CNO himself.

Admiral Wilkinson: That's why I wish you would tell it.

Admiral Wilkinson: Well, all right. I was selected early for admiral, as I told you. Later on, lots of people were selected early, but in the beginning, at that time I was the youngest guy that had been selected. And I was selected early for admiral because the selection board was told to select a nuclear-trained officer. And because I was selected

---

* The submarine *Scorpion* (SSN-589) was lost with all hands while en route from the Mediterranean to Norfolk. She was last heard from on 21 May 1968. On 27 May she was reported overdue and on 5 June presumed lost with her entire crew of 99 officers and men. The wreckage was located on 30 October of that year. No definitive conclusion has been reached as to cause.

way early, I was the junior man on the list. And, strangely enough, there was a provision in the law that if you were selected in a special category, because the selection board was advised to do so, that the next year's selection board if there was anyone selected on it that had been senior to you as a captain, he then became senior to you on the lineal list as a flag officer.

Well, as it happened, when the next year's selection came out, all 31 of them had been senior to me as a captain, and so although I had been selected the year before and now had made my number and I was a rear admiral, suddenly I lost 31 numbers on the lineal list.* Well, as OP-31 when I first went there I was a captain that hadn't been frocked yet. As an admiral selectee who was still a captain, I didn't rate a parking place. Well, I came early to work, so that didn't bother me unless I wanted to grab my car and run somewhere in the daytime, over to talk to Levering Smith or something, and come back. Eventually I became more and more senior, and eventually, by golly, I rated a parking place on the mall.

But when the next selection board came out and I lost my 31 numbers, I was not senior enough for a parking place. So, lo and behold, they took that for decision right up to the Chief of Naval Operations? Someone said to him, "Admiral Wilkinson has a parking place on the mall, and he's not senior enough for a parking place because there are only so many parking places."

The CNO nodded sagely, and he said, "Let me tell you. Losing 31 numbers is bad enough. Let him keep his parking place." [Laughter]

Paul Stillwell: Was that Admiral McDonald?†

Admiral Wilkinson: Yes. Good man.

Paul Stillwell: Do you have any other recollections from that Pentagon job?

---

* The law allows so many numbers of flag officers in each rank on the lineal promotion list. Even after an individual is selected for admiral, he or she has to wait until a retirement opens up a number on the list for that person to move into. An officer may be frocked in the higher rank when doing the job and wear admiral's insignia but doesn't get the pay of the higher rank until making the number.

† Admiral David L. McDonald, USN, served as Chief of Naval Operations from 1 August 1963 to 1 August 1967. His oral history is in the Naval Institute collection.

Admiral Wilkinson: That pretty well goes through the OP-31 time, except for my leaving, which was a bad situation in that I had talked to a man named Leary, who was the correspondent for some magazine. Articles were written that were pro-submarine and against a lot of other things in the Navy, and that really antagonized some higher authority. I was accused of having buddy-buddied up with him and got what in some people's minds was a pro-submarine touch. It was absolutely not true at all. But before I knew it, I had my orders to go to other duty. That's how I was fortunate enough to be the Chief of Staff, U.S. Forces Japan. A subsequent investigation cleared me totally of any involvement, including a statement from my yeoman, a young lady who was there for the interview. When Leary himself was accosted, "Where did he get this information?" he was able to reach up and pull down this page or that page in the *Congressional Record*. [Laughter] But it was sensitive at the time.

Paul Stillwell: What publication did he represent?

Admiral Wilkinson: You know, it's amazing that something that was so important in my life and I don't even remember what magazine the articles were in. It was some magazine.

Paul Stillwell: What was the substance of what you had told him?

Admiral Wilkinson: I had really told him nothing about classified information in any way. I wouldn't dream of doing that. I probably talked submarines to him some but certainly not the data that he used to embellish his article in the magazine.

Paul Stillwell: So the main accusation against you was that you had disclosed classified information?

Admiral Wilkinson: Oh, yes.

Paul Stillwell: It was not that you were pro-submarine?

Admiral Wilkinson: Oh, no. [Laughter] As soon as I was detached and on my way to Japan, I put that behind me. It was only in getting ready for you coming that I pulled some of this stuff out. There I had saved some of the correspondence, including, of course, the statements of my yeoman and the statements later that showed that I was innocent of what I was thought to have done. But the damage was already done. But I had had a tour in OpNav. It was the right time to leave anyway, and there isn't any doubt that my wife was really happy for us to go to Japan. I had a fantastic tour of duty in Japan. I was there at a good time.

Paul Stillwell: Who did the banishing? Was it in the Navy?

Admiral Wilkinson: I presume it was the Secretary of the Navy.

Paul Stillwell: That would have been Nitze at that time.[*]

Admiral Wilkinson: Maybe it was. Anyway, I left under a sort of a cloud and went to Japan. Before I left Washington, I went around and saw the powers that be. I went over to the State Department, saw the man in charge of that desk, and said, "Tell me what our goals and objectives are for dealing with the Japanese. What are you trying to accomplish? Let me read them, please."

He said, "We don't have that."

I said, "Come on. You're putting me on. I'm going out there as Chief of Staff, U.S. Forces Japan. I'll be the representative on the Joint Committee for the Status of Forces Agreement, and I need to know that. Let me see your goals and objectives for Japan and also for Taiwan and Korea."

He said, "We don't have that."

I said, "Hey, maybe you've got an old one that's out of date. Just let me see that."

He said, "We really don't have that written."

I said, "I can't believe that. Let me tell you, before I come back I'll see you've got them." [Laughter]

---

[*] Paul H. Nitze served as Secretary of the Navy from 29 November 1963 to 30 June 1967.

Then I went and saw Admiral McDonald, who said, "Well, what do we want?"

I said, "I'm going out there, and what would you like to get done in Japan?"

He said, "I'd like to get nuclear-powered ships into Japanese ports."

So I went on, and when I went through Honolulu I asked the same thing of CinCPac and told him what the CNO had said, and the people there concurred with that. They wanted to get nuclear ships into Japan.

So I became the U.S. representative on the joint committee, and during my time there I had three counterparts, one of whom later became the Japanese ambassador to the United States. One of my counterparts was Togo, which is a pretty famous name in Japan.[*] Fumihiko was his first name. I said, "Fumihiko, your job is to look out for the interest of Japan, and my job is to look out for the interest of the United States. And I would never expect you to do anything else but that. But, other things being equal, let me tell you that professionally in my career this means a lot to me. Let me show you this letter from the CNO, that he'd really like for me to get entry of nuclear ships into Japan." And, let me tell you, there wasn't any doubt nuclear ships, by God, were going to get in Japan, and Togo was going to see that they did.

Paul Stillwell: Just on the basis of that personal appeal?

Admiral Wilkinson: Yes, yes, yes. And so he did, and we did get the entry of nuclear ships into Japan.

I developed quite a close relationship with the Ambassador Alex Johnson, who was a tremendously capable person.[†] He'd have a meeting of the country team, as it was called, every couple of weeks, and I was always invited to that meeting. He got so that he dealt with me on any matters that involved the military, not with the Commander of U.S. Forces, Japan, the three-star general that was my boss, McKee, but Alex dealt with me.[‡] He would call me up and say, "Dennis, let's talk on the secure phone," which was

---

[*] In the 27 May 1905 Battle of Tsushima Strait (which connects the Sea of Japan with the East China Sea), Japanese forces under Admiral Heihachiro Togo overwhelmed the Russian Baltic Fleet led by Admiral Zinovy Rozhdestvensky.
[†] U. Alexis Johnson, a Foreign Service Officer, served as ambassador to Japan, 1966-69.
[‡] Lieutenant General Seth J. McKee, USAF.

one deck travel for him in the embassy. It was a block and a half for me from my office over to where the secure phone was. And I would run. I'd get there completely out of breath [laughter] to be there by the time the ambassador got to the secure phone to talk to me. I don't know how many times that happened.

Time went by, and I got a really good relationship with the Japanese. One time there were representatives there from the State Department, and they were talking about really wanting to get rid of military scrip at the U.S. bases in Japan.* They wanted to be able to use green money, and they had been trying for many years to get this resolved with the Japanese.

Paul Stillwell: What was the reason for the scrip—to avoid black market dealings?

Admiral Wilkinson: In the beginning to avoid black market. Instead of U.S. green money at various countries, military scrip was used, and then if there was a black market business they could replace all that with a new issue of military scrip. At one time there were probably 30 or 40 places where military scrip was used. As I said once in my speech to the people involved in Japan when I was talking about it, "There used to be military scrip in many, many places. Now it's only left in the three backward places of Libya, Vietnam, and Japan. And Japan is an economic power."

Paul Stillwell: What was the Japanese view on this?

Admiral Wilkinson: It was the Japanese position not to let that happen. They were happy with the way things were and wanted to preserve the status quo. The Japanese always found some reason not to acquiesce to that with the American government. In fact, the U.S. Government's effort to get rid of the military scrip in Japan had been going on for many, many, many years, with no success. So these two State Department senior officers from Washington were there and talking it over with the ambassador. I was at the country team meeting, and I listened, and finally I said, "Ambassador, sir, why that

---

* The military payment certificates, widely known as MPC, came in the same denominations as U.S. dollars.

really involves the military. Why don't you quit trying to do that through the State Department and the embassy and let me take care of that in the joint committee?"

The two guys from Washington hoorahed and said, "Hey, we've got a stack of correspondence back and forth with the Japanese on that subject that high," and I'm pointing at the middle of your chest there.

But Alex Johnson said, "Why don't you try to do that, Dennis?" And so it was. I talked to the Japanese and said that I'd like to get rid of military scrip at the bases in Japan. They allowed as how they'd be happy to talk to me about that. I said, "Well, I don't want to just talk about it. I want to get it done."

"Oh, yes. That's possible." So we had some meetings and came in with a proposal and resolved the answers to a lot of questions like, "What denominations of green money?" and so on we'd be talking about. They said that they, of course, had to take it over to the Diet.[*] So a period of time went by, and back they came—just like in the years before—with six pages of new problems from the Diet.

I said, "Hey, we talked about this, and I thought you people were sincere. If you just don't want to do this, let's not waste each other's time. Just say so." And then I gave them that little speech about the military scrip being left in the three backward countries of Libya and Vietnam and Japan. No, they allowed as how they really were sincere, but they had this problem from the Diet and all these conditions. Some conditions were more important than others, some of them petty little items. I said, "Well, instead of fooling around with these, why don't we go back and get them all? Why don't we get all the conditions and see if we can resolve it if you people are sincere." And they said, no, they had done that, that that was all. So I said, "Well, in that case the United States agrees to all those conditions, and why don't we just get it done?"

They said, "No, you have to send that back to the State Department to get it reviewed."

"No, no," I said. "I'm the U.S. representative on the joint committee, and I'll sign for the United States. We agree to those conditions and let's get the paperwork done."

That threw them into a panic. As Togo said to me in an aside later, "Dennis, you just can't realize what you did and the position you put all those people in." But they

---

[*] The Diet is the Japanese legislative body.

didn't get it typed up and get it done. A little more time went by, and I had my orders back to the United States to go to New London and be the flotilla commander at the sub base. I felt bad that I hadn't got rid of the military scrip for Ambassador Johnson in Japan.

We haven't talked about it, but I graduated from San Diego State in 1938, and in 1956 I had the pleasure of going back and giving the commencement address. If you're involved in a commencement, it's awkward handing over the diploma and giving a handshake. They really have a better system in Japan. A guy would come up to get his diploma. It's handed out to him with two hands. He takes it with two hands. He holds it up in the air and says, "Hai," and marches off. Well, I was leaving Japan on a Saturday morning, and they'd passed in the Diet on Thursday the approval to get rid of military scrip and use green money in Japan. Friday they came over with two hands and handed that to me, and that was my going-away present from Japanese authority. [Laughter]

Paul Stillwell: Well, in a way when they handed you all those conditions that was like a bluff, and you called their bluff.

Admiral Wilkinson: As a matter of fact, when it was done none of those conditions were in there. They could have done it all the time.

I had one other going-away present from the Japanese. They also gave me an award, the Second Order of the Sacred Treasure, but the real present was the Diet passing the measure to get rid of the scrip in Japan. The next morning, Saturday morning, Janice and I were due to leave on a commercial flight. I've even forgotten which airline it was now, but somebody recognized that there were important people involved, because at 7:00 in the morning there was a nice lounge with drinks and tomato juice and Bloody Marys and coffee and orange juice and sticky buns. Down to see me off were the head of the Defense Facilities Administration and Togo and officials from the Gaimusho and the Chairman of the Joint Chiefs of Staff and the head of the Air Force and the head of the Army and the head of the Navy for Japan—all in all, maybe 70 people like that.*

---

* Gaimusho is the Ministry of Foreign Affairs of Japan.

Finally the airline came around, and they loaded all the other passengers on. Then they moved the airplane over to where I was with these people to say good-bye, and they rolled out a red carpet and said, "Admiral, your plane is ready." [Laughter] And I was just a commercial passenger on a plane. The Japanese took pictures and said good-bye. Janice and I walked out, up the red carpet, and all the 70 people came out and snapped their cameras and waved good-bye. We came up the first class stairs, of course, and turned and waved good-bye and got in the airplane and went through and sat in our coach seats. [Laughter] As we transferred flights in Hawaii, they took care of us again, and then it was all gone. [Laughter] But I always thought that was cute. That even amused you.

Paul Stillwell: That had to be a very satisfying moment to have that kind of a sendoff.

Admiral Wilkinson: Yes. "Admiral, your plane is ready." A commercial flight was moved over to where I was and a red carpet laid out.

Paul Stillwell: The rest of the passengers must have wondered what was going on.

Admiral Wilkinson: Yes. [Laughter] We had an exceptionally good tour in Japan, and we did really a lot of good things, and I won't go through them all. There had been a war and a surrender and a treaty and a status of forces agreement, a provision for stationing U.S. forces in Japan, and a provision for a joint committee with one representative from the United States and one representative from Japan. And their representative was a very senior one. What we signed was binding on both governments, independent of going through the State Department, and so it was important. I signed a piece of paper that gave them back the Bonin Islands, Iwo Jima and all that.*

Paul Stillwell: Ha Ha Jima and Chi Chi Jima.

---

* U.S. Marines had captured Iwo Jima in March 1945 after bloody fighting against Japanese defenders.

Admiral Wilkinson: Yes. I signed the piece of paper that gave them back the Bonin Islands. I also signed the piece of paper that gave them Narita Airport and little things like that.*

I had a really good relationship with my Japanese representative. There were the two of us. Of course, each of us had extensive staff that was there supporting us, and they would talk things over in Japanese. I had one member of my staff that could speak Japanese fluently. He would sit and hear it all, but he never said anything, and so that was sort of accepted. And, of course, they all understand English. The United States had good records of every meeting that there had been of the joint committee since it was started. It was started just after the surrender in 1945, and initially the advantages were pretty much on our side.

If a thing was brought up, I had the kind of support that I could say, "In the 125th meeting at such-and-such a time in 1956 it was agreed that—" And I'd say, "Gomenasai."†

The Japanese were honorable men. I mean, their word was good. One time there was an issue, and I said, "Hey, in such and such a meeting and such and such this was agreed to."

Togo said, "Dennis, let's look at that." We looked at it, and he was right. It was written very ambiguously, and it was really not clear what was meant.

I said, "Sir, let me show you the memo to file that my people wrote at that time." I had a 30-page memo that said exactly what was, and he looked at it. If that's what it meant, that's what it meant. Fine.

I probably reached a good relationship with them by starting right out saying, "Hey, I'm not experienced in this, and I need help. If there's any doubt or question or something I don't understand, let's go through it thoroughly so that we make sure that we both agree that that's what we've said." And let me tell you, the Japanese loved that. They wanted every dot made and everything tied up. They liked to understand exactly what was said, which wasn't really true of our State Department people. They love to

---

* Narita is the name of the airport that serves Tokyo.
† This means, "I'm sorry."

dance around something. But I had great relations with the Japanese in making sure that there wasn't any doubt that we were in accord of what we were talking about.

We had a joint committee meeting every six weeks. One time I was going to a meeting, and I stopped by Mr. Togo's office. He was the Japanese representative from the Gaimusho. After he was replaced there, he became the Japanese ambassador in Washington to the United States.[*] He was the person in the Gaimusho in Japan responsible for their relations with the Japanese community in North and South America. There's quite a few Japanese down in countries like Brazil and whatnot. So we had good relations, and he's the one that ensured that nuclear-powered ships got into Japan. And he did it. He made it happen.

Paul Stillwell: Well, I'd be interested in details on that, because I remember the protests they had over there during those years. Big ritual scripted things almost.

Admiral Wilkinson: And yet in spite of that they were brought in, weren't they?

Paul Stillwell: Yes. Was this after you had known him a while?

Admiral Wilkinson: Oh, yes, after we had worked on the joint committee.

One time we were having a joint committee meeting, which happened every six weeks, and I stopped by his office an hour ahead of time. I said, "Mr. Togo, could we talk over a problem here? I'd like to accomplish this."

He looked at it, and he said, "That's a new item."

And I said, "Well, yes, sir."

He said, "Our staffs have never looked at that."

I said, "Yes, sir, but you're the best and most knowledgeable man on the Japanese side, and I am on the American side. Why can't we just work it out between us and make it so?"

That appealed to him. He said, "None of my staff has seen that."

---

[*] Togo was Japan's ambassador to the United States in the late 1970s.

"I know, but there's nobody more capable to do that than you." And so it was. It wasn't that big a thing. We worked it out and reached agreement, and when we got to the joint committee meeting finally I brought this item up. He replied, and his people were all turning through their papers. Finally one of them went up and tugged at his coattail, and Togo pushed him back and we kept talking. The guy came up again and tugged at his coat and finally whispered in his ear. Togo pushed him back, and we resolved the item and went all through it. We said this, and we both agreed to that, and it had to be typed up to be signed. [Laughter]

Paul Stillwell: Do you remember what the issue was?

Admiral Wilkinson: No, it was a long time ago. I could look it up. But the interesting sequel was that not the next meeting but maybe a couple of meetings later Togo asked me to stop by his office before the meeting. So I did, and we had a cup of tea and pleasantries. I said, "What have you got in mind?"

He said, "Nothing. Have you got anything?" [Laughter] That approach I'd taken earlier had really appealed to him. [Laughter] So we really did have good relationships. Later on, after we came to the United States, Janice and I were invited any time we were in Washington to stay at the Japanese Embassy, which we never did. But our relationships were quite close. Togo ensured that the U.S. ships got into Japan and they did. The protests you were talking about, they're true and they happened, but the ships got in anyway.

Paul Stillwell: And the demonstrations kept on happening even after the ships got there.

Admiral Wilkinson: Yes.

Paul Stillwell: Do you remember when the first nuclear-powered ships went in there?

Admiral Wilkinson: No, but it was during that period that we were out there. The Navy CNO and CinCPac were happy to see it happen, and that's the only thing they'd asked me to get done out there.

Paul Stillwell: In January '68 I remember the *Enterprise* was at Sasebo when the *Pueblo* was seized, so it had been done by then.* I don't know if she was the first one or not.

Admiral Wilkinson: I thought the first one was in Yokosuka, but I'm not sure.

Paul Stillwell: It may have been.

Admiral Wilkinson: Yes, I'm not sure. It's hazy in my mind now. Not the part about getting the Japanese support for getting it done, but the actual exact time I don't remember. But I know it was done, and I know it was important to us, and I know how it happened. It happened because a friend of mine in Japan with the authority and the influence made it happen.

Paul Stillwell: You had a specific agenda item going over there, that of getting nuclear-powered ships into Japan. I was wondering if Togo also had some agenda items or desires or goals on the Japanese side that he was trying to accomplish in dealings with you.

Admiral Wilkinson: Well, naturally. They wanted to get the prefecture there that was on the slope of the sacred mountain, Fuji, and I managed to get that piece of land given back to them. They wanted the land on which Narita Airport is now built, and I got that back to them in some accommodation from us. There were those kinds of things that went on all the time in the joint committee. Our relations were good, and they were honorable. Remember, right after the surrender every agreement was in our favor. As things went by, no longer did you have segregated trains. No longer this, no longer that. So

---

* USS *Pueblo* (AGER-2), an electronic intelligence ship, was seized on 23 January 1968 in the Sea of Japan by North Korean naval forces. The ship's crew members were held as prisoners until 23 December of that year. Of the 83 officers and men on board, 28 were intelligence specialists.

frequently there would be a request from the Japanese to reconsider something or bring something to issue. I had such support from staff that I was able always on any item that was brought up to be able to refer to exactly to where that was in the record and how it was taken.

I don't remember what the item was now, but there was a question that Togo had. I went and checked on it with my staff before our next meeting. We got the record out and looked at it, and it was very poorly written. It was really quite ambiguous, and Togo said, "Dennis, it's really not clear what that says."

I said, "Let me show you this 30-page memo to file of our staff at the time as exactly what that meant," and which it was very clearly in the 30-page support staff memo.

Togo would look at it and say, "Hey, if that's what it was, that's what it was." Bang. There wasn't any question like that. On the other hand, when they asked you to look at something there was no obligation on your part to change it, but there was an obligation to review and reconsider it. You didn't have to make the change, but you certainly had to accede to a request to look at things.

Paul Stillwell: Well presumably it would have been a request such as that that led to the return of the land for the Narita Airport.

Admiral Wilkinson: This was something they wanted and we looked and we didn't need that land anymore so we accommodated. Yes.

Paul Stillwell: What do you remember of those events when the *Pueblo* was seized?

Admiral Wilkinson: I had some involvement. My boss, Commander U.S. Forces Japan, had that position because he was the senior U.S. military person in Japan. The commander of the Army in Japan was a major general, and the commander of the Navy in Japan was a two-star rear admiral. But the Commander of the Fifth Air Force was a lieutenant general in the Air Force, General McKee. He was the senior person, and I was his chief of staff. But we weren't in any way an operational command, in command of forces for actions. But with his Air Force hat as Commander of the Fifth Air Force he was. At the time that the *Pueblo* was taken, I saw the dispatch about it immediately. I am an operator, and I abandoned my non-operational position as the chief of staff. I went up to my boss's office where he was Commander Fifth Air Force.

I said, "Boss, may I talk to you a minute and give you some recommendations and suggestions?" And I came out with a page full. The first was, "Immediately start making a log of time and of every communication you get and every communication you give back. And immediately, just as fast as you can, deploy your jet forces from Yokota and move them to Korea and from Okinawa and move them."*

He said, "Well, they wouldn't get there till—"

I said, "If something happens, they'll be there where they are in time." I guess he hadn't had that kind of comment from his own people. Well, it was only the first few minutes, but he did all those things. And later in the investigation, when many other operational commands were blasted in that report, there were only very commendatory comments about the Fifth Air Force.

There was another interesting connection through the Fifth Air Force. The Seventh Air Force was down at Vietnam, and for reasons of pressure on people and whatnot personnel from Fifth Air Force would swap with Seventh Air Force. They'd go down and do some time in Vietnam and then come back. So I would run into a lot of the officers there who didn't know my background from Adam, and they would talk about their tours down in Vietnam. And we would talk about the Navy command ship that was a control ship out in the Gulf of Tonkin. They'd say, "There was one that was the best."

"Yeah, which was one was that?"

"That was the *Long Beach*. When the *Long Beach* had control of you and talked to you, they knew exactly where you were." And I would grin deep in my heart although keeping a poker face. The *Long Beach* had a fantastic air control system. We had the ability to track 256 targets at once and update every one of them every second. And we helped make those systems work as the ship was being built and modified.

In the Gulf of Tonkin off Vietnam the first Navy ship to shoot down a MiG was *Long Beach*, and the second Navy ship to shoot down a MIG was the *Long Beach*.

---

* Yokota, Japan is the site of a U.S. Air Force base.

[Laughter] And I don't know if any other ship ever did it. The Vietnamese would come down from Hanoi, and if any Air Force fighters were approaching, they'd turn around and scurry back. And so *Long Beach* watched that for a couple of days, and finally *Long Beach* plugged them with a Talos, 60 miles.[*] And a while later they did it again and they plugged him [Laughter] within 60 miles, and they didn't ever come across again. When I was in Japan, hearing some of these stories, I was really proud of my old home. I guess Jim Watkins was the exec of the ship at that time.[†] What a crackerjack guy.

Paul Stillwell: Yes.

Admiral Wilkinson: But he went to a good ship.

Paul Stillwell: What do you recall about living in Japan during that period?

Admiral Wilkinson: Gee, that job was one the greatest things that ever happened to me, because my wife used to put the arm on me all the time: "If we're in the Navy why don't we go somewhere?" And she didn't mean New London and Norfolk and certainly not Washington. So when I got the tour of duty and we were going to live in Japan, Janice thought that was really great. If you look around our house now and see all the memorabilia and souvenirs and pictures about Japan and Japanese art, you'd think we'd never lived anywhere else.

Janice had a lot of fun in Japan and belonged to the Japan Time Ladies Club. It went on trips all over Japan, so Janice really got to see all the dirty dish shops and all that stuff. And anytime I got time off, we would fly space available outside Japan. We went to Korea and Taiwan and the Philippines and Bangkok, and we got as far as India, all space available. So we really enjoyed that period.

---

[*] On 23 May 1968 the *Long Beach* fired two Talos missiles at a MiG fighter at 65 miles. The first knocked the plane down, and the second hit the falling wreckage. In September 1968 a Talos from the *Long Beach* shot down a MiG that was 61 miles away. For details on this and other aspects of the career of the *Long Beach*, see Malcolm Muir, Jr., *Black Shoes and Blue Water: Surface Warfare in the United States Navy, 1945-1975* (Washington, D.C.: Naval Historical Center, 1996).

[†] At the time, James D. Watkins, future Chief of Naval Operations, was a commander.

I had good relations with my boss. I had especially good relations with the Japanese authority both in their Gaimusho, in that phase of the section of the government, with all their military, with many civilian people and companies. I was fortunate to be in that position at a time of importance. I was recommended for and got my first Distinguished Service Medal. And I won the Air Force Pacific tennis doubles. And, as I said a few days ago, I won a lot of money playing poker from the Air Force. My wife spent it buying memorabilia from Japan, and we have some pictures in there by pretty famous artists that are worth a lot of money now. It was a really good tour.

Paul Stillwell: Please tell me about your relationship on a day-to-day basis with General McKee, the types of things he handled, the types of things you handled.

Admiral Wilkinson: General McKee, and after him General McGee [Laughter], who was his replacement, wanted to spend more time with the double-hatted position as Commander Fifth Air Force, and they were doing things. Their personnel were interchanging with the personnel in the Seventh Air Force down fighting the war in Vietnam. We were pumping a million gallons a day of fuel to support the air going through. All the burn victims were coming back. My boss was really busy in his role as Commander Fifth Air Force, which was an operational command. And so although he did everything that was required as Commander U.S. Forces Japan, it wasn't an operational command, so he had the tendency to delegate to me and have me do more of that.

So I became the guy that did all the interactions with the U.S. ambassador, who was a crackerjack guy, Alex Johnson, and it got so that he never called my boss. He always called and talked to me and frequently on the secure telephone. And there were an awful lot of social obligations. We were invited to receptions by all the other embassies and ambassadors in Japan and by the Japanese. Janice and I probably had an average of ten such invitations a week, which is more than one a day. We lived at Fuchu, Higashi, which is out toward Hachioji, and the traffic was terrible.* It was an hour ride

---

* Fuchu Air Force Base, on the outskirts of the Tokyo metropolitan area, then housed the headquarters of U.S. Forces Japan. That command has since moved to Yokota Air Force Base.

into Tokyo, an hour ride back. My general boss didn't care for the receptions that much. I'm not saying that I did. But he also really didn't care for an hour ride into town and back, so a lot of that I did.

I gave the speech at Law Day with all nine members of the Japanese Superior Court—it's the equivalent of our Supreme Court—present. And so I ended up taking care of a lot of those kinds of functions, and my boss discharged his more urgent business as the operational Commander of the Fifth Air Force. Also, it sort of tied in with the joint committee. I was the guy that did the business with the embassy and the ambassador and went to all those damned social functions and gave a lot speeches and so forth. I also had some other little jobs like I was the vice president of the Eastern Council of the Boy Scouts, 10,000 Boy Scouts, and the Eastern Council of the Girl Scouts, about 2,500 Girl Scouts. I showed you marks of recognition and appreciation from both those organizations, because I did square away their finances.

Paul Stillwell: How large a staff did you coordinate as chief of staff?

Admiral Wilkinson: Not very big—30 to 40 officers.

Paul Stillwell: Was it mainly a coordinating organization for the individual services?

Admiral Wilkinson: Oh, no. Mainly it was an organization that did relations with the Japanese.

Paul Stillwell: I see. How much of a relationship did you have with the U.S. Naval Forces Commanders?

Admiral Wilkinson: And also an Army general down in Azima. I had a lot of personal communication; I was the point of contact with the Japanese related to all of our installations in Japan. They were living in those installations, so if there was any problem or question relating to a base or whatnot, I was the final point of contact between the United States and Japan. So naturally I had communication in that problem with the

Navy commander who had Yokosuka and other bases. What's the one you were telling me about over in the Sea of Japan?

Paul Stillwell: Sasebo.

Admiral Wilkinson: Sasebo and other places. The Army had places like Azima. The Navy had Iwakuni. Any problems related to those, there was a communication between me and the Navy commander and the Air Force commander or between my staff and his staff. More the latter, of course. So I had good relations, and I'd go down and visit there frequently and talk to those people. It was a good relationship that was largely a logistic link where we were taking care of some of their problems with the Japanese and ensuring that they had the support for their bases.

And it wasn't just the bases that they had their forces on. Remember we also had a bunch of land for golf courses, and an awful lot of facilities were provided by the Japanese to the United States. I was that point of contact. For example, on all our installations we had about 60,000 Japanese hires. When there were any labor relations problems, they weren't taken care of by the Commander Naval Forces or Commander of Army Forces or the Commander of Fifth Air Forces. They were taken care of by me. I did the negotiation with the Japanese on all the labor contracts and pay that was given to them and so forth, and I could tell you an amusing story on that.

Paul Stillwell: All right.

Admiral Wilkinson: Every year they would threaten to strike, and I would say, "Well, gee, we think an awful lot of those employees of ours, and I'd hate to have them strike because I know they need the money. But we are short of funds, and if it has to happen it will really help us out budget wise, because we've done our utmost not to lay anybody off." So every year they would strike, and they would be out less than four hours. Then the labor leaders would announce that there had been a settlement and that they gained an increase. And the increase was what we'd already offered a long time previously, which was equivalent to what the Japanese Government gave to their people. It wasn't exactly,

So my staff and I handled those kinds of things, and really any logistic relations with the Japanese Government came through me. So I did have contact with the gentlemen you were talking about, but it was not an operational line. It was a logistic line.

Paul Stillwell: When there would be disciplinary problems and an American serviceman committed crimes against Japanese, did you get involved in those?

Admiral Wilkinson: No. I did get involved with some of the civilians that were there. I can remember the Japanese were very, very intense about things involving traffic or automobile accidents. For example, to avoid that it was decided that I wouldn't drive in Japan, and so I was provided a car with two drivers so I could have 24-hour-a-day coverage, day and night. And my wife was provided a car and two drivers, and we never drove in Japan.

If there's a traffic accident in Japan, it doesn't work quite the same as in the United States. First of all, in the United States the car on the right has the right of way. The guiding principle in Japan is "Thou shall not run into the other car." [Laughter] Let's say there are a couple of lanes of cars bumper to bumper; a guy wants to shift lanes, but he can't. He'll get a chance and he'll get over four inches. And then there's another chance, and he'll get over another four inches. Another chance and he may make six or eight inches. Eventually, it gets into the point that he's far enough over that the other guy's worried about running into him, at which point all traffic stops in both lanes. Then he gets all the way over into the lane, and then they start up again. And if there is an accident nobody moves. Everything is stopped until the police get there. And it's not acceptable to not tell the truth. So they may stay right there for a few hours while all the traffic is stopped or until the police really resolve that and, "What do you mean you were only doing 20 miles an hour?

I mentioned I was involved with the scouts. One of my civilians over there was a Boy Scout leader. He was in an accident where there were injuries. I resolved it with the Japanese and kept him out of prison. But as far as the disciplinary business of our people, I wasn't in any way involved with that. I really didn't have disciplinary problems because of the nature of the people we had on the joint U.S. Forces Japan staff. I'm talking mostly senior officers, captains in the Navy and colonels in the Air Force and Army.

Paul Stillwell: Did you live in government-furnished quarters?

Admiral Wilkinson: I had government-furnished quarters. We had two cars and four drivers. My quarters had a maid, Yoshi-san, who was tremendous. And I had two stewards. We lived very well.

Paul Stillwell: Did you do a fair amount of entertaining?

Admiral Wilkinson: Yes and no. Not at our quarters, but sometimes we were the host at one of the functions. Like I said, the functions that we would be invited to, ten every week, we also hosted things in downtown Tokyo with all the invitees, and it was interesting going to those functions because they'd be hosted by the English or the French or whatnot, or Headquarters, U.S. Forces Japan.

Paul Stillwell: You had the same waitresses no matter who was the host?

Admiral Wilkinson: Yes. And so they all knew that they brought me a glass of plain water. Eventually, I didn't even have to tell them what I wanted to drink. I went to an awful lot of those functions, and that's what I got.

Paul Stillwell: How much did you travel throughout the country of Japan?

Admiral Wilkinson: Not a great deal. I went to the bases in the general vicinity of where we were. Obviously I had business in Kannamura and I had business at Azima, and I had business at Iwakuni and I had business at Yokosuka. I'd see the general in charge of the Army forces and the admiral in charge of the Navy forces. It was only to listen to their logistics problems that I could take action with the Japanese Government on. The one that traveled around Japan was my wife with the ladies of the Japan Time group. Where I did my travels was on vacation, space available, we always went outside Japan.

Paul Stillwell: I see. So you didn't get out to places like Kyoto or Kamakura?

Admiral Wilkinson: Well, of course, I've been to all those places [laughter] and an awful lot more you could name. When you said "travel to them," I sort of put in my mind time and time again. I went to all those places once, and there was a sort of an expression that covered that: "Did you do thus and so? Did you go to that?"

"Oh, I did that last year." For an awful lot of those things, once was enough. We went to the Goat-sai [phonetic], which is like the Rockettes and the Nichi-geiki and those shows and we did all those things but not a multitude of times.

Paul Stillwell: Did you climb Mount Fuji?

Admiral Wilkinson: I did not, but my kids did, and they got a stick for every height. My kids went to 14,000 feet, and they tell me right up on the top of Mount Fuji are the same dirty dish shops you'd see anywhere else. [Laughter]

Paul Stillwell: How much did you get to Tokyo?

Admiral Wilkinson: Oh, a lot. A lot. Day after day. Fuchu is in the outskirts of Tokyo, and we'd probably go down to one of these functions five nights a week. We'd be invited to them, of course, seven nights a week, but we in fact went five nights a week, and sometimes we'd do two functions in the same day. Then I went officially to a meeting of the joint committee every six weeks.

Paul Stillwell: Did you have any occasion to exchange experiences with Japanese naval veterans of World War II?

Admiral Wilkinson: Only a limited number of times. I was talking with one retired Japanese naval officer about our wartime experience, and our submarine had sunk his ship. When that was disclosed and we talked about it, it was a big experience. That was a big event in his life. After the war he was out of the Navy and retired, and he wasn't mad at me. He threw his arms around us. I mean, it was pretty surprising. There was no animosity or resentment at all. It was the chance for him to go back to part of his glory. It was hard, of course, for the Japanese military to lose.

Paul Stillwell: What kind of ship had he been in? Do you recall?

Admiral Wilkinson: Oh, I don't remember now, but we had sunk it.

Paul Stillwell: And each of you recognized the other was just doing his job at the time.

Admiral Wilkinson: Yes. I went and gave some talks and presented the diplomas at some graduations, but not too much of that. My counterparts, the people I was working with—like the morning we left Japan to say good-bye—were the Chairman of the Joint Chiefs, the head of the Army, head of the Navy, head of the Air Force. So I guess they were older than I. After all, in World War II, I was sort of a junior guy.

Paul Stillwell: Were the members of their Self-Defense Force pushing to get a bigger role militarily?

Admiral Wilkinson: No, not really. They do have more now, but in the aftermath of World War II the military was fairly well held down by the government. You were there at that time in the late 1960s.[*]

Paul Stillwell: Well, it was just about literally a Self-Defense Force.

---

[*] From 1966 to 1969 the interviewer served in the crew of the tank landing ship *Washoe County* (LST-1165), which was based in Yokosuka, Japan.

Admiral Wilkinson: Yes. I have many fond memories of Japan. Let me tell you, their word was good. If my counterpart on the joint committee said they'd do something, that's the way it was. My wife stopped in a little Japanese shop in downtown Tokyo and bought some Sanguay crackers. In those days the exchange rate was 360 yen to the dollar. I don't know what it is now, maybe somewhere between 110 and 120 to the dollar, but it goes up and down. My wife bought 100 yen worth of Sanguay and walked out of the shop because she had some of this and some of that and gave the guy 100 yen. But she didn't have 100 yen worth, and she walked out of the shop with her bag of crackers. The little shopkeeper chased after her and took a block and a half to catch her. He couldn't speak any English, but he got her by the arm and got her back and gave her some more crackers until she had 100 yen worth.

Once I was riding a taxi and going to the Sanno, which was our hotel downtown, and a 100-yen coin dropped out of my pocket in the taxi.*

Paul Stillwell: So it was worth about 26 cents American.

Admiral Wilkinson: Sure enough, quite some later the taxi guy came back to the hotel and tracked down who this was and identified me and gave me back my 100 yen. So the Japanese were quite honest, but this wasn't so in Korea. We had a terrible time in Korea maintaining communication because we'd string wire and, gee, that's valuable material; that wire would be stolen and you lost your telephone line. Finally heroic action was taken by our military in Korea, and they got their supplies and had a compound and a double fence with space in between. But they came up, click, click, click, and stole the fence because that was good material. [Laughter] And that's true. But it wasn't that way in Japan. I could have laid down a sheaf of bills on my desk, and let me tell you, they'd be there all day. And, similarly in my dealings with the Japanese authority, there was the same honesty and integrity.

I can remember when I first got to Japan, which was earlier than this now. It was when I was skipper of the submarine *Volador*. We went into Yokosuka during our six-month WestPac deployment. I rode the train from Yokosuka up to Tokyo, and they

---

* The Sanno Hotel in Tokyo was run by the U.S. military for members of the services and their families.

still had segregated trains where Americans had a compartment of their own. I'd look out at that countryside, and there was nothing. Those people had nothing. I could only say to myself, "How did it take us so long to beat them?" The answer was they worked really hard. I could tell you a lot of stories that would be amusing, all in all, since you shocked me. I was trying not to. I'll tell you a couple.

One of the great things was the fish market. Tokyo was 12 million people, and they ate a lot of fish and seafood. Every morning it was all assembled at the fish market and sold out. And beautifully done, sold out to a lot of merchants and sold from wholesalers out to smaller things and down through the system. And I'm not just talking fish. I'm talking whale and I'm talking a whole lot of sea items.

Paul Stillwell: Squid. Eel.

Paul Stillwell: Squids and eel and all that stuff. That was something to see. We've all gone down and seen the Japanese fish market at dawn at least once. You didn't have a tour in Japan without, by golly, seeing that fish market. One of my friends, a colonel, was going to see the fish market. So he went down into downtown Tokyo and got his room in the Sanno Hotel. He got up at 3:15 and went out, and finally he got to it. "Yes, this is the fish market." But the wind was cold, and some paper was blowing, because the Japanese did put trash around. There was nothing there, and he was trying to find the right place. It was before dawn, and finally he found somebody, a Japanese that could speak English, and had it explained to him. "Fish market no Sunday." [Laughter]

I had a couple of really fascinating experiences in Japan. One of them was that we got to go to the royal duck netting. Under the Emperor there's a preserve with a lake that is on the flyway for the ducks, and tens of thousands of ducks would land on this lake.* If you were out on the lake and looked toward the shore, there was a bunch of stakes driven in and a wooden picket fence all around the lake. If you were on the

---

* Hirohito became Emperor of Japan in 1926 and was given the status of a descendent of the ancient sun goddess. He was above politics but wielded influence nonetheless. When Japan surrendered in 1945, the Allies forced him to renounce his divinity, but he remained Emperor and continued as the symbolic head of state until his death in 1989.

outside looking in, you saw beautiful green land sloping up to the top of these stakes. At intervals all around were little canals that went through it with gates in them.

Under the Emperor, they would invite special people out, and we were invited. At the end of this channel behind a barricade you'd be assembled and given guidance and instruction as to what to do. Maybe there'd be eight of you in the party, and you were handed big butterfly nets. Down in the depths of the channel on the lake an opening would be lifted, and corn would be sprinkled in this little channel. And out on the lake there were a lot of tame Judas ducks. They understood that that was free corn, and so they would quickly swim in there and start peck-peck-pecking the corn. Then some of the wild ducks would go along with them and start pecking.

Then we would be given our signal, and we would rush out four to the side on top of this ditch. The Judas ducks paid us no mind, but the wild ducks would look up, and that would terrify them, and so they would take off as we were coming up. Our instructions were, "Everybody go the same direction." And with just amateurs having been given some instruction, on our first time we would catch far more than 50% of those ducks in butterfly nets. Then with not the Emperor himself but some royal prince who certainly was our host we would go up to a lodge and have among other things strawberries and cream and ducks cooked over a charcoal brazier. It was quite a thing, once.

That was continued a few times until everybody in the party had caught at least one duck. And then, since they'd caught far more ducks than we cooked on the charcoal braziers, the women were allowed to release the wild ducks that weren't consumed. I have a picture of my wife as she was just releasing this duck. He was just flying away, a foot or two from her hands en route at his departure. It shows the joy on my wife's face as she let this duck go; I'll treasure that picture forever.

Another time we were invited to a no play. The actors were doing their part, and the support cast was totally in black. They'd come out on the stage, and you could hardly see them. They do the support functions that support the actors, and they're the little men that aren't there.

Paul Stillwell: Pretending to be invisible.

Admiral Wilkinson: Yes, and they're so cloaked in black and all, and in fact they are hard as hell to see. They have nothing to do with the no play, and I used to refer to them as the people that weren't there.

Another time we were invited to the royal fishing, and so we went high, high in the mountains. There are some pretty scenic mountains in the neighborhood around Tokyo. We went up to a stream, and everybody was given fishing rods and salmon eggs, and we were all fishing for trout. Then, just like in the no play, there were these little men that weren't there. Suddenly out of the background came some men with big tubs filled with hungry trout, which they dumped into the stream just above our fishing party. Suddenly everybody was catching trout right and left. Then they dumped another tub full and another tub full, and when everybody had caught some trout off we went. So it was sort of interesting to go to some of those functions and, of course, in my position we were invited to all those kind of things.

But that kind of fishing doesn't really appeal to me. I did that only once, and I went to the royal duck netting only once, although I was invited more than once. And there the old phrase that applied. "Oh, I did that last year." [Laughter] So we had that part of Japan, too, but now I've digressed in the telling of sea stories. That was only one of the perks but not the job, if you understand what I'm saying.

Paul Stillwell: What was life like for your children in Japan?

Admiral Wilkinson: My children weren't living there. They were of such an age that they were away in college. I think my daughter did one year in the university out there. But they came in the summertime, and they really enjoyed it. My daughter met a young man she later married, but my kids were there and had jobs as lifeguards in the pool and made money. They weren't as restricted in their traveling out on the economy as Janice and I were, and so they really enjoyed Japan.

My oldest son lives in Japan now and is married to a Japanese girl. We have a little Japanese grandson, Eugene-San. He has just entered the first grade and tested second highest of any six-year-old in Japan. And that's a lot. [Laughter] He is Eugene Kanichi Wilkinson. He's named after me and named after his grandfather on the other side. My son's wife's parents were Samurais. Little Gene-san speaks Japanese, but he also speaks English fluently. And he can do all kinds of arithmetic.

Paul Stillwell: The young man your daughter married, he was an American Air Force man?

Admiral Wilkinson: Air Force, and he came back and got out of the Air Force and has had a very successful career and is now president of his own company.

Paul Stillwell: I have exhausted my questions on Japan. Do you have any more items related to that?

Admiral Wilkinson: No. In my Navy career it was a good tour. It was a very good tour for me, and certainly it was the most enjoyable part of all my military service as far as my wife was concerned. My kids did come in the summertime, and they enjoyed it. So although I had not been totally wild to go out there, it was really a great tour.

Paul Stillwell: And it was really a complete contrast to almost everything else you did in your naval service, which had some tie-in with submarines or nuclear power or both. After that, of course, you did return to submarines, this time as Commander Submarine Flotilla Two in New London.

Admiral Wilkinson: I went back to the Submarine Force after having been gone a long time, and so I worked hard at getting acquainted with everybody again and going around to all my ships. I met the people, two crews on the Polaris submarines. We'd already built them, and they were operating hard. Our ships had a lot of problems, so I spent a lot of time going on board ships.

One of the problems I encountered came from the Polaris crews in their off period between patrols. They would come back there for relaxation and for training until the next patrol. There were a lot of bachelors and not much supervision. They were living up in barracks and weren't taking care of them very well. I mean, the fire extinguishers were down and had been used to cool beer, and the pool balls were all lost from the tables. Covers were ripped and beds with no mattress covers over them and unmade; the barracks more or less looked like a mess.

I went up there and looked at those, and I said, "This has to be squared away." Then I followed up on it, and it didn't immediately get squared away. I said, "If I have to have every off-crew commanding officer inspecting one wing of this barracks and living here, it's going to get squared away." Well, it got squared away. But, anyway, I was up taking a look through the barracks shortly thereafter. The phone rang from Rickover, and he wanted to talk to me, so as soon as I got back I got him on the line.

He said, "Dennis, what in Christ's name are you doing up inspecting barracks when we've got all these ships with all our problems. Why aren't you down looking at the ships and seeing what ought to be done and doing that?"

I said, "Admiral, it all goes together."

He said, "Yeah, yeah, I know." And he hung up. [Laughter] And it's true. If you've got a problem in one area, you've got problems in another, and if your people do well at one thing they do well at everything. People and their performance and all are much the same regardless of what they're involved in.

But I wasn't SubFlot 2 very long. It must have been only six months before I was chosen to be Commander Submarine Force Atlantic Fleet, promoted to three stars, and moved to Norfolk. So I didn't have a long time in that job.

Paul Stillwell: Were you the senior submariner in New London?

Admiral Wilkinson: Yes.

Paul Stillwell: Did you have any cognizance over the Submarine School and training facilities there?

Admiral Wilkinson: No. Neither the commanding officer of Submarine School nor the commanding officer of the submarine base reported to me for writing their fitness reports. I was a commander of forces afloat, not shore-based commands. I hadn't thought of that.

By golly, I should have been but I wasn't. Those weren't under me. But certainly just age and weight and seniority, obviously they would listen to me, and obviously we had interactions and conversations. But I wasn't their Navy reporting senior.

Paul Stillwell: Anything else to recall about that time in New London?

Admiral Wilkinson: I liked to play tennis, as I told you earlier. My knees are shot now, and I can't move from side to side, and I haven't played tennis for several years. But there was a time when I was a fair club player. When I was in Japan, I entered the Air Force's tennis competition, and my partner and I did win the Air Force senior doubles for the Pacific Ocean Area, which was frustrating to the Air Force. When I went back after that and became the flotilla commander in New London, we did win the New London doubles, and I'm not talking senior doubles, I'm talking the doubles championship. So I played tennis quite a little bit, and I had some interesting experiences.

I had a friend up in Boston who was good enough to have played in the U.S. doubles championship, and he hadn't won, but he was in the quarterfinals I think. He invited me out to Longwood, and he went out and he was my partner. We played with a couple of young ladies that were playing in the ladies doubles, and they just waxed the hell out of us. [Laughter] And they didn't pick on me either. They hit it wherever you should in doubles. So it's fantastic how good some of these people are. But as a club player when I was SubLant I still played tennis. Somebody told me we had a young officer that was really a good tennis player, and so I talked to him and said, "Gee, how good are you? Who can you beat?"

He said, "I can beat anybody. I would be a pro if it wasn't that I was in the military." His brother was a club pro somewhere, and he probably couldn't beat everybody, but he was really good. He could hit that ball right through the wall. I mean, I never saw such a hard serve. And so once I was up visiting the superintendent of the Coast Guard Academy, who was an admiral and was a very, very superior tennis partner. He challenged me to a doubles match, and I thought, "Gee, I better get a good player," so I got my young officer who said he could beat anybody. And maybe he could. He was really good. The superintendent's partner was their football coach, who was Otto Graham.* I don't know if you've ever heard of Otto Graham.

Paul Stillwell: Oh, yes. He used to be with the Cleveland Browns.

Admiral Wilkinson: But it was really amazing, because there is a difference with a real natural athlete. He hadn't perhaps played all that much tennis but what an athlete. Quick as a cat, and in doubles at the net it was incredible how quick that guy was and how quick in reaction and how fast he could move. I was really afterwards entranced with my game and association with Otto Graham. But they didn't win because my young officer who could beat anybody was there.

Later I was OP-02, and I was in Washington. We were at a reception one Friday night, and among the people there was an admiral from Taiwan, a Chinese admiral who was a considerable tennis player. We were having a bit of cheer, and we talked about playing tennis. We arranged that we'd play tennis on Sunday morning, and we'd play doubles. He said to me, "How good a partner should I get?" [Laughter]

Having had quite a bit of cheer, I said, "You better get the best partner you can get." [Laughter] On the next morning, Saturday morning, I got to thinking about that, and I thought, "You know, that guy might really go out of his way to get somebody really good." So I asked my young officer that could beat anybody if he'd come and give me a little support. So Sunday morning when we went out to play tennis, and this Chinese admiral's partner was a Chinese young man that was 6-foot-4, had arms that hung down below his knees, and played first singles for UCLA.† And this was back in the days when UCLA dominated tennis. But I had a partner that could beat anybody, so the first singles champion from UCLA wasn't as good as my partner. [Laughter]

---

* Otto E. Graham, Jr., was quarterback for Northwestern University during World War II and later quarterback for the Cleveland Browns, 1946-55. He was elected to both college and pro football halls of fame. He was head football coach and athletic director at the Coast Guard Academy, 1959-66; head coach of the Washington Redskins, 1966-68, and athletic director of the Coast Guard Academy, 1970-85.
† UCLA – University of California at Los Angeles.

Paul Stillwell: What was the name of this man who could beat anybody?

Admiral Wilkinson: I don't know. I can't remember it right now. But he was a good player. He had a fantastic serve, and he was good enough to carry me to beat a pretty good Chinese admiral and the first singles from UCLA. And he was good enough to carry me to beat Otto Graham and the Superintendent of the Coast Guard Academy, who was a better player than I. Maybe he couldn't beat anybody, but he thought he could.

Paul Stillwell: Did he go on to a full Navy career?

Admiral Wilkinson: No.

Paul Stillwell: What do you remember about retention problems for submarine officers in that era?

Admiral Wilkinson: Things were very bad. A lot of those things go with the economy, and they go with the temper of the country. We're talking 1969; there was the business in Vietnam. You go back to World War II, and everyone was in service. It was the thing to do. In '69 it was not necessarily the temper of the country that the thing to do was to be in the military. Our submarines were operating hard. The Polaris people were out there keeping the strategic weapons system on the line, and they were away from home half the time. It was possible for a young man to make more money on the outside. We had maybe 2,200 nuclear-trained officers in the Submarine Force Atlantic Fleet, and because of all those competing factors we were running one officer resignation a day. That was 365 a year, and out of 2,200 that's a significant number.

So it was a considerable worry to the thing, because there have to be replacements. They have to be selected and go through a long period of training. You didn't have a guy become a qualified nuclear submariner overnight. That included going through Nuclear Power School and going through a prototype and coming to a boat and then starting training and finally getting qualified in nuclear submarines. We're talking surely a two- or three-year lead-time. So it was a worry to us.

When the guys resigned, the Navy didn't want them out. They gave them one more year of service, and then they'd get out. So now we had on all our submarines some officers who had put in their resignations and who were being held aboard against their will. So they groused, and that had an impact on the other young officers and so they could see, "Gee, if I have to stay another year after I ask to get out, I'd better ask now." So that generated more resignations, probably from some people that didn't really want to resign at all. [Laughter] So we had a lot of officers who were on board their submarines against their will and were a bad influence.

When I had the good fortune to become SubLant, I was asked by the CNO to try to do something about the problem. That was because I had had a good reputation as the commanding officer of quite a few ships, and certainly our retention was high and the reenlistment of our troops was high and morale was good on all the ships I had been skipper of. We got the bonus passed for nuclear submarine officers, where if they signed up for longer they got paid a good bonus. And, as luck would have it, the economy changed on the outside so it wasn't as easy to get a job. And I visited every submarine and talked to all the officers. I also went to the CNO, who took me to the Secretary of the Navy.* I said, "I want authority to get rid of all those people on the submarines that are being held against their will. It's a canker in there."

So with a little bit of trepidation on the part of higher authority, they said, "All right, go ahead." I made all those people that were being held fish or cut bait, and an awful lot of them didn't get out. [Laughter] Anyway, with the bonus and change in economy and whatever, one thing and another, when my three-year tour at SubLant was finished, we were down to one officer resignation a month. The last two months I was there, we didn't have any. So I felt really pleased with that.

Paul Stillwell: That was down from one a day.

Admiral Wilkinson: Yes. We still had the same tempo of operations. They were still gone the same amount, but someway or other it got turned around.

---

* The Chief of Naval Operations at the time was Admiral Thomas H. Moorer, USN; the Secretary of the Navy was John H. Chafee.

Paul Stillwell: What do you remember about the impact of Admiral Zumwalt's arrival as CNO in 1970 and the Z-grams and so forth?*

Admiral Wilkinson: It was tough for us, for the submarines. There's the organizational diagram on the wall, and there's the real structure, and for many years I set policies in submarines regardless of what job I was in. Certainly I controlled what happened in submarines when I was OP-31 and when I was OP-02 and when I was ComSubLant. But then we got some of the Z-grams in the form of messages to the entire Navy: "All the forces afloat are working too hard, so we're going to go to a watch section in six, a duty in six."

Well, we had the nuclear plants to look out for and nuclear weapons, and with our small manning in a submarine we didn't have enough people to stand a watch in six. I'd sit down and write a dispatch back to the CNO, "We can't properly take care of our ships and our weapons and our responsibility and ensure the safety of our nuclear plants and do that, so we're staying on one in three." It's easy to write that dispatch to the CNO, but it's not so easy to say, "Hey, they don't really mean us, fellows." Because your guys would like to go home five nights out of six instead of two nights out of three when they're in port, because they're at sea a hell of a lot. So some of the Z-grams that were supposed to boost the morale of the Navy just made it a little tougher for us in the Submarine Force.

Paul Stillwell: Well, surely you were successful having the argument that you can't compromise on safety.

Admiral Wilkinson: Oh, once I'd sent the dispatch that said that we're not doing it that way there was never any problem. I never took an action ever in all that time that was ever countermanded. We knew what we were talking about. There might have been a

---

* Admiral Elmo R. Zumwalt, Jr., USN, served as Chief of Naval Operations from 1 July 1970 to 29 June 1974. His oral history is in the Naval Institute collection. Z-grams were consecutively numbered policy directives from Zumwalt that attempted to deal with such issues as enlisted rights and privileges, equal opportunity, and Navy families. Junior personnel viewed them much more favorably than did their seniors. See *U.S. Naval Institute Proceedings*, May 1971, pages 293-298.

little grousing: "The damn submarine people aren't supporting us." But nothing was ever countermanded. And eventually the Navy had to protest change somewhat. It was a destructive force in our country. Not all the Z-grams were right. Hey, a lot of stuff was good, but not all the Z-grams were right. Sometimes you do have need to maintain a little order and discipline. And some of the Z-grams were really just a search for popularity. Maybe I'm being overly critical.

Paul Stillwell: What can you say about your relationship with Admiral Rickover when you were ComSubLant?

Admiral Wilkinson: Sometimes in dealing with Rickover you had to stand up for your own as he became more and more powerful. When I was ComSubLant many was the time I'd get a call from Admiral Rickover: "Your guy, Whats-n-whats, has screwed up, and I want you to fire him."

"Well, Admiral, I'll look into it, and I'll get right to you as quick as I can," said I.

"I don't have to look into it. I've already looked into it. I just want you to fire him."

"Admiral, [laughter] I'll investigate it thoroughly as fast as I can, and I'll give you a report." But you couldn't just say, "Aye, aye," on something like that. That's not the way to run an organization.

I had Rickover get really mad at me, and I guess the maximum time he wouldn't speak to me was for six weeks. But, by and large, we did a lot of business together. One time, again when I was ComSubLant, Rickover wanted me to do something, and I said, "No, we can't do that, Admiral." And he kept after me and this went on a month or two, and I said, "No, we just can't do that."

Let me come back to that story in a minute and digress a little. At every shipyard Rickover had a representative, and whenever our submarines were in there his representative would have access and come down and come up with a multitude of problems, and they loved to tell about things that were wrong. And Rickover had the weakness that he loved to hear about things that were wrong. He decided he was getting a lot of good information from these things and that what he really ought to have was one of his representatives on every ship. So he told me, "Yeah, I'm going to have a new policy. I'm going to have one my people ride every one of the ships and give me a report."

Then you've got to think back a minute. Rickover was born in Russia, and I said right back to him, "Admiral, we're not going to have a commissar on our ships."

And he kept talking. He said, "I'm going to have—"

I said, "Admiral, you didn't hear me again and the way I said it. Let me tell you again. There isn't going to be a commissar on each one of our Navy ships." And he thought about that for a while and backed away. [Laughter]

Another time Rickover was on my back as SubLant. He wanted me to do something, and I won't go into the details of what it was except I just told him, "No, we can't do that." And so one day I get an order from the Chief of Naval Operations to do that. Head of the Navy, Admiral Moorer. So I called Admiral Rickover up, and I said, "Admiral, you and I have discussed this thing for a couple of months, and I told you we couldn't do it."

"Yeah," he said.

I said, "I just got an order from the Chief of Naval Operations to do that."

"Yeah," he said.

I said, "Admiral, I just called up to tell you that you can't have it both ways. You can deal with me informally as much as you want, or you can go through the chain of command. I'm willing to do it either way, but you can't have both. Just to show you what I mean, I'm still not going to do it."

He said, "But the CNO has ordered you to do it."

I said, "I know. He did it because you put pressure on him, and if you want to make an issue of it, you can probably hurt me. Be my guest." [Laughter]

I never heard any more about that. He never tried that ploy again. [Laughter] But Rickover would do anything to have his way. You had to watch him. I've seen him cry, get tears in his eyes, and say, "You've got to do this."

If you say, "All right, yes, I will," bang, he'd turn it off just like that and go on to the next item. [Laughter] I mean, you could not let Rickover force you do to something you knew wasn't right. You could look into it, and if you were wrong you could come around, but you really had to hold the line if you were right. Now, there probably wasn't any other submarine officer that had the guts and the strength that way that I did, but it was easier for me. I was first. I was there in the beginning. I wasn't that bent on Navy success. I had a lot of fun and a good career in the Navy, and I wouldn't have cared if I'd have got out sooner. So I had a tendency to stand up for what I thought was right. That's the way it was, and we didn't back down from that very much. [Laughter]

Paul Stillwell: What inputs did you make during that period to the development of the 688 class?[*]

Admiral Wilkinson: It was support for a higher speed. Also, Rickover did an awful lot to ensure quiet. We wanted better submarines, and the 688 class had very, very superior characteristics. With the operational guys that worked for me, we participated in the studies that made the suggestions in some of those characteristics. My guy was Joe Williams, and Joe was an awfully goddamned good experienced submarine operator.[†] And Joe was smart enough to get him supported by a lot of other people. And a lot of other people were involved in the characteristics of those ships. Of course, Admiral Rickover and all the nuclear expertise, and by that time we were controlling any money that was spent on submarine research and development. So we got the inputs from sonars and depth control and other things and the spin-off from the SubSafe and operational letters, the lessons. But from the operator side the major input was my guy, Joe Williams. And the operating submarines worked for him.

I tried to explain to you, back to the prototype and when submarines are built, how we really looked at, "How am I going to get that end bell off for maintenance when this pipe in the way?" We wanted to make sure that pipe wasn't built that way. So one of the looks was, "How can I do maintenance on all the equipment in these two sections

---

[*] USS *Los Angeles* (SSN-688) was commissioned on 13 November 1976 as the lead ship of a class of 39 nuclear-powered fast-attack submarines. They were followed in 1988 with the commissioning of the USS *San Juan* (SSN-751), lead ship of what is known as the "improved *Los Angeles* class." As a captain, Williams was the chief of staff for ComSubLant.
[†] See the Naval Institute oral history of Vice Admiral Joe Williams, Jr., USN (Ret.). It provides a detailed account of the steps involved in the development of the *Los Angeles* class.

of hull at the prototype?" And let me tell you, the guys that were pointing that out were not the designers. They were the operators. And, similarly, the 688 class had all the expertise of the designers, but it also needed, before it was laid down and built, to have the input from the operators. And so that was us. [Laughter] My senior agent was Joe Williams, but there were other guys as well.

Paul Stillwell: Well, there was really a committee that was studying inputs.

Admiral Wilkinson: Yes, and the dominant force on that committee was Joe Williams.

Paul Stillwell: How much of this was specifically aimed at responding to Soviet advances?

Admiral Wilkinson: Well, I started to say it wasn't, but I guess you're right, it was. It was more so in numbers. But also they were faster and deeper, and so part of it was that. But mostly it was responding to doing better than the things we had. The 688 is a superior submarine to the ones we had before. As the skipper of the *Nautilus* I had a way of answering that. "Yeah, I know that's better in every way. But let me tell you, it won't run any better." [Laughter] But that was the only thing we had left. They didn't run any better, but the capabilities were certainly orders of magnitude better than the stuff we had before. And that was really based on lessons learned from the ships that we had and the improvements that ought to be made, both technically from Rickover's side but operationally from Joe Williams's side. It wasn't comparison with the Soviets. It was comparison with ourselves. You understand what I'm saying?

Paul Stillwell: Yes, but certainly there was consideration of the Soviet capabilities. I talked to Vice Admiral Kent Lee, and when he was the skipper of *Enterprise* he had a Soviet submarine in trail, and he was surprised by how high a speed he could make and still have that submarine stay with him.* This information was communicated back to Washington.

Paul Stillwell: Oh, there isn't any doubt. [Laughter] Hey, any surface ship truly is helpless against us. If it came to that, it's really only a question of how long they'd survive. I mean, seriously. I understand what you're saying, and it ties in with what I said. They'd go deeper and faster, and we needed to get that information about the Soviets. We knew that. I mean, we didn't need to get that information from the *Enterprise*. Submariners all knew that. [Laughter] We full well knew the characteristics of the Soviet submarines.

Admiral Wilkinson: What do you remember about Joe Williams's work when he was your chief of staff at SubLant?

Admiral Wilkinson: Joe Williams worked for me more than once. He was a crackerjack officer. He worked for me at SubLant, and he worked for me in OpNav. And he's a close personal friend and a pistol.

Paul Stillwell: He is feisty.

Admiral Wilkinson: We communicate and are friends to this day. He did a fantastic job. The first time I was the submarine guy on the selection board there were four submariners selected, and Joe was one of them. I think Joe was one of the best and most capable, and he's a hard guy to shave. Joe's tough. He said, "Admiral, when you leave, look behind you," and I did. And Joe became ComSubLant in his day.† And even when I was long retired, more than once he'd call me up and kick an item around with me. I think very, very highly of Joe. He was right 98% of the time, and the 2% he was wrong there was no dealing with him at all. [Laughter] If you tried to get into that item, he'd

---

* See the Naval Institute oral history of Vice Admiral Kent L. Lee, USN (Ret.), and Patrick Tyler, *Running Critical: The Silent War, Rickover, and General Dynamics* (New York: Harper & Row, 1986).
† Vice Admiral Joe Williams, Jr., USN, served as Commander Submarine Force Atlantic Fleet from 24 September 1974 to 20 June 1977.

just start talking louder and louder. I would say, "Joe, listen to yourself talk. You're talking louder and louder because you know you're wrong." And then he'd laugh. But we were friends and had a good relationship. He's a pistol.

Paul Stillwell: Yes, he is. Had the problems already started up at that time, the difficulties with General Dynamics? In the work at Electric Boat there were questions about the quality control and claims for additional payments to General Dynamics.

Admiral Wilkinson: I know that existed, but I didn't have a function. I wasn't really in on that.

Paul Stillwell: What more do you recall about your years as ComSubLant?

Admiral Wilkinson: I was the first nuclear-trained guy to be SubLant, and there was a lot of morale problem in the beginning. We were talking about the officers that were resigning. There were a lot of pressures on them. They operated hard. Their wives didn't like them being away from home so much, and that was a pressure. And the Nuclear Weapon Examining Board exams and the ORSE exams, the Operational Reactor Safeguard Exams under Rickover's people were a pressure. And I was concerned that all the submarines would be as good as they could be.

So on every one of those exams, whether it was a weapons exam or the Board of Inspection and Survey, I got copies of the reports and read them. I said, "Gee, that sounds bad. I want that straightened out." I did that ship by ship and item by item, and that's more than a guy can do. After a while I said, "Gee, that's the third time I've seen that item on the ORSE Board. I want that fixed for everybody." So we took some actions of support like that so that no longer was a deficiency, and things got better. During my time at SubLant it got turned around so we didn't have any failed ORSE exams, and we didn't have any failed nuclear weapons exams. I never had a submarine that had a collision and never had a submarine that ran aground. And I never had any submarine that had any people killed. And we made some changes in our supply systems and improved our spare parts support and still saved money at it. And we were the

All-Navy softball champs and the All-Navy basketball champs every year. And we kept our strategic weapons submarines on line, where we were doing the refits ourselves on the tenders. We never missed having one sail on time in those three years. And we had none of our ships that missed any operational commitments. I had some awfully good people working for me. My supply officer went on to become the Chief Porkchopper in the Navy.

Paul Stillwell: Who was that?

Admiral Wilkinson: Oh, one of my supply officers. I'd have to think back a minute. He came to see me a couple of times afterwards. And I had other guys that did well and got promoted. And I could show you in the other room a letter I got within the last couple of weeks from one of my yeoman of that time. I still hear from those people.

Paul Stillwell: What was the connection between ComSubLant and CinCLant in operating the strategic missile submarines?

Admiral Wilkinson: Actually, ComSubLant used to be in New London. As the Submarine Force got the strategic weapons system and the requirement for command and control and all, that's why ComSubLant was moved from New London to Norfolk in the first place and why ComSubLant became a three-star billet instead of a two-star billet. So ComSubLant headquarters were close to CinCLantFlt headquarters, and opcon was there. We certainly had command and control of our forces. So we had such a relation with the Commander in Chief Atlantic Fleet, and, of course, he's only an agent, all the way up to the President himself.

Admiral Wilkinson: What do you remember about the two Atlantic Fleet commanders you dealt with, Admiral Holmes and Admiral Duncan?*

---

* Admiral Ephraim P. Holmes, USN, served as Supreme Allied Commander Atlantic, Commander in Chief Atlantic, and Commander in Chief Atlantic Fleet from 17 June 1967 to 30 September 1970. Admiral Charles K. Duncan, USN, held the same three billets from 30 September 1970 to 31 October 1972. His oral history is in the Naval Institute collection.

Admiral Wilkinson: I thought both of them were capable, and I liked them both personally. I had good friendship and good relations. Frequently, especially in Admiral Duncan's time, my wife and I were invited to be guests for dinner at more than one function, and certainly I had no criticism, real or implied, operationally. As far as I was concerned, they were both capable officers and did their jobs well. I don't know what they thought of me, but as far as I know our relations were fine, and that was no problem at all.

Paul Stillwell: What do you recall about the business of providing direct support in attack submarines for carrier task groups?

Admiral Wilkinson: Submarines got more and more capability as time went by. Certainly we couldn't have done that with the *Nautilus*. But by the time we got the 688 class we were able to keep up with high-speed surface forces, and we had the capability to detect submarines at speed when they couldn't. We could speed and slow down and detect and then move again, so we had an ability to contribute information to a task force commander. We were hampered by a lack of the ability to do communications, and so we endeavored design-wise to try to do something to improve that communicational link. But we recognized that this was something of the future that we needed, and so I had no problem. Submarines always operated independently before that, and we liked it that way, but we could see that the day was coming when for our high-speed carrier task force we could contribute something. And so I in no way was against that.

Paul Stillwell: Just to jump ahead when you were OP-02 were you involved in the efforts to develop the extremely low frequency communications links?

Admiral Wilkinson: Yes.

Paul Stillwell: Any details on that? That was a highly political thing.

Admiral Wilkinson: Yes. I was really involved personally, and I can remember putting it on the line once that we were going to do that, and we won that battle. But I don't remember all the details. But, yes, we were vehemently strong supporters of that, and we did our utmost to see that that happened. We needed to be able to go deep in order to make use of our speed and sonar layers and whatnot, but we needed to be able when the guy was deep not to lose contact with him. When a submarine is towing a wire that's close to the surface you can communicate and even have rather rapid communications. It's tougher deep, and it was with the ELF that we could have a low-rate message get down that really told the guy, "Come up so we can talk to you."

There was lot of Mickey Mouse that those installations out there would do damage, radiation damage to people.* Just like the great confusion in the public mind between nuclear weapons and nuclear power and a great lack of knowledge of some of the things related to nuclear power, there was a real lack of knowledge on some hazards related to ELF transmission. A lot of do-good environmentalists who didn't know what they were talking about that said, "This is a danger to people," which wasn't really so. I can remember being in on that. But we got our capability.

Paul Stillwell: I remember even concerns that livestock would be contaminated and so forth.

Admiral Wilkinson: Yes.

Paul Stillwell: Anything else to say about your ComSubLant years?

Admiral Wilkinson: As SubLant I lectured to the PCOs and moved the PCO School to SubLant so I could talk to them.† I talked to every class for about ten hours. I'd tell them, "Each one of you guys is going to be a commanding officer, and each one of you is going to want to have the very best ship in the force, and you can't all do that. And we would also like each one of you to have the very best ship, just as best as it can possibly

---

* The concern was in the areas where the transmitters would be located near farms and other populated areas in the northern United States.
† PCO – prospective commanding officer.

be, but you can't do that. I want to tell you some basic truths. You're got 95 guys involved, and you're a crackerjack guy. It's not how you do. It's how all 95 guys do, and now I'll tell you a simple truth. They'll do better if you ask them." That was the thrust of one of the start-out talks to the guys. Some people never recognize that it's not them alone; it's all their guys. Some COs don't ask them, and they don't know what to ask for anyway.

A leader has to be able to communicate with his people. When I was Commander Submarine Force Atlantic Fleet, my material guy was a fellow named Jack Williams.* He was a crackerjack guy whom I'd known earlier when he was younger. Guys can't help it, but they fall into patterns of things, and probably more than one time in my life I've looked very sincerely at one of the people working for me and said, "Gee, Joe," or Paul, or whatever: "Paul, have I told you lately what a really great job I think you're doing?"

The guy would say, "Well, no, Captain."

I'd say, "Well, god damn it, I've been so busy and all, and I just should have done that. I know better, and you are a great guy doing a great job, and I'm happy as hell that you're working for me. And now that the subject's come up I just want to tell you how really much I appreciate your being here and the job you're doing." I've probably used some variation of those words more than once in my naval career, and certainly I had said those words to Jack Williams. So one night we were working late at SubLant. It was probably 8:00 o'clock, and there were not many of us left. Jack Williams was in the office, and I went in and said, "Jack, what are you doing?"

"Such and such."

"Well, Jack, have I told you what a really great job you're doing for me and how much I appreciate it?" This was probably the third time in his life I'd given that spiel to Jack or some variant of the words.

He said, "Well, no, you haven't, Admiral."

I said, "Well, damn it, Jack. That's because you're not, and you've got to get this crap squared away." [Laughter] And then we both were roaring and rolled on the floor with laughter, because Jack knew he was really doing a really good job, and he really

---

* Captain John G. Williams, Jr., USN.

knew I knew it, and he really knew I appreciated it. So the words didn't matter. I shouldn't say this out of context, but eventually Jack put in his chit to retire from the Navy. I got him in and I told him, "Hey, you really shouldn't do that, Jack. You're the kind of a guy they really need in the Navy. If you stay in the Navy, you'll make admiral. That will be for the value of the Navy, and with the time you've put in you owe that." He told me, no, his career wasn't like that. He wasn't going to make it.

Then I ran through the spiel again and told him if he'd stay in he was going to make admiral, and the second time he told me that, no, he wanted to retire. He felt that his career was about over. And I said, "Jack, god damn it, who do you think's running things around here?" [Laughter] He stayed in the Navy. He did make admiral. He did make four stars. [Laughter]

Paul Stillwell: Chief of Naval Material.[*]

Admiral Wilkinson: When I retired from the Navy and came back, Jack Williams was in charge of the San Diego submarine area here.[†] He made his manners and said, "Admiral, we've got this room reserved for you and this suite of offices laid aside for your use and whatnot."

I thought, "Gee, I certainly wouldn't want to get Jack into any trouble." So I said, "Jack, I really would appreciate it if I could park a car here and have it looked out for for a couple of weeks while I get squared away. But really that's all I need." So Jack wanted to take care of me even after I retired. He was a crackerjack officer.

Paul Stillwell: Well, you moved in '72 from Norfolk back to Washington to be the head submarine man in OpNav. How did OP-02 differ from what OP-31 had been several years earlier?

Admiral Wilkinson: The boss was more senior. [Laughter]

---

[*] Admiral John G. Williams, Jr., USN, served as Chief of Naval Material, 1 July 1981 to 31 July 1983.
[†] In the mid-1970s, as a rear admiral, Williams served as Commander Submarine Group Five.

Paul Stillwell: Was that the only difference?

Admiral Wilkinson: And OP-02 was a three-star job. As a consequence, it had a little more muscle. But it was still the submarine warlord, and we had the same kind of problems. There wasn't really all that much difference.

Paul Stillwell: In what ways did you benefit by having one more star in that position?

Admiral Wilkinson: I had more access in the higher-level committees. Surely I had some more people working for me and some more experienced people. I wasn't now the only admiral in OP-02. I had, for example, Yogi Kaufman.* There aren't many people can compete with Yogi Kauffman in many fields, including physical. [Laughter] Yogi Kaufman is a guy that accomplished a lot, and I made him my front guy to make the Trident program happen, and he did a great job for me.† And I had other very capable people, so I probably had more people and more talent supporting me and more access myself. I was on a Navy selection board again, and I was in a little more powerful position than when I'd been the junior guy on a selection board years before.

On the other hand, I had the handicap that the CNO was Admiral Zumwalt, and he wasn't a strong supporter of submarines. He thought we were spending too much of the Navy's money. So there were pros and cons and checks and balances. But essentially the job was the same, to look out for and take care of submarines and see that they were doing right.

Paul Stillwell: What do you recall of your personal relationship with Admiral Zumwalt?

Admiral Wilkinson: He was not really pro-submarine, and I was the guy responsible for submarines, and so we didn't always see eye to eye or always have a happy relationship.

---

* Captain Robert Y. Kaufman, USN.
† USS *Ohio* (SSBN-726), the first of a class of nuclear powered submarines armed with the Trident ballistic missile, was approved in the early 1970s. She was laid down 10 April 1976, launched 7 April 1979, and commissioned 11 November 1981. The ship is 560 feet long and displaces 18,750 tons submerged.

Paul Stillwell: Was it difficult for you to get access to him?

Admiral Wilkinson: Oh, no. Oh, no. I didn't have any problem in that regard. But when I had access he might not happily support what I'd like to see happen. He had his responsibility for the whole Navy and his own agenda, and his own agenda was not to worry about submarines very much.

Paul Stillwell: How much support did you get from him on the Trident program?

Admiral Wilkinson: You know, that's a good question, and I don't remember very much, and certainly I never asked for any. I mean, I didn't need any, so I didn't ask for any. But now, since you put the question that way and I think back, I didn't have opposition from him at all, whereas from many other things that had to do with our attack submarines and funds and whatnot we had desperate opposition to cut those funds out. But on the Trident, there was not any negativism from Admiral Zumwalt like there was for some of our other things. If I'm giving you impression that I failed to get support, I can't ever remember asking the CNO, Admiral Zumwalt, for support for anything. We supported ourselves. If I had asked, I probably wouldn't have got it either.

Paul Stillwell: Probably some of his negativism was countered by the support on Capitol Hill that Admiral Rickover had fostered.

Admiral Wilkinson: Oh, absolutely. We've seen them come and go, and just like Admiral Martell, OP-95 in his day and OP-31 or Admiral Zumwalt in his day in OP-02, we never lost. We had the support in the Congress. It's just like when Admiral Martell's chief of staff came in and started measuring our spaces in OP-31 and said, "Admiral Martell's going to take over these offices."

We said, "Hey, we were here, and we saw such and such come and go. We'll see OP-95 come and go. We've been in these offices since the building was built, and we're not moving." And we didn't. [Laughter] I'm giving you the wrong picture, but it's just like in World War II. I did submarine operations. I've been fired at by the French and the Germans and the Brits and the Japanese and the Army Air Forces. There were an awful lot of those people. All they'd see was a big medal down there. They didn't differentiate that much. There's just a submarine, and they were against it. I mean so it was in other things. The submarine outfit tried real hard to look out for themselves. Especially with Admiral Rickover in the congressional thing, we had the support. We kept it. Not very many people took it away from us, no matter how hard they tried.

Paul Stillwell: So what you're saying is that not all your enemies were foreign.

Admiral Wilkinson: It's not a question of enemies. There are only so many resources, and each outfit is competing for them. The President has his budget. They want to spend resources of so much on Medicare and so much on this and so much on that. If you go to the military, sincerely the Army thinks he should have more than he's got at the expense of the others, and the Navy and the Marines and the Air Force all feel likewise, and there's really a competition for resources between them. And if you come into the Navy itself really, truthfully and sincerely the aviators feel they ought to have more for carriers and planes, and the black shoes feel they ought to have more for the surface ships, and the submarine people feel they ought to have more. And if you go down into other little divisions, other people would like to have more for research and development and so on.

It just happened that my responsibility always was to look out for submarines, and I did that as best I could. And I was fussed at once by higher authority that I was getting more than my share, and I said, "Gee, that's the job I've been assigned. That's my responsibility. If you'd like to put me in charge of the resources for all the Navy, I'll do my best I can there, but as long as I'm the submarine guy that what I'm going to do." And I did. I didn't always win, but we did pretty well.

Paul Stillwell: What specifically do you recall about Yogi Kaufman's work in connection with the Trident?

Admiral Wilkinson: Yogi Kauffman was great, and he was my front guy, and he's very personable and very knowledgeable and very enthusiastic. And certainly he carried the torch with an awful lot of congressional people and within the Navy. Yogi's highly respected. The development against the calendar of the authorization of the Trident program, the Trident missiles, authorizations involved, the building of the ships—I'm sure it happened earlier in time because of Yogi Kaufman than it would have otherwise. Yogi Kaufman in my book is great and did a great job for me there.

The Trident system was important. It gave us a better, less vulnerable, and harder to detect submarines that could carry more missiles and the longer-range missiles and operate over a much broader ocean area. After all, we're talking about the survivable deterrent. It was necessary for the United States to have a deterrent system in the nuclear weapons, but also that word survivable is an important word, because we needed to be able to survive any surprise attack. And finally the point was got to that if some Soviets had wanted to launch a surprise attack against us, they could have knocked out every silo in the Great Plains 100%. They could have destroyed any submarine that was moored in port. They could have destroyed any carrier that was moored in port. They would have a greater chance of destroying a carrier at sea that could be seen by global satellites, although they're a little more survivable because they're moving. But one of the design concepts for survivability was to move silos around on trains so they wouldn't know for sure just where they were all the time.

But the submarine, once it was out and submerged and undetectable, reached that word survivable. Well, the Trident makes it easier to be survivable, because it puts out across against a much greater ocean area. So the Trident was the next step that was sensible after Polaris and Poseidon. If you look against the calendar I'm sure that Yogi's efforts moved that ahead a little in getting authorizations and funds and whatnot. He was my front man and he did it well.

Paul Stillwell: What do you recall about the issue of where the Trident submarines would be based?

Admiral Wilkinson: The longer-range missile concept was important. As the Soviet nuclear submarines were developing and becoming better and their worldwide naval stance and their naval capability, it seemed that we should disperse our strategic missile systems into both oceans. We did a study of more than a hundred possibilities of where we would base the Trident submarines. And for various reasons to make the problems more complex for the Soviets, to broaden their problem, it seemed we should have some in the Pacific. We finally settled on Bangor, Washington.

There was lots to do and lots to think about. I was sitting there in my office one day, and I said, "God damn it, I've never cut in Senator Jackson."* So I went over and apologized and told him that this was just happening, and there was going to be an announcement some day. And Senator Jackson didn't need extra business in his district to get elected or anything like that. As a matter of fact, by those times there was a certain animosity to nuclear with a little confusion in the public's mind between nuclear power and nuclear weapons. And so Jackson was not totally happy, but he sat there, and he said, "Dennis, are you certain that's the right decision?"

"Absolutely, sir."

"Fine," then he said. And that's the way Jackson was. From my interaction and experience, he was a totally sincere and dedicated professional guy that as far as I could see always did what he thought was right. He was a very good supporter of Admiral Rickover's.

Paul Stillwell: So what you're saying is that Bangor was not picked for political reasons.

Admiral Wilkinson: No, absolutely not. It was to open up a whole new ocean area in case sometime downstream the Soviet capability got better and better, that would still be tougher for them to ever track and surprise our strategic weapon systems deployed at sea. For the strength of the submarine nuclear weapons system over the strategic missiles in the silos in the Great Plains is that actually the Soviets knew exactly where everyone of those was. But once a submarine was at sea nobody knew where it was. I even took action so that we didn't know where it was except it was in a general area. So there was no way to make a surprise attack and destroy a large portion of our strike capability. For years and years and years and years we managed to keep more than 55% of our strategic

---

* Henry M. Jackson, a Democrat from the state of Washington, served in the House of Representatives from 1941 to 1953 and then in the Senate from 1953 until his death in 1983.

missiles at sea, location unknown. And when I say unknown, I mean even the operational commander ashore didn't know exactly where it was. He knew within a geographical area.

Paul Stillwell: Were there any political considerations in the choice of the Kings Bay site on the Atlantic?

Admiral Wilkinson: I didn't do that, but I was involved in a different decision. Remember each succeeding class, each succeeding weapon, Polaris, A-1, A-2, Poseidon, Trident, has longer range.*

Paul Stillwell: Which gave you more flexibility.

Admiral Wilkinson: Which gave you more area. In the beginning with the A-1 we needed to be closer and so our submarines, the first ones operated out of Holy Loch up off Norway and up in there, that area, so they could reach any target in Russia. And we had a base at Rota, Spain, and those submarines went into the Med and operated closer to the target because their range was limited. But as technology and development improved, we went from the A-1 to the A-2, we got a longer missile. And then we got a longer missile in Poseidon that would carry more warheads. And then we got a longer and bigger missile in the Trident. And so we could get back farther and farther from the target area. And the actual accuracy at target wasn't a function of the range of the shot. The latest ones are just as accurate on target as the first ones. It's just that they can shoot from farther way. For a limited time they're going straight up. They have a certain impact on them of a wind and the atmosphere, but then once they go out of the atmosphere it's a straight ballistic shot for thousands of miles with nothing affecting it.

---

* The first version of the submarine-launched Polaris ballistic missile, the A-1, was 28 feet long, 4 feet in diameter, and weighed about 30,000 pounds. It had a range of 1,200 nautical miles. The A-2 version was 31 feet long; 4 feet, 6 inches in diameter; and weighed about 30,000 pounds. It had a range of 1,725 nautical miles. The A-3 version was 32 feet long; 4 feet, 6 inches in diameter; and weighed about 35,000 pounds. It had a range of 2,880 nautical miles. The first version of the Trident missile, the C-4, was 34 feet long, 74 inches in diameter, and weighed about 65,000 pounds. It had a range of approximately 4,000 nautical miles.

And then they come down through the atmosphere for only a limited time. And those atmosphere times are the same whether it's gone 500 miles or 5,000 miles. So we're just as accurate—if not more so—with the longer-range missiles than we were in the beginning.

Back then we had to be closer, so we had bases in Holy Loch and Rota and there were some political considerations and payoff. You couldn't have a base in Rota without Spain getting something out if it. And finally their price became too large, and we no longer needed it, so I guess I had some involvement in the recognition that we didn't need Rota anymore.* And then we fell back to the United States and we had the base at Kings Bay. I wasn't as involved in the decision for the location at Kings Bay as I happened to have been at a different time in the decision for the location of the base at Bangor.

During that same time, of course, we were also looking at the design of the Trident submarines. What you really want is your strategic weapon to be survivable. We were authorized to have 656 missile tubes in our submarine strategic weapons system. Now, the absolutely safest way to do that would be to have 656 submarines, each with one missile tube, and the Soviets did have some missile submarines that only had one, two or three tubes, but that would be a lot of submarines and quite expensive. Or the cheapest way would be to have one great big submarine with 656 tubes, but that would be putting all your eggs in one basket and be hard to operate and whatnot.

On the Polaris/Poseidon submarines, 41 for freedom, we had 16 tubes each, but it was decided in the Trident to put more tubes in. We did lots of studies and plotted lots of curves, and we finally came out with 20 tubes as the optimum. But some way or other that got screwed up, and Secretary Laird got confused.† In talking to Congress he told them it was 24 tubes, and my people came back appalled with that information. And I said, "Hey, those curves are absolutely flat up there. It's 24." [Laughter] And that's the way we shifted from our studies of 20 to 24 tubes in the Trident submarine, and actually

---

* In January 1976, the negotiators initialed a draft treaty between Spain and the U.S.; it called for withdrawal of the Submarine Squadron 16 from Rota, Spain, by July 1979. The U.S. Congress ratified the treaty in June 1976. The submarine tender *Simon Lake* (AS-33) arrived at the new base at Kings Bay, Georgia, on 2 July 1979. Four days later, USS *James Monroe* (SSBN-622) entered Kings Bay and moored alongside the tender, and the new base was in operation.
† Melvin R. Laird served as Secretary of Defense from 22 January 1969 to 29 January 1973.

it wasn't a bad decision because we might not have been able to get that many hulls at 20 tubes. But it's interesting how some decisions are made.

Paul Stillwell: How much were you personally involved in testimony before Congress?

Admiral Wilkinson: I've done it, of course, but really not too much. Not like Admiral Rickover with his hundreds and hundreds and hundreds of hours. And, "Swiss education's better than ours." Four hundred pages it took. And I used to have people make snide comments about Admiral Rickover, and here he's testifying to something that is not what is his primary mission.

Paul Stillwell: What sorts of things did you testify on?

Admiral Wilkinson: Our submarine operations, the drug business, and support for a submarine program. But really not very much. Since I was at INPO later on I've also testified on some things related to the country's nuclear electric generating plants, but again not very much.

Paul Stillwell: Admiral Zumwalt essentially set up the surface and submarine barons at three-star level. The OP-05 had existed already, and he set up OP-02 and OP-03 as the fellow barons.* What were your relations with OP-03 and OP-05?

Admiral Wilkinson: We had reached the point where we were beginning to have a capability with our submarines to perhaps operate in company with carriers and support them, and we had good coordination with OP-05. I've even let them have a little bit of my money for a couple of projects, seriously, and that's about as friendly as you can get.

Paul Stillwell: What would be examples of those when you gave them some of your money?

---

* OP-05 – Deputy Chief of Naval Operations (Air Warfare).

Admiral Wilkinson: Some of the problem of communication links. And obviously we saw each other as human beings and friends, but we didn't have much of an interaction with 03.

Paul Stillwell: Well, I have a note here under the OP-02 period about surface effect ships. What kind of an issue was that?

Admiral Wilkinson: Being a senior officer in OpNav, Admiral Zumwalt had a group of the leading warlords and some others who reviewed all the proposals. Admiral Zumwalt was an advocate of a surface effect ship, which I'm talking about a large ship that would conceptually be able to operate at up to 60 knots and have great capability and could catch any submarine. It wasn't quite clear how they would detect them or how they would get out on deck and handle weapons with a wind of 60 knots. But the capability was going to have the 60 knots, and it wasn't quite clear how they would put a submarine detection device down into the water. But the concept was there to build a great big surface effect ship.

Frankly, I thought it was a bunch of crap, so I was against it and so stated verbally and in writing as I stated the submarine position for that review group on many things. Not that that's why, but in fact no such ship was ever built. It wouldn't really have been feasible. Just after I got out of the Navy, I was offered a consulting job by the company that was trying to get the contract to work on such a ship. There would be a triad of a submarine guy and a surface ship guy and a flier. The flier was Admiral Connolly, and the surface ship guy was Admiral Holmes, and the submarine guy was going to be Dennis Wilkinson.* We were offered a consultant contract of $1,000 dollars a day with a minimum of $5,000 a month, regardless of how much time you had to put in but more than five days, then it at $1,000 a day more.

I can remember telling them that, "Gee, I was pretty vehemently against that when I was in the Navy. I'd have a hard time changing for only $1,000 a day." So I didn't take that. I was offered a lot of jobs when I got out that I didn't take because my wife wanted to come back and live in San Diego, so we did.

---

* Vice Admiral Thomas F. Connolly, USN (Ret.); Admiral Ephraim P. Holmes, USN (Ret.).

Paul Stillwell: I have a note here also about home-porting in Australia. What did that involve?

Admiral Wilkinson: That was another concept that was whipped up. On that same review group we put it pretty strong being against and why. And again that's another item that didn't happen.

Paul Stillwell: What was the basis for the objection?

Admiral Wilkinson: Some of the historical problems we had in other countries and the fact that we didn't have support from the Australians for it and some minor things like that.

Paul Stillwell: What were the perceived benefits from doing that?

Admiral Wilkinson: I don't know. [Laughter]

Paul Stillwell: Anything else to wrap up your time in OP-02? You really were at the pinnacle of the submarine warfare hierarchy.

Admiral Wilkinson: Well, the other thing. OP-02 was my last job in the Navy, and I finally voluntarily retired the first of September 1974. I wasn't asked to retire from the Navy. My separation from the Navy was at my own initiative, not at the Navy's. My wife was happy to see me retire and was eager to go live where she'd grown up in San Diego, and that was one of the contributing factors to getting out when I did.

I like to do my share, and after I retired there was not a damn thing that I could do as well as Janice. I couldn't make a bed. I couldn't cook. I ended up washing the dishes, and I'd wake up every morning at 6:00 o'clock feeling guilty. One morning my wife leaned over and said I ought to go back to work. And I always sort of wondered if I could make it on the outside. So I went back to work, and I think the first year and a half I made more money than I had made in the 34 years in the Navy. And now I have a really nice Navy retirement, thanks to having been retired a long time and the increases for cost of living. Mendel Rivers, bless his heart, having put the retired military on the cost-of-living basis that is maintained to this day.* Certainly my overall retirement now is more than twice of my Navy retirement. So I've had just as much fun and just as many nice things to do since I retired from the Navy as I had while I was in it. And, truthfully, the *Nautilus* was a great big job, and the *Long Beach* was a great big job, but the INPO was even a bigger job. So I agonized about getting out of the Navy at the time, but afterwards I was pleased that I had, because you only have one life to live, and it was fun to try something else.

Paul Stillwell: What was that first job you took off when you went back to work?

Admiral Wilkinson: I didn't take a job right away. It took a while for that worry to get to me. At first we made the trip to Hong Kong and the Greek Island cruise and the fjord trip, and we spent six or seven months in Mexico and Central America. Back in those days it was safe to travel down there, and there isn't anyplace I haven't been in Mexico and all the South American countries. And I owned a penthouse in Costa Rica, in San Juan, but the kids won't go that far. Eventually I went back to work, and I took a job as a vice president for a technical company called Data Design Laboratories. We made printed circuit boards and things like that. So I was fortunate enough for things to be successful and make money.

Paul Stillwell: What specific things were your duties in that job?

Admiral Wilkinson: I was the executive vice president, and I worried about everything. There's a difference between a vice president and the executive vice president. The executive vice president for the president is sort of running things, and that was what I did.

---

* L. Mendel Rivers, Democrat from South Carolina, served in the U.S. House of Representatives from 1940 until he died in 1970. He was chairman of the House Armed Services Committee from 1965 till his death.

At some time after I retired in 1974, the Navy's oceanographer asked me to do a study on what R&D, research and development, should be done in the Arctic Ocean. I had eight members on a committee, of which I was chairman, to help me do that, and I think all eight of them were members of the National Academy of Science. I made quite a few trips up to the North Slope and North Cape and the Arctic, and we did a lot of study and came out with a document some 80 pages of findings and recommendations of what ought to be done in the Arctic. I was awarded a Meritorious Civilian Citizen award for that.

I really had eight brilliant people, all of whom belonged to the National Academy of Science. But when it came time to write a report of our work I had a hell of a time getting anything out of them. Finally I got mad, and I said, "I will write it, and I'll give you a draft." So I just wrote the whole report, some 80 typewritten pages, and distributed it to the eight of them. Then I got lots of comments. [Laughter] They didn't like this, and they didn't like that, and they didn't agree with this. So I incorporated all those comments, and I had another draft and sent it out. Again I got a bunch of comments, and that sort of annoyed me. So I wrote the third draft, and I said, "This is it. If there's anybody that doesn't agree with this, that's simple. We just won't put your name on the report." And, you know, those scientists really it's publish or perish, I guess. Suddenly everybody agreed totally with everything that was written, and so the report was issued with everybody's name on it. That was in about 1977. [Laughter]

Paul Stillwell: When did you get involved with INPO?

Admiral Wilkinson: When was it the accident happened at Three-Mile Island.*

Paul Stillwell: That was in 1979.

Admiral Wilkinson: In March of '79. It really concerned the nuclear utilities in our country, and they had been complying with government regulation from the Nuclear

---

* On 28 March 1979, at the Three Mile Island commercial nuclear power plant near Middletown, Pennsylvania, a partial meltdown occurred and released radioactive material.

Regulatory Commission. They had the mistaken idea that if they did everything the government told them to do that they would be safe. And that wasn't really so, because the government didn't get into some of the things that are important, like personnel selection and training and education and training and qualification and continuing requalification of personnel and the exchange of information from plant to plant.

The plant operators decided they should set up an independent—that's a key word—organization to set the proper standards for running our country's nuclear plants. It should also check on them to see that each and every one of them—there were 60 companies and 100 reactors—were in fact doing what they should. So in about June of '79 some headhunters came and talked to me, and I gave them names of a couple of good people. They came back in August, and I gave them two or three more names, and I guess none of those people appealed to them, or they didn't appeal to the people. But they had some 100 and some odd names on a list. It was interesting. They had Dennis Wilkinson and E. P. Wilkinson on their list.

But Bill Lee, the head of Duke, who was a pistol, was one of those.[*] He was probably the dominant company guy in that hierarchy, and he had gone and kept Three-Mile Island from being any worse a casualty than it was. He was determined that something should be done to minimize the probability of that happening again. An awful lot of these names they had were people that had been in the Navy's nuclear program, so he would call and check them with Admiral Rickover, and Rickover was a pretty critical guy. He would say, "He's no damn good. He's no damn good. He's no damn good."

Lee then asked him about Dennis Wilkinson, and Rickover said, "He's too good for you. He wouldn't do it." And that was like a challenge to Bill Lee, and there wasn't anybody that was a better man or a better salesman. Bill Lee could truly sell refrigerators to the Eskimos, so he came out to California and saw me, and he talked me into doing this thing. So I bowed out of Data Design Laboratory, where I was the executive vice president, and we were doing a lot of things. During the time I was the executive vice president of Data Design our sales had quadrupled, and our earnings per share had more than doubled, and our stock had gone from three to 20, and I had stock options on 15,000

---

[*] William S. Lee, president & chief executive officer of Duke Power Company, Charlotte, North Carolina.

shares, and things were going well. So it was quite a little decision to give all that up and go off and maybe start this new organization.

But it sounded like fun and a good thing to do, and Bill Lee was a good salesman. It wasn't for the money. I went to INPO without even any discussion of money. I just agreed to do it. And I agreed to be there by the first of February. Now, there was a lot of stuff to get finished at Data Design, of which I was the guy that was really knowledgeable. So I finished all those on the 30th of January and came home here. Then I caught the flight out the 31st of January and arrived at INPO at 5:00 in the morning, like I said I would, on the first of February. And it was cold. It was about 12, but with the wind chill factor it was such and such below zero, and I wondered, "What the hell am I doing here?" [Laughter]

Paul Stillwell: Why was it located in Atlanta?

Admiral Wilkinson: The utility industry did a study and made that decision. There were a lot more nuclear electric generating plants in the Eastern United States than there were out here. Out here there were just a very few. And it was a good travel hub. We had teams going and inspecting all these plants, and it was a good place to catch airplanes and travel. The housing was more reasonable, and there was good university support. It was a good decision. It was a good location.

When I went out to INPO they were all in one room, and they had only one typewriter, and there was even something wrong with it. It got so it would only type caps. They had five people loaned from industry, and some of them weren't all that good. I had a secretary, and that was it. I didn't even have enough people to properly interview job candidates. So I had a dickens of a time manning the place to start with. I'd been promised the resources, money and people. There was no question about the money being available, but the people were really tough. And I used to talk to the utilities. We made a deal where they loaned us a man to stay a year and go back, and I'd say, "Don't pull a Castro on me. I don't want him unless he's a good man." But that was something we'd have to struggle at, and we worked hard at that.

My money lasted me even better than my resources because I couldn't man at the rate that I wanted, so I was always undermanned. [Laughter] Your money's a large part of your budget. Eventually we built up to the 400 people we needed, and I interviewed and chose every one of them.

I jump shift in time to when I was the operations officer at Pittsburgh area office of the Atomic Energy Commission back in early '49, when Westinghouse was starting the Bettis plant. I helped pick and choose some of the people, and you'd interview and talk to this guy and he'd say, "Well, what are you going to do?"

"Glad you asked. We're going to develop a nuclear propulsion plant to drive a submarine."

"Yeah, what are you going to do when you've finished that?" [Laughter] Well, that actually happened to me. It wasn't that easy. Well, I was interviewing people at INPO, and the question was, "Yeah, this is an organization set up by the plant operators. Why should I come to your organization? How do I know this is going to survive?"

All I could say was, "Well, friend, we didn't come to lose." And that was the way I felt: "We didn't come down here not to succeed." INPO was a truly great success. I mean, we finally got up to our 400 people. We ran a budget of about $40 million a year. We saved the nuclear utility industry billions.

Paul Stillwell: How did you do that?

Admiral Wilkinson: Well, I'd have to pull out the charts and show you, but things involving nuclear fuel make nuclear waste. It has to be properly disposed of, and there's high-level waste, very highly radioactive waste, the actual nuclear core that's run for a few thousand hours and really is tremendously radioactive. That's never been taken care of. All that highly radioactive waste is in the swimming pools under the reactors to this day, because the government has never done what it should and provided a place to put the radioactive material.

But there's also a lot of low-level radioactive waste in America, and the majority of it does not come from nuclear electric generating plants. It comes from hospitals and radiation of food and X-rays and dental offices and whatnot. All that stuff just can't be thrown in the street. It's got to go somewhere, and, let me tell you, it costs a lot to send it there. We made heroic efforts to have actions taken by the utilities that decreased the amount of radioactive waste, which we managed to get decreased by over a factor of 10. There was less than a tenth after INPO was established than there was before. And just the expense paid out of pocket in money of storing that would have been more than the money that was spent on INPO, for example. But that's insignificant compared to the money we saved them. Another thing that you can't quite equate with money is the decrease in radioactive exposure of their workers. Several factors of four or five decrease in that, in truth, probably saved them money in not having as many suits later on. The fact that they had accurate records that could stand up that they could show.

We could say, "The records would show that this guy reported this day. He's worked at the company this time. This is the exact amount of this kind of radiation and that kind of radiation that he had in all the years that he's worked for us. And, look, it's only a quarter of what the governments had established as regulated tolerances." We had the accurate record, the bringing it down to quarter. The first year I was there, one of my guys ran a utility that had a certain amount of people that had overexposed past the government standard. And I got my guy in, and my guy told me about it. I said, "I don't want to hurt your feelings, but I haven't got you here to keep score. [Laughter] I can hire some accountants that could add those numbers up. I hired you to see that it never happened. [Laughter] In this nuclear utility industry I don't want anybody to ever be overexposed again. And, by God, if I have to have a report from every plant in the country every day, we're not going to ever have anybody overexposed."

Well, there's never been a guy overexposed since, and we don't have to get a report every day, but somewhere their attitudes got changed, and the exposure of people has gone down by a factor certainly of five. I can't put dollars to that, but you could make some estimates on dollars on suits. The big thing was that the percentage of time that they stayed on the line, the amount of power that they generated was in the low 50% of what it would be if was running at 100% power for the whole year.

At the end of the year, because of problems and staying on line and whatnot, as an average across all the 100 reactors in America, they were generating about 53% of that. Now they're averaging 78%. If you will, 53 to 78, that's the same as 25 1,000-megawatt reactors. At the cost of electricity, that's a lot of money. And we didn't do it. The plants did it. We were just the agent to make sure they did. But the amount of money that represents is what? A third of their revenue for all their plants. So if you go to talk to knowledgeable utility executives, CEOs of this or that company, there's a great respect for INPO. Then INPO led on to WANO, the world association, and now all countries in the world belong.* And it was a good tour. Now it's well over 90%.

Paul Stillwell: Well, I'm guessing the impetus for this was a perception that Three-Mile Island was not an isolated situation. It was a symptom of a widespread problem.

Admiral Wilkinson: It was, and if you look back in time, it was not just Three-Mile Island, but there was this casualty with that reactor, there was this casualty with that. If you plotted them, how many reactors, how many hours they were running, statistically you would say there was a high probability that there'll be another one in another 19 months or something. That was March '79, and there hasn't been one since. [Laughter] Hey, a lot of things changed. INPO didn't do that. The utilities did that. The government, the Nuclear Regulatory Commission changed. And INPO had a little impact on the NRC changing.

It wasn't just chance that Lando Zech and Ken Carr became chairmen of the Nuclear Regulatory Commission.† I picked them and sold them on the willingness to do it man for man and helped it happen. And they made a big difference. The Nuclear Regulatory Commission is not like it used to be, and the utilities aren't like they used to be. INPO didn't do that, but we were the agents. We were sort of the conscience. And I always had tremendous support from my board of directors, the 11 CEOs of utilities.

If I were to go over and pick up that phone today and call one of those companies and say, "This is Dennis Wilkinson. I'd like to speak to the CEO," he'd be on the phone in a couple of minutes if he was there. I'm talking companies that have revenues of four or five billion dollars a year. It's been a long, long time, but mine is still a respected

---
* WANO – World Association of Nuclear Operators.
† Vice Admiral Lando W. Zech, Jr., USN (Ret.), was chairman of the Nuclear Regulatory Commission from 1986 to 1989; Vice Admiral Kenneth M. Carr, USN (Ret.), served as chairman, 1989-91.

name in the nuclear utility industry. I got the Henry DeWolf Smyth Nuclear Statesman Award. Hey, that was only two or three years ago.*

I jump aside. It was a lot of fun to me when they made the *Nautilus* a national historic monument. And then a few years later it was fun to me when the submarine force named a building after me in New London. And I'm president emeritus of INPO, and there's a room of memorabilia about me at INPO. And I'm not even dead yet. [Laughter] So a lot of the fun and accomplishment, if you will, in my life has been after I got out of the Navy. Not while I was in it. And that accomplishment includes my own financial well-being. I'm a little better off financially than I was when I was in the Navy. I had four kids in college at one time, and they were all bright kids and they had scholarships. I used to help support it moonlighting playing poker. And I'm going to play poker tomorrow night, but it's just for fun. I don't really need the money anymore.

I really agonized at getting out of the Navy when I did, because it was an irreversible decision. But I heard my wife talking. I'd said, and that's an exact figure, I was out of Atlanta 165 days the first year. I got Janice out of my hair by sending her off on a seven-week trip to Nepal and Tiger Top. I used to go work in the morning at about 6:30 and come home at 6:00 at night with a pile of paperwork till 11:00, and Janice would say, "What are we trying to prove?" And she was right. But once I got involved and emotionally involved, it was an enormous job and total commitment. And finally it was, by God, I'll do anything, anything to win.

So I guess really the toughest period in my life was the starting of INPO. That was a harder job and a bigger job than the *Nautilus* or the *Long Beach*. I was dealing all the time with CEOs of over 60 companies, and I decided I needed to have a workshop with the CEOs. So I started the first year a CEO workshop where they came to Atlanta for two or three days, and we went through all the problems with them. And I had Pat Haggerty from Texas Instruments, who had been on the Kemeny Commission, come and talk to them and, God, he was good and just as comfortable as an old shoe.

I called up Shapiro, the head of DuPont, and said, "Hey, I'm down here, and I've got a workshop with the CEOs of 60 utilities. And there isn't anybody that is as safety

---

* Admiral Wilkinson received the award in 1994.

conscious as DuPont. I'd like to have you come down here and preach a little safety."*

I was talking big companies, and that impressed even the head of DuPont a little bit. He said, "Well, yes, I'd be happy to do that."

I said, "Well, can I give you any help? Can I get you any information or can we meet you and provide transportation when you arrive?"

He said, "Oh, my people will take care of all of that." I mean, it shows you how people think differently, and I was young and naïve in some of those things. But then the accident happened at Bhopal in a plant.

Paul Stillwell: Union Carbide.

Admiral Wilkinson: Union Carbide, yes.† DuPont, as a leader in the industry, decided that something needed to be done. So they called me up and asked if they could have an interview for three of their vice presidents to come down and talk to me and maybe learn some lessons from what we had done in INPO in the nuclear utility industry that would be applicable to the chemical industry as a follow-up to the action at Bhopal. I told them, "Well, yes, I'd be happy to do that." I looked at my calendar, and I gave them a date and time about three weeks hence. They wanted to do it faster than that, and they said, "Well, how about a Saturday or a Sunday?"

I said, "Hey, friends, that time I'm giving you is the first time that I'm free, including Saturdays and Sundays."

They said, "Is there anything? What are you doing?"

Well, then I told them, "I'm doing this. I'm going to fly in an airplane."

"Hah," they said. "You have to fly from such and such to such and such. Well then, why don't we just send a plane to pick you up and take you from there to there, and our executives can meet with you en route?"

I said, "Well, that would be fine and we can do it day after tomorrow." And that's the way it was. You've got to think different sometime. We never put it on the tape, but

---

* Irving S. Shapiro was chairman and chief executive officer of DuPont Corporation from 1973 to 1981.
† In December 1984, a Union Carbide chemical plant in Bhopal, India, leaked 27 tons of the deadly gas methyl isocyanate. Safety systems designed to contain such a leak were not operating.

it was just like when I had one of my meetings with Vice President Bush. Things can be done.

Paul Stillwell: What was the case for your meeting with Vice President Bush?

Admiral Wilkinson: The background is that I had had the good fortune to be a member of a highly technical group that met quarterly with the CIA. And when Bush was head of the CIA I met with him every three months.[*] And I had done some of the talking at those meetings, which would last about six hours every three months. So I guess he had remembered my name. So I mentioned earlier one of the things that we needed to do was improve the Nuclear Regulatory Commission. Among the important things were the commissioners, and so I went down and saw Mr. Bush three times about getting good persons chosen as the commissioners. And the first time it happened and the second time it happened. The third time he said, "Hey, you've already had two successes."

I said, "Sir, I'd like to bat three for three." [Laughter] And so we picked one more commissioner and I guess it was an interaction with me and Mr. Bush that caused the Nuclear Regulatory Commission to improve. And first I had to talk them into being willing. It was the interaction between me and Mr. Bush that caused Lando Zech to be a commissioner and chairman of the Nuclear Regulatory Commission and Ken Carr to be a commissioner and chairman of the Nuclear Regulatory Commission and another gentlemen also I won't mention but who is still on it.

Paul Stillwell: What was the relationship between INPO on one hand and the Nuclear Regulatory Commission on the other?

Admiral Wilkinson: We fully cooperated with them and made available the information from ourselves. We did not try to tell them what they ought to do. We didn't try to be a public spokesman or advocate for nuclear power. Later I caused to be formed some other organizations whose job was to deal with NRC. INPO wanted to maintain itself as above

---

[*] George H. W. Bush served as Director of Central Intelligence/Director of the Central Intelligence Agency from 30 January 1976 to 20 January 1977. He was later Vice President of the United States from January 1981 to January 1989 and President from January 1989 to January 1993.

reproach as the outfit that called it like they saw it, independent, just for the safety reasons. INPO has quite a good reputation.

Paul Stillwell: Were those 165 days you spent on the road mostly doing nuclear plant inspections?

Admiral Wilkinson: Yes.

Paul Stillwell: What would be a typical inspection? What did you look for? What did you find?

Admiral Wilkinson: I got a team of as expert people as I could. I augmented that team with peers from the industry, chosen people of qualification in similar plants, including a peer executive from another company. We went with a team and looked at the multitude of things, and I'd have to show you a whole book. They inspected for two weeks, and obviously I didn't go for two weeks, but I came at the end and went through everything. Certainly I was at the part of the inspection at the end of every one of the plants on the first round, and I was the spokesman to talk with the CEO afterwards.

It would take longer than we've got to put on that tape for me to tell you everything they looked at, but they looked at essentially everything. And they got better at it. I think I alluded to how tough it was in the beginning to get personnel to work for us doing that. We used loan people from the industry and from other plants; they'd come for a year or two years and then go back home. Later on we had reverse loans where we loaned an INPO man to go help a company out. After a while I was advised by the headhunters that if a man had a tour at INPO it raised his salary an average of $9,000 a year. So it's no longer difficult for INPO to get people. INPO now can pick and choose.

Paul Stillwell: Did you have a procedure in place to deal with discrepancies and get them corrected?

Admiral Wilkinson: Yes, we did. We had a system that we listed all discrepancies. And I'm talking sometimes 50, 100 pages worth, typewritten pages' worth.

Paul Stillwell: For one plant?

Admiral Wilkinson: For one plant, for one inspection. And, incidentally, I thoroughly briefed the committees of Congress how we were doing this, and they said, "Gee, that sounds great." I really had congressional concurrence on what I was doing. One of the things we did was after we'd written our first draft report of all the discrepancies was get a commitment from the utility as to what they were going to do about that item and how and when. In the report the discrepancy and the commitment to resolution were all typed in the final report. So no report that was ever issued showed something that it didn't also show a plan and a commitment to do something about it. Then INPO would go back and follow up to see that that commitment was met. Over time it made a considerable difference. Also as time went by we got more experienced and better at what we were doing in finding all the things that were wrong.

In the first year or two I inspected all the nuclear plants in the United States. An awful lot of those plants had personnel in them who had been enlisted men in the nuclear Navy and had finished their time and got out of the Navy and got that kind of job on the outside in a nuclear plant. And when I made the first inspection of every utility plant, every civilian power reactor for generation of electricity program, there was only one plant that I went to that I didn't see somebody I knew. That was a TVA plant where they had grown their own people.* But every other one I saw some guy that I had known in the Navy. They would come up and say, "Captain," or "Admiral, we know we weren't doing it right." Let me tell you, it didn't hurt in squaring those plants away. I might go into an electric generating plant, and the man on watch would be in an old dirty sweatshirt and feet up on the table and sending out for pizza and saying, "Kelly's Pool Hall," on the phone. Hey, that was not the way to run the thing, and they knew it. When I went in those plants and saw something like that, those guys were embarrassed. They knew they shouldn't be acting like that.

---

* TVA – Tennessee Valley Authority.

I got people like Claude Cross and Ken Strom and others who back in their Navy tours had been the senior members of the Navy's Nuclear Power Examining Board. And I had a procedure that, in addition to a lot of other qualifications, I didn't count a guy as qualified to be a member of a team until he had made two trips. So I was off on a trip with Claude, and I said, "Claude, how many trips have you made?" I wanted to find out whether he'd made his two trips yet or not. He said, "A hundred and thirty-five." [Laughter] He was referring to the 135 inspections he had done in the Navy when he was senior member of the examining board. Claude retired the other day, and we laughed about the 158 trips he's done now. Claude was the one we picked to go where it was hardest, when there was a real problem. INPO has done a good job, but they were only the agent, so partly it was because of the supreme desire of the utility industry to do something in support and the performance of the people that I was fortunate enough to get at INPO. I'm telling you they were really great.

Certainly over the years we've been, as I said, more than worth the money to the utility industry than they spent. It was a unique industrial organization in that INPO has 100% membership. There isn't anybody that runs a nuclear power electric generating plant in the United States that doesn't belong to INPO. I can remember speaking to the CEOs and saying, "Gentlemen, it's not enough for us to identify the deficiencies. You have to fix them. If for some reason you've got other commitments, other ways you've got to spend your money, some reason you don't have the people—if there's some reason you can't fix these discrepancies I understand that. But then we'll give you your money back, and you just can't belong to our organization."

Well, that was tongue-in-cheek a little bit, because there wasn't any utility that could afford not to belong to our organization, because they had two billion dollars' worth of insurance that had the provision that the insurance consortium was provided a copy of our report with actions of the company to straighten it out. They'd have lost that two billion dollars' worth of coverage. And if we had of thrown somebody out of our organization, the Nuclear Regulatory Commission would have been, "Oh, why, why, why?" and they would have been all over them. So there wasn't anybody that could afford not to belong. But it was a unique industrial organization.

Paul Stillwell: You've shown me a resolution that was issued on February 1, 1980.

Admiral Wilkinson: I don't know who they are, but those are the heads of those companies, see. And so I really had great support. And here is something. I picked Zach Pate to be my deputy to relieve me, and here's the kind of things—see the little words he's penned on it. There are a lot of different measurements, but you see how things improved over time—this is ten years' worth. One concern was the lack of availability when a plant doesn't happen to be there, but some of those improvements also represent a lot of money. I mean money value and sometimes actual money spent. When I first went to the utility industry I was horrified when I went to those plants. I thought, "My God!" I come from the Navy where we knew what we were doing. I've got to write a book here telling these people how to run a nuclear plant." Then I laughed at myself and said, "You know, if God had helped me to write the perfect book, it wouldn't do any good if they wouldn't use it."

So we backed into it. We had guidelines and best practices. We didn't even call them best practices but good practices and so on. And we finally covered it all. Now if you go around and talk about something with a utility they say, "Oh, gee, we're doing the INPO guideline on that." And they know that's okay.

I made a speech to the CEOs of the nuclear utility industry. It addressed a major weakness. The reason they couldn't live up to Bill Lee's commitment was that they didn't have an adequate number of trained people to run the plants. And so it was a major weakness, and it was important. So when Lee and my board of directors didn't come through with the people they said they would, I got mad. One day told my board, "Hey, if you don't give me these people like you said, I'm going to get the job done anyway. I'll go elsewhere."

They said, "Gee, why don't you do that, Dennis?"

So I picked up the phone that day and I called eight retired Navy captains. I said, "Hey, I'm down here with this damned job and I'm in trouble. I need help." Eight of them said they'd come down and help me, and that day we had eight crackerjack retired Navy captains, some more crackerjack than others but all certainly experienced, and on their way. They all came down, and we paid them $41,000 a year, which wasn't very much. And we laid out the methodology. Not exactly the goals and objectives, because I guess some of those were in my mind and head. But certainly we laid out the mechanical procedure for getting that place started. I could have done what any one of the eight did, but there was no way I could do what all of the eight guys did.

Also, we founded the National Academy of Nuclear Training, and I made each and every utility put people in the training pipeline. Because there's a hidden threat in there. We changed the industry in standards for education, training, qualifying, occasionally continuing re-qualification of your personnel. Not just the licensed operators but all the people involved in the operation, maintenance and support of your plants. We changed that and management. And then we made the executives take courses, and we changed the nuclear utility industry. And part of this I was thinking, there's a little bit of exaggeration and poetic license of our own perspective, but, Paul, not very much.

It's just like that old thing, "And when she began to peel, everything that she had was absolutely real." Mostly it's fairly close to what I tell you. As a matter of fact, sometimes I've toned it down a little because it sounds ugly.

Paul Stillwell: You've shown me this speech you made on the first anniversary of taking over as president and CEO of INPO. The major thrust of it is that there were not enough people in the nuclear industry who were properly trained and qualified. And so rather than increase the supply, they were hiring away from each other, which didn't solve the problem.

Admiral Wilkinson: No. Steal from Peter to pay Paul. I mean ridiculous. The whole utility industry had to operate safely because a TMI impacted them all. That cost the utility industry billions and billions and billions of dollars, and it shouldn't have happened. I say again that INPO didn't do all those things. But we were the agent. I used to give the industry full credit, and the only thing I would ever say about INPO was, "Well, it happened at about our time," [Laughter] which was true. Truthfully, Paul, I've had a lot of excitement in my life, but really the one biggest thing I ever did was INPO. Oh, the *Nautilus* was a part of the thing that made the Navy change, but INPO was involved in the changing of the nuclear electric generating plants in the United States and had some impact worldwide. And even though nuclear is in a little bit of disrepute they still form 20% of the electricity in the United States. There's nothing that complies, that matches as closely with the standard of living of a country as its utilization of electricity. It tracks all just whiz-bang. Not nuclear electric. That's electricity.

Paul Stillwell: How long did you stay with INPO?

Admiral Wilkinson: A little over four years. When I asked Bill Lee what he wanted to get accomplished and he told me, I said, "Hey, that would take five years." In my heart I set myself a goal of getting it done in three. I got a pretty good cut at it in four years, and my wife was really eager to get me home some more and get back to San Diego where we live so we turned over to a—always pick a guy better than you to replace you. Then he won't let things get screwed up. I picked a much better man than myself, Zack Pate, as my replacement at INPO and he has done a fantastic job. And a little bit of that's reflected on me.

Paul Stillwell: What have you done in the years since 1984?

Admiral Wilkinson: It was ironic in a way. I had quite a good reputation in the nuclear utility industry, and here I was ready to retire again. I've retired about three times and flunked retirement every time. I was ready to retire again, but never, never had I been so marketable. Any time a utility got in real trouble, like when the plants were shut down at Peach Bottom, they would come to me for help.* I've received as much as $4,000 for a day of consultant work. And I earned it. So I have from time to time provided some support to some of the nuclear utilities, always one that was in trouble. The danger is you get emotionally involved, and then you can't back away until it gets squared away.

I've also been on the board of directors of quite a few companies. One of the largest, I was on the board of directors of Commonwealth Edison Company, the big

---

* The Peach Bottom nuclear plant serves Philadelphia Electric. It was one of the first in the nation to become operational.

utility in Chicago, with 12 nuclear reactors and other generating plants. I'm old now and can't hear very well, and I've had this big bad problem with my knee for the last couple of years that I'm just getting taken care of. But I'm still on the board of directors of a couple of companies. I'm the chairman of the board of MDM Services, and we're quite successful. Our job's to make money, and we make money. And so although I'm almost retired now at 79, I still am on those two boards.

It's hard for me to explain how much mail and correspondence I get related to the nuclear business, related to the Navy, and so on. Jumping back, one of the most fun things that happened to me on the *Nautilus* was I got to go back in 1956 and give the commencement address at San Diego State. And having graduated there in '38, that was a lot of fun. I guess it was when I was SubLant, the mayor of Long Beach had an E. P. Wilkinson Day. I was having lunch with the mayor and the city council and all formal in uniform, and during the conversation I said I was born in Long Beach, which I guess not every one of them knew. You know, Paul, that they had a copy of my birth certificate there in less than 20 minutes. And when we looked at the birth certificate, back in 1918, I was not born in a hospital. I was born at home. There on the certificate was the address. Afterwards, as we finished lunch, the mayor asked me if I'd like to see where I was born, and I said, "Yeah, I certainly would." So they wheeled out the great big limousine, and they took me over to the address where I was born, and now it was a Safeway Store. [Laughter] What a letdown! [Laughter]

Also on that trip I went over and gave a speech to a group of people on the *Queen Mary*.[*] There were, oh, 300 or 400 people there I was talking to. And I was given support by a local military guy who was a Marine, a one-star brigadier general. He was about 6-foot-3 and slim and really a military alert-looking guy. So I got up and started my speech, and I said, "I'm in the Navy and I'm glad of that. And I'm a submariner and I'm glad of that. But if I hadn't been that, I'd have liked to have been a Marine." And then without thinking I ran my hands up both sides of my head, and I said, "And my hair's still short enough." [Laughter] This was in the days of the long-haired Navy, and,

---

[*] RMS *Queen Mary* was a large British passenger liner converted for use as a fast troop transport in World War II. She was built by John Brown & Company, Clydebank, Scotland; her first voyage as a commercial ship was in August 1936. In the early 1970s she became a museum and tourist attraction in Long Beach.

Paul, I got a much bigger hand for that comment than I got for my whole damned speech. [Laughter] That's it.

Paul Stillwell: Well, I've got just a few more questions. How would you assess Admiral Rickover's overall contribution to the Navy and to the nation as a whole?

Admiral Wilkinson: Some of the things that were done you couldn't do today in the same time. Because of the nature of things, I'm sure that by now there would be nuclear electric generating plants. And I'm sure that by now there would be nuclear-propelled ships. But there wouldn't have been at the time there was. And it wouldn't have been done as well as it was done unless you had somebody like Rickover doing it. There wasn't anybody else like Rickover. So he made it happen sooner.

There was a time when our country was dominant. We had nuclear weapons, and nobody else did. Then you look forward in history, and there was a time when the Soviets had the strength and the nuclear that they did that our country actually was at risk. It was the real availability to our country of our survivable strategic weapons system that for years and years and years must oppose the threat that kept the Soviets in line. And it was the superiority of our submarines overall, which was really due to Admiral Rickover making our boats silent, that gave us the superiority over the Soviet submarines.

Rickover built the first commercial nuclear plant at Shippingport.* We wouldn't have had nuclear electric generating plants as soon as we did if it wasn't for Rickover. If it wasn't for me, coming out of the Rickover program, they wouldn't have been as safe as they were as soon as they were. [Laughter] I was the first operator to go to the Navy's nuclear power program. Rickover and a group of his officers interviewed me, so really I was the first one ever interviewed for that program. And I wasn't trying to sell myself. What did some damn EDO captain mean to me in those days? It didn't mean a damn thing to me. I wasn't even sure I was going to stay in the Navy. I'd only stayed in the

---

* The nation's first large-scale nuclear power plant opened in 1957 at Shippingport, Pennsylvania, about 30 miles northwest of Pittsburgh.

Navy if I had something I enjoyed doing in those days. And so I wasn't trying to sell myself to be chosen to go into the nuclear thing.

I grabbed one of the officers. It happened to be Lou Roddis, who was a pretty fantastic guy. He was first in his class at the trade school, '39, and '39 was a stellar class. And he at that time had come out with a record that was better than anybody they'd ever had before. I got him aside and said, "Hey, tell me about this guy." I was asking about Rickover, because he threw his weight around.

Lou said, "Well, there's a part that's good, and there's a part that's bad, and there's a part you wouldn't believe." You know, in all the years I never heard a better description of Admiral Rickover than that. But the good part accomplished some amazing things. Rickover didn't really give much credit for people's opinions other than his own, and once he decided to do anything he would do anything to have his way. I've had him put pressure on me six ways from the Jack. I've had him sit there and have tears streaming down his face. And he recognized I'm an honorable man. If I somewhere along that said, "I'll do that," he turned off just like that, on to the next problem.

Paul Stillwell: Turned off the tears?

Admiral Wilkinson: Yes, turned off the tears instantly. It's just on to the next problem. "I've got a commitment there from Dennis, and so I know it'll happen." So I had to be very careful giving my commitments in dealing with Admiral Rickover, because I do feel that. A commitment is a commitment and, by God, it's going to happen. And so I don't make all my commitments easily.

Paul Stillwell: Was he ever abusive to you?

Admiral Wilkinson: No. No. No, he really wasn't. I could show you also quite a few very nice letters in the other room, and not many people have Admiral Rickover's signature. I'll bet you won't find another skipper with a very friendly nice letter from Admiral Rickover inviting him to stay at his home. And I have three or four hands full of those letters in there. When Rickover came to Pittsburgh he stayed at our house and slept in one of the kid's bunks.

He picked on me. He told me time and time again I was young and immature and didn't know what I was doing. But that's not abusive. That's why I hesitated to answer you. He told me I didn't know what I was talking about, and he said I didn't play poker with really important people, which by the way isn't true. He was wrong there. But he wasn't ever abusive, and he was really nice as hell to my wife, and that meant a lot to me. My wife sometimes heard us on the phone. I used to get a call from him every night at Pittsburgh, and like I say, sometimes you've got to hold up your own. And Janice would say afterwards, "Dennis, why are you speaking so tough to that nice old man?" [Laughter]

I'd say, "Honey, you don't understand." [Laughter] But my wife loved Admiral Rickover. He was really always nice to her, and when our son Rodney had a lymphoma above his eye, Rickover gave her a lot of advice on not getting nuclear radiation there and whatnot. He worried about my wife. He worried about our kids. I had said sometimes that it didn't matter with Admiral Rickover. You could have 20 years of stellar performance for him, and that didn't mean a damn thing. It was what about this item. But that isn't completely true. After all those years there isn't any doubt Rickover was on my side.

It may not mean much to you but when I got the George Westinghouse Gold Medal from the American Society of Mechanical Engineers in 1983—and that's a prestigious thing in the United States—I discovered later that there was a glowing letter of endorsement from Admiral Rickover, who was far behind me. He wasn't in the Navy anymore and things like that. In describing Admiral Rickover I don't want to use the word "friend," because he wasn't a friend. But after all those years together he was on my side. Push came to shove he was on my side. Let me say, on the other hand, that when push came to shove, by God, I was on his side too. [Laughter]

Paul Stillwell: Well, he recognized that you had done a lot for him too.

Admiral Wilkinson: Well, I don't know. He knew that I had supported the nuclear program. He wouldn't have put in the words you just did, done a lot for him. I had supported the nuclear program. That was for him, I mean if you get the difference of that nuance.

Paul Stillwell: Well, you had supported the program, and you had also contributed a great deal to its success.

Admiral Wilkinson: Yes, that's what I mean. It's not what you try to do. It's how you make out that counts.

Paul Stillwell: We've been talking a lot about the past. If I can indulge your patience, I have a letter from Captain Jim Hay of the Naval Submarine League, and he asked me if I'd pose a few questions to you about the future.* One is, considering the history of nuclear submarine development, use and influence over the past 40 years and the current Navy emphasis on littoral warfare and away from ASW, what place do you see for submarines in the next couple of decades?

Admiral Wilkinson: You know, we had the years and years and years of our strategic weapon people out on patrol, the survivable deterrent. We had a large force of nuclear attack submarines of the greatest capability that could help in sea control, the sea control submarine. We developed the capability in those submarines to help escort carriers, for projection of power ashore. There were some really important missions for submarines, and they did them well. We won the Cold War. Actually we bankrupted Russia in trying to keep up. In my opinion we bankrupted ourselves too. We just haven't fully realized it yet, but that's another thing.

Then, after the Russian threat was greatly minimized, we really didn't have the need for the submarine forces that we had had before either in the survivable deterrent or the sea control submarine. And so although I've been involved in the authorization of a lot of those submarines to start with, properly so for our country's utilization of

---

* Captain James C. Hay, USN (Ret.).

resources, we've put a lot of submarines out of commission. As a matter of fact, the only reason we didn't put them out faster was because we didn't have the yard capability to take care of the nuclear plants properly. So we're still in the business of reduction in number of submarines as we do it right.

Looking at the world as it exists today, we don't have the requirements for as many highly capable, very expensive nuclear submarines, either as sea control or survivable deterrent as we used to have. And certainly we ought to keep enough so that we retain the people and the expertise and so we have the nucleus to grow from if that should come. But in the next 20 years you'd have to look at your political crystal ball and your international crystal ball, but I don't see the threat coming that requires us to have an increase in submarine forces in that time frame. I think it's really important that we maintain all our know-how and continue to make developmental improvements but as a nucleus for expansion if a threat comes and grows. That's my own personal opinion. I'm not speaking for the Navy Department or anything.

Paul Stillwell: Whom would you consider to be the architects of the submarine strategy that won the Cold War? Who were the giants of submarine development and who were the best, really the aces, among the skippers in the Cold War?

Admiral Wilkinson: The important people in the development were 08, Admiral Rickover and his outfit in BuShips and the Atomic Energy Commission and SP, Levering Smith and his outfit in BuShips. Without them and what they did, we wouldn't have had the capabilities that we had. The strategy sort of grew and flowed naturally from the capability. And what was the rest of that question?

Paul Stillwell: Whom would you single out as really the top skippers and operators during the Cold War?

Admiral Wilkinson: It was the sustained effort from the whole force in keeping as many as possible of the strategic missile submarines at sea to ensure that they were survivable. That wasn't the individual talent of any skipper. There are some things that you do with genius, and maybe one genius is worth a thousand men, a Nobel Prize winner or that kind of a guy, but there are other things that you have to do with numbers. So it wasn't any brilliant deal of any one strategic submarine or any one captain. It was the combined efforts of all of them and all their people, blue and gold crews, officers and men, support from the tenders and whatnot that kept those strategic submarines at sea hidden a larger and larger percentage of the time. So the problem here isn't with my answer. It's with the question. [Laughter] My answer is the right one. You've got to change the question to fit that.

Paul Stillwell: How do you feel about the construction of special mission submarines versus multi-mission capable ships of admittedly higher cost?

Admiral Wilkinson: I am absolutely and have been vehemently committed all my life and fought it, hip and thigh, against the single-purpose cheap submarine. I want a multi-purpose, expensive, high-capability submarine that can defeat the enemy in battle. I feel that way very, very strongly because I defy you to project for the lifetime of Navy ships, 25 or 30 years, exactly all the requirements that will be imposed upon them. The problem with the little cheap single-purpose thing is that that's not the problem you'll have at the time. Whatever your problem may be, that thing won't be able to handle it. So let me say again, and it's the way I always conducted my fights for resources, and I have used those very same words paraphrased a little, and I don't want any cheap special-purpose submarine. I want an expensive multi-purpose submarine that can defeat the enemy in battle, and I feel that way still.

Paul Stillwell: I presume that would rule out any future diesel submarine construction by the United States.

Admiral Wilkinson: Yes.

Paul Stillwell: This fourth question. The submarine building debates of the last few years have really been about whether or not the U.S. will continue to have a nuclear submarine force. Now that the pure existence question has been answered, and they will in fact stay in service, should serious objections be raised to the projected force level of 55 SSNs by 1999? And this is talking about reductions that have come about since the Reagan administration. The Clinton projection in the bottom-up review for the Navy was 346 ships with 45 to 55 SSNs, a maximum of almost 16% and a minimum of 13%. So the question is whether the percentages or absolute numbers are what counts. What do you see as an optimum force level going out to the future?

Admiral Wilkinson: As I said for some time, we were above numbers because they couldn't put them out that fast, but you need other forces than submarines. You really need carriers to be able to project forces, project power ashore. The problem with submarines is that really they're for big war, where you're really going to destroy the enemy, whether it's his use of the sea or whether it's with nuclear weapons or whatnot. But submarines, except for use of a few of our systems like Tomahawk, mostly they're not for projecting any power ashore. So I can't come down to a number of 55 or 45. You've got to talk about the threat at the time. That wouldn't have been enough when the Soviets were at full strength. With any opposition we have now, we could sink all their ships with less than that. What really counts is to continue to develop the next generation of greater capability, to continue to have a cadre of really trained and experienced people, to not stay static but keep a viable nucleus on which you could expand if you had to. You just talked SSNs. Remember we keep also a force of Tridents, a strategic thing.

Paul Stillwell: Right.

Admiral Wilkinson: But I suspect before we're through that you'll see a further reduction in SSNs. But I hope it's not enough that we don't continue to get a new development from time to time and maintain a well-trained, disciplined nucleus.

Paul Stillwell: Well, we have seen one of those new developments in the SSN-21, the *Seawolf*.[*]

Admiral Wilkinson: It hasn't been easy to get.

Paul Stillwell: No, it hasn't.

Admiral Wilkinson: And I think it's important that those things happen.

Paul Stillwell: And part of that is an issue of maintaining the industrial base to be able to expand if need be.

Well, Admiral, we've talked a lot about your Navy and civilian careers and the various legacies. Yet another legacy is your family, so I'd appreciate it if you could close by talking about your children and grandchildren.

Admiral Wilkinson: I have a fantastic wife who's been the loyalist supporter. Let me tell you, if we were to pull out some of those pictures of my first days in the Navy, Janice was a doll, and she has been a great wife. This year, March 28, my number-two grandson, Eric, is getting married. By chance that happens to be our 56th wedding anniversary. So Janice has put up with me for a long time. We have four kids, and they're all bright as hell, and they were honorable, high-standard kids. And to me, more important than that, they all like one another. They like their mother and they're nice to me. They keep turning up like bad pennies, and we've maintained a close relationship with our kids.

If you look back at the Wilkinson generations, you don't get many girls. There was my sister in that generation, and there's Mary Lynn in that generation, but in the grandson generation my sister had four boys, and they don't have any granddaughters.

---

[*] USS *Seawolf* (SSN-21), the first of a two-ship class of nuclear-powered attack submarines, was commissioned 19 July 1997. She displaces 7,460 tons surfaced and 9,137 tons submerged. The ship is 353 feet long, 40 feet in the beam, and has a maximum draft of 36 feet. Her top speed on the surface is 15 knots; top speed submerged is 35 knots. The submarine is armed with Tomahawk missiles and has eight 26½-inch torpedo tubes.

They're all boys. And all my grandchildren are boys. We don't get many girls. My daughter in her day was the pick of the litter. I've got four grandsons, and they're all bright and they're all doing well, and I feel very fortunate to have them.

Looking back, I didn't spend as much time with my family as I should have. I was busy in total commitment, and the *Nautilus* kept me very busy. Even the first year at INPO, as I said, I was out of Atlanta 165 days. That was a lot of time away from my wife. When our children were born, we had four when the oldest was five, and I was only there for one of them being born, who was my daughter, born when I was in that tour at Oak Ridge, our little hillbilly. My wife was there alone for the birth of the other three and was taking care of those kids when I was off at sea having all that fun. Looking back, I didn't think anything of it then, but having had a little more maturity and experience now I don't see how the hell she did it. But she did it in some way or other. The kids turned out all right.

Paul Stillwell: I wonder if you could just run through them individually and mention what each one is doing now.

Admiral Wilkinson: My number-one son, Dennis or Skipper, is out in Japan, and he's teaching English in college there. My kids are all smart, as I said, but Skipper's the only one that got an 800 on the College Board. He got a master's degree. He is married to a Japanese girl who comes from a Samurai family and is a pretty smart girl. She's a qualified pharmacist. She owns a pharmacy and is qualified to run and operate a pharmacy.

My number-two youngster is Stephen, and he got a law degree. He is smart also. He stood number one in his class at law school at Texas, and he eventually quit being a lawyer. Oh, he still has the license, and became a banker. He owns his own bank in Texas and makes a lot of money.

My number three is my daughter, Mary Lynn, who's the pick of the litter, and she works for Quality Assurance International, which certifies companies or production places that they comply with the regulations for being able to use the word "organic."

My number four, Rodney, lives up in Seattle and he works for Microsoft, and he has some Microsoft stock and some stock options and he's doing well.

I've got four grandkids and they're all boys. The oldest one is my Bryan, and he's quite photogenic and you met him here. He just had an accident like you had and broke his collarbone, and we're worrying about that getting properly taken care of. He's an assistant writer on a TV program called "Nothing Sacred," and that's what he wants to do in life. He's quite artistic. I don't know what he's going to do in the TV industry, but he's going to do something.

My number-two grandson is Eric. He graduated from Cal Poly summa cum laude and with a 3.86 grade point average. He's pretty smart. He got a good job coming out, his first year out, making $36,000 a year plus overtime. He's been out a year and seven months, and now he makes $78,000 a year. He's about to get married to a nice girl.

My number-three grandson, Stephen in Texas, is just bright as hell and he is a swimmer and made AAU top 10 in the United States swimmers' times.[*] And he speaks fluently Russian and French. And he's over in France at Institute Polytechnique. If you go to France there isn't anybody that runs a technical company that didn't go from there, and so he's taking his education there.

Our number-four grandson is a Japanese-American, Eugene. I told you about him earlier. They just tested him and all the first graders in Japan and he placed second highest of any six-year old in Japan. They evaluated him as an IQ of 205, which ain't possible. But it's because his folks have worked with him. When he came here I was always posing mathematical problems to him, and long before he started school he could add and subtract in his head two-digit numbers easily. He understands fractions, and he can read and write and speaks English and Japanese fluently. He's ready for first grade.

Paul Stillwell: Now that we've talked about your entire career, what can you say to sum it up?

Admiral Wilkinson: I know I'll be repeating some things I've said, but let me tell you in overview I had a career in the Navy that meant a lot to me. I was fortunate enough to be

---

[*] AAU –Amateur Athletic Union.

involved at times in development of some very interesting things, the development of the missile systems and nuclear power and so on. When I was in the Navy some of the things resulted in a bunch of awards. I got things like the Silver Star and the Navy Commendation Medal and the Legion of Merit and the Distinguished Service Medal three times. And the Joint Service Commendation Medal and numerous area medals and ribbons and the Second Order of the Sacred Treasure from Japan. And certainly the keys were presented to me for several cities like Miami Beach and New Orleans and Long Beach. And all those things were nice. I'll come back to it in a minute.

In my career after the Navy I also had some things that meant a lot to me: for example, the Meritorious Public Service Citation from the Secretary of the Navy for service to the Navy's oceanographic programs, specifically Arctic Research and Development. And the George Westinghouse Gold Medal from the American Society of Mechanical Engineers and the Oliver Townsend Medal from the Atomic Industrial Forum and the Gold Medal from the Uranium Institute. That was an international award. The Henry DeWolf Smyth Nuclear Statesman Medal from the American Nuclear Society.

And it meant a lot to me to be elected to the National Academy of Engineering. I came home and sort of said it low key to my wife that I was elected to the National Academy of Engineering and Janice said, "Engineer? Engineer? If you're an engineer why don't you fix the washing machine?" [Laughter] Also probably the biggest individual best performance in my life was as the first president of INPO, the Institute of Nuclear Power Operations, in which we had a part in increasing the safety of operation of all the nuclear electric generation stations in the United States.

That went really well and led on to the formation of the World Association of Nuclear Operators, which has quite an impact on the operation of all the nuclear electric generating plants in the world. And I had really great relations with all the electric companies in the United States that own or operate nuclear electric generating plants. And I worked hard at that business and I got a lot of satisfaction out of it. And so a lot of recognition has been given to me with some medals and awards in the Navy and a couple of gold medals, and I mean real gold medals—big and round and heavy, and some other awards.

But I'll tell you true what's meant more to me is also over the years to have the satisfaction to see an awful lot of young people that worked for me that proceeded on to greater glory. You've got to have a little satisfaction when one of your junior officers, Jim Watkins, eventually becomes Chief of Naval Operations and then Harry Train has his four stars. But there were many, many others. Ken Carr and Lando Zech got to three stars and became chairmen of the Nuclear Regulatory Commission. And then there's Vice Admiral Nicholson, who was a crackerjack guy and one of my engineers on the *Nautilus*. Also, Jack Williams who went on to four stars and Paul Early.[*] If I sat here I could name an awful lot of my people that made admiral, and that's a good mark of success in the Navy. But not just the officers. A multitude of my enlisted men, I saw them get promoted. Gee, when I was SubLant I had four commanding officers that had progressed from being enlisted men. I saw a lot of those men go up and become captains in the Navy and commanding officers of ships.

I had a lot of people, a lot of my troops that after they got out of the Navy became vice presidents of companies and some of them presidents and owners of companies. And certainly they had good careers in the Navy while they were in and many, many, many of them good careers in civilian life after they got out. And many, many of those people have come back and told me so, and you can't help but get a tremendous amount of satisfaction out of that. So I guess that truly I've enjoyed that more than the medals I got myself.

So after the Navy, from '74 to '98, I did have a very good career and I was a director of many companies like Commonwealth Edison in Chicago, which is a big company, and although I'm 79 now I'm still director of a couple of companies. The Advanced Resource and Development, Environmental in Maryland, and I'm chairman of the board of MDM Services Corporation and still keep my hand in a little. So life since the Navy had been very, very active and very, very gratifying to me, and I've made enough money out of it so that my retirement is more than double my Navy retirement. So I've enjoyed what I've done in life and I just wanted to say that the 24 years since I got out of the Navy have been just as full and just as much fun and just as satisfying day by day and year by year as the 34 years I spent in the Navy, which were great.

---

[*] Rear Admiral Paul J. Early, USN (Ret.). He was one of the junior officers in the *Nautilus* in the 1950s.

Paul Stillwell: Is there anything else you'd like to add to all we've talked about?

Admiral Wilkinson: Yes. It was shocking to me how much I've forgotten. It's only in your way of doing things and asking things that you've jogged my memory time and time again. And I know that I've left out a lot of the best stuff. I was always so busy in my life with total commitment that when I quit the *Nautilus* I wasn't all that unorganized. I put all that stuff away. Gee, I've got the "Well Done" file, all those letters of commendation and all those commendatory dispatches including the ones from some enlisted wives and mothers that I also considered as "Well Done" file. And I've got a multitude of dispatches commending *Nautilus* on her performance. And the same on *Volador* and same on *Long Beach*.

And it's just like this speech that we looked at a minute ago in which when I went over and talked to the Guild Hall for the Uranium Institute, and I wrote a speech something like this and my wife said, "That sounds like the same old thing." But I have copies of all my speeches I've ever given, including the commencement address in '56. I opened boxes that I hadn't opened for 40 years. And I didn't have enough time before you came to really look through it all and get organized and get myself some notes. But I know that in there there's quite some few things that are of much more value than any of the things we've talked about.

Before I throw that stuff away or send it to the Submarine Museum or something, I'm going to go through it again. And maybe this time I'll pull out at least the important things. I know that a lot of the best of it, talented as you were, it never got out of me.

Paul Stillwell: Well, I am grateful to you for two years ago or whenever it was making the commitment to do this project, because, as you said, you carry through on commitments, and we've both had some health situations that have delayed the process.

Admiral Wilkinson: We have. Your accident and my legs and all this time my memory's fading and my hearing's going away, so I really wish we'd have done this 20 years ago. But then I wouldn't have been able to tell you about INPO and all those things that have happened since.

Paul Stillwell: Admiral, it has been a genuine privilege for me to meet and get acquainted with you. You're one of the most fascinating people I've ever met.

Admiral Wilkinson: Paul, the pleasure's all mine.

Paul Stillwell: I'm grateful to you for your patience and your hospitality and for what I know is a superb contribution to the record of naval history. And grateful also for the medium of oral history to preserve these recollections, so I thank you very much.

Admiral Wilkinson: Well, you bet, Paul, but I tell you there's a lot of crap in that and when you go through it you'll do me a service if you erase a lot of that nonsense. And I recognize we've duplicated a lot, and I defy you to put all that stuff in the right chronological order.

Paul Stillwell: That's a challenge I'm willing to accept.

Launched in 1969, the Naval Institute's oral history program is among the oldest in the country. Used in combination with documentary sources, oral histories offer a richer understanding of naval history. Often they contain candid recollections and explanations never entered into contemporary records. In addition, they can help depict the atmosphere of a particular event or era in a manner not available in official documents.

The Naval Institute gratefully accepts tax-deductible gifts to strengthen its oral history initiatives. This support allows the Institute to preserve the life experiences of today's service men and women so they may teach and inspire future generations.

For information about opportunities to underwrite Naval Institute oral history projects, please contact the Naval Institute Foundation at 291 Wood Road, Annapolis, Maryland 21402; by phone at (410) 295-1054; or by e-mail at foundation@usni.org.

Index to the Oral History of
Vice Admiral Eugene P. Wilkinson, U.S. Navy (Retired)

Advancement of Enlisted Personnel
On board the nuclear submarine *Nautilus* (SSN-571) in the mid-1950s, 169, 231
On board the nuclear cruiser *Long Beach* (CGN-9) in the early 1960s, 327-329

Air Force, U.S.
In the mid-1960s was involved with the Navy in a joint study on offshore ranges, 339-341
In the late 1960s the Fifth Air Force was based in Japan, 16-18, 364-367

Alcohol
The crew of the nuclear submarine *Nautilus* (SSN-571) purchased a large quantity of liquor in Bermuda in the mid-1950s, 214-215
Unauthorized liquor on board the *Nautilus* in the 1950s, 219-220
Much beer was consumed during a softball game in the mid-1950s between the crews of the cruiser *Boston* (CAG-1) and the nuclear submarine *Nautilus* (SSN-571), 237-239

Anderson, Commander William R., USN (USNA, 1943)
In the early 1950s served in the submarine *Tang* (SS-563) and later commanded the submarine *Wahoo* (SS-565), 154, 157, 161
Commanded the nuclear submarine *Nautilus* (SSN-571) in the late 1950s, 255-256, 258, 269-270, 273

Antiair Warfare
Against German planes flying over England in early 1943, 59-60
Training device used at Submarine School in early 1945, 88-89

Antisubmarine Warfare
German action against the submarine *Blackfish* (SS-221) in the Bay of Biscay in February 1943, 57-58, 61
Japanese action against the submarine *Darter* (SS-227) in June 1944, 74-75
U.S. exercises against the submarines *Volador* (SS-490) and *Wahoo* (SS-565) in the early 1950s, 132-135, 139-144
Exercises in the mid-1950s against the nuclear submarine *Nautilus* (SSN-571), 196-197, 206-213, 222-226, 231-232, 249-250, 254-255
Vice Admiral Charles Martell was Director of Antisubmarine Warfare Programs in OpNav in the mid-1960s, 345-347, 397
In the early 1970s CNO Elmo Zumwalt advocated surface effect ships as ASW platforms, 404-405

Antrim, Ensign James E., USNR
Attended Submarine School in early 1942, 54

Arctic
    The nuclear submarine *Nautilus* (SSN-571) operated under the icecap in the late 1950s, 205, 236, 269-272, 276
    The nuclear submarine *Skate* (SSN-578) surfaced at the North Pole in August 1958, 269-272, 276
    In the mid-1970s Wilkinson did a study on research and development in the Arctic Ocean, 407

Argonne National Laboratory, Illinois
    Site of early development work in the Navy's nuclear power program in the late 1940s, 112-113

***Atago* (Japanese Cruiser)**
    Sunk in October 1944 by the submarine Darter (SS-227), 76-77

Atomic Energy Commission
    Role in the early development of nuclear power in the late 1940s, 118-120
    Role in connection with the construction of the nuclear submarine *Nautilus* (SSN-571) in the 1950s, 177, 185

Australia
    Visited by the U.S. submarine *Darter* (SS-227) between war patrols in 1944, 68-69
    Survivors from the *Darter* went to Australia on board the *Dace* (SS-247) after their boat was lost in October 1944, 84
    In the early 1970s was contemplated for home-porting U.S. submarines, 405

Axene, Lieutenant Commander Dean L., USN (USNA, 1945)
    Served as the first executive officer of the nuclear submarine *Nautilus* (SSN-571) in the mid-1950s, 167, 221, 227

***Badoeng Strait*, USS (CVE-116)**
    In December 1951 a helicopter from the ship crashed at sea while transferring *Collier's* magazine correspondent Charlotte Knight, 133-135

Baer, Captain Donald G., USN (USNA, 1937)
    Commanded a submarine tender at New London, Connecticut, in the 1950s, 186-188

Bakutis, Lieutenant Commander Fred E., USN (USNA, 1935)
    In October 1944 was shot down during the Battle of Leyte Gulf and rescued at sea, 85

Bangor, Washington, Submarine Base
    Selected in the early 1970s as the base for West Coast Trident submarines, 399-400

Barkley, Lieutenant Commander Henry Brock, Jr., USN (USNA, 1949)
Served in the first crew of the nuclear cruiser *Long Beach* (CGN-9) in the early 1960s, 283-285

Basketball
Successful team in the early 1950s in the crew of the submarine *Volador* (SS-490), 129-131

Baskett, Commander Thomas S., USN (USNA, 1935)
In 1946 was the first commanding officer when the submarine *Dogfish* (SS-350) was commissioned, 96-97

Beach, Commander Edward L., USN (USNA, 1939)
In the early 1950s was the first commanding officer of the submarine *Trigger* (SS-564), 152-153
Was a candidate to be first skipper of the nuclear submarine *Nautilus* (SSN-571), 164
In 1960 commanded the nuclear submarine *Triton* (SSRN-586) during a voyage around the world, 274, 281

Beijing, China
In 1989, at the time of the Tiananmen Square riots, the Wilkinson family visited the city, 4

Benson, Commander Roy S., USN (USNA, 1929)
Served as an instructor at Submarine School during World War II, 52

Bergner, Lieutenant Commander Allen E., USN (USNA, 1940)
During the Korean War commanded the submarine *Pomodon* (SS-486), 145-147

Bermuda
Visited by the nuclear submarine *Nautilus* (SSN-571) in the mid-1950s, 196-198, 211-215, 237-239

Bethlehem Steel Company, Quincy, Massachusetts
Construction of the nuclear cruiser *Long Beach* (CGN-9) in the late 1950s-early 1960s was slowed by a strike, 289-294, 310-311

Bettis Laboratory, West Mifflin, Pennsylvania
Site of early development work in the Navy's nuclear power program in the late 1940s, 112-120, 127-128

***Blackfish*, USS (SS-221)**
New submarine that operated in the Atlantic and European waters in 1942-43, 56-66

Boller, Lieutenant Commander Jack W., USN
 In the early 1960s was the first navigator of the nuclear cruiser *Long Beach* (CGN-9), 300

Boston, Massachusetts
 Hosted a heroes' welcome for the crew of the nuclear submarine *Skate* (SSN-578) in 1958, 273

***Boston*, USS (CAG-1)**
 In the mid-1950s her crew played a beer-soaked softball game against the crew of the nuclear submarine *Nautilus* (SSN-571), 237-239

Boyd, Lieutenant (junior grade) David S., USN (USNA, 1950)
 Served in the first crew of the nuclear submarine *Nautilus* (SSN-571) in the mid-1950s, 167, 228

Brown, George E., Jr.
 Future congressman who grew up in Holtville, California, in the 1920s and 1930s, 9-10

Brown, Dr. Harold
 In the early 1960s served as director of Defense Research and Engineering, 338, 341-343

Brown, Rear Admiral John H., Jr., USN (USNA, 1914)
 As Commander Submarine Force Pacific Fleet in the early 1950s, was interested in fleet basketball, 129-131

Budgetary Issues
 Quest for funds for submarines in the early 1970s, 396-398

Bureau of Medicine and Surgery
 Survey concerning venereal disease in the fleet in the early 1950s, 131

Bureau of Naval Personnel
 Manning of the nuclear cruiser *Long Beach* (CGN-9) as she approached completion in the early 1960s, 287-288

Bureau of Naval Weapons
 Role in the early 1960s in the installation of weapon systems on board the nuclear cruiser *Long Beach* (CGN-9), 309-312, 318-320

Bureau of Ships
 Involvement with the nuclear submarine *Nautilus* (SSN-571) in the mid-1950s, 177-179, 185, 200-201, 203, 234-235

Role in the early 1960s in the installation of weapon systems on board the nuclear cruiser *Long Beach* (CGN-9), 309-312, 318-320

Burke, Admiral Arleigh A., USN (USNA, 1923)
As Chief of Naval Operations, visited the nuclear submarine *Nautilus* (SSN-571) in the mid-1950s, 205-207
In the late 1950s told Wilkinson why he was selected to command the nuclear cruiser *Long Beach* (CGN-9), 281

Bush, George H. W.
As director of the Central Intelligence Agency, met with Wilkinson in the mid-1970s and as Vice President in the early 1980s, 415

Calvert, Commander James F., USN (USNA, 1943)
In the late 1950s commanded the submarine *Skate* (SSN-578), 158, 167, 265-266, 268-269

Canadian Navy
Interaction with the U.S. Navy in the late 1950s about nuclear submarines, 267-268

Carney, Admiral Robert B., USN (USNA, 1916)
Chief of Naval Operations who went to sea in the nuclear submarine *Nautilus* (SSN-571) in 1955, 208

Carr, Vice Admiral Kenneth M., USN (Ret.) (USNA, 1949)
Served as a junior officer in the nuclear submarine *Nautilus* (SSN-571) in the mid-1950s, 216, 228-230, 257
In the 1970s served as aide to the Deputy Secretary of Defense, 344
Served 1989-91 as chairman of the Nuclear Regulatory Commission, 412, 415

Castle, Commander Hal. C., USN (USNA, 1944)
In the early 1960s was the first executive office of the nuclear cruiser *Long Beach* (CGN-9), 285, 324

Cavenagh, Rear Admiral Robert W., USN (USNA, 1926)
In 1961, as Commander Cruiser Force Atlantic Fleet, embarked in the nuclear cruiser *Long Beach* (CGN-9), 297-299, 301-302

China
In 1989, at the time of the Tiananmen Square riots, the Wilkinson family visited Beijing and rode the Yangtze River, 4-5

Coast Guard Academy, New London, Connecticut
Results of a Navy-Coast Guard tennis match circa 1970, 380-381

Cobean, Lieutenant Commander Warren R., Jr., USN (USNA, 1947)
    Operated the Navy prototype reactor at Arco, Idaho, in the early 1950s, 165
    Served as executive officer in the nuclear submarine Nautilus (SSN-571) in the mid-1950s, 221

Communications
    In October 1944 the submarine *Darter* (SS-227) sent in a vital sighting report of the Japanese fleet, 75-76
    Radio communications by the submarine *Volador* (SS-490) in the early 1950s, 138-141
    In January 1955 the nuclear submarine *Nautilus* (SSN-571) sent a flashing-light message to report she was under way for the first time, 182-183
    Use of underwater telephone between the submarines *Seawolf* (SSN-575) and *Nautilus* (SSN-571) in the mid-1950s, 213-214
    Development in the 1970s of extremely low frequency radio communications with submarines, 392-393

Congress, U.S.
    Provided solid support for the Navy's nuclear power program from the late 1940s onward, 120-122, 256-258
    Secretary of Defense Melvin Laird's testimony in the early 1970s concerning Trident submarines, 402-403

Crossick, Chief Fire Controlman, USN
    In the mid-1950s did some expert photography while in the crew of the nuclear submarine *Nautilus* (SSN-571), 195-196, 198-199, 221, 270

Cruiser-Destroyer Force Atlantic Fleet
    As type commander for the nuclear cruiser *Long Beach* (CGN-9) in the early 1960s, 301-309, 326

Cuba
    Pre-deployment training of the nuclear cruiser *Long Beach* (CGN-9) at Guantánamo Bay in the early 1960s, 320-322

***Cusk*, (SSG-348)**
    Operations in the Pacific in 1947-48 included tests of Loon guided missiles, 103-110

Cutter, Captain Slade D., USN (USNA, 1935)
    Commanded the submarine *Seahorse* (SS-304) in 1943-44, 77-78
    Commanded the submarine *Requin* (SS-481) at the end of World War II, 95
    While on the SubLant staff in the mid-1950s went to sea on board the nuclear submarine *Nautilus* (SSN-571), 208-210, 233

Dace, USS (SS-247)
    In October 1944 rescued the crew of the submarine *Darter* (SS-227), which had run aground on Bombay Shoal, 79-81

Damage Control
    On board the heavy cruiser *Louisville* (CA-28) in 1941, 31-32

Darter, USS (SS-227)
    Torpedo testing in October 1943 off Maine, 66
    Guns and gunnery practice in 1943-44, 67, 69-70
    Pacific war patrols against the Japanese in 1944, 68-74, 144-145
    Role in the October 1944 Battle of Leyte Gulf, 75-79, 85-86
    Ran aground on Bombay Shoal on 24 October 1944 and had to be abandoned, 78-81

Data Design Laboratories
    Wilkinson's role as executive vice president in the late 1970s, 406, 408-409

Davidson, Commander John F., USN (USNA, 1929)
    In 1942-43 served as the first commanding officer of the submarine *Blackfish* (SS-221), 56, 60-63
    In 1945 ordered Wilkinson to the crew of the submarine *Dogfish* (SS-350), 96

Deane, Commissaryman Second Class Thomas J., Jr., USN
    Got married in 1957 while on leave from the crew of the nuclear submarine *Nautilus* (SSN-571), 245-247, 254

Dennison, Vice Admiral Robert L., USN (USNA, 1923)
    As Commander First Fleet, visited the nuclear submarine *Nautilus* (SSN-571) in 1957, 252-253

Disciplinary Matters
    Captain's mast cases on board the nuclear cruiser *Long Beach* (CGN-9) in the early 1960s, 306-308

Dogfish, USS (SS-350)
    Shortly after World War II had a mix-up on who would serve as executive officer, 96-97

Dornin, Lieutenant Commander Robert E., USN (USNA, 1935)
    In 1944-45 served as aide to Admiral Ernest J. King, 85-86

Duncan, Admiral Donald B., USN (USNA, 1917)
    Was Vice Chief of Naval Operations when the nuclear submarine *Nautilus* (SSN-571) first went to sea in 1955, 182

Dunford, Lieutenant Commander James M., USN (USNA, 1939)
  Early involvement in the Navy's nuclear power program in the late 1940s, 111, 113

Early, Lieutenant Paul J., USN (USNA, 1948)
  Served in the nuclear submarine *Nautilus* (SSN-571) in the mid-1950s, 250

Ebersole, Lieutenant John H., Medical Corps, USN
  Served in the crew of the nuclear submarine *Nautilus* (SSN-571) in the mid-1950s, 198

Education
  Wilkinson's studies in California in the 1920s and 1930s, 1, 3-4, 8-12, 19-20, 24, 116
  Wilkinson taught at San Diego State College, 1938-40, 21-23

Eisenhower, President Dwight D.
  Espoused an Atoms for Peace program in the 1950s, 174, 180

Eisenhower, Mamie
  The President's wife christened the nuclear submarine *Nautilus* (SSN-571) at the time of launching in January 1954, 170-172, 237

Electric Boat Company, Groton, Connecticut
  Early involvement in the Navy's nuclear power program in the late 1940s, 114, 116, 119-120, 129
  Keel-laying in June 1952 for the nuclear submarine *Nautilus* (SSN-571), 163-164
  Construction of the *Nautilus* in the early 1950s, 167-176, 181-182, 184, 192-193, 202-204

England
  In early 1943 the U.S. submarine *Blackfish* (SS-221) went into the Royal Naval Dockyard at Devonport for repair of battle damage, 58-60

Enlisted Personnel
  In the crew of the heavy cruiser *Louisville* (CA-28) in 1941, 39-41
  Shortage of submarine personnel following demobilization after World War II, 97, 101
  In the crew of the submarine *Cusk* (SSG-348) in the late 1940s, 105, 108-109
  In the crew of the submarine *Volador* (SS-490) in the early 1950s, 129-131, 133-135, 147-148
  In the crew of the submarine *Wahoo* (SS-565) in the early 1950s, 150-153, 155-158
  In the crew of the nuclear submarine *Nautilus* (SSN-571) in the mid-1950s, 167-169, 174, 177, 183-184, 189-190, 195-196, 198-199, 218-220, 224-225, 230-231, 237-239, 244-247, 251-253, 259
  In the crew of the nuclear cruiser *Long Beach* (CGN-9) in the early 1960s, 282-283, 286-288, 293, 296-297, 302-304, 306-308, 327-329

In the early 1960s OP-31 worked to increase the manning for Polaris submarines, 347-348

Enterprise, USS (CVAN-65)
Deployment to the Mediterranean in 1963, 326-327

Fields, Torpedoman First Class George W., USN
Served in the nuclear submarine *Nautilus* (SSN-571) in the mid-1950s, 189-190, 259

Fitness Reports
Difficulty for the first commander of Submarine Squadron 14 in evaluating top-performing skippers, 278-280

Food
On board the submarine *Darter* (SS-227) in 1944, 68
On board the submarine *Dace* (SS-247) in 1944, 81
Flying fish wound up on the deck of the submarine *Volador* (SS-490) in the early 1950s, 132

France
Wilkinson spent some leisure time in Paris in 1963 after being relieved of command of the nuclear cruiser *Long Beach* (CGN-9), 334-336

French Navy
The battleship *Richelieu* was stationed at Dakar, West Africa, in late 1942, 56-57

Gardner, Ensign George Peabody, Jr., USNR
In 1941 served in the heavy cruiser *Louisville* (CA-28), 42-43

General Line School, Newport, Rhode Island
In 1946-47 provided training to former Naval Reserve officers, 103

German Navy
Action against the submarine *Blackfish* (SS-221) in the Bay of Biscay in February 1943, 57-58, 61

Germany
Former German V-1 rockets were used as Loon missiles by the U.S. Navy in the late 1940s, 106-109
Visited by the nuclear cruiser *Long Beach* (CGN-9) in the early 1960s, 316-318

Glenard P. Lipscomb, **USS (SSN-685)**
Quiet nuclear submarine built in the early 1970s, 346-347

Graham, Otto E. Jr.
  Played in a Navy-Coast Guard tennis match around 1970 while serving as Academy athletic director, 380-381

Great Britain
  In early 1943 the U.S. submarine *Blackfish* (SS-221) went into the Royal Naval Dockyard at Devonport for repair of battle damage, 58-60
  In the late 1950s the Royal Navy sent officers to the United States for nuclear training, 16, 266-267

Grenfell, Rear Admiral Elton W., USN (USNA, 1926)
  As ComSubPac rode the nuclear submarine *Nautilus* (SSN-571) in 1957, 255-258

Guantánamo Bay, Cuba
  Site of pre-deployment training of the nuclear cruiser *Long Beach* (CGN-9) in the early 1960s, 320-322

***Gudgeon*, USS (SS-567)**
  New fast attack submarine commissioned in 1952, 156-157

Gunnery – Naval
  Practice by the heavy cruiser *Louisville* (CA-28) in 1941, 33, 41
  Practice by the submarine *Darter* (SS-227) in November 1943, 67
  Use of the saluting battery by the nuclear cruiser *Long Beach* (CGN-9) in the early 1960s, 316-318

Hawaii
  In 1941 the heavy cruiser *Louisville* (CA-28) was one of the ships based there, 37-44
  Japanese attack on in December 1941, 45-46
  In the early 1950s Pearl Harbor served as homeport for the submarine *Wahoo* (SS-565), 158

Hébert, F. Edward
  U.S Congressman who visited the nuclear submarine *Nautilus* (SSN-571) in New Orleans in the mid-1950s, 235

Helicopters
  In December 1951 crewmen from the submarine *Volador* (SS-490) rescued *Collier's* magazine correspondent Charlotte Knight after a helicopter crash at sea, 133-135
  In the mid-1950s a helicopter dropped a pilot on the deck of the nuclear submarine *Nautilus* (SSN-571), 196-198

Hensel, Commander Karl G., USN (USNA, 1923)
  In 1942 served as officer in charge of Submarine School, 49-51

Ingles, Chief Torpedoman Leroy, USN
Served as first chief of the boat in the nuclear submarine *Nautilus* (SSN-571) in the mid-1950s, 167-168, 218-220

Institute of Nuclear Power Operations (INPO)
Staff members from the organization have become executives in the nuclear power industry, 155
Wilkinson's role in running the organization from 1980 to 1984, 407-423

Jackson, Henry M.
U.S. Senator who was supportive of the Navy's nuclear power program for many years, 122, 237, 256-258, 400

Janney, Lieutenant Commander Frederick E., USN (USNA, 1937)
In 1946 commanded the submarine *Raton* (SS-270), 97-101

Japan
Visited by the submarine *Volador* (SS-490) in the early 1950s, 374-375
In the late 1960s the Fifth Air Force was based in Japan, 16-18, 364-367
In the late 1960s the U.S. Navy was able to introduce nuclear-powered ships into Japanese ports, 353, 355, 361-363
Japanese talks with the Wilkinson, the U.S. representative, on various issues in the late 1960s, 355-364, 367-371, 374
Life in Japan for the Wilkinson family in the late 1960s, 366-378

Japanese Navy
Action in the October 1944 Battle of Leyte Gulf, 75-79
In the late 1960s Wilkinson met a Japanese naval officer whose ship had been sunk by Wilkinson's submarine in World War II, 373

Johnson, Lieutenant John D., USN
Future three-star admiral who served in the crew of the submarine *Wahoo* (SS-565) in the early 1950s, 149-150, 153, 156

Johnson, U. Alexis
U.S. ambassador to Japan in the late 1960s 355-357, 368

Kaufman, Captain Robert Y., USN (USNA, 1946)
In the early 1970s worked in the OP-02 organization in OpNav, 396, 398-399

Kefauver, Carey Estes
U.S. Senator who was involved with the nuclear submarine *Nautilus* (SSN-571) in the late 1950s, 274

Kelly, Lieutenant Leslie D., Jr., USN (USNA, 1946)
Operated the Navy prototype reactor at Arco, Idaho, in the early 1950s, 165

In the mid-1950s was chief engineer and executive officer of the nuclear submarine *Nautilus* (SSN-571), 176-177, 191, 221

In the early 1960s was chief engineer in the nuclear submarine *Triton* (SSRN-586), 274-275

King, Admiral Ernest J., USN (USNA, 1901)
In 1944, as Chief of Naval Operations, directed that the crew of the lost submarine *Darter* (SS-227) be transferred to put the *Menhaden* (SS-377) in commission, 85-86

Kissinger, Captain Ralph, Jr., USN (USNA, 1937)
Engineering specialist who was involved in tests on board the nuclear submarine *Nautilus* (SSN-571) in the mid-1950s, 185-186

Knight, Charlotte
In December 1951 crewmen from the submarine *Volador* (SS-490) rescued *Collier's* magazine correspondent Knight after a helicopter crash at sea, 133-135

Learned about relative capabilities of submarines and ASW forces, 140, 142-143

Korea
In the late 1960s U.S. armed forces in Korea had problems with theft of materials, 374

Korean War
During the war the U.S. Navy suspended promotion examinations for officers, 145-146

Korth, Fred H.
As Secretary of the Navy had a trip on board the nuclear cruiser *Long Beach* (CGN-9) in April 1962, 323

Laird, Melvin R.
Congressional testimony in the early 1970s concerning Trident submarines, 402-403

Laney, Captain Robert V., USN (resigned) (USNA, 1939)
Nuclear-trained officer who worked for the Bethlehem Steel shipyard at Quincy, Massachusetts, in the early 1960s, 290

Laning, Commander Richard B., USN (USNA, 1940)
In the mid-1950s commanded the nuclear submarine *Seawolf* (SSN-575) during exercises against the nuclear submarine *Nautilus* (SSN-571), 212-214

Layman, Lieutenant William H., USN (USNA, 1948)
Served in the original crew of the nuclear submarine *Nautilus* (SSN-571) in the mid-1950s, 187

Leave and Liberty
 For the crew of the nuclear submarine *Nautilus* (SSN-571) in New Orleans in the mid-1950s, 235
 Wilkinson spent some leisure time in Paris in 1963 after being relieved of command of the nuclear cruiser *Long Beach* (CGN-9), 334-336

Lee, William S.
 Power company executive who had a key role in bringing Wilkinson to the Institute of Nuclear Power Operations in 1980, 408-409, 419

Leyte Gulf, Battle of
 Role of the submarine *Darter* (SS-227) against the Japanese in the October 1944 battle, 75-79

Long Beach, California
 Wilkinson was born in the city in 1918 and subsequently honored there in the early 1970s, 282, 422
 Wilkinson gave a speech on board the retired liner *Queen Mary*, 422-423

Long Beach, **USS (CGN-9)**
  Changes in the design of the ship during construction, 283-284, 286-288
  Increase in the size of the crew during construction, 283, 286-288
  Construction at Quincy, Massachusetts, in the late 1950s-early 1960s, 289-294, 310-311
  Nuclear power plant, 275, 282-285, 309-310
  In the 1960s stocked missile parts for the rest of the Navy, 220, 312-313
  Enlisted crewmen in the early 1960s, 293, 296-297, 302-304, 306-308, 327-329
  Ship handing, 158, 295-296, 315-316, 323-324, 330
  At-sea operations in the early 1960s, 293, 297-299, 301, 320-321, 324-327, 330-333
  Spent time at the Philadelphia Naval Shipyard for repairs and equipment installation in the early 1960s, 299-300
  As a unit of Cruiser-Destroyer Force Atlantic Fleet from late 1961 onward, 301-309, 326
  Sports teams made up of crew members, 305
  Commissioning in September 1961, 295-296
  Industry technical representatives on board ship during the first few months in commission, 309-315
  Installation and testing of weapon systems in the early 1960s, 310-315, 318-320
  Visited Germany in the early 1960s, 317-318
  Deployment to the Mediterranean Sea in 1963, 324-327, 333-334
  In 1968, in the Vietnam War, the ship shot down MiG fighters with Talos missiles, 314, 365-366
  Decommissioning in May 1995, 295-296

Loon Missiles
   Former German V-1 rockets were used as Loon missiles by the U.S. Navy in the late 1940s, 106-109

Los Angeles **(SSN-688)-Class Submarines**
   Capabilities of this class, which was developed in the early 1970s, 280-281, 350, 387-389
   Role in direct support of carrier task groups, 392

***Louisville*,** **USS (CA-28)**
   In 1941 was based at Pearl Harbor while operating in the Pacific, 30-31, 33, 37-45
   Engineering department and damage control in 1941, 31-35, 42
   Gunnery in 1941, 33, 41
   Reserve officers in the crew in 1941, 36-37, 42-43
   In 1941 the ship's sailing team was successful in competition around Pearl Harbor, 37-41

Lowrance, Vice Admiral Vernon L., USN (USNA, 1930)
   Served as Commander Submarine Force Atlantic Fleet from 1964 to 1966, 349-351

Lynch, Captain Richard B., USN (USNA, 1935)
   In the mid-1950s commanded Submarine Squadron Ten, 186-188

Lyon, Lieutenant (junior grade) Harvey E., USN (USNA, 1946)
   In the early 1950s served in the submarine *Wahoo* (SS-565), 149, 153-154

Martell, Vice Admiral Charles B., USN (USNA, 1930)
   In the mid-1960s was Director of Antisubmarine Warfare Programs on the OpNav staff, 345-347

McClintock, Lieutenant Commander David H., USN (USNA, 1935)
   Commanded the submarine *Darter* (SS-227) during war patrols in 1944, 68-78, 82, 85-86, 144-145
   Was first commanding officer when the submarine *Menhaden* (SS-377) was commissioned in 1945, 85-86

McDonald, Admiral David L., USN (USNA, 1928)
   As Chief of Naval Operations in the mid-1960s approved Wilkinson's parking spot outside the Pentagon, 351-352
   Objective of getting nuclear-powered U.S. Navy ships into Japan, 355

McKee, Lieutenant General Seth J., USAF
   In the late 1960s commanded the Fifth Air Force and U.S. Forces Japan, 355, 364-365, 367-368

Medical Problems
Survey concerning venereal disease in the fleet in the early 1950s, 131
A helicopter pilot was injured when he fell on the deck of the nuclear submarine *Nautilus* (SSN-571) in the mid-1950s, 196-198

Menhaden, USS (SS-377)
First crew, when commissioned in 1945, was from the lost *Darter* (SS-227), 85-86
Trip down the Mississippi River shortly after commissioning, 92-94
Site of the Pacific Fleet change of command in November 1945, 94

Michaelis, Captain Frederick H., USN (1940)
Commanded the aircraft carrier *Enterprise* (CVAN-65) in the early 1960s, 326-327

Mine Warfare
In early1952 the submarine *Sea Robin* (SS-407) did a mine-laying exercise, 162-163

Missiles
Former German V-1 rockets were used as Loon missiles by the U.S. Navy in the late 1940s, 106-109
In the 1960s the nuclear cruiser *Long Beach* (CGN-9) stocked missile parts for the rest of the Navy, 220, 312-313
During the Vietnam War, the *Long Beach* shot down MiG fighters with Talos missiles, 314, 365-366
The increasing range of submarine-launched ballistic missiles provided larger operating areas, 401-403

Mississippi River
In 1945 the submarine *Menhaden* (SS-377) made a trip down the river in a floating dry dock, 92-95

Moorer, Admiral Thomas H., USN (Ret.) (USNA, 1933)
As Chief of Naval Operations, relationship with submarines in 1969-70, 383, 386

Morin, Commander George F., USN
Interaction with the Canadian Navy about nuclear submarines, 267-268

Murrow, Edward R.
Television broadcast from the nuclear submarine *Nautilus* (SSN-571) in the mid-1950s, 216-217

Nautilus, USS (SSN-571)
Keel-laying at Groton, Connecticut, in June 1952, 163-165
Process involved in the early 1950s for selecting the first commanding officer, 164-165, 170
Construction of the new ship at Electric Boat in the early 1950s, 167-177, 181, 192-193, 202-204

Launching on 21 January 1954, 170-171
Enlisted crew members in the mid-1950s, 167-169, 174, 177, 183-184, 189-190, 195-196, 198-199, 218-220, 224-225, 230-231, 237-239, 244-247, 251-253, 259
Commissioning on 30 September 1954, 169-173
Sea trials in 1955, 177-179, 181-185, 191-192
Based in New London, Connecticut, 1955-57, 186-190
Nuclear-fired steam propulsion plant, 169-185, 191-193, 241-244
In April 1955 the *Saturday Evening Post* published a two-part series on the ship's sea trials, 193-195
Operations at sea, 1955-57, 195-202, 206-213, 222-226, 231-232, 247-250, 254-255
Tours and trips for visitors in the mid-1950s, 121, 188-190, 195-196, 229-230, 239-241, 250-253, 261-262
Oxygen supply during extended periods underwater, 199-201
Vibration problems early in the ship's operations, 202-204
Purchase of a large quantity of liquor in Bermuda in the mid-1950s, 214-215
Operations under the Arctic icecap in the late 1950s, 205, 236, 269-270, 276
Reception in New York in 1958 after trip under the North Pole, 272-273
In the 1970s the condition of the submarine had declined, 251

Naval Reactor Test Station, Arco, Idaho
Served as a prototype for training nuclear power plant operators in the 1950s, 165-167, 174, 228

Naval Reserve, U.S.
In the latter part of 1940 Wilkinson went through the V-7 officer training program, 24-30
Reserve officers in the crew of the heavy cruiser *Louisville* (CA-28) in 1941, 36-37, 42-43
Reserve officers as students at Submarine School in 1942, 48-49

Naval War College, Newport, Rhode Island
Curriculum in the late 1950s emphasized strategy and political science, 260-263

Naval Weapons Station, Yorktown, Virginia
In April 1962 the nuclear cruiser *Long Beach* (CGN-9) went to the naval weapons station to off-load missiles, 323-324

Navigation
The submarine *Darter* (SS-227) ran aground on Bombay Shoal on 24 October 1944 and had to be abandoned, 78-81
On board the submarine *Cusk* (SSG-348) in 1947, 104-105

Navy Ships Parts Control Center, Mechanicsburg, Pennsylvania
Involvement with the nuclear cruiser *Long Beach* (CGN-9) in the early 1960s, 312-313

New London, Connecticut, Submarine Base
 Homeport for the nuclear submarine *Nautilus* (SSN-571) in the mid-1950s, 186-190
 Problems with Polaris off-duty crews in New London in 1969-70, 378-379

New Orleans, Louisiana
 Visited in the mid-1950s by the nuclear submarine *Nautilus* (SSN-571), 235

News Media
 In December 1951 crewmen from the submarine *Volador* (SS-490) rescued *Collier's* magazine correspondent Charlotte Knight after a helicopter crash at sea, 133-135
 Coverage of the nuclear submarine *Nautilus* (SSN-571) in the mid-1950s, 183, 256-257
 In April 1955 the *Saturday Evening Post* published a two-part series on the sea trials of the *Nautilus*, 193-195
 Edward R. Murrow television broadcast from the *Nautilus* in the mid-1950s, 216-217
 Wilkinson was sent to an overseas assignment in 1966 amid concern that he had divulged classified information in a magazine interview, 353-354

New York City, New York
 Hosted a heroes' welcome for the crew of the nuclear submarine *Nautilus* (SSN-571) in 1958, 272-273

Nicholson, Lieutenant Commander John H., USN (USNA, 1947)
 Served as main propulsion assistant and executive officer in the nuclear submarine *Nautilus* (SSN-571) in the mid-1950s, 185-186, 208, 252
 Served in the nuclear submarine *Skate* (SSN-578) when she surfaced at the North Pole in August 1958, 270-271

Nimitz, Fleet Admiral Chester W., USN (USNA, 1905)
 In November 1945 was relieved as Commander in Chief Pacific Fleet on board the submarine *Menhaden* (SS-377), 94

Nimitz, Commander Chester W., Jr., USN (USNA, 1936)
 Headed the gunnery department at Submarine School in early 1945, 87-92
 Retired from the Navy in the mid-1950s, 336

North Africa
 In November 1942 the submarine *Blackfish* (SS-221) supported the U.S. invasion of Africa, 56-57

Northwestern University, Evanston, Illinois
 In 1940 was one site for the V-7 Naval Reserve officer training program, 24-28, 30

Nuclear Power
 Origins of the Navy's nuclear power program in the late 1940s at Oak Ridge, Tennessee, Argonne National Laboratory, and Bettis Laboratory, 111-128

Operation of the Navy prototype reactor at Arco, Idaho, in the 1950s, 114, 119, 165-167, 174, 228

Steam plant on board the nuclear submarine *Nautilus* (SSN-571) in the mid-1950s, 169-185, 191-193, 241-244

Role of Admiral Hyman Rickover in selecting officers for the nuclear power program, 227-229

Access to various ports by nuclear-powered ships, 236

In the late 1950s the Royal Navy sent officers to the United States for nuclear training, 16, 266-267

Two-reactor plant in the nuclear submarine *Triton* (SSRN-586) in the early 1960s, 274-275, 280

Power plant in the cruiser *Long Beach* (CGN-9) in the early 1960s, 275, 282-285, 288-289, 309-310

In the late 1960s the U.S. Navy was able to introduce nuclear-powered ships into Japanese ports, 353, 355, 361-363

Role of the Institute of Nuclear Power Operations (INPO) in the early 1980s, 155, 407-423

Overall contributions of Admiral Hyman Rickover, 423-424

Nuclear Regulatory Commission
Relationship with the civilian nuclear power industry, 407-408

In the 1980s and 1990s retired Navy admirals served as chairmen, 412, 415

Nuclear Weapons
The Trident program advanced in the early 1970s, 398-401

The increasing range of submarine-launched ballistic missiles provided larger operating areas, 401-402

Oak Ridge National Laboratory, Tennessee
Site of early development work in the Navy's nuclear power program in the late 1940s, 111-112, 117, 123-127

Oil Fuel
Competition for fuel economy among Pacific Fleet cruisers in 1941, 33-35

O'Keefe, Lieutenant Commander George F., USN (USNA, 1925)
In 1941 served as chief engineer of the heavy cruiser *Louisville* (CA-28), 31-32, 37-40

Osborn, Commander James B., USN (USNA, 1942)
In the early 1960s was the first commanding officer of the ballistic missile submarine *George Washington* (SSBN-598), 277

Panama Canal
Transit by the nuclear submarine *Nautilus* (SSN-571) in 1957, 247-248

Paris, France
    Wilkinson spent some leisure time in Paris in 1963 after being relieved of command of the nuclear cruiser *Long Beach* (CGN-9), 334-336

Pay and Allowance
    Payment of the crew of the U.S. submarine *Blackfish* (SS-221) in England in early 1943, 59

Pearl Harbor, Hawaii
    In 1941 the heavy cruiser *Louisville* (CA-28) was one of the ships based there, 37-44
    Japanese attack on in December 1941, 45-46
    In the early 1950s served as home port for the submarine *Wahoo* (SS-565), 158

Personnel
    Shortage of enlisted submariners following demobilization after World War II, 97, 101

Philadelphia Naval Shipyard
    In the early 1960s the nuclear cruiser *Long Beach* (CGN-9) spent time at the yard for repairs and equipment installation, 299-300, 318-320, 324-325

Philippine Islands
    Action of the U.S. and Japanese navies in the October 1944 Battle of Leyte Gulf, 75-79

Photography
    Through-the-periscope photography by U.S. submarines in World War II, 144
    In the early 1950s the crew of the submarine *Volador* (SS-490) took pictures through periscopes to demonstrate the success of her attacks against surface ships in ASW exercises, 141-144
    In the mid-1950s Chief Fire Controlman Al Crossick did some expert photography while in the crew of the nuclear submarine *Nautilus* (SSN-571), 195-196, 198-199, 270

Point Mugu, California
    In the late 1940s the Pacific Missile Test Range was involved in Loon missile testing by the submarine *Cusk* (SSG-348), 106-109

Poker
    Throughout his life, Wilkinson enjoyed great success in the game of poker, 13-18, 81-83, 147-148, 267-268

***Pomodon*, USS (SS-486)**
    During the Korean War her skipper, Lieutenant Commander Allen Bergner, studied diligently for promotion exams, 145-147

Portsmouth Naval Shipyard, Kittery, Maine
   In the early 1950s built the fast-attack submarine *Wahoo* (SS-565), 148-150, 159-160

Princeton, **USS (CVS-37)**
   Involved in a war game off the coast of California in 1957, 254-255

Prisoners of War
   Submarine officers who had been captured during World War II were slow in reacting when they returned to operations after they were released, 100

Promotion of Officers
   During the Korean War the U.S. Navy suspended promotion examinations for officers, 145-147

Propulsion Plants
   Steam plant in 1941 on board the heavy cruiser *Louisville* (CA-28), 33-34, 42
   Origins of the Navy's nuclear power program in the late 1940s at Oak Ridge, Tennessee, Argonne National Laboratory, and Bettis Laboratory, 111-128
   Difficulty with pancake diesel engines in the submarine *Wahoo* (SS-565) in the early 1950s, 151-153, 156, 161
   Water-cooled plant on board the nuclear submarine *Nautilus* (SSN-571) in the mid-1950s, 169-185, 191-193, 241-244
   Liquid-sodium-cooled nuclear plant on board the submarine *Seawolf* (SSN-575) in the mid-1950s, 212-213
   Two-reactor plant in the nuclear submarine *Triton* (SSRN-586) in the early 1960s, 274-275, 280
   Nuclear power plant in the cruiser *Long Beach* (CGN-9) in the early 1960s, 275, 282-285, 288-289, 309-310

Public Relations
   In December 1951 the Navy publicized film of a rescue at sea by the crew of the submarine *Volador* (SS-490), 134-135
   The crew of the nuclear submarine *Nautilus* (SSN-571) had to respond to many requests from the public in the mid-1950s, 236, 239-240

Pueblo, **USS (AGER-2)**
   Reaction in Japan when this intelligence ship was seized by North Korea in January 1968, 363-365

Puerto Rico
   In the early 1960s the nuclear cruiser *Long Beach* (CGN-9) visited San Juan, 315-316

Queen Mary, **RMS**
   Wilkinson gave a speech on board the retired liner in the early 1970s, 422-423

Radio
    In October 1944 the submarine *Darter* (SS-227) sent in a vital sighting report of the Japanese fleet, 75-76
    Communications by the submarine *Volador* (SS-490) in the early 1950s, 138-141
    Voice call sign "Aggravate" used by the nuclear submarine *Nautilus* (SSN-571) in the mid-1950s, 216
    Development in the 1970s of extremely low frequency radio communications with submarines, 392-393

Raton, USS (SS-270)
    In 1946 served as a school boat for Submarine School at New London, 97-101
    Shortage of personnel shortly after the end of World War II, 136-137

Reece, Engineman First Class Thomas, USN
    In 1954-55 was in the initial crew of the nuclear submarine *Nautilus* (SSN-571), 183-184

Rescue at Sea
    In December 1951 crewmen from the submarine *Volador* (SS-490) rescued *Collier's* magazine correspondent Charlotte Knight after a helicopter crash at sea, 133-135

Richelieu (French Battleship)
    Stationed at Dakar, West Africa, in late 1942, 56-57

Ricketts, Admiral Claude V., USN (USNA, 1929)
    In the early 1960s, as Vice Chief of Naval Operations, had several dealings with the nuclear cruiser *Long Beach* (CGN-9), 299-301

Rickover, Admiral Hyman G., USN (Ret.) (USNA, 1922)
    Early involvement in the Navy's nuclear power program in the late 1940s and early 1950s, 111-128, 165-166
    Role in the selection of Wilkinson as first commanding officer of the nuclear submarine *Nautilus* (SSN-571) in the early 1950s, 163-165, 170
    Work in the design, construction, and testing of the *Nautilus* in the 1950s, 168, 174, 180-181, 183-185, 191-193, 204-205, 213, 236, 242
    Role in selecting officers for the nuclear power program, 227-229
    Personality of, 263-265, 379, 386-387, 424-426
    Involvement with the nuclear cruiser *Long Beach* (CGN-9) in the late 1950s-early 1960s, 283, 287-289, 292-293, 309-310
    Relationship with OP-31 in the mid-1960s, 346-347, 349-350
    Relationship with Wilkinson in the early 1970s, 385-387, 397-398
    Connection with Wilkinson after the latter's retirement from the Navy, 408
    Assessment of his overall contributions, 423-427

Rivero, Admiral Horacio, Jr., USN (USNA, 1931)
    As VCNO in the early 1960s, had questions about the SubSafe program, 339

***Robert E. Lee*, USS (SSBN-601)**
    Built in the early 1960s at Newport News, Virginia, 154

Rockets
    Former German V-1 rockets were used as Loon missiles by the U.S. Navy in the late 1940s, 106-109

Roddis, Lieutenant Commander Louis H., USN (USNA, 1939)
    Early involvement in the Navy's nuclear power program in the late 1940s, 111, 113, 117, 424

Royal Navy
    In early 1943 the U.S. submarine *Blackfish* (SS-221) went into the Royal Naval Dockyard at Devonport for repair of battle damage, 58-60
    In the late 1950s sent officers to the United States to learn about nuclear submarines, 16, 266-267

Sailing
    In 1941 the team from the heavy cruiser *Louisville* (CA-28) was successful in competition around Pearl Harbor, 37-41

San Diego State College
    Wilkinson graduated from the school in 1938 and later taught there, 1, 3-4, 8, 12, 19-23

San Juan, Puerto Rico
    In the early 1960s the nuclear cruiser *Long Beach* (CGN-9) visited San Juan, 315-316

Satterford, Captain Robert B., USN
    In the early 1960s served as deputy to OP-31 on the OpNav staff, 340-341, 345

Saturday Evening Post
    In April 1955 the magazine published a two-part series on the sea trials of the nuclear submarine *Nautilus* (SSN-571), 193-195

***Savannah*, NS**
    First U.S. nuclear-powered merchant ship, built in the late 1950s-early 1960s, 184

Schlesinger, James R.
    In the late 1950s taught at the Naval War College, 261-262

Schwab, Lieutenant Commander Ernest L., Jr., USN (USNA, 1939)
    In 1944 was executive officer and navigator of the submarine *Darter* (SS-227), 70-71, 78-79, 86

Seattle, Washington
   First visit by the nuclear submarine *Nautilus* (SSN-571) was in 1957, 256-257

***Sea Robin*, USS (SS-407)**
   Wilkinson had temporary command in 1952 when the regular skipper had physical problems, 161-163
   Involved in a mine-laying exercise in 1952, 162-163

***Seawolf*, USS (SSN-575)**
   Exercises at sea in the mid-1950s against the nuclear submarine *Nautilus* (SSN-571), 212-214

Selection Boards
   Naval Academy graduates now compete on an even basis with officers from other sources, 50-51
   Difficulties selection boards have in evaluating large numbers of naval officers, 278-279

Shipbuilding
   Construction of the submarine *Wahoo* (SS-565) by the Portsmouth Naval Shipyard in the early 1950s, 148-150, 159-160
   Construction of the nuclear submarine *Nautilus* (SSN-571) by the Electric Boat Division of General Dynamics in the 1950s, 167-176, 181-182, 184, 192-193, 202-204
   Construction of the nuclear cruiser *Long Beach* (CGN-9) by Bethlehem Steel in Quincy, Massachusetts, in the late 1950s-early 1960s, 289-294, 310-311

Ship Characteristics Board
   Role in making changes to the nuclear cruiser *Long Beach* (CGN-9) during her construction in the early 1960s, 287-288

Ship Design
   Changes in the design of the nuclear cruiser *Long Beach* (CGN-9) during her construction in the late 1950s-early 1960s, 283-284, 286-287

Ship Handling
   By Lieutenant Commander Frederick Janney on board the submarine *Raton* (SS-270) in 1946, 99-100
   In the submarine *Volador* (SS-490) in the early 1950s, 137
   In the submarine *Wahoo* (SS-565) in the early 1950s, 158-159
   In the nuclear submarine *Nautilus* (SSN-571) in the mid-1950s, 247-248, 250, 252-253, 257, 261-262
   In the nuclear cruiser *Long Beach* (CGN-9) in the early 1960s, 158, 295-296, 315-316, 323-324, 330

Shor, Lieutenant Commander Samuel W. W., USN (USNA, 1943)
   Engineering duty specialist who was involved in the construction and testing of the nuclear submarine *Nautilus* (SSN-571) in the mid-1950s, 172-173, 191

Shugg, Carleton Shugg
   Was president of the Electric Boat Division when the nuclear submarine *Nautilus* (SSN-571) was built in the early 1950s, 175-176

Skate, USS (SSN-578)
   Was commissioned in 1957 as one of the earliest nuclear submarines, 167, 241, 266
   Surfaced at the North Pole in August 1958, 269-271, 276
   Reception in Boston in 1958 after trip to the North Pole, 273

Smith, Vice Admiral Harold Page, USN (USNA, 1924)
   In the late 1950s served as Chief of Naval Personnel, 274

Smith, Rear Admiral Levering, USN (USNA, 1932)
   In the mid-1960s was heavily involved in strategic missile systems, 342, 348-349, 427

Snowe, Chief Ship Repair Technician Marvin L., USN
   In the early 1960s served in the nuclear cruiser *Long Beach* (CGN-9), 282, 300-301

Softball
   Game in the mid-1950s between the crews of the cruiser *Boston* (CAG-1) and the nuclear submarine *Nautilus* (SSN-571), 237-239

Sonar
   Use of by the nuclear submarine *Nautilus* (SSN-571) in the mid-1950s, 209-210, 222-226, 231-232, 254-255

Speck, Rear Admiral Robert H., USN (USNA, 1927)
   Role as head of the Ship Characteristics board in the early 1960s, 288, 305
   In the early 1960s served as the first Commander Cruiser-Destroyer Force Atlantic Fleet, 301-309
   Wife of, 304

Spencer, Captain William A., USN (USNA, 1947)
   In the early 1960s was the first chief engineer of the nuclear cruiser *Long Beach* (CGN-9) and later became the commanding officer, 282, 330-331

State Department
   Role in relation to Japan in the late 1960s, 354-356. 360-361, 368

Submarine Division 102
    In the late 1950s included all of the U.S. Navy's nuclear-powered submarines, 266, 269
    In the late 1950s the Royal Navy sent officers to the United States for nuclear training, 16, 266-267
    Interaction with the Canadian Navy about nuclear submarines, 267-268
    Two of the division's submarines went to the North Pole in August 1958, 269-272

Submarine Flotilla Two
    Problems with Polaris off-duty crews in New London in 1969-70, 378-379

Submarine Force Atlantic Fleet
    In the early 1950s gave a pre-deployment inspection to the submarine *Wahoo* (SS-565), 150-151, 160
    Involvement with the nuclear submarine *Nautilus* (SSN-571) in the mid-1950s, 209-210, 227, 233-234, 241
    Retention problems for nuclear submarine officers in the late 1960s, 382-383
    Impact of CNO Elmo Zumwalt's Z-gram messages on the submarine force in the early 1970s, 384-385
    Emphasis in the early 1970s on correcting inspection deficiencies, 390
    Relationship in the early 1970s with CinCLantFlt in control of ballistic missile submarines, 391
    Course in the early 1970s for prospective submarine skippers, 393-394

Submarine School, New London, Connecticut
    Training of prospective submariners in early 1942, 47-58
    Training of prospective commanding officers in 1945-46, 86-92, 98-101

Submarine Squadron 14
    In the early 1960s was the first with Polaris submarines, 277-279

Submarine Warfare
    Operations by the submarine *Blackfish* (SS-221) in the Atlantic and European waters in 1942-43, 56-66
    War patrols by the submarine *Darter* (SS-227) in 1944, 71-79, 144-145
    Capabilities of modernized Guppy submarines in the early 1950s, 135-136
    Role of the submarine *Volador* (SS-490) in ASW exercises in the early 1950s, 132-135, 139-143
    Role of the submarine *Wahoo* (SS-565) in ASW exercises in the early 1950s, 160
    Role of the nuclear submarine *Nautilus* (SSN-571) in ASW exercises in the mid-1950s, 196-197, 206-213, 222-226, 231-232, 249-250, 254-255
    Work of the Submarine Warfare Division, OP-31, in OpNav, from 1963 to 1966, 338-354
    Work of the DCNO (Submarine Warfare), OP-02, in OpNav, from 1972 to 1974, 395-405

Wilkinson's assessment of the submarine force of the Cold War and beyond, 426-427

SubSafe Program
Loss of the nuclear submarine *Thresher* (SSN-593) in April 1963 led to SubSafe corrective measures, 339, 342, 349, 351

Summers, Commander Paul E., USN (USNA, 1936)
In the late 1940s commanded the submarine *Cusk* (SSG-348) during missile tests in the Pacific, 104-106, 110

Surface Effect Ships
Advocated by CNO Elmo Zumwalt in the early 1970s for antisubmarine warfare, 404-405

Takao (Japanese Cruiser)
Damaged in October 1944 by the submarine Darter (SS-227), 76-78

Talos Missile
In 1968, in the Vietnam War, the cruiser *Long Beach* (CGN-9) shot down MiG fighters with Talos missiles, 314, 365-366

Tang, USS (SS-563)
Fast attack submarine commissioned in 1951, 154, 185

Teixeira, Quartermaster First Class John P., USN
Served with Wilkinson in the submarine *Nautilus* (SSN-571) in the 1950s, 185

Television
Edward R. Murrow broadcast from the nuclear submarine *Nautilus* (SSN-571) in the mid-1950s, 216-217
Disney program from the *Nautilus* in the 1950s, 217

Tennis
Wilkinson played the sport on many occasions, 19, 318, 380-382

Thomas, Charles S.
As Secretary of the Navy, visited the nuclear submarine *Nautilus* (SSN-571) in the mid-1950s, 188-189

Thresher, USS (SSN-593)
Loss of in April 1963 led to SubSafe corrective measures, 339, 342, 349, 351

Togo, Fumihiko
Japanese representative in nation-to-nation talks with the United States in the late 1960s, 355, 357-364

Torpedo Data Computer
   Use of as a fire control device in World War II, 56, 58, 71-73, 86-92

Torpedoes
   Testing by the submarine *Darter* (SS-227) off Maine in October 1943, 66
   Use of by the *Darter* against the Japanese in 1944, 71-74, 76-77
   Firing practice by the submarine *Menhaden* (SS-377) in mid-1945, 94
   Reload of torpedoes in new fast-attack submarines in the early 1950s, 156-157
   In the mid-1950s the nuclear submarine Nautilus (SSN-571) carried torpedoes left over from World War II, 189-190

Train, Admiral Harry D. II, USN (USNA, 1949)
   Future four-star admiral who served in the crew of the submarine *Wahoo* (SS-565) in the early 1950s, 149, 151-152, 154, 275

Training
   In the latter part of 1940 Wilkinson went through the Navy's V-7 officer training program, 24-30
   At Submarine School in early 1942, 47-54
   Training of prospective submarine commanding officers in 1945-46, 86-92, 98-101
   In early1952 the submarine *Sea Robin* (SS-407) did a mine-laying exercise, 162-163
   In the late 1950s the Royal Navy sent officers to the United States for nuclear training, 16, 266-267
   Pre-deployment training of the nuclear cruiser *Long Beach* (CGN-9) at Guantánamo Bay, Cuba, in the early 1960s, 320-322

Trident Program
   Advancement of in the early 1970s, 398-399
   Selection of bases in Georgia and Washington for Trident submarines, 399-400
   Increased range of Trident missiles provided greater operating areas for the submarines, 401-402
   Decision on the number of missile tubes per submarine, 402-403

Trigger, **USS (SS-564)**
   Engineering problems in this fast-attack submarine commissioned in 1952, 152-153

Triton, **USS (SSRN-586)**
   Though officially a radar picket, was actually a test platform for a two-reactor nuclear plant, 280-281
   In the spring of 1960 made a submerged transit around the world, 274-275

Truman, President Harry S.
   In June 1952 was involved in the keel-laying for the nuclear submarine *Nautilus* (SSN-571) at Groton, Connecticut, 163-164, 170

Tucker, Lieutenant (junior grade) Houston Clay, Jr., USN (USNA, 1939)
Served in 1942-43 in the submarine *Blackfish* (SS-221), 64-66

Turkish Navy
In the early 1960s a Turkish submarine received repairs at the Philadelphia Naval Shipyard, 324

Tyree, Captain John A., Jr., USN (USNA, 1933)
Role in the selection of the first commanding officer of the nuclear submarine *Nautilus* (SSN-571) in the early 1950s, 164-165

V-1 Rockets
Former German rockets were used as Loon missiles by the U.S. Navy in the late 1940s, 106-109

V-7 Program
In the latter part of 1940 Wilkinson went through the V-7 Naval Reserve officer training program, 24-30

Venereal Disease
Survey concerning venereal disease in the fleet in the early 1950s, 131

Vietnam War
In 1968 the cruiser *Long Beach* (CGN-9) shot down MiG fighters with Talos missiles, 314, 365-366

***Volador*, USS (SS-490)**
Deployment to the Western Pacific in the early 1950s, 129-144, 147-148, 374-375
Ship's basketball team, 129-131
Tangles with U.S. antisubmarine forces, 133-135, 139-144
Ship handling, 137
Poker playing on board the boat in the early 1950s, 147-148

***Wahoo*, USS (SS-565)**
Construction of at Portsmouth Naval Shipyard in the early 1950s, 148-150, 159-160
Shakedown training of the crew, 160
Enlisted crew members, 150-153, 155-158
Difficulty with pancake diesel engines, 151-153, 156, 161
Ship handling, 158-159

Wakeman, Samuel
In the late 1950s-early 1960s managed the Bethlehem Steel shipyard at Quincy, Massachusetts, during the building of the nuclear cruiser *Long Beach* (CGN-9), 290-291

Walsh, Ensign John J., USN (USNA, 1938)
Served in 1941 in the heavy cruiser *Louisville* (CA-28), 36-37

Ward, Captain Norvell G., USN (USNA, 1935)
In the early 1960s commanded Submarine Squadron 14, the first with Polaris submarines, 277-279

Watkins, Rear Admiral Frank T., USN (USNA, 1922)
As ComSubLant, rode the nuclear submarine *Nautilus* (SSN-571) during ASW exercises in the mid-1950s, 210-211, 233-235

Watkins, Admiral James D., USN (USNA, 1949)
Future Chief of Naval Operations served as a junior officer in the submarine *Volador* (SS-490) in the early 1950s, 138, 275-276
In the late 1960s was executive officer of the nuclear cruiser *Long Beach* (CGN-9), 366

Weapon Able/Alfa
Used by surface ships in antisubmarine exercises in the mid-1950s, 223-224

Westinghouse Corporation
Involved in development work in the Navy's nuclear power program in the late 1940s and early 1950s, 112-120, 123, 127-128, 168, 176-177, 212
Manufactured components that were used in building the nuclear cruiser *Long Beach* (CGN-9) in the early 1960s, 299

Whales
Ability to sense where ice is thin in order to break through to get air, 271-272

Whitmire, Lieutenant (junior grade) Donald B., USN (USNA, 1947)
In the early 1950s served in the submarine *Gudgeon* (SS-567), 156-157

Wilkinson, Vice Admiral Eugene P., USN (Ret.)
Grandparents, 1-3, 5-8, 10-11, 19
Parents, 1-3, 6, 8, 10-11, 19
Sister Lillian, 4-5, 9, 19, 257, 260
Wife Janice, 4-5, 17-18, 20, 25, 46-47, 54, 61, 64, 67, 81-83, 86-87, 124-125, 162, 170, 233, 261, 281, 336-337, 358, 362, 366-367, 370-372, 374, 376, 378, 404-406, 421, 425, 430-431, 433, 435
Children, 3, 61, 67, 125, 217, 261, 337, 372, 377-378, 406, 413, 425, 430-432
Grandchildren, 377-378, 430-432
Youth in California in the 1920s and 1930s, 1-14, 19-21
Throughout his life, Wilkinson enjoyed great success in the game of poker, 13-18
In the latter part of 1940 went through the V-7 Naval Reserve officer training program, 24-30

Served in 1941 in the crew of the heavy cruiser *Louisville* (CA-28), 30-46
As a student at Submarine School in early 1942, 47-54
In the spring of 1942 served briefly in the submarine *R-10*, 55-56
Served 1942-43 in the submarine *Blackfish* (SS-221), 56-66
Served 1943-44 in the submarine *Darter* (SS-227), 66-84, 144-145
In early 1945 taught in the PCO course at Submarine School, 86-92
In 1945 was executive officer of the submarine *Menhaden* (SS-377), 86, 92-95
In early 1946 was executive officer of the submarine *Raton* (SS-270), 97-101
Was a student at General Line School in 1946-47, 103
In 1947-48 was executive officer of the submarine *Cusk* (SSG-348)
Involvement in the origins of the Navy's nuclear power program in the late 1940s, 111-128
In 1950-51 commanded the submarine *Volador* (SS-490), 129-148, 374-375
From 1951 to 1953 was PCO and then commanding officer of the submarine *Wahoo* (SS-565), 148-165
Had temporary command of the submarine *Sea Robin* (SS-407) in 1952, 157, 161-163
From 1953 to 1957 was PCO and then commanding officer of the nuclear submarine *Nautilus* (SSN-571), 165-262
In 1957-58 was a student at the Naval War College, 260-263
In 1958-59 commanded Submarine Division 102, 15-16, 220-221, 266-282
Short tour in 1958 as commanding officer of the *Nautilus*, 273-274
From 1959 to 1963 was PCO and then commanding officer of the cruiser *Long Beach* (CGN-9), 158, 275, 281-334
Selected for flag rank in the early 1960s, 336-337
Served from 1963 to 1966 as Director, Submarine Warfare Division, OP-31, in OpNav, 338-354
From 1966 to 1969 was Chief of Staff, U.S. Forces Japan, 354-378
Served as Commander Submarine Flotilla Two, 1969-70, 378-383
From 1970 to 1972 was Commander Submarine Force Atlantic Fleet, 383-395
Final active duty billet, from 1972 to 1974, was as OP-02, 395-405
Post-retirement employment, including serving as head of INPO, 405-422

Williams, Vice Admiral Joe, Jr., USN
In the early 1970s served as chief of staff to Commander Submarine Force Atlantic Fleet, 387-389
In the mid-1970s served as ComSubLant, 389
Personality, 389-390

Williams, Admiral John G., Jr., USN (USNA, 1947)
In the early 1970s was material officer on the ComSubLant staff, 394-395
Was selected for flag rank despite earlier thoughts of leaving the Navy, 395

Wilson, Charles E.
In 1955 was Secretary of Defense when the *Saturday Evening Post* published a two-part series on the nuclear submarine *Nautilus* (SSN-571), 194

Woodall, Commander Reuben F., USN (USNA, 1943)
    In the early 1950s served in the submarine *Wahoo* (SS-565), 149, 153-154
    In the early 1960s commanded the submarine *Robert E. Lee* (SSBN-601), 153-154

Wright, Admiral Jerauld, USN (USNA, 1918)
    Spoke at the commissioning of the nuclear submarine *Nautilus* (SSN-571) in September 1954, 171-173

***Wyoming*, USS (AG-17)**
    Former battleship that in 1940 served as a training ship for midshipmen, 27-30

Yorktown, Virginia
    In April 1962 the nuclear cruiser *Long Beach* (CGN-9) went to the naval weapons station to off-load missiles, 323-324

Youman, Commander Harold R., Jr., USN
    In the early 1960s was the first chief operations officer of the nuclear cruiser *Long Beach* (CGN-9), 285-286

Zech, Vice Admiral Lando W., Jr., USN (USNA, 1945)
    Commanded the nuclear submarine *Nautilus* (SSN-571), 1959-62, 154
    In the mid-1960s was a submarine detail officer in the Bureau of Naval Personnel, 343-344
    Served 1986-89 as chairman of the Nuclear Regulatory Commission, 412, 415

Zumwalt, Admiral Elmo R., Jr., USN (Ret.) (USNA, 1943)
    As Chief of Naval Operations in the early 1970s wrote some highly laudatory fitness reports on subordinates, 279
    Impact of Z-gram messages on the submarine force in the early 1970s, 384-385
    As CNO did not provide strong support for submarines, 396-397
    Advocated surface effect ships, 404-405